DAVID HOCKNEY

Also by Christopher Simon Sykes

AS AUTHOR

The Visitors' Book
Private Palaces
Black Sheep
Country House Camera
The National Trust Country House Album
The Big House
Eric Clapton (with Eric Clapton)
David Hockney: The Biography, 1937–1975

AS AUTHOR AND PHOTOGRAPHER

Ancient English Houses

AS PHOTOGRAPHER

The Front Garden
The Rolling Stones on Tour
The Perfect English House
English Country
Private Landscapes
Scottish Country
Corfu: The Garden Isle
At Home with Books
At Home with Art
Great Houses of England and Wales
Great Houses of Scotland
Great Houses of Ireland
The English Room
English Manor Houses
The Gardens of Buckingham Palace

HOCKNEY

THE BIOGRAPHY, 1975–2012

A PILGRIM'S PROGRESS

Christopher Simon Sykes

NAN A. TALESE

Doubleday

NEW YORK   LONDON   TORONTO   SYDNEY   AUCKLAND

www.nanatalese.com

Originally published in Great Britain as *Hockney: The Biography,* Vol. 2, by Century,
the Random House Group Ltd, London. This edition published by arrangement with
the Random House Group Ltd.

DOUBLEDAY is a registered trademark of Random House LLC. Nan A. Talese and the
colophon are trademarks of Random House LLC.

Jacket design by John Fontana
Jacket photograph by John Angerson, Camera Press London

Library of Congress Cataloging-in-Publication Data

Sykes, Christopher Simon, 1948–
[Hockney]
David Hockney : the biography / Christopher Sykes.—1st United States ed.
p.   cm.
Originally published: Hockney: the biography. London : Century,
the Random House Group, 2011
Includes bibliographical references and index.
1. Hockney, David.   2. Artists—Great Britain—Biography.   I. Hockney, David.   II. Title.
N6797.H57S95   2012
740.92—dc23   [B]   2011041629

ISBN 978-0-385-53590-8 (hardcover)   ISBN 978-0-385-53955-5 (eBook)

PRINTED IN THE UNITED STATES OF AMERICA

1   3   5   7   9   10   8   6   4   2

First American Edition

This book is dedicated to the memory of Dominic Elliott,
who died far too young.

CONTENTS

ILLUSTRATIONS IN THE TEXT

PLATES

Section I

Kerby (After Hogarth) Useful Knowledge, 1975, oil on canvas, 72 x 60"
© David Hockney. Photo credit: Prudence Cuming Associates.
Collection: Museum of Modern Art (MOMA), New York

'The Old Guitarist' from *The Blue Guitar*, 1976–77, etching, edition of
200, 20½ x 18" © David Hockney

Self-Portrait with Blue Guitar, 1977, oil on canvas, 60 x 72"
© David Hockney. Photo credit: Richard Schmidt. Collection:
Museum of Modern Art, Vienna

Looking at Pictures on a Screen, 1977, oil on canvas, 74 x 74"
© David Hockney

My Parents, 1977, oil on canvas, 72 x 72" © David Hockney.
Photo credit: Richard Schmidt. Collection: Tate, London

Act I, Scene III. Sarastro's Kingdom from *The Magic Flute*, 1977,
gouache on foamcore, 26½ x 41" © David Hockney.
Collection: The David Hockney Foundation

David Hockney applying colour dye with a turkey baster to newly
pressed paper for the 12-panel *Le Plongeur* while looking at *A
Diver* on wall with *Piscine avec trois bleus* pool framed as a screen
in the background, from his *Paper Pools* series, Tyler Workshop
Ltd artist's studio, Bedford Village, New York, 1978, colour
photograph by Lindsay Green, courtesy of the National Gallery
of Australia, Canberra, gift of Kenneth Tyler, 2002

Day Pool with Three Blues (Paper Pool 7), 1978, coloured and pressed
paper pulp, 72 x 85½" © David Hockney / Tyler Graphics Ltd.

Canyon Painting, 1978, acrylic on canvas, 60 x 60" © David Hockney

Santa Monica Blvd, 1978-80, acrylic on canvas, 86 x 240"
© David Hockney. Photo credit: Richard Schmidt. Collection:
The David Hockney Foundation

Divine, 1979, acrylic on canvas, 60 x 60" © David Hockney. Photo
credit: Richard Schmidt. Collection: Carnegie Museum of Art,
Pittsburgh

Section 2

Section 3

Section 4

ACKNOWLEDGEMENTS

Writing the two volumes of this biography has been a journey, in the progress of which I have been helped by a great number of people who have crossed David Hockney's path at some time or other in their lives. I have already acknowledged in the first volume the part many of them have played, and would like to add to that list the following:

Peter Adam * Jonathon Brown * Don Cribb * Edith Devaney
Marinka Ellidge * Sid Felsen * John Fitzherbert * Martin Friedman
Martin Gayford * Peter Goulds * Paul Joyce * Aaron Kasmin
Karen Kuhlman * Bing McGilvray * Riggs O'Hara * David Plante
Maggie Silver * Robin Silver * Zoe Silver * Joanna Taylor
Ken Tyler * Lawrence Weschler * Bruno Wollheim

Thank you all, and, of course, many thanks again to David Hockney and his siblings, without whom there would be no book.

DAVID HOCKNEY

'I never do a painting as a work of art. All of them are researches.'

Picasso

PROLOGUE

When David Hockney's mother was once told by one of his friends, 'You must be very proud of your son,' she replied, 'Oh yes! To be Mayor of Bradford!' She was referring to her eldest son, Paul. David was the fourth of five children born before and during the war to a working-class couple, Kenneth and Laura Hockney. Kenneth, a radical thinker, was a clerk in a dry-salter's, earning a meagre wage, and the fact that he was also a conscientious objector meant that the family received no government assistance when he lost his job. He therefore had to rely on his wits, and he started a business restoring prams, which he painted to look like new. This was the young David Hockney's first introduction to any kind of 'art'. He was soon drawing with chalk on the lino floor, on a blackboard in the kitchen, and scribbling in pencil all over his brother's comics.

Despite the hardship and lack of money, the Hockney children wanted for little, least of all a good education, which their parents saw as the most important thing in their lives, and in 1947 David won a scholarship to Bradford Grammar School. But, in spite of being one of the brightest boys in the school, he mostly languished in the bottom classes, having discovered that these were the only ones in which art was taught on a regular basis. Even here, however, he found little encouragement, his form mistress at one point writing on his report, 'He should realise that ability in and enthusiasm for art alone is not enough to make a career for him.' Eventually, he was allowed to apply for a place at Bradford College of Art, and he now views the four years he spent painting and drawing chiefly from life as having been vital to all his later work.

Hockney's output at Bradford secured him a place at the Royal College of Art in London, where he went in the autumn of 1959, joining an intake that included Allen Jones, Derek Boshier and R. B. Kitaj. On many levels this was an eye-opener for Hockney. He found a freedom among the rebellious students that set his work in a new direction, and he discovered his sexuality, coming out unashamedly as being gay. His work blossomed. He dabbled in pop art, with his 'Tea' paintings, and produced several gay propaganda pictures such as *Doll Boy* and the 'Love' paintings, all of which were shown in the *Young Contemporaries* exhibition of 1961, a defining moment in his career as he attracted the attention of his first dealer, John Kasmin, whose gallery in Bond Street was to be the first to show his work.

It was while he was a student at the Royal College that Hockney made his first trip to the USA, another highly significant experience for him. He was blown away by New York, and by American culture in general. After watching an advertisement on TV for a hair-colouring product, Clairol, which suggested that 'Blondes have more fun', he went out and dyed his hair, returning home a peroxide blond, wearing white shoes and smoking cigars. It was a look which, along with his large round-rimmed spectacles, was to define him for years to come. He also returned fired up with inspiration, the result of which was one of his most memorable works, *A Rake's Progress*, his own version of Hogarth's series of paintings depicting the downfall of a young ne'er-do-well in eighteenth-century London, now transported to twentieth-century New York.

After leaving the Royal College in July 1962, complete with the rarely awarded Gold Medal, Hockney set himself up in a flat in Powis Terrace in London's Notting Hill, then an area noted for its profusion of slum properties, mostly divided up for West Indian tenants or poor students. It had two large rooms, one of which became his first studio. He slept in the other room, and at the end of his bed was a chest of drawers on which he painted in large capital letters the words 'GET UP AND WORK IMMEDIATELY', a practice he has followed throughout his life. With Kasmin's encouragement he had soon painted enough pictures to hold his first exhibition, *Paintings With People In*, which opened to great acclaim at the Bond Street gallery in December 1963. By then his name was beginning to be on everyone's lips as the new wunderkind of the London art scene.

The show's success gave Hockney enough money to realise his next ambition, which was to spend a year in America. When he visited Los Angeles he was blown away by the beaches, the boys and the architecture, and driving through the streets one day, he realised that no one had ever really painted the city, and decided that he would become 'the Piranesi of LA'. He soon found himself a small studio and began to paint the local architecture. He also explored the art scene on La Cienega Boulevard, and made a number of artist friends, such as Bill Brice and Ed Ruscha. More importantly he struck up a friendship with Christopher Isherwood and his boyfriend, Don Bachardy, which was to prove one of the most significant of his life. It was the first time he had come across a gay relationship that was like a marriage.

Over the next few years, Hockney returned to LA frequently, and it was on one of these trips, in the summer of 1966, when he had a job teaching art at UCLA, that he met and fell in love with a young student, Peter Schlesinger, who was the first real love of his life. They set up house together in a tiny apartment on Pico Boulevard, and it was here that Hockney produced some of his most iconic paintings, starting with *Beverly Hills Housewife* and including *A Bigger Splash*, both pictures establishing him as *the* chronicler of life in LA. It was one of the happiest and most productive times of his life. In the autumn of 1968, they moved to London so that Schlesinger could take up a place at the Slade School of Art. Hockney was only too keen to show off his boyfriend, and Powis Terrace became the setting for large weekend tea parties, to which invitations became much sought-after.

Though Hockney had been friends with, and eventually the lover of, the fashion designer Ossie Clark for a number of years, it was through Schlesinger that he became friends with Clark's wife, Celia Birtwell, who was to become his muse, and who features in one of his best-loved paintings, *Mr and Mrs Clark and Percy*. Their friendship blossomed during a period in which her marriage to Clark was breaking down, and Hockney's relationship with Schlesinger was also foundering, a situation which eventually broke his heart. They cried on each other's shoulders, and Hockney's many beautiful drawings of Birtwell were a testament to what was in effect a love affair. After the break-up with

Schlesinger, Hockney began to spend more time in America, where he was taken on by two highly influential dealers: André Emmerich in New York and Nick Wilder in Los Angeles.

In 1973, still smarting from the loss of Schlesinger, he moved to Paris, where he set up a studio in a house rented from his close friend, the film director Tony Richardson. Here he studied under Aldo Crommelynck, Picasso's master etching printer, who taught him different techniques, including the 'sugar lift', and his own ingenious method of etching in colour. Hockney, who was at something of a crossroads in his working life and trying to avoid what he considered to be the dangers of obsessive naturalism, now buried himself in drawing, producing in particular a series of beautiful images of Birtwell, many of which were exhibited in 1974 at the Musée des Arts Décoratifs. He worried constantly, however, that he might be forever labelled a portrait painter, particularly since he was also embarking on a new double portrait of two Paris friends, Shirley Goldfarb and Gregory Masurovsky. But help came from an unexpected quarter.

In the summer of 1974, the director John Cox approached Hockney, asking him to design an opera, Stravinsky's *The Rake's Progress*, for the Glyndebourne Festival the following year. Hockney immediately saw this as a possible way out of the rut he was in, since it would give him an opportunity to let his imagination run riot. Drawing on Hogarth's own engravings from his original suite of paintings, and using the technique of cross-hatching, he brilliantly took an eighteenth-century idea and gave it a twentieth-century look, and the result was a triumph. 'Suddenly I realised,' he said, 'I'd found a way to move into another area. In a sense I'd broken my previous attitudes about space and naturalism, which had been bogging me down. I'd found areas to step into which were fascinating: the space of the theatre.'[1]

When he returned to Paris, he did so happy in himself. He had recently begun a relationship with a young Californian, Gregory Evans, which had brought him contentment, but most of all he was excited by a new sense of freedom after finding the means of breaking the chains of naturalism that he felt had been holding him back. It was the beginning of a period of great discovery.

CHAPTER ONE

MY PARENTS
AND MYSELF

At the beginning of the third week of August 1975, exhausted by the gruelling weeks spent on designing *The Rake's Progress* for Glyndebourne, and by a month's painting in Paris, David Hockney took up the invitation of his close friend Henry Geldzahler to spend some time on Fire Island, which lies five miles off the south shore of New York's Long Island. It is no ordinary place. What gives it its special charm is the fact that motor vehicles are banned owing to the absence of any paved roads, and access to the various communities is by boardwalks. This creates a highly romantic relationship between human beings and the sea which has been attracting people of an artistic nature since the 1930s. More notably, however, since the sixties, when John B. Whyte, a former fashion model, bought up and developed a lot of property there, a large gay community has established itself in a district called Fire Island Pines, a hamlet in the town of Brookhaven that derives its name from the extensive growth in the vicinity of pine trees and holly.

'Fire Island was a really amazing place in the summer of 1975,' Hockney recalled, thirty-five years later, on a bitterly cold winter's day in Yorkshire. 'It was just mad fun, a very, very lively sexy place.'[1] As he spoke, he was standing on Bridlington's South Beach by a row of wooden beach huts, looking out across an empty expanse of damp sand to a grey and bleak-looking North Sea, a place as far removed from the fleshpots of Fire Island as it is possible to imagine.

Geldzahler and Hockney's host was their banker friend Arthur Lambert, who had been a regular visitor to the island since 1964, when he used to rent a house in Cherry Grove, another gay-friendly Brookhaven hamlet, in whose Perkinson Hotel Oscar Wilde is reputed to have stayed. 'Cherry Grove is very old,' says Lambert, 'and was popular with gay people even as far back as the late 1800s, but it is much camper, and respectable gay people were much more comfortable living in the Pines. I rented in the Grove until 1972, when more and more of my friends moved down to the Pines and I then decided to buy a house there.' Lambert's place was a small craftsman's house in a great location with a deck on the water. It looked, he says, 'like a child's drawing of a house'.[2]

By the time Hockney arrived in the Pines, he was ready for a break. Apart from a brief holiday in Scotland after the opening night of the opera, he had been constantly working. '. . . in all these mists up here,' he had written to John Cox in June from Inverlochy Castle, 'I'm thinking of my Hogarth painting again and my parents' portrait.'[3] The Hogarth painting to which he referred was a work he had begun in May, inspired by a book he had come across during his research into *The Rake's Progress*. Titled *Dr Brook Taylor's Method of Perspective Made Easy*, it was a manual based on the work of Dr Taylor, who, after Isaac Newton and Roger Cotes, was regarded as the most important mathematician in eighteenth-century England. Its author was the Suffolk-born painter and topographer Joshua Kirby and it had a frontispiece by William Hogarth, *Two Anglers by a River*, which wittily demonstrated the results of not observing the rules of perspective. To begin with, anyone looking at this picture would think it was just a normal scene, with a river, two men fishing, a bridge, sky and buildings at the side. But closer inspection reveals that the perspectives are all wrong – the inn sign on the building in the foreground, for example, is obscured by trees that are way in the distance, a woman leaning out of a window in the same building is somehow lighting the pipe of a man climbing a faraway hill, while the fishing rod of the man seated by the river passes in front of that of his companion who is far behind him.

'. . . the Hogarth picture . . . caught my eye,' wrote Hockney, 'probably because of its rather whimsical feeling. You could see what it was about, how Hogarth meant it: If you did not know the rules of perspective, ghastly errors like this would occur. But I was attracted to what Hogarth thought were the ghastly errors and I thought I

*Two Anglers by
a River*, William
Hogarth

also saw that they created space just as well, if not better, than the
correct perspective he was praising.'[4] Looking at this picture had made
Hockney realise that it was possible to paint a picture that ignored all
laws and conventions and yet still looked convincing, so he painted his
own version of it, titled *Kerby (After Hogarth) Useful Knowledge*, which
turned out to be of greater significance than he thought, in that it was
to help him escape the constrictions of one-point perspective. However,
as he later told the writer Lawrence 'Ren' Weschler, 'At the time I
did it, I did not yet realise what my painting was all about. It took
me almost ten years to understand how, for instance, the reverse

perspective in the foreground, far from being a mistake, gives the image greater reality.'[5]

Hockney completed *Kerby* on his return to Paris in July, and then turned his mind to the long-standing project of painting a double portrait of his parents. Throughout his career, starting in 1955 with the striking oil of his father, they had remained the one subject to which he returned time and time again. Since the impatience that Kenneth had shown while posing for *Portrait of My Father* made him the more difficult subject of the two, the majority of Hockney's parental studies were of his mother, Laura, who was always willing to help her son with his work by sitting for him. After he left home, there were few visits to Bradford that were not marked by some representation of her, whether it was a drawing, a painting or a photograph, and in all of them her modest and unassuming nature comes across, together with the steeliness that was an integral part of her character.

The one thing Hockney had never attempted was a painting of his parents together, yet it was an idea that had its origins back in September 1970, when his mother had been in hospital in Bradford undergoing an operation for a tumour on her bowel. 'My father could go to the hospital every day for a few hours,' he told the art historian Marco Livingstone, 'but he wasn't used to sitting and talking to her for a few hours every day at home. He would be doing something, my mother would be doing something else. It was then I noticed that people communicate in other ways, it's not always just talking, especially people who know each other well. They'd been married forty-five years, and if you've been living with somebody forty-five years, you know a lot about the face, the little actions, what they mean. You know how to interpret them. I think it was then I decided there was a subject there I somehow wanted to try and deal with.'[6]

He called his mother on his birthday, 9 July, to suggest a sitting, though she was not feeling her best after suffering a prolonged bout of diarrhoea. 'David suggests we go to Paris near the month end,' wrote Laura Hockney in her diary, 'as he needs another sitting for the picture he is painting of Ken & I. I feel miles away from having a picture of myself in this condition.'[7] In spite of still feeling under the weather, however, the end of August found her and Ken in Paris, the lure of a weekend with her son too great to miss. 'Not feeling too good,' she noted, 'but hoping to enjoy stay in Paris. David started work on picture almost immediately. Sitting can be quite hard work.'[8]

Over the next three days Ken and Laura sat constantly for their portrait, with the occasional break for a trip to the shops or a meal with friends. On the first night, Jean Léger and Alexis Vidal gave them dinner in their apartment – 'What a lovely meal,' Laura wrote, 'vegetarian – made on my account'[9] – while on the following day Shirley Goldfarb joined them for lunch and took Ken shopping in the afternoon, an expedition that caused him some anguish – 'Ken complains about having to spend (own) money at shops with Shirley.'[10] The next day it was Laura's turn. 'Yves-Marie came to lunch. David suddenly broke off and said we would go to the shops and buy a dress – which we did . . . Yves-Marie being spokesman as he speaks French perfectly. Went and returned by 2 taxis, I the richer for a beautiful dress & in an hour we were back at the easel . . . I sat again for David – so many alterations – but he was happy – worked very hard and said he was getting on well.'[11]

After Kenneth and Laura returned to Bradford, and with enough material to make a solid start on the new picture on his return, Hockney now set off to New York to join Geldzahler for their trip to Fire Island. He left on 13 August, a Wednesday, finally ready after months of hard work to let his hair down. The social season on Fire Island went on from May through till Labor Day in early September, most of the activity taking place at the weekend when the Long Island Railroad would fill up with crowds of young people and transport them down to the Long Island South Shore to catch a ferry to their chosen destinations, the gay communities of Cherry Grove and the Pines being reached from Sayville. The rich wouldn't bother with the three-hour train journey. They flew in by seaplane from the 23rd Street Skyport. When they arrived, everyone headed on the wooden boardwalks, pulling the luggage and groceries behind them in little red metal wagons, for their rented beachside cottages, many of which were supported on stilts dug into the sand dunes. Houses were usually shared for the season by a group of friends who went there for one reason only – to cruise, to dance, to take drugs, to have fun.

'Fire Island was such an idealised state of nature and human promiscuity, in a more profound way than just sexually,' recalls Don Cribb, a photographer friend of both Hockney and Arthur Lambert. 'It was promiscuous in every way because it was all new things coming together, and the temptation to explore a little bit and to meet people randomly, not just by design or because of a formal introduction, but just random people coming together, converging and dissipating. It was fascinating. The people were good-looking, all the music was interesting, either topical and right for the moment, or classical, and the combinations were always overlapping. The people were either well-accomplished musicians or trendy young people in fashion or the photographers of the moment, or all these people aspiring to meet famous people, or the famous people themselves. It was just a convergence of all this energy and a very polite kind of social atmosphere. David used to refer to himself as "a little artist on the boardwalk of life".'[12]

Life in the Pines revolved around the beach in the daytime, and the harbour area from late afternoon when the crowds would begin to gather at the Pines Dune and Yacht Club, a waterside complex that included the Botel, a hotel with pool and bar, the Elephant Restaurant, the Pavilion Disco and the Blue Whale Bar. Central to the scene were the happy-hour 'tea dances', originally inaugurated by John Whyte at the Blue Whale. 'The gay community played a substantial role in how the area felt, and what it did with its time,' Cribb remembers. 'For example, after a certain hour the restaurants turned into gay bars, so late afternoon, after all the beach and stuff, you'd go home, take a shower and then go out.'[13]

Each day consisted of a series of rituals, beginning with the afternoon swimsuit tea dances, 'Low Tea', at the Blue Whale around 5 p.m., followed by 'High Tea' at the Pavilion around 8 p.m. Groups of friends would then drift back to their houses for dinner, then take a nap and head out again at midnight when the hardcore fun began with disco dancing at the Ice Palace or the Pavilion – most people out of their heads on a combination of poppers, cocaine and Quaaludes. 'It was totally sex and drugs and rock 'n' roll,' Hockney recalls. 'I would take anything there that people gave to me. They'd give you a pill and whether it was acid or anything you would just take it. The bars closed at 4 a.m. I remember people telling me one time that I was dancing on the counter. I was probably on acid or some other strong thing.'[14]

When the dancing finally stopped, action moved to the wooded glen that lies between the Grove and the Pines, popularly known as 'the Meat Rack', as described by the American author and literary critic Edmund White in his memoir *City Boy*. 'After the disco finally closed shop at dawn, beautiful, sweaty men would stagger off into the scrub bush between communities to have group sex. At Versailles no titles were used in conversation, though everyone was conscious of exact gradations in rank; in the same way on Fire Island penniless beauties and millionaire lawyers all laughed and made love together, all dressed in the same swim trunks or jeans and sandals.'[15] For Don Cribb 'it was totally hedonistic. Everything was sexual, from what you ate, what

Henry Geldzahler and David Hockney at Arthur Lambert's house on Fire Island

you did, what you heard, I mean the whole thing, visually, tangibly, you could feel the throbbing in the soil. You felt that the whole world was having sex and you just latched to it. Next thing you knew it was daybreak and you were thinking "How did time go by so fast?"[16]

Hockney loved his summer spent on Fire Island. The photograph of him and Geldzahler taken by Arthur Lambert perfectly sums up the mood of the holiday. They are sitting stretched out on wooden beach recliners, Geldzahler in bow tie and straw hat, Hockney in a white suit with bow tie and white flat cap, both holding parasols as if they were on the deck of an ocean liner and had not a care in the world. The other guests were Don Cribb, Larry Stanton and Hockney's old friend, the fashion model Joe McDonald, all of whom he drew. Having no penchant for either swimming or sunbathing, he spent his time on the beach with his camera, eventually filling a whole album with photographs of bronzed young men.

However caught up he was in the whirlwind that was life on Fire Island, Hockney never forgot his mother. 'David phoned from New York,' Laura recorded on 3 September, ' – he is enjoying holiday & stays another week. Hopes to come up to Bradford on return. It was lovely of him to phone. He asked Dad if he was taking care of me – Dad said Yes!!!'[17] When his holiday was over, he flew directly back to Paris, much to the disappointment of his mother, but not before arranging a special surprise for her. 'Phone call from London,' wrote Laura on 25 September. 'Julie Cavanagh [sic] on behalf of American paper "Women's Wear Daily". David had given my name as a "beautiful woman" along with Celia Birtwell – how I laughed – but if it is for American publication, it won't matter.'[18] The next day, however, the *Yorkshire Post* called. 'Did I know about the "beautiful women"?'[19] And on Saturday morning she woke to find the story in that day's paper, and a photograph of her under the headline 'BEAUTY FOR DAVID HOCKNEY'. '. . . she is something special to her 38-year-old, David,' commented the 'People' columnist, 'who when asked what he would describe as beautiful replied, "My mum." . . . Mrs Hockney was somewhat embarrassed at the unexpected publicity. "I didn't know I was any beauty. I'm just ordinary and I don't like a fuss. But it was nice of David to say so," she said.'[20]

In Paris, Hockney was eager to get back to work on his parents' portrait, something that had been causing him some anxiety. He was beset with problems, not least of which was that, in his desire to paint a loving son's account of his parents, he was forced to address highly personal issues. 'It's a very traditional thing to do, I know, painting one's parents,' he told his biographer, Peter Webb, 'but I think it could be a lot more than just that – their predicament, their lack of fulfilment, the desperate-not-knowing what they could have had out of life. And their relationship with me.'[21]

Hockney approached the project gingerly. He was a little out of practice using oils and was aware that he was embarking on a return to naturalism, his last experience of which, the double portrait of George Lawson and Wayne Sleep, had ended in disaster. He began by sketching out the composition in a series of line drawings made in ink and crayon, his initial plan being to include himself in the painting, using the contrivance of placing his face as a reflection in a mirror. In *My Parents and Myself*, the seated figures of Laura and Kenneth are placed

'My Parents Posing for *My Parents and Myself*', photograph by David Hockney

on either side of a green tabouret, on the surface of which stands a
bowl of yellow tulips and a dressing-table mirror in which the artist
is reflected. To concentrate attention on the subjects, they are shown
against a background of bare canvas on which is painted a large red
triangle. This was intended to act as a device to unite the three heads
and function as a visual metaphor of their mutual dependence. The
picture was not a success. The triangular device was too contrived; he
reworked the figure of his father until he began to look wooden; and
the face in the mirror distracted the viewer from the main subject. '. . .
it looked too much like earlier work,' Hockney said later, 'it looked as
though I've gone back a bit and don't quite know what to do. So I was
never truly satisfied, nor was I satisfied with it as a portrait of <u>them</u>, it
wasn't quite right. So I had to struggle on. Now I might have abandoned
it had it not <u>been</u> my parents . . . Because it was them they would want
to <u>know</u> why I'd abandoned it and everything and I couldn't do that.
And I thought anyway it <u>is</u> an interesting thing to do . . . and I should
pursue it.'[22]

He distracted himself with another project, after being approached
by Nikos Stangos, who had left Penguin and was now working as a
commissioning editor at Thames & Hudson. He was keen to revive
the idea of the book suggested by Henry Geldzahler which had never
materialised, in spite of the work he and Hockney had put into it on
their trip to Lucca in August 1973. This may have been laziness on the
part of Geldzahler, who had a reputation as someone who liked to leave
the office early. Ron Kitaj loved to tease Hockney with his story of
meeting Diana Vreeland, the formidable and throaty-voiced editor of
American *Vogue*, and asking her if she knew Geldzahler. '"Oh we all
know Henry," she replied. "He's very well read, isn't he?" continued
Kitaj, to which Mrs Vreeland replied, "You'd be well read if you went
home every day at one o'clock."'[23]

Stangos realised that the only way such a book would ever appear
would be if he took it over completely and acted as ghostwriter. Taking
as his model the autobiography of Benvenuto Cellini, who had dictated
his life to his young assistant, he persuaded Hockney to come to London
and spend some time with him at his flat, speaking into a tape recorder.

The sessions, which took place over three days, were fuelled by copious quantities of white wine, and Stangos's questions were sparked off by a large collection he had amassed of black-and-white reproductions of the artist's work. 'He would stay from ten in the morning till ten in the evening with no one around,' Stangos recalled. 'It was like conducting an extended psychoanalytical session. David would lie on a couch and I would sit at the other end of the room and I would put questions to him and would just let him talk in a rambling way . . . What I did was to keep in mind always that I wanted a *narrative*, a Cellini-like narrative, that would be almost like a work of fiction.'[24]

The twenty-five hours of taped conversations that resulted were then edited down into narrative form. 'I did that very quickly, in about ten days. I wrote a lot of it myself and I put words into his mouth, but not any words that he wouldn't have used.'[25] The resulting text of about eighty thousand words was then sent over to Hockney in Paris, who was at first quite taken aback. 'David was shocked,' Stangos said. 'He hadn't expected a narrative account at all. He felt it was rather revealing, perhaps embarrassing, maybe even harmful to himself. And he wondered if anyone would be interested. It was like *A Bigger Splash* all over again – he said he hadn't realized what had been going on . . .'[26] Stangos had great faith in the book, however, and managed to persuade Hockney that it would do him more good than harm, and he consequently agreed to its publication the following year.

Hockney's abandonment of *My Parents and Myself* coincided with a general disillusionment about his life in Paris. To start with, the successful release there of *A Bigger Splash* had brought him new and unwanted fame. 'The French loved it,' he wrote. 'I suppose it was a kind of French-style film. And so people would come up to me on the street and they'd come round to my place.'[27] Then there was the fact that he had originally gone to Paris for peace and tranquillity, to get away from the social whirl of London in order to work, but by the time he'd been living there for a year, everybody knew where he was and people started to come over from England to visit him. 'They would say, "Oh, David Hockney will make us a cup of tea,"' he recalls.

'"He's always there, just painting away," and people did start dropping in and not leaving until midnight. Well, I couldn't work under those conditions, so I thought I'd better go back to London. So I just got a van and Gregory and I spent two days packing everything into it and we drove back to London. It's always a good reason to move when people start to be a nuisance.'[28]

When he returned to London at the beginning of November, it was clear to Hockney that he needed to make changes in his life. His flat in Powis Terrace depressed him, holding as it did so many memories of Peter Schlesinger, and things were not helped by the fact that his friend and studio assistant Mo McDermott was back on heroin. 'I phoned Mo (again),' wrote mutual friend Ossie Clark in his diary on 16 November, 'but he . . . sounded smacked out,' while on 22 November he noted, 'Mo behaving ridiculously – all kinds of junkies at his place.'[29] This scenario is supported by Marinka Watts, who lived across the road from Hockney. She shared a flat with Nicky Rae, a knitwear designer, who was one of Hockney's regular models and a boyfriend of Henry Geldzahler, and had made friends with Mo after meeting him on the street and agreeing to help look after his cat, Arthur, while he was away in LA. From cat-sitting, she had then graduated to occasional flat-sitting.

'Every time I went back to that flat,' she remembers, 'it got worse, and in the end there were people from down the street moved in there. It had become a den of iniquity, like Bedlam in *The Rake's Progress*. At the beginning it was all very bright and lovely and inspirational, and there was always fantastic music playing. A few years later, when I was going out to work early in the morning, I would have to leave the flat at about 7.30 and I would have to walk over bodies lying all over the place. I remember a revolting person who was probably the drug pusher, really dreadful-looking, who thought he was important, but was likely to die at any minute . . . I found one boy trying to commit suicide in the bathtub. You were fighting a losing battle.'[30]

Luckily for Hockney, Maurice Payne, his printer on the Cavafy poems project, was around to assist him while Mo was out of action. Payne was at that time employed by Petersburg Press, but he was permitted to take this job as it was seen as a means of keeping in touch

'Self-portrait with
Maurice Payne',
1977, photograph
by David Hockney

with what Hockney was up to. The two men worked at 2 Pembroke
Studios, Pembroke Gardens, part of a complex of small studio houses
in Kensington built in the 1890s by Charles Frederick Kearley, and as
luck would have it, the owner of number 10, the artist Bernard Cohen,
was looking for a tenant. He asked Payne if he thought Hockney might
like to rent it. It was perfect timing, and he jumped at the opportunity.
He had already decided to sell his flat in Powis Terrace to Tchaik
Chassay, who had been responsible for its remodelling, and had bought
the apartment on the top floor of number 17, with a view to converting
it into a new studio. Chassay was to carry out the work.

    10 Pembroke Studios turned out to be the perfect haven he was
looking for. 'Not too many people knew I was there,' he wrote. 'Each
time you move back you have a nice period when it's quiet, the phone
doesn't ring much, you can get on with work and see only a few friends.
Despite what some people may think, I tend to live in a rather intimate

world of a few people, close friends who are very respectful of my time, and if I want to work they let me. I started feeling much better.'[31]

Hockney planned to spend Christmas in Bradford as usual, before heading off to New York to meet up with his lover, Gregory Evans, and drive to California. 'David arrived about 12 noon,' Laura wrote on Christmas Day, '& we went to Pauls – very good Christmas lunch at 2pm – then opening gifts – & what surprises! David gave watches to Ken and three of the children (digital watches) except Ken's which was a "Gollywog". . . I received a beautiful fine gold chain . . . Ken gave David a cassette of his "Billy Williams".[32] That was his limit! Seems to miss out on the Christmas Spirit tho' he has bought some expensive photographic gadgets for himself.'[33] The following day her irritation with Ken was cancelled out by a special treat. 'David up first – made two drawings of me – then suggested we had a run – left Dad to make his own breakfast. What a beautiful clear morning! Drove to Ilkley, Heber's Ghyll, Baildon & home by Paul's. All in little more than an hour – I enjoyed David – alone.'[34]

When Hockney returned to London, it was to find Mo in a poor state, junked up to the eyeballs, so he booked him into a clinic. A week later, on 10 January, Laura noted in her diary that 'David . . . has plans to help Mo – by asking Rod Taylor to give him work in his weaving shed when recuperating . . . We are all anxious he should keep well.'[35] Rod Taylor, a contemporary of Hockney's who had been a textile student when he was at Bradford College of Art, was now living near Howarth in West Yorkshire, where he and his wife, Brenda, had bought Ponden Hall, a seventeenth-century farmhouse which was said to have been the model for Thrushcross Grange, the home of the Linton family in *Wuthering Heights*. Here they ran both weaving courses and a bed-and-breakfast business. 'David came before noon with Mo,' wrote Laura on 17 January, 'who looks very frail but says they have done wonders for him at the hospital – he brought a beautiful white cyclamen for me . . . We had fish & chips from the shop for lunch & I had made apple tart . . . we went to Ponden Hall, near Howarth, where Brenda and Rod Taylor have made their home and cater for "Pennine Way" hikers and travellers. There was a crowd around the table when we went in – the place is huge & one room with about 5 double beds in it all unmade – not a tidy bed anywhere. But that is typical . . . Mo will find it Spartan but I'm sure he will find plenty to do.'[36]

With Mo temporarily in good hands, Hockney left for the US. Other than seeing Gregory, there was a purpose to the drive to California. Ken Tyler, who had printed both *A Hollywood Collection* and *The Weather Series*, had left Gemini to set up his own business in Bedford Village, New York, and his former partner Sid Felsen had asked Hockney to come to LA to work on a new series of lithographs on the subject of 'Friends'. So he and Gregory set off from New York, armed with nothing more than some guidebooks and a set of Rand McNally road maps, on what he later described to Henry Geldzahler as 'that marvellous drive'.[37] They took two weeks, passing through Pennsylvania, Virginia, Tennessee, Arkansas, Louisiana, Texas, New Mexico, Arizona and finally California. 'It was a new experience for me,' Evans recalls, 'I hadn't really been back to the States since I'd been living in Europe, so I was coming back with a different perspective. We had a good time, enjoying each other's company and sense of humour. We stayed in a lot of motels, and at that time you couldn't really get any decent wine in the US. Since David and I had been well and truly "Parisified", there were a lot of jokes about that.'[38]

It was supposed to be partly a holiday, but that is a word that Hockney scarcely understood. 'If everybody is asleep,' Henry Geldzahler observed, 'he draws them sleeping, and if he's alone he draws his luggage lying on the floor. He'll work until he drops . . . There's a line of poetry: "He rests from art in art". If David is tired of drawing then he'll take photographs; if he's tired of taking photographs he'll paint; if he's tired of painting he'll design an opera. He's constantly thinking he hasn't worked hard enough recently.'[39] Needless to say, the entire trip was chronicled in many drawings and hundreds of photographs.

Though their accommodation on the journey was mostly in motels which, Hockney told his parents, were 'reasonably cheap and convenient but monotonously alike, which is a bit depressing after driving a few hundred miles',[40] there was the occasional exception, such as the Arlington in Hot Springs, Arkansas. This massive Spanish

Renaissance-style hotel, built in the 1920s, and famous for its thermal baths, had been host to both Presidents Roosevelt and Truman, as well as to Al Capone, who used to take an entire floor for his staff and bodyguards. 'I have been here for two days,' Hockney wrote to Ken and Laura on 29 January, 'drawing and reading and taking the baths every afternoon, they make one feel very good . . . This hotel was built about 1925 – quite old for this part of America and makes a pleasant change from the usual motel. The landscape is very beautiful – mountains and pine forests and hot springs and hot lakes.'[41]

After New Orleans, where they stayed in a Howard Johnson motel, they drove up to Phoenix, Hockney becoming increasingly entranced by the colours he was seeing around him. 'I've now driven 4,000 miles from New York,' he told his parents, 'and at a 55 mph speed limit it seems quite slow (but safe) yet here in the west it's very beautiful at that speed. In the late afternoons the mountains seem to be a vivid purple and the desert all orange and red. Occaisonaly [sic] it rains. Jan and Feb are the only rainy times here and it does bring out the flowers in the cacti.'[42] In Phoenix they enjoyed another spot of luxury. 'Wherever we were,' Evans remembers, 'David would always say, "Look in the guide. See what hotels there are." So when we got to Phoenix, I said, "Well, here's one with two dining rooms," but it didn't really say anything else about it, and it wasn't until we were checking in and looking around that we noticed anything special about it.'[43] It turned out to be the Arizona Biltmore, designed by Albert Chase McArthur, a pupil of Frank Lloyd Wright's, and built in 1929, when it was crowned 'The Jewel of the Desert'. 'This hotel,' wrote Hockney, 'is still kept exactly as it was then. Very beautiful indeed.'[44] Among some memorable images he created while he was there are a coloured crayon drawing of a large vase in the hotel gardens, and some beautiful studies of water in the hotel pool, which was said to be Marilyn Monroe's favourite swimming pool in America.

When Hockney and Gregory finally reached LA on 7 February, they moved into a penthouse suite at the Chateau Marmont, and Hockney immersed himself in the 'Friends' project that had been suggested by Sid Felsen. This had come along at a perfect time, as he was once more facing doubts about the direction in which he was going, and required something to take his mind off his problems, just as he had done in Paris a few years previously when he was trying to break away from obsessive naturalism. The struggle he had faced with the portrait of his parents had shaken him and he needed to engage in some academic drawing again. At the Gemini studio on Melrose Avenue, he made a series of large coloured lithographs of friends, both old and new, that were done in the traditional manner, drawn directly onto the stone. They were meticulous and detailed, if in the end a little lifeless, featuring, among others, his 'gang' – Joe McDonald, Gregory Evans, Nick Wilder and Mo McDermott – all seated full-length in chairs; two new friends, Billy Wilder and Brooke Hopper, both similarly posed; a new double portrait of Christopher Isherwood and Don Bachardy; and several studies of Henry Geldzahler. 'We are pleased to say,' wrote Sid Felsen to Paul Cornwall-Jones, 'that David is doing an extraordinary series, which we believe will become recognized as one of the most important graphic portraiture projects done by him or anyone else in our time.'[45]

'I've always liked the idea of doing academic drawings at times,' Hockney told Marco Livingstone. 'It's something that's reasonably necessary to do if you want to draw at all . . . If you want to make depictions of anything, it's just something as old-fashioned as training your eye to look and observe again. They're done really as exercises, you're not that interested in what it's going to look like when you've done. It's the doing of it that's the exercise . . . I've always thought then immediately afterwards all the drawings are better, whatever you draw. The line drawings are better: the line can tell you more of what's there after doing this.'[46] The truth of this can be seen in the few lithographs he completed immediately after the 'Friends' sessions, in particular a freely drawn nude of Gregory wearing gym socks that positively flows with energy, and a charming small study made with the simplest of brush strokes of Henry Geldzahler smoking a cigar. 'Henry was always willing to pose,' Hockney recalled. 'One time he saw me drawing and he thought I was posing him, so he sat rigid. And I didn't say anything, but for twenty minutes I kept looking up and drawing, and I drew a very careful drawing of Mickey Mouse on a piece of paper. And he sat

rigid for twenty minutes. He was very annoyed, but I couldn't resist. It was naughty of me, I know!'[47]

Christopher Isherwood's diaries from this period show that Hockney, while in Hollywood, led a social life that was every bit as relentless as his working life. At its centre was Isherwood and Don Bachardy's house at 145 Adelaide Drive, Santa Monica, where they presided over a southern Californian salon for philosophers, writers and artists. At regular dinners held around their circular dining table, which had come from a sale at the props department at Warner Bros, Hockney mixed with Aldous Huxley, Allen Ginsberg, the Stravinskys, Wystan Auden, Lauren Bacall and Tony Richardson. He ate at the most fashionable restaurants, such as Ma Maison, L'Ermitage and Mr Chow's. He hung out with David and Angie Bowie after Bowie's show at the Forum, and attended a party given by John Schlesinger, along with Warren Beatty, Elton John, Roddy McDowall and Charlotte Rampling. He attended dinners at George Cukor's, where guests were invited for six o'clock on the dot, and would all be lined up outside his house at five to for fear of his temper if they were two seconds late. His new friend Billy Wilder said of him, 'Any Hollywood hostess is honoured to have him at her party – they fight for him because he brings life . . . he's always interesting and if he has got nothing to say, he just keeps his mouth shut. It's fascinating how a working-class Englishman has become so much part of our community. If you only have one friend and it is Hockney, you are not lost in this world.'[48]

On 1 April Christopher Isherwood noted in his diary, 'Said goodbye to David Hockney and Gregory Evans who leave for Australia tonight.'[49] It was to be Hockney's first visit to Australia – home to his brothers John and Philip – where an exhibition of his prints was to be mounted in Adelaide. They flew first to Tahiti, where they took a small boat to Cook's Bay and 'sailed into the most beautiful bay just as Captain Cook did about 1760'.[50] From there they travelled to the tiny island of Bora Bora, where they stayed, Hockney wrote to Kitaj, 'in a little cabin over the water like a peasant'.[51] He told his parents, 'The sea is warm and inviting, clear and blue and full of brightly coloured fish. Everyone here goes "snorkelling" – a goggle mask with a tube to breathe through so you can look at the fish and coral as you swim around. It's all marvelously relaxing after working hard in Los Angeles.'[52] On hearing his news, Laura noted, 'I do like his letters & I wish I was with him – to be with a good companion who enjoys and shares his pleasure is so great!'[53]

Hockney also told Kitaj, 'It's stunningly beautiful, but a week is enough for me. In the end I prefer culture to nature . . . I've been doing a lot of drawing and must have already taken a thousand photographs . . . and have lots of ideas for paintings.'[54] He talked of his excitement at visiting Australia and staying with John in Sydney, but could not resist the usual Australian jokes. 'I hope we can keep our feet on the ground there . . . I'll let you know what down-under is like, if I can find a pen that writes on the cieling [*sic*] – we've started joking already about how the coffee flies up in your face etc, etc, etc.'[55] He wrote him a postcard in similar mode a few days later from New Zealand. 'Watcha Digger, here we are in New Zealand sat on the ceiling of a little restaurant. The food is not so good but with the kitchen up in the basement what can you expect. They are big on sheep here, talk about sex + animals, they even have a magazine about sheep that strip – it's called The New Zealand Sheep Shearer. I'll send you a copy when the shops open next week. PS Gregory just went and pissed on his head.'[56]

The subject of Mo was never far from Hockney's mind, even on the other side of the world. By now he had moved from Ponden Hall and was living with Hockney's brother Paul. 'Mo seems to be fine with Paul in Bradford,' Hockney wrote to Kitaj, 'and I must confess that one of the nice things about California is the absence of all that other worrying I have to do in London. Everybody, even Henry, says I'm so much more relaxed in California, and it's terrific to devote all one's energies into work – a bit selfish perhaps, but a relief for a while.'[57] On 16 April, a day on which Laura received 'a lovely card from David from Boa Boa [*sic*]', she was able to record, 'Mo went off to London yesterday & hopes to go to California on Tuesday, I do hope he keeps up the good living. Paul and Jean have made a new man of him physically – He looks fine.'[58]

Mo flew to California on 20 April, arriving just in time to meet Hockney back from Australia and help him prepare for an exhibition of his work, which opened on 9 May at Nick Wilder's. Hockney was happy to see him looking so much better, but while Mo may have been on the mend, it soon transpired that things in the family home in Bradford were not so good. Kenneth, who had developed an interest in Christian

Science, was simply ignoring his diabetes and was subsequently behaving in an irrational and aggressive manner. Laura, meanwhile, was in constant pain from a bad hip, which was to require an operation, and for which she received little sympathy from her husband. Things came to a head at the end of April when, on a holiday in Llandudno, Kenneth, much to his fury, had to be forcibly hospitalised in order to stabilise him. On his return home, he made the lives of all around him a misery. 'Ken got up full of accusations this a.m,' recorded Laura in her diary on 5 May. 'Still on about . . . hospital & blaming all and sundry for having to go there.'[59] And on 11 May she described Ken as 'very difficult. He has no pain but I'm sure he is uncomfortable & is fighting his own way back to normal to avoid Doctors – says he is afraid to go into hospital again. That is a confession!'[60] A week later they were both hospitalised, Kenneth in St Luke's for further stabilisation of his diabetes, and Laura in Woodlands for her hip operation.

Hockney returned to England and went straight up to Bradford for a few days. 'David came up to hospital each day,' Laura recorded, '– not only visited but did drawings and took a few snaps. Brought sherry to celebrate Mrs Bent and Kathleen Symons going home on Saturday. – Could not have it Friday night so had it after lunch. David arrived in time to share & they drank his health. Dr came round. I unexpectedly decide to return home . . . as beds are needed. David picked me up . . . & left for London after lunch.'[61] Back in town he found Christopher Isherwood and Don Bachardy, who had arrived from LA for a month. Isherwood was to be featured in a big show in London at the National Portrait Gallery, *Young Writers of the Thirties*, and he was keen while in England to visit his brother Richard in Cheshire.

Before the exhibition opened, Isherwood and Bachardy persuaded Hockney to take them on a 'Mr Whiz Tour' to East Anglia, Oxfordshire, Scotland, the Lake District and Yorkshire. They had chosen the ideal summer to do this, the weather being perfect throughout June and July of 1976, and the day on which they set off, 9 June, was, noted Isherwood in his diary, 'very warm'.[62] Their first stop was lunch with the writer Dodie Smith and her husband, Alec Beesley, in Finchingfield, Essex, before driving across to Suffolk to dine with Benjamin Britten and Peter Pears in Aldeburgh. The following morning they drove to Stow-on-the-Wold to see Tony Richardson, who was filming *Joseph Andrews*, with Ann-Margret and Peter Firth, afterwards taking in a tour of Blenheim Palace and a spot of punting on the river in Oxford.

On 11 June they left their billet, Hillside Farm, Adelstrop, at 7.45 a.m. and drove to Durham for lunch and a look round the cathedral, arriving in Edinburgh in time for tea. They stayed at the Caledonian Hotel and ate haggis for dinner at the Café Royal. In the morning they took in the National Gallery, and lunched with Hockney's old friend George Lawson, who had been brought up in Edinburgh and had attended the Royal High School, 'then saw the portrait gallery, drove up Arthur's Seat and all had tea with George's mother'.[63] They ended the day dining with George's eccentric uncle, Robin Stark, who with his wife Christine had been instrumental in setting up the Edinburgh Festival in 1947. They also provided money towards the upkeep of the giraffe in Edinburgh Zoo, and had paid for a bench outside the compound on which they could sit and watch it. After dinner, Stark took them to look at the Water of Leith, a stream that flows through the suburbs of Edinburgh to the Port of Leith.

Isherwood's diary entry for 13 June gives credence to the name 'Mr Whiz Tours' for these Hockney-led excursions: 'Left at 7:45, driving via Glencoe, Fort William (lunched Alexandra Hotel), Urquhart Castle on Loch Ness, to Inverness. Back via Blair Atholl, Perth (supper at Station Hotel), Forth bridges, arriving back in Edinburgh 10:30pm.'[64] They must have been exhausted by the end of the day. At ten o'clock the following morning they were on the road again, to Lindisfarne Castle on Holy Island, had a walk on the Roman wall at Housesteads, and then drove cross-country to Keswick, where they stayed at the Royal Oak Hotel and took a motor launch on Derwent Water.

On 15 June, the final day of the tour, it was time to visit Yorkshire and take in Brontë country. 'We left Keswick at 8:00 a.m., saw Wordsworth's Dove Cottage. Drove via Hawes to Haworth – bad road over the fells above Semer Water. We had lunch at Ponden Hall (original of Thrushcross Grange) with Roderick and Brenda Taylor. We saw the Brontës' house at Haworth. Saw David's mother at her home in Bradford.'[65] After tea with Laura, Hockney and Bachardy drove Isherwood to his brother's home, Thornway, in Cheshire, and then returned to Bradford, where Kenneth was about to undergo an operation on his bladder, something he was very unhappy about. 'Dad . . . unsettled about operation,' Laura noted. 'Christian Scientists don't operate.'[66] In the end the surgeon managed to get his bladder working again without a full operation, and Kenneth was finally allowed home at the end of the month.

On Hockney's return to London, he found himself involved in another fight about gay rights. Ever since the public stands he had taken in the late sixties, he had been something of a hero to the burgeoning gay rights movement, and had even been appointed vice president of the Campaign for Homosexual Equality. Aside from his celebrity, it was because his name was on the notepaper of the CHE that he received a telephone call at his studio in late June from the proprietor of Incognito Books, a gay bookshop in Earls Court, to say that they were being raided by the police, and a selection of their stock, all considered pornographic, had been confiscated. This included magazines such as *Hung Heavy*, *Taste of Beefcake*, *Black Studs*, *Him Exclusive* and *Leather Studs*, as well as *Playguy*, in whose pages Hockney had himself recently appeared. The January 1976 issue had featured blown-up Polaroids of Gregory Evans, Mark Lippiscombe and himself posing in the bathroom of his flat in the Cour de Rohan in Paris. In some of the shots they were wearing white socks and underpants, while in others they were nude, sitting on the edge of the bath, though all the photographs were consciously erotic, with the sheen of water on their flesh and the light giving the effect of a painting by Caravaggio. Hockney had been quite proud of the shoot, but when a friend of Ann Upton's had seen the pictures, they had said to her, 'My God, what's somebody in his position doing in a magazine like that?', to which she had replied, 'What position?'[67]

This was not the first time that Incognito Books had been targeted. There had been several raids in 1975 – during one the entire September issue of *Him Exclusive*, which had its editorial offices there, had been confiscated. At that time, the editor, Alan Purnell, had commented to the *Guardian* that these raids were entirely discriminatory. 'The magazine is clearly marked for adults only,' he said, 'and it has been openly on sale for almost a year . . . Him Exclusive contains nothing that would not be perfectly acceptable in any heterosexual magazine.'[68] Since the Incognito bookshop was not far from Pembroke Gardens, Hockney responded to the call by going straight over there to add his weight to the remonstrations with the police. He later told *Gay News* that he had every intention of following up his action with strong complaints to the Home Office about police harassment of gay bookshops and gay publications, because 'when people become aware of oppression, they should do something about it . . . I think censorship is quite bad here and nobody does anything about it. Nobody complains.'[69]

Having someone as well known as Hockney prepared to take a stand on their behalf was of enormous significance to shops like Incognito, a measure of his fame at the time being his inclusion in a series run in the *Observer* called 'The Superstars', in which he featured alongside Marilyn Monroe and Rudolf Nureyev. A further demonstration of his ever-increasing celebrity was his invitation to the royal reception for the president of France, Valéry Giscard d'Estaing, on a state visit to London at the end of June, as his mother proudly noted in her diary. 'David . . . had an invitation to meet the French President & was introduced – also met the Queen whom he thought was P. wife.'[70] When he read of the Incognito incident, Denis Lemon, the editor of the pioneering *Gay News*, saw an interview with Hockney as a way of further raising their profile. This was at a time when the paper was already in the news as a result of a private prosecution for blasphemy being brought against it by Mary Whitehouse, president of the National Viewers' and Listeners' Association, for the inclusion in the 3 June issue of James Kirkup's controversial poem 'The Love That Dares to Speak Its Name', which contains graphic descriptions of a Roman centurion making love to the dead body of Christ.

Keith Howes, the features editor who was sent to do the interview, made two visits to Hockney's Pembroke Gardens studio, and was quite charmed by both his subject and his surroundings. 'One expects to find an Aladdin's cave of fascinating objects in an artist's studio,' he wrote after their first meeting, 'and David Hockney's high, white room with its gallery does not disappoint. A discarded pair of canary-yellow braces speckled with Cambridge-blue paint. A woolly panda sitting next to a Bradford Grammar School old boys' magazine. On the work bench is a leather bound photograph album with over two hundred pictures waiting to be slotted in. Pictures of comfortable, grey-haired ladies (David's aunties), of comfortable young men with wet straggly hair and white shorts. Pictures of swimming pools and wire chairs in the Californian sun. And isn't that Christopher Isherwood with Benjamin Britten and Peter Pears in Aldeburgh? . . . Dominating the studio is an unfinished painting of David's mother and father, sitting somewhat uncomfortably on Habitat chairs against a chintz-less, white wall. And between them is a mirror in which the artist's little Dutch Boy face is plainly visible. The little Dutch Boy himself is resplendent in bright blue shirt and black pin-stripe trousers with tennis shoes and a big fat cigar to complete the shimmering effect.'[71]

The fact that Howes refers to Hockney's parents looking so uncomfortable in his portrait of them is a reflection of the struggle that he was still having with this picture, which remained unfinished in spite of endless attempts to get it right. A few days after this first session with *Gay News*, Laura Hockney came down on a day trip from Bradford for yet another sitting. 'David met me at King's Cross – we drove straight to Pembroke Gdns Studios, had cup of tea and I "sat" until 1pm. David went to shop & made lunch while I sat in the sunshine in his little garden – lunch of omelet, Tomato Salad, cheese, apple juice. Back at work by 1.45pm. How hot we were even just sitting. David was pleased with his achievement tho to me it is very slow work, but he took many photographs for detail. At 4pm we finished work.'[72]

When Howes returned for a second visit, he found Peter Schlesinger at the studio, hovering 'edgily round the scene – hosing the garden, fetching a louvred screen and then a ladder and probably going out of his mind that although he and David are supposed to be going over to a friend's for dinner at 10, David is still talking to me over an hour late. But as he's known David for ten years, he breathes deeply and manages a few retailer's smiles in my direction and finally defrosts the fridge next door with a vigour Nanook of the North would have envied.'[73] In spite of his relationship with Gregory Evans, Hockney was still a little bit in love with Schlesinger and liked to have him around as much as possible, arranging jobs for him and even a small monthly salary. 'He knew I didn't have any money,' Schlesinger recalls, 'so he employed me to do things for him, like sticking all the photographs in his photo albums, of which there were thousands, and then I would get a little monthly cheque from Paul Hockney. With hindsight it should just have been a clean break, but it wasn't easy.'[74]

Questioned by Howes as to whether or not they still had sex together, Hockney commented, 'No. I would like it in a way, but I can understand his point of view a bit. I just think it would be nice one day to do it . . . I certainly wouldn't press it. I think he knows that I keep trying to engineer situations that might . . . But I think it was Bernard Shaw who said "the single-minded should stay single".'[75] He finally admitted that he was probably too self-absorbed to have a successful relationship. 'You can't,' he said. 'All artists are like that. In the end they're gonna put their work first. You read about them – what Tolstoy was like with his wife, what Matisse was like . . . very few artists actually had a good relationship with a close person. In the end it's because of what you put first. There are certain things you won't give up.'[76] The success of his liaison with Gregory Evans lay in the fact that Evans understood this and was quite independent. 'After David went back to London,' he recalls, 'our relationship was ongoing, but it wasn't exclusive. I had other relationships and also freedom to go where I wanted to go when I wanted to go.'[77]

Howes finished his interview by asking Hockney if he ever bought pictures, to which he replied, 'No. But I'd love to have that Della Francesca [*The Baptism of Christ*] just so I could look at it every day for an hour. That picture behind us of my parents, apart from painting it, I bet I've sat and looked at it for many, many hours.'[78] Such close scrutiny day after day, and the eventual realisation that he was getting nowhere with it, led to his decision to abandon the painting once and for all. 'David phoned,' wrote Laura on 3 August, ' – has decided to scrap his painting of Ken & I. Much depressed yesterday but feels better now after his decision. I sympathise and hope he will do what is best – compare it with sewing when seeking perfection – a creation.'[79]

One person who did not take kindly to this decision was his father, now home from hospital, but moody and difficult. 'Kenneth raves,' Laura noted, 'and blames everyone but David – his friends taking advantage of him, particularly Henry who he says is not good for David.'[80] His 'ravings' continued into the following day when he telephoned the studio. 'K. phones David and "spills over". David hurt and says he will please himself.' After Laura remonstrated with him, Kenneth had a change of heart. 'Eventually says should he phone again? I leave it with him! Phones & just said David! Disregard what I have just said.'[81] Difficult though these calls were to deal with, they probably did make him think hard about having another attempt at the painting, and two days later he called his mother again.

'David phones again,' she recorded on 6 August. 'Started again on portrait. I asked what changed his mind & what influenced him? He says had new inspiration – anyway only a few days and he goes away – so he will be able to collect himself. I only want him to be happy and satisfied with his work – nothing less will do!!'[82]

Three days later, Hockney was on his way to New York, to meet up with Henry Geldzahler then return to Arthur Lambert on Fire Island, where he was to be inspired by a famous poem to make one of his most memorable works.

CHAPTER TWO

THE BLUE GUITAR

In the mad gay resort that was Fire Island Pines, amid the tea dances, the drugs and the discos, there were moments of calm, when Hockney was drawing or painting pictures of his bedroom and portraits of Larry Stanton, Christopher Isherwood and Henry Geldzahler. One evening the latter introduced him to a poem by the American philosophical poet Wallace Stevens, which utterly intrigued him. 'The only poem of his I'd ever come across,' he wrote, 'was . . . "The Emperor of Ice Cream"; the title alone had always attracted me. Now I came across "The Man with the Blue Guitar" . . . I was thrilled with it.'[1] The poem was written after Stevens had seen an exhibition of Picasso's work in Hartford, Connecticut, in 1936, the first ever Picasso exhibition in an American museum. It was inspired by one of the most celebrated paintings from his Blue Period, *The Old Guitarist*, and deals with the inextricable conjunction between things as they are and things as they are imagined.

> The man bent over his guitar,
> A shearsman of sorts. The day was green.
>
> They said, 'You have a blue guitar,
> You do not play things as they are.'
>
> The man replied, 'Things as they are
> Are changed upon the blue guitar.'
>
> And they said then, 'But play you must,
> A tune beyond us, yet ourselves,
>
> A tune upon the blue guitar
> Of things exactly as they are.'

'It seemed to express,' said Hockney, 'something I felt about my own work at the time.'[2] Geldzahler persuaded Hockney to read the poem aloud, the effect of which was magical, both on the reader and the assembled company. 'When I first read it,' Hockney said, '. . . I wasn't quite sure what it was about, like all poems like that, but I loved the rhythms in it and some of the imagery, just the choice of words is marvellous. Then, when I read it out loud . . . I loved it even more, because I got the music that it has.'[3] At Geldzahler's suggestion, and using what he had to hand – namely paper, coloured inks and crayons – Hockney immediately set to work on a series of ten drawings inspired by the poem, and when he returned to London in September he made an attempt to transfer these images onto canvas, with unsatisfactory results. Instead he decided to abandon the paintings, and make a portfolio of etchings with Picasso as his muse, using imagery derived directly from the master's work, with references throughout to several of his paintings and drawings and the different styles he employed.

Hockney chose the method of etching in colour that he had been taught in Paris by Picasso's printer, Aldo Crommelynck. This ingenious procedure allowed the artist to dispense with different plates to register the colours, instead letting him draw directly onto a single plate. There was a poignancy to Hockney using this process, since, even though it had been invented for Picasso, he did not in fact live long enough ever to use it. 'The etchings themselves weren't conceived as literal illustrations of the poem,' Hockney wrote, 'but as an interpretation of its themes in visual terms. Like the poem, they're about the transformations within art as well as the relation between reality and the imagination, so there are pictures within pictures and different styles of representation juxtaposed and reflected and dissolved within the same frame, this "hoard of destructions" that Picasso talked about.'[4]

Maurice Payne was on hand to help him turn his ideas into reality. To get inspiration for the opening image, which was to be based on *The Old Guitarist*, which depicts a blind old man hunched over his guitar, they flew to Chicago to look at the original picture hanging in the Art Institute. On their return, they set to work in the etching studio in Pembroke Gardens. 'It was a good period for him,' Payne recalls. 'He made the drawings directly onto the plates. He would come over in the morning quite early and say, "Oh, I've had another idea . . . I had a dream last night and it's given me a great idea." *Tick It, Tock It, Turn it True* came from a dream. He would virtually do another image there and then. He just never stopped once he had started, just went through the whole thing from beginning to end, and I can't remember any rejects at all.'[5] Hockney exhausted all the possibilities the project had to offer, creating a series of images that celebrated the imagination and were the first flowering of what was to be his own reinterpretation of Cubism. 'The ideas for these etchings quickly started developing and moving about,' he wrote, 'and I got excited and realised that I was breaking out of naturalism.'[6] He wrote to Henry Geldzahler in the new year: 'I've finished *The Blue Guitar*. I did two more, making eighteen in all, and I must say I'm sad I'm finished. I loved working on them – I think the finish has left Maurice sad as well.'[7] The final version of twenty images was to be published by Petersburg Press in the autumn of 1977, both as a portfolio, in an edition of two hundred, and as a small book, its subtitle pointing to the double and triple takes to be found inside – *Etchings by David Hockney Who Was Inspired by Wallace Stevens Who Was Inspired by Pablo Picasso.*

Hockney's autobiography, *David Hockney: My Early Years,* edited by Nikos Stangos, was published in October 1976. Henry Geldzahler wrote the introduction, which began, 'David Hockney's art has been lively from the first because he has conducted his education in public with a charming and endearing innocence. The pictures are of the distinctly autobiographical, confirming Hockney's place in the grand tradition of English eccentricity.'[8] It was a good time in Hockney's life, when he was finally beginning to feel that his work was going somewhere again. The launch took place in Bradford on 21 October, much to the delight of his mother. 'GREAT DAY FOR DAVID,' she recorded, 'launching his book DAVID HOCKNEY by David Hockney at Cartwright Hall . . . David arrived 20 mins late. Had dropped off at Leeds – train arriving early – to visit Art Gallery with his friends, Nikos, David and

Henry. Very pleasant assembly 200/300 – good buffet – Lord Mayor
& Mr Davis, Bradford Librarian to whom David returned library book
(stolen) 20 years ago[9] . . . Donated picture and book to Library Fund.'[10]
Hockney signed the book for the mayor to auction as part of his annual
Lord Mayor's Appeal, and it greatly amused him that as he was leaving,
Henry Geldzahler said to the mayor, 'I hope you sell the book, Lord
Mayor, and I also hope you win your appeal.'[11] The following morning,
beneath a photograph of Hockney standing with a copy of the book
balanced on his head, the *Yorkshire Post* ran the caption 'David shows he
is an artist with poise'.[12] He returned to London in the evening, and
the following day Laura noted, 'Spoke to David, he is very tired after
another day of "launching" in London.'[13]

  The book opened with a warning to the reader – 'It is very good
advice to believe only what an artist does, rather than what he says
about his work' – and what followed was a down-to-earth, candid
account of his life, his work and his philosophy. In true Hockney style,
it ended with a joke. Referring to his print *Homage to Michelangelo*, he
told how a line from the T. S. Eliot poem 'The Love Song of J. Alfred
Prufrock' had inspired it.

> In the room the women come and go.
> Talking of Michelangelo.

'When I was talking about it to Jasper Johns,' he wrote, 'he told me
about a scene in *The Maltese Falcon* where a man says to the detective
"What does it mean, 'In the room the women come and go, talking of
Michelangelo?'" And the detective says "It probably means he doesn't
know much about women." Pretty good. I like that.'[14]

  The Times called the book 'a clear-headed, beautiful and often
very funny book' that 'returns Hockney's art to the centre of his life'.
The critic, Michael Ratcliffe, went on to call Hockney's work 'one of
the most cheering aspects of life in England today'.[15] Emma Tennant
in the *Listener* liked 'the mixture of the personal and the technical'[16]
though John McEwen, writing in the *Spectator*, found that 'the insistent
"I" becomes oppressive, the tone is monotonous, the common sense
and drollery he has often demonstrated have either been dulled by the

nature of the work or are untranslatable'.[17] 'I read all the reviews of the book yesterday,' Hockney wrote to Geldzahler on 9 December, ' – quite interesting really. The only people who seem to be a little disappointed are the professional art writers (jargonists all) who hate its simple prose (undermining their profession?) A number overpraise it a little [The *TLS* called it 'the most remarkable autobiographical work any artist, scientist or man of letters of his generation has written'][18] . . . Anyway the bookshops keep running out of it which naturally makes people more eager.'[19]

The huge success of the book came as a surprise to everyone apart from Nikos Stangos. 'Somehow I did not feel confident that we would sell a lot of copies of the Hockney book,' wrote Trevor Craker, the editorial director at Thames & Hudson who was in charge of sales. 'I suggested we should print 3,000 and . . . the form was duly signed off for this quantity. When Nikos caught up with the situation he came to me in the nicest way and suggested that I had greatly underestimated the demand. With 24 years of experience behind me I stuck to my guns – and made the biggest under-calculation of a print run in my career. Our 3,000 copies were sold before publication. It took three reprints totalling another 20,000 copies just to catch up with the demand . . . I regard Nikos as little less than a saint for resisting the temptation to say, "I told you so".'[20]

Hockney found the resulting publicity tiresome. 'The book has been an enormous success here,' he told Geldzahler, 'and overpraised almost everywhere. It's put me off going to parties – the last one I went to a lady told me she had three copies given for Christmas. I laughed but I can't face talking about it to another person.'[21] It began to get him down and, with the sense of loss he was feeling since the completion of *The Blue Guitar*, together with some homesickness for America, he began 1977 in a gloom. 'It's January 2,' he wrote, 'it's 1977, it's Celia's birthday and I'm feeling a bit down . . . London life is getting to me now. I honestly don't know why I'm here. Nothing excites me or stimulates me outside, with few exceptions . . . I saw John Schlesinger and Michael Childers the other evening. Michael hates London . . . and said to me "how do you get a hard on in this country?" I laughed, but I know exactly what he means.'[22]

He went on to tell Geldzahler that he didn't want his letter to reek of self-pity. 'I want it to be a confession,' he said. 'A confession that I never really get America out of my head, a confession that I'm very lonely here (I never seem to be in America), a confession that I wish I were leaving here tomorrow.' The winter weather got him down, he continued, the lack of colour and the fact that there were no shadows anywhere, and he also missed Gregory Evans enormously, who was still living in Paris. His relationship with Kasmin also appears to have become somewhat strained. 'Kas is away in Africa with Bruce Chatwin,' he wrote. 'He doesn't help me much – always ringing up with trivial requests – Would you draw so and so? I got mad with him, saying "Look Kas I want to paint; every silly request you make would be at least a day off painting – why do you want me to do it?" – then it gets me down that he doesn't seem to understand.'[23]

He also felt a sense of cowardice, that he was clinging to England out of love for his parents and a few friends, the only glimmer of hope on the horizon being the fact that his younger brother, John, was seriously considering returning from Australia. If that were to happen, he said, it would make him feel less guilty about leaving. What he missed above all was stimulation. '. . . stimulation means a great deal to me,' he told Geldzahler. 'I know I can have it from books but when I put them down I day dream again about N.Y or L.A . . . Apart from my evenings with Ron, which are stimulating, it's always the same. Perhaps I should meet some new people – yet in London that's not easy unless one leads an intense social life that I'm not prepared to do . . . Powis Terrace is nearly finished, yet going back up there depresses me a bit. It's cost quite a bit more than I thought, yet I don't care. I'd love to leave it all and just come to New York with a pen and paper.'[24]

In spite of his depression, Hockney did not leave London at this point. Instead, as always, he threw himself back into his work, and a month later was writing to Geldzahler, 'I have been painting non-stop since the beginning of the year – bolder, surer and more confidently than 76 or 75. If you come and stay in a month there should be quite a bit of work.'[25] The pictures to which he was referring further explored the cubist influence of Picasso that he had begun in *The Blue Guitar*, and were a return to the spatial games and pictures-within-pictures with which he had toyed in the early sixties. They examined the theme of painting as the subject of painting. The first, a self-portrait, was embarked on quite spontaneously with no real plan and no reference to a drawing, and in painting it Hockney allowed his mind to run free. The result was that *Self Portrait with Blue Guitar* invited the viewer to look at the picture on two levels, firstly as the portrait of an artist at work, in his case on a drawing of a blue guitar, and secondly as a portrait of his imagination, represented by the various images taken from his recent work that were floating around him.

The second work, *Model with Unfinished Self-Portrait*, which featured the sleeping figure of Gregory Evans, continued the game of perplexing the viewer by appearing to place the two figures depicted in the same room, when the reality was that Evans was painted from life, while the figure of Hockney sketching in the background existed only on a canvas propped up against the wall. 'My self-portrait, which was not finished at the time,' he recalled, 'was leaning against the wall of my London studio. Gregory posed on a bed in front of it and a great deal of his figure was painted from life. That gave it a kind of power. It looks as though it's a painting of two completely different kinds of space. It seems as if there's a stage behind Gregory with a curtain. The curtain has been pulled back and there I am, about to draw a guitar.'[26]

Evans's presence in London was extremely welcome to Hockney, who had been keenly missing him. He drew him asleep, and it is a touching and emotional representation, suggesting that he felt this was the only way he ever had his lover totally to himself. Evans certainly enjoyed the sitting, which was a far cry from his normal experience of posing. 'David's coloured drawings were very hard to sit for because they could take two or three days. To begin with it is seductive and you feel flattered, then reality sets in, when you think about how many times your leg goes numb or your arm goes numb or you're drifting off to sleep.'[27] On this occasion he had no such problems, and the days drifted by in a pleasurable and languid way. 'David would wake me at

8 am,' he told the biographer Peter Webb, 'I would then put on his bright-blue dressing-gown, go downstairs to the studio, lie on the couch and go back to sleep again. When I woke up he was very good, he allowed me breaks for cigarettes and tea and we would go out to a pub for lunch. By 4 pm we would have to stop as people would always drop in for tea. We would eat out unless he could persuade me to cook dinner, and he would always sit and look at the painting for some time before coming to bed. The picture seemed to take a long time . . .'[28]

'Gregory posing for *Model with Unfinished Self-Portrait*', 1977, photograph by David Hockney

Because the painting took so long and Evans had to leave London for Paris before it was completed, Hockney finished it using Peter Schlesinger as his stand-in, and in the completed version the feet of the sleeping model were based on Schlesinger's. Evans felt no jealousy over this. 'I didn't care about what David's feelings for Peter were,' he recalls. 'After all, I had known Peter before I knew David, and the situation was that as long as I was in the picture, David paid me a lot of attention and wasn't going on about Peter. But he was friendly with Peter and Peter was around a lot, and we did a lot of things together. The thing is David doesn't like to be alone. In fact he's never been alone.'[29]

Hockney also took Schlesinger on a trip to France, to stay with Baron Philippe de Rothschild, who had commissioned him to paint the label for that year's vintage of Château Mouton Rothschild. Of his decision to go, Schlesinger later wrote, 'How could I say no? Even hard-to-please Cecil Beaton said Baron Philippe . . . was the most thoughtful and stylish of hosts.'[30] 'I'm down here with Peter,' Hockney wrote to Geldzahler, 'staying for two days to do the wine label . . . Naturally it's very charming, the food is superb and the "ordinary" wine we had for lunch was from 1927. Tonight it's 1901 we were told.'[31] Among the guests at the Château was Joan Littlewood, the theatre director, who was a long-time friend of Baron Philippe. When Hockney commented at dinner, 'I must tell you, Baron, that this is the best home-made wine I've ever drunk,' she leaned over and whispered to him, 'I don't think, David, that the Baron has any experience of a Boots Wine Kit.'[32] She later insisted that they go together into the local village to drink plonk at the nearest bar 'to remind us of what we're drinking at the Château'.[33]

Commissioning contemporary artists to paint the Château's labels had been the idea of the 22-year-old Philippe, and had begun in 1924 as a one-off with Jean Carlu, the famous poster designer. It had then continued annually from 1945, with artists such as Picasso, Chagall, Kandinski and Miró all contributing, in return for a number of cases of two different vintages from the Château. In the end, Hockney's design never materialised. 'It was difficult working on such a small scale,' he says, 'and I just never got round to doing it.'[34] Baron Philippe chose instead to make the 1977 label a special tribute to Queen Elizabeth the Queen Mother, the vintage being the year of her daughter's Silver Jubilee.

When the two new paintings were finally completed, Hockney persuaded Kasmin to accompany him on a trip to India, a country which intrigued him, but which he had never visited, his plans to visit Delhi with Mark Lancaster a few years previously having been thwarted by war between India and Pakistan. It was not the best of ideas since their relationship at the time was delicate, with Kasmin continually pressing for more work to sell and Hockney erring on the side of caution, a not unknown situation between artists and their dealers. He admitted to Geldzahler, 'I'm having quite a bit of trouble with Kas . . . He talks to me like a child which is pretty depressing and I don't honestly know how to reply to him without being outrageous and hurting his feelings. I am not naive in the least and I think he misinterprets my caution as naivety – a great pity.'[35] Kasmin, however, who had been to India before, was only too keen to oblige as he both loved travelling and thought he might get some good drawings out of the trip. Unfortunately for him things did not turn out quite as he might have liked.

The trip got off to a bad start. '. . . at London Airport,' wrote Kasmin in a diary he kept of the journey, 'David asked suddenly why we were travelling tourist class on a cheap ticket. I spent thirty minutes on the problem of changing seats to first and found our ticket valueless in the exchange required – it would cost £420 each to sit for 10 hours in the wider seats of the select. After much bartering, chat and criticism of my mean prudence we agreed to spend the extra only to find that first was full from Bahrain, so why bother. A slightly sour taste was deposited in my mouth nevertheless.'[36] Things took a turn for the better on the plane, a night flight on a crowded jumbo, when 'David was recognised . . . and given free cigars – we were both taken to the cabin and spent half an hour with the crew, learning about the controls as we flew over Baghdad and surrounding oil wells flaring in the darkness'.[37]

Their first stop was Mumbai, where they checked into the Sunset Suite of the Taj Hotel, £950 per day securing them a large air-conditioned sitting/dining room and a vast bedroom and bathroom. After lunch and a siesta, wrote Kasmin, 'we went for a walk past the museum and up Gandhi Street full of evening crowds and obviously many beggars. At the Jehangir gallery I show David the exhibits of local art . . . He sits on the steps in his white suit and polka dot bowtie and draws a boy selling nuts on the pavement. Locals stand over him to watch. Later drive to the hanging gardens on Malabar Hill and saunter with the families in growing dust. David says he's exhausted . . .'[38] At breakfast the following morning Hockney poured his heart out about his unhappiness in London and his desire to move to New York. 'I tried suggesting this was quite consistent,' Kasmin commented, 'and no upheaval in that he shifts his base every year or two and being free and rich enough to do so would probably continue this as long as he thought the perfect life was somewhere else, and the right lover or companion might be there.'[39]

Rather than allow him to become a slave to his self-pity, Kasmin decided to take Hockney on the ferry to Elephanta Island, 'the City of Caves', in the Sea of Oman, close to Mumbai Harbour, where there are a number of famous temples, dedicated to Shiva, carved out of the rock. 'We climbed the hundred or so steps beneath tamarinds and banyans and monkeys and birds playing about, and rested twice on the way . . . The temple was superb, a great feat of rock-cutting in the 6th Century. Many voluptuously fluted and carved columns and figures of Shiva in a confusion of roles. Before the Lingam, a splendid big fat one, our guide dealt skilfully with phallic worship. "Do you really believe I would pray to sex? This is also a symbol of the divine and universal flame . . ." David bored fast and withdrew to draw a capital and then went down the hill again to the colourful little bar and drew clients drinking coke.'[40] Back at the hotel they ate sandwiches in their room and took a siesta before heading off to look at the Prince of Wales Museum. Here, 'David sat drawing a fire-extinguisher, in bright red crayon, adjacent to a medieval male sculpture which was pale and secondary on his paper. Several puzzled art lovers studied his work over his shoulder and a guard kept watch against disturbances, which turned out to mean prohibiting me from snapping the scene.'[41]

Their evening turned into a disaster, after Hockney agreed to dine with an old friend of Kasmin's, Suruchi, and her husband. All looked hopeful, 'Till we got going. Suruchi lives with her husband, Ramesh, in a flat on Cumbala Hill high above hutments of the poor. A modern décor and all the art by her. Ramesh is a businessman as his big bag of golf clubs proclaimed – he has a glass factory employing a thousand people. He tells a rather alarmed David "Forgive

Kerby (After Hogarth) Useful Knowledge, **1975**.
Oil on Canvas, 72 × 60˝

'The Old Guitarist' from *The Blue Guitar*,
1976–77. Etching, edition of 200,
20 ½ × 18˝

Self-Portrait with Blue Guitar, 1977. Oil on Canvas, 60 × 72″

My Parents, 1977. Oil on Canvas, 72 x 72"

Looking at Pictures on a Screen, **1977.** Oil on Canvas, 74 × 74″

Act I, Scene III. Sarastro's Kingdom from The Magic Flute, 1977. Gouache on Foamcore, 26 ½ × 41 ˝

David Hockney applying colour dye with a turkey baster to newly pressed paper for the 12-panel *Le Plongeur*, from his *Paper Pools* series

Day Pool with Three Blues (Paper Pool 7), **1978**. Coloured and Pressed Paper Pulp, 72 × 85 ½″

Canyon Painting, **1978**. Acrylic on Canvas, 60 × 60″

Santa Monica Blvd., **1978–80.** Acrylic on Canvas, 86 × 240″

Divine, **1979.** Acrylic on Canvas, 60 × 60″

my partiality but I am a fascist, believe in authoritarian dictatorship because my people are too foolish to be trusted." Much talk over thali dinner of caste and politics. Ramesh's mother cannot travel because airport security police are low caste and, opening her suitcases, would touch her clothes and would pollute them. She keeps a naked 158 year old guru in a hut in her garden . . . Such a lot of confused and silly prattling.'[42]

Being a true North Country Fabian, Hockney was finding both the extremes of poverty and the inequalities of the caste system hard to take, and this, combined with the fact that he was suffering from jet lag and also found the extreme heat and humidity uncomfortable, caused him to fall into a deep despondency, something that did not go unnoticed by Kasmin. 'David is such a strong personality,' he recalls, 'that when he gets in a depression, a cloud of gloom descends over everything and everybody.'[43] It settled in on the way back to the hotel. 'After midnight we seem to be going home in a cab,' Kasmin noted in his diary. 'I fail to notice David's fatigue. First we stop to visit a street of Christian Indians, picturesque, quiet, rows of sleeping bearers on the sidewalk, but clean and of very odd architecture . . . then to a tank near Malabar Hill – more bodies stunned to sleep and we thread between them, avoiding dogs and faeces to admire the moon in the insect dappled waters. I love it. David's anger grows . . . we get to the hotel at 1.30am with David raging at my insensitivity. Perhaps dehydration has hurt him. No words. He goes to bed and I silently sit for hours in the other room . . .'[44]

His mood had not lightened by the following morning. 'At 10.30 he woke to curse the world and promised to leave for London. So I went to the Crawford Market and marvelled at fruit, birds caged in crowds, and bought a dozen white lilies and some spider lilies too so that my delicate entry to the sullen suite was perfumed and prophylactic at least. An hour of discussions . . . and the usual examination of his "situation" (suggested psychotherapy as proper course when consistently self-muddled) and criticism of selfishness of his friends . . . I cannot seem to fix on the right perspective and fail to do much except be comradely and calm. Anyway I booked Udaipur and flights and left for lunch feeling like a dentist faced with a set of steel false teeth in a crying client.'[45] Back at the hotel a few hours later, however, Kasmin found an encouraging sight. 'He had when I returned at 5.15 done a rich picture of his briefcase and panama hat which I guess was an act of reassurance though solipsistic . . .'[46]

Having been persuaded to give up any ideas about returning to London and to journey on to Udaipur, Hockney appeared to be quite taken with the Lake Palace Hotel, where they had booked, for £550 a night, the only suite with air conditioning. 'Dear Mum and Dad,' he wrote to Kenneth and Laura, 'we are staying in this hotel in the middle of a lake. It's an old 17th Century palace built by the Maharajah. We look out of the window at another palace on the lake shore. It's extremely beautiful and peaceful. Bombay was very very hot and humid . . . but the poverty takes some getting used to. There are a great number of beggars and deformed people . . . The country though has great beauty, with a strange bright light and wonderful sunsets. I cannot tell whether the people are happy or not . . .'[47]

They took a taxi to the Saheliyon Ki Bari gardens where they saw a fountain featuring four marble elephants, though any hopes of getting some drawings out of the expedition were soon dashed. 'Well he liked it,' Kasmin noted, 'but by this time had taken hold of a camera and like the veteran smoker at the end of an abstinence clicked happily instead of wielding the pencils promised before in London. On to Jagdish temple in town and the collection of an always-growing retinue of small boys out for fun and "ball-pens". Actually we wandered about for a couple of hours in little streets, looking at shops and houses and ghats and temples . . . It is apparent now that India does not really interest him. He keeps talking of American boys and life in New York and wonders what "gay" Udaipur does with itself. We did see lads bathing on the steps by the lake but their modesty forbad comparison with Santa Monica and their Gods seemed strange and furthermore worshipped – horror to the Fabian.'[48]

Back in the air-conditioned luxury of the Lake Palace, Kasmin, fed up with the heavy atmosphere, 'hit the scotch hard' while Hockney cheered up considerably when he was recognised by a young half-

Indian girl, a former art student to whom he was able to show the dummy he had with him of *The Blue Guitar*. '. . . the girl admired his book,' Kasmin recorded, 'and made him glow by talking of the Slade etc and encouraging words on the need for figure drawing. This fierily-eyed girl led David into every one of his familiar patterns . . .'[49] But all this did was make him long for home again, and the atmosphere in the hotel room later that night was once again tense. 'Woken at 4a.m. by David with the lights on, reading then noisily showering – grumpily twisting about under the covers I failed to regain sleep. His endless worries torment his nights and he sleeps little himself . . .'[50] Kasmin's patience finally ran out later the next day when, during a frustrating visit to the Indian Airline's office to organise the flights to their next destination, they were told by a clerk that there was 'not a room in Delhi'. 'Of course he means in the grand hotels,' Kasmin wrote, 'and I know there are dozens of respectable little places, but David plans once more to take a London flight. My calmness provokes him to tetch more . . . At last I offer my view – that David's ego is so large his self-pity is commensurate, that he lacks humour in his self-view, etc. He smiles wryly and is silent . . .'[51]

The trip ended in Delhi, where they found accommodation with Michael Pakenham, the First Secretary at the British Embassy, at his new house on Aurangzeb Street, done up in true English style with heavy mahogany furniture, golf clubs and guns, naval books and trophies. By now Hockney had decided that he wanted to go to Egypt, and talked incessantly of Luxor and Karnak 'in between berating me', Kasmin commented, 'for bringing him here without a luxury hotel. Just at this moment his company is insufferable and I wish I was elsewhere . . .'[52] When it proved impossible to get tickets to Egypt, flights were booked back to London on Maundy Thursday. In celebration, Kasmin took them to Moti Mahal, the famous Delhi restaurant from where the original recipes for tandoori and butter chicken are reputed to have come and where they ate 'a very good meal'. Then, at Hockney's choice, 'a cycle rickshaw through the old town's alleys to Conna Circus – lean man standing barefoot on the pedals and straining at the burden of our bodies behind him. In the old souk it fitted and was exotic – on the new straight and wide roads outside, each thrust of his legs accused us (or rather David) of the poverty and injustice of India.'[53]

On their last day they had lunch at Michael Pakenham's, eating an Irish stew on their own, their host being in bed with flu. With home in sight, the atmosphere was lighter. 'David's humour is fine,' Kasmin wrote, 'and he is obviously happy at the thought of London tomorrow. He drew Michael's blue and white checked chairs in the reading gallery while I siestered. After collecting our tickets (3rd visit to Cook's) I posed for an hour for a coloured crayon drawing. Held the pose easily since I was sat facing the window and a tree that was busily visited by birds and a chipmunk too that just avoided the hungry hawks that came by. The head David drew was very tender and I believe extraordinarily exact. He is being solicitous now too.'[54]

On his return from India just before Easter, Hockney felt he needed more space so he moved out of his Pembroke Gardens studio and lent it to Peter Schlesinger. 'Pembroke Studios . . . was fairly small,' Hockney recalled, 'and the studio had to be the living room as well. I might not go out much but I like people around, coming to visit, and when you start working a lot the room gets messy, especially if you're not a very tidy painter.'[55] He now moved himself into his new premises, on the top floor of 17 Powis Terrace, which Tchaik Chassay had converted into a large studio, twenty-five feet square and eighteen feet high with wall-length windows and a long north-facing skylight that drenched the room with light, plus a kitchen, bedroom and bathroom. The equipment included a large tubular-framed mirror on wheels, two easels, a blue folding screen to use as a backdrop, a huge sink, a gym-finished polished parquet floor, Mies van der Rohe chairs, plenty of built-in shelves and cupboards, movable drawer systems and nine overhead halogen lights with a rheostat switchboard. 'The whole thing,' wrote the art historian Anthony Bailey, 'complete with unfinished canvases stacked against a wall, looked like the film set for the studio of an internationally known artist.'[56] 'David phoned,' his mother noted on 16 April. 'He is in Powis Terrace & says it looks very nice.'[57] At that point it was not finished, however, and when his parents visited a month later to sit for him, Laura was unimpressed by the lackadaisical attitude of the workmen. 'Went to London on 7.20a.m. train, and had taxi to David's. Posed for camera for nearly three hours – had lunch and looked around flat, which is very good, but takes some completing. Indifferent workmen I guess – one sat down reading paper – not lunch hour.'[58]

An early visitor to the new studio, and witness to the continuation there of the tea ceremonies, was Jonathon Brown, a young Scottish student who had sent Hockney an essay he had written in which he had discussed the common ground between his work and that of Caspar David Friedrich. Much to his surprise he had received not just a reply but an invitation to tea, acceptance of which had necessitated a journey from Edinburgh to London. 'He had told me the address,' he later reminisced, 'and how to zig-zag from the tube to find it all; and how to press the button marked "Bell" at the top of the outside steps. '"It is a bell after all", he had joked, my first experience of this instinctive goonery . . . I followed a long series of narrow stairs and came in on the great room . . . There were four or five people there and, while he chewed on the stump of a fat cigar, a sort he told me he liked since they had the look of something you'd picked off the pavement . . . David showed me the proofs of *The Blue Guitar*. They were on the floor with tissue between them and I could scarcely make out head or tail of them . . . I fingered through the sheets in amazement; they seemed to bear no resemblance to any of the measured more or less representational paintings I had been so clever about in my essay.'[59]

On this, his first visit to Hockney's studio, Brown was struck forcibly by the feeling that he was entering another world. 'My immediate perception was of everything in the large room bathed in a light that had a light of its own. The room itself was an amalgam, I think, of more or less all the front rooms of a top-floor flat, with their attics incorporated as well, so that much of the ceiling was glass and decorated entirely by the endlessly teasing London skies . . . At a time at which London was still filthy, the seats of the Bakerloo Line still gritty and springy, some carriages still of wooden construction, or so it seemed, and even in the centre of town with gap sites that may have been from the Blitz, this bathingly benign light and sense not only of ease but of endless possibility was a paradise . . . This paradise was all the more unexpected given the neglected state of the local streets, and then that rudimentary slightly battered narrow little steep-staired corridor taking you up to the great room.'[60] When later he found himself in Langan's, something else made Brown aware of the very different world he had entered. 'Peter Schlesinger was there and I was amazed by the fact that he stirred his drink with his finger. I just thought Insurance-Brokers' sons reading philosophy don't meet people who stir their gin and orange with a finger. It was another world.'[61]

One of the first people to model for Hockney in the new studio was Marinka Watts, whose testimony bears out Laura Hockney's worries about indifferent workmanship. 'I worked with David in the top-floor studio. It had a leak in the ceiling, and he did nude drawings of me there with a bucket under the drips!'[62] Marinka, who had worked as a seamstress in Lachasse, a leading couture house in Mayfair, and was then waitressing in Peter Langan's new restaurant, had been introduced to Hockney by Mo McDermott. In spite of the fifteen-year age gap between them, they hit it off and when he returned from India he invited her to sit for him. 'We modelled on Sundays,' she recalls. 'I'd go over there very early and we'd have breakfast and he'd read the papers. Then he would start drawing and he wouldn't stop until he'd finished. He did five drawings, three clothed or semi-clothed and two nude. He was very meticulous. I remember he used to peer over his glasses. That was a very particular look. I think he was a little bit shy of me, because he was mad about Celia, and with another girl around, he might have worried that she minded.'[63]

The drawings of Marinka, including the only female nudes he produced, other than those of Celia, were undertaken at a time when Hockney was taking a public stand with his friend Kitaj on the case for the figurative in art. Their argument was that form was not everything, citing Matisse and Picasso as two modernists who never abandoned the art of representing people. 'It's not a coincidence,'

Kitaj commented, 'that those two people were the greatest draughtsmen of the human figure, as well as being the two greatest modernists,'[64] while Hockney soundly defended sentiment in art, also citing Matisse: '. . . anyone studying [Matisse] will say a great deal of his painting is about colour and form, but to deny the poetry and the sentiment in his painting is to deny some of the art, to diminish it . . . The very fact that he drew and painted mostly women, not men. Why? Because he liked women. It's unrealistic to deny that sentimental aspect of the pictures.'[65]

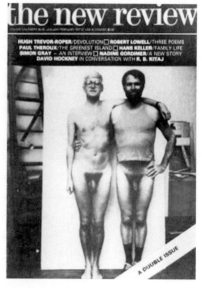

David Hockney and Ron Kitaj pose nude for the *New Review*

These views, which were published in the January/February edition of the *New Review*, caused some controversy, leading certain supporters of the avant-garde to label them as two old reactionaries. As far as Hockney was concerned, however, his point was proved by the reaction that many people had to the cover of the magazine, which featured a full-frontal nude photograph of Hockney and Kitaj, taken as a dare by Peter Langan. 'It was kind of innocent,' Hockney told Anthony Bailey. 'I was drawing Peter Langan. Ron Kitaj came over – he's working on a painting of me nude, so he took a few photos of me nude against a canvas. Then Peter said "That looks easy." He grabbed a Polaroid, said, "Well, take your pants off Ron," and snapped a few of the two of us. He gave one to Ron, and the next week Ron had this big blow-up of it on his wall. The *New Review* girl interviewed us there . . . and later she asked Ron for the photo.'[66] What surprised Hockney about the furious objections people had to the cover was that 'all our discussions inside was of how figurative art meant more than abstraction. And there's other people saying "Oh, you're all wrong," yet they're complaining about the cover. Our whole point was made. Amazing!'[67]

*

Shortly before moving into Powis Terrace, Hockney had written to Henry Geldzahler, 'When were you planning to come? Perhaps I'll do an imaginative portrait of you in London — although I do want to do my parents first . . .'[68] Hockney had worked on the first painting of his parents for months, agonising and fussing over it to such an extent that it had eventually lost its freshness. He had also struggled with how to depict himself in relation to them. On the second attempt he worked much faster, and the result was far more successful. Before he began, however, he practised on Peter Schlesinger, spending a week painting him seated in a comfortable chair, wearing a purple suit and a bow tie, staring out at the viewer, with a Polaroid camera on a tripod to one side. He later described it as 'an experiment in bold colour',[69] and as well as getting his hand in it also meant having Peter to himself for a whole week.

Since he had failed to find a way of putting himself successfully in the original picture of his parents, he now removed himself from the equation, which greatly simplified matters. He had prepared for the first portrait by establishing the composition in a series of line drawings. This time he took dozens of colour photographs, which proved particularly helpful in his final decision as to how to depict his father, whose seated figure had seemed so wooden in the original. That is because in real life, Kenneth was incapable of sitting still, something he did not have to do during the photographic sessions, during one of which, in a fit of boredom, he had simply picked up a book and started reading, oblivious to what was going on around him. This was the Kenneth that Hockney recognised, and was how he eventually chose to paint him, reading a copy of Aaron Scharf's *Art and Photography*, his restlessness shown in the way his feet are not firmly on the ground, while opposite him, and some distance away, Laura sits serenely, looking directly at her artist son, as lost in her own world as her husband is in his.

As in all Hockney's greatest double portraits, there is drama in the picture, in that the subjects appear to just miss relating to one another, something that he himself felt reflected his own failure 'to really, really, connect with another person'.[70] 'The thing about the painting of David's parents,' says Maurice Payne, 'is it is a painting of two people who have been married for forty-eight years yet appear to be hardly aware that the other one is there.'[71] Though they had been together for so long, Kenneth and Laura's marriage was by no means perfect, he being totally wrapped up in himself, she longing for love and companionship, feelings which were reflected in outpourings of anguish to her diary. 'My great regret,' she wrote in August 1973, 'is that Ken and I are incompatible and the more I think of it the more I realise how the war and his attitude to it changed and embittered him.'[72] 'How I wish he could love,'[73] she sighed, at the end of March 1975, while two months later she was bemoaning the fact that 'Ken is always hot-tempered and aggressive – invites no confidence or gives comfort. He has <u>no feelings</u> – hence our unhappiness – tho' he would not admit he was anything but right and perfect. I'm so sorry because he is not frank and open and makes it hard for anyone to love him and show it.'[74] Kenneth's untidiness also drove her to distraction, something he completely failed to notice. 'The house is still a tip,' she wrote in September 1976, '. . . mixture of newspapers – accounts – photography films, crayons – cameras & bags – never an attempt to clear up, just more and more – my efforts are hopeless. Ken just wallows in it. He gave me <u>two</u> bars of chocolate – how can they compensate for consistent chaos?'[75]

What kept Laura going in the face of Kenneth's total obliviousness to her feelings was both her religion and her deep and unselfish love of, and pride in, all her children. When Philip and John both came over from Australia at the end of September 1976, it was an excuse to gather all the children together for a lunch at the Devonshire Arms in nearby Bolton Abbey, where their parents had first met back in 1928. '. . . we had our own room, and family meal, and drank toast in champagne. I tried to express my thanks for their loyalty – achievements & health & families. It is a pity Ken being deaf did not join in & I did not say all I felt. I do hope they all realise how proud we are of them . . .'[76] And when Paul was publicly announced as the next Lord Mayor of Bradford in December 1976, she wrote, 'Out of all our blessings this must surely be my greatest day. Paul our first-born son – always from childhood considered kind . . . faithful and loyal, blessed with a grand wife and children. He deserves them all . . .'[77]

My Parents went on show in July 1977 at the Hayward Gallery, as part of a new series of annual exhibitions, called the Hayward Annual, which were designed to show off the best recent British art. It opened on 19 July, ten days after Hockney's fortieth birthday. The family came down from Bradford for the opening, Paul, the new Lord Mayor, combining his trip with a visit to a Buckingham Palace garden party. 'Arrive David's 12.30pm,' Laura recorded. 'Lunch with David, Henry, Maurice, Gregory and ourselves. Driven to Buckingham Palace by Maurice – long long queues – Paul & party arrive and we take photos. Taxi to Harrods. Sale on . . . but prices fantastic! Waste of time really. Bus back to David's & cup of tea & change for evening – David meanwhile has made progress with picture of Henry.'[78] The picture to which Laura refers is the 'imaginative portrait' that Hockney had promised to paint of his friend, who now, courtesy of Mayor Ed Koch, held the grand position of Commissioner of Cultural Affairs, New York City. The painting showed Geldzahler as an important man, sharply dressed in a white suit and bow tie, looking at a series of reproductions of famous paintings stuck onto a screen with tape. The works were all by past 'masters': Vermeer's *A Young Woman Standing at a Virginal*, Degas's *After the Bath*, Van Gogh's *Sunflowers* and, Hockney's own personal favourite, Piero della Francesca's *The Baptism of Christ*. It was a clear statement by him of his unashamed alliance with the tradition represented by these artists.

Along with Howard Hodgkin, Peter Blake and R. B. Kitaj, Hockney had a room to himself at the Hayward, in which he showed the suite of etchings for *The Blue Guitar*, alongside *Self Portrait with Blue Guitar*, *Model with Unfinished Self Portrait* and *My Parents*. He had also hung a drawing his father had done of Bertrand Russell, who, like Kenneth, was a leading supporter of CND. The brutalist architecture of the South Bank gallery did not appeal to Laura Hockney. 'All visit Hayward Gallery,' she wrote. 'Very depressing gallery. David's Salon of pictures in the show much brighter than any others. Picture of Ken & I the Chief!!, Crowds of students and visitors all acclaim picture good. My own opinion – Ken absolutely typical – myself rather stiff – unrelaxed – but true. David has put so much into his work – I'm disappointed he has taken his self-portrait from the mirror. I wish I had been occupied rather than sat bolt upright. We are very proud of his work & so seemed everyone else. A great surprise and honour for Kenneth – David had hung a picture of Bertrand Russell drawn by Ken in the 50s during the CND marches. David felt it was as good as many others on show.'[79]

They dined at Odin's, still Hockney's favourite restaurant, in spite of the fact that Peter Langan had recently opened the even more fashionable Langan's Brasserie, for which he had drawn the cover of the menu. By then, Laura wrote, 'Was so very tired. Ken & I went home with David – had adjoining flat & used double bed – which we have not done for years – slept well. Ken up & down – he had overeaten & not feeling good.'[80] The following morning, Henry Geldzahler joined them on a trip to Hampton Court and Kenwood House, and they also went to Bertram Rota, the antiquarian bookshop in Long Acre, where George Lawson had his office. 'David had sent them along to see me,' he recalls, 'and I got a message to say they were in the shop. So I went down to meet them, and I said to his mother, "Goodness me, you must be very proud of your son," to which she replied, "Oh yes! To be Mayor of Bradford!"'[81] Kenneth and Laura returned to Bradford the next day when, writing up her diary, Laura gave her final verdict on her portrait. 'The Picture!? – Well everyone says it is good! David has put so much into it. For myself, I liked the first one better – I look so stiff and highly coloured – but of course I don't relax & David has just painted what he sees – I don't feel vain at all – but don't feel it is the best of me! I hope I look happier & not so tense usually. Maybe I should have been better if occupied – it is difficult to be a critic, but it is very TRUE.'[82] Ken's only opinion was 'It shows I concentrate'.[83]

Hockney's work at the Hayward had a mixed reception. William Feaver, writing in the *Observer*, loved the 'fascinating mixture of Picasso motifs and pure Hockney whims and capers' of *The Blue Guitar* etchings, though he was cautious in his appraisal of *My Parents*. 'At first sight, this is an uneasy composition, the figures being stiff and curiously lurid at the joints, the whole richly varnished. But as it settles on the eye, the subtleties of handling and feeling begin to emerge. Mannered though this painting may be, it is neither jokey nor sub-Ingres, but devoted and altogether fine.'[84] In the *Guardian*, Caroline Tisdall was happy that *The Blue Guitar* 'appears to have reawakened his old awareness of representational artifice, and some of his youthful zest appears in a recent series of etchings'.[85] But the *Times* critic Paul Overy considered Hockney's performance 'dismal'. 'These new paintings are not well painted,' he wrote. 'This may be because Hockney has moved back to painting in oils rather than the acrylics he's been using for some time. Technically they are very tacky . . .'[86]

Generally the Hayward Annual was roundly criticised in the press, poorly attended by the public, and led Hockney into some controversy. Those who reviewed the show were by and large united in their feelings that the selection was too safe and retrospective, and was without inspiration. Feaver called it the 'Chums Annual'[87] since 50 per cent of the artists came from the Waddington and Tooth Galleries. 'An unsuspecting visitor to London might be forgiven for thinking,' wrote Tisdall, 'that we have been overrun by a State art of boredom.' The problem, she suggested, was a cliquey art world pushing 'art for art's sake', and a public without 'the courage to ask "art" questions like "What the hell is it all about?"'[88]

One man who was prepared to ask these questions, however, was Fyfe Robertson, the Edinburgh-born television reporter who had made his name on the BBC magazine programme *Tonight,* always sporting a tweed trilby and beginning every piece with the words 'Hello there, this is Fyfe Robertson reporting', delivered in a slow Scottish drawl. On Saturday 13 August, as part of a six-part documentary series titled *Robbie,* he used a tour of the Hayward Annual to launch a scathing attack on avant-garde art. 'This exhibition baffles me,' he said. 'Is there anything that *isn't* art, in avant-garde eyes? I think these people are in retreat from art. They're degrading it to an undisciplined, despairing, free-for-all meaninglessness.' He had coined his own phrase for the work. 'The Hayward Gallery's lunacies have been called non-art,' he told the viewers. 'But I think they're much worse than that. They're phoney-art. You can condense these two words into one which has the proper flavour of contemptuous derision, *Phart*.'[89] It angered him that 'art which requires no artistic talent or ability as I know it' was being supported by taxpayers' money, citing in particular Bob Law's installation of four empty white canvases and one black one, Barry Flanagan's arrangement of rope coiled on the floor, and the performance artist Stuart Brisley, horror of horrors an art teacher from the Slade School, who crawled through detergent foam while retching. 'I can remember a time,' Robertson said, 'when somebody doing this sort of stuff would have been an instant candidate for a plain van.'

Eventually he came to the room housing Hockney's own work, where he spoke to the artist himself. 'When I first walked through this exhibition,' he told him, 'and came on your pictures I felt like the Sahara explorers starving for water who suddenly came on an oasis – an oasis here of what I call art.' Pressed to give his opinion on 'some of the more way-out stuff', Hockney was at first reluctant to comment, other than to say, 'Maybe there's something in it,' but when further pushed to elaborate he admitted, 'I don't understand it at all . . . it seems to me that if you make pictures there should be something there on the canvas. I don't understand four lines of ballpoint pen round the edge of the canvas. I've no idea really what it's about . . .' As for the term 'avant-garde', he remarked, 'I think it was an American artist who said that the term should be given back to the French Army, from which it came. The concept of the avant-garde in a way is rather old-fashioned now so it's a paradox – I mean the avant-garde is not avant-garde.'[90]

For Fyfe Robertson to air his views was just about acceptable so far as the art establishment was concerned. He was, after all, 'confessedly ignorant', having described himself as being 'art-wise just the intelligent man in the street', and admitted that 'just as I listen to music though I don't know much about it, so I look at art . . .'[91] For David Hockney, however, one of the leading artists of his generation, to come out publicly with what they regarded as such reactionary nonsense was positively blasphemous.

The result was that in the letters pages of the *Guardian,* in articles in art magazines and across the airwaves of the BBC, a veritable hornets' nest was stirred up, and suddenly in London there were echoes of Paris in the late nineteenth century when the Impressionists came under sustained attack. At the beginning of September, Michael Compton of the Tate Gallery, and one of the curators of the Hayward show, felt it necessary to hold a public meeting 'to air some of the problems of presenting contemporary art to a largely suspicious and indifferent public'.[92] Compton, the painter John Hoyland, Hockney and Robertson all attended, but when Robertson attempted to ask a question, 'I was told to shut up,' he told a *Guardian* reporter, and stormed out of the meeting, dismissing it as 'the verbal diarrhoea our art establishment is so skilled at producing'.[93]

Hockney, however, was not prepared to shut up, and subsequently gave a long interview to a new and lively magazine, *Art Monthly*, in which he reiterated his views, invoking the respected opinions of his mother, who on seeing the Barry Flanagan installation of coiled rope had asked, 'Did he make the rope?' This seemed to him a good question. 'Modern art generally ignores skills and crafts,' he told the interviewer Peter Fuller, 'or assumes they are not necessary. But the real world of ordinary people is full of them. So they question things by asking "Where is the skill?" I suppose the skill Flanagan knows is that of deciding to do a piece and placing it. But an ordinary person finds that hard to take. They see the skill as *making* the actual rope. I don't think their question can be just dismissed, unless you think art is just for a few people . . . Instead of trying to hide behind the struggles of the past, the art world should begin to deal with the questions people are asking.'[94]

An invitation to spend some time in France with Jane Kasmin provided the perfect opportunity to escape from all the art-world bitching, so Hockney took off with Gregory and travelled to Balme in the Dordogne, where Jane was spending the last summer in the holiday home that she and Kasmin had bought together and which was about to be sold. It was a beautiful old farmhouse in faded yellow stone, set in a pretty village nestling beneath dramatic limestone cliffs. The river flowed close by, and all around were luscious meadows where maize and tobacco grew in abundance. The house had a lovely garden, looked after by an old man who had worked on the farm, and a railway ran along the hill above the village, which was a source of fascination for the Kasmin children, Paul and Aaron, who loved to watch the little trains as they passed by. It was as idyllic a spot as Carennac had once been, and was the perfect place for Hockney to prepare himself for his next venture, designing *The Magic Flute* for Glyndebourne Opera.

CHAPTER THREE

PAPER POOLS

Sitting next to Hockney on the opening night at Glyndebourne of Stravinsky's *The Rake's Progress*, the director John Cox had an idea. 'In one of the intervals between the scenes,' he recalls, 'I leant over to him and whispered, "What would you think about doing *The Magic Flute*?" There was a pause. "Why?" he asked. Then after another pause he said, "Well, that needs imagination, doesn't it?" And finally, after another silence, he said, "Well, let's just say that you've planted the seed." Afterwards, because *Flute* can be a very difficult opera to fathom, I wrote him a working storyboard for him to have with him when he was thinking about it.'[1] Hockney took this with him on his trip to Balme, along with the score, which he had recorded onto cassettes so that he could play it on the car stereo on the journey down. This also proved useful on arrival, as the house had no music system. 'Because we had no stereo there,' Aaron Kasmin remembers, 'David used to bring his car round and park at the front, where there was a gravelly terrace with a low wall, and we all used to sit out on the grass and listen to *The Magic Flute*, which was blaring out the whole time to give him inspiration.'[2]

Aaron and his brother Paul were also subjects for his pencils, for, typically, the music could not distract him from his drawing. The results, however, were not a success. 'One day,' Aaron recalls, 'he went to Albi, which was a couple of hours away, and made a day's expedition. It is where Toulouse-Lautrec was born and there is a museum in the town dedicated to him, and he came back completely inspired and did some very bad drawings of my brother and myself which he didn't like at all, because they were very chocolate-boxy, using very bright colours. I remember he tore them up and threw them away.'[3] He then immersed himself in the original libretto of *The Magic Flute*, written by the German impresario Emanuel Schikaneder, who was also the director of the Theater auf der Wieden in Vienna. This was famous in its day for its magical stage effects that included flying machines, trapdoors, thunder, lightning, fires and waterfalls, and was the setting for a series of fairy-tale operas, culminating in the premiere of *The Magic Flute* in September 1791.

After the stay in Balme, Gregory Evans went to visit friends in Spain, while Hockney arranged to meet his parents in Chester, from where he had arranged to take them for a few days to Portmeirion in North Wales, the extraordinary village built in the Italian style by the architect Sir Clough Williams-Ellis. Situated on the estuary of the River Dwyryd, south-east of Porthmadog, it is a mixture of Arts and Crafts and classical buildings, all painted in ice-cream colours, and has been an inspiration over the years for writers such as Noël Coward, who wrote *Blithe Spirit* while staying there. It was also been the setting for numerous films and television programmes, the most famous being *The Prisoner*, with Patrick McGoohan, which was filmed there in the late 1960s.

On their last day, Laura noted, 'David did some drawings of Ken and I – & we were invited for drinks to Sir Clough Williams-Ellis, the owner of Portmerion & architect of all we surveyed. He lived about 4 miles away at PLAS BRONDANW. He is a tall ruddy rural man who wears knee britches & yellow stockings, very striking & a wonderful personality. He took us round the house – rather dark & with mahogany furniture, but electric light (which he knew where every light was) tho' just had operation for cataracts. We must have walked two miles thro grounds & woods & gorgeous views & surprise views of Snowdon & surrounding hills. Pools & water fountains – sculptures in all sorts of little niches & corners. Ken very languid all the time – went without cameras!!'[4]

The holiday was a great success and, though Hockney did not know it then, it was to be the last time he would go on such a trip with both his parents. When he got back to London he met up with John Cox, who was about to leave the country for several months to work in Australia, and was keen to get across his own ideas for the opera before he left. For this purpose he had written a long scenic analysis for guidance, though it turned out to be of limited use. Faced with the prospect of being alone in Powis Terrace, where he was still haunted by memories, and keen to escape the London art world, he decided to go and work on designing the opera in New York, where he would also find greater peace and quiet. By now he had his own strong ideas and every intention of forging ahead with them, and he knew what he could get away with. 'The nice thing about working with John Cox,' he told the music journalist Gillian Widdicombe, 'is that he always adapts if I won't budge. I mean I'll budge a lot of the time, but it's my job to make it look exciting.'[5] His base was to be a large and spacious apartment of six and a half rooms at 30 Sutton Place South, borrowed from Melissa North's* sister, Mary Clow. It was on the eighth floor, with views across to the East River, and Clow had taken the sensible precaution of putting all her furniture and pictures in storage. This allowed Hockney to create his own studio there, and Maurice Payne, his assistant, had already travelled out in advance to prepare the ground, so he settled in quickly.

It was a propitious time for him to be in New York as André Emmerich was putting on the first new show of Hockney's work since 1973, which included *The Blue Guitar* suite of etchings, drawings of Marinka Watts and of his parents, and the five big paintings, *Self Portrait with Blue Guitar*, *Model with Unfinished Self Portrait*, *The Honourable Beast*, *Looking at Pictures on a Screen* and *My Parents*. Among those who attended the opening was the British art historian Anthony Bailey, who was working on a profile of Hockney for the *New Yorker* and who reported to Laura Hockney, when interviewing her for his article, that 'David's Exhibition had done exceedingly well & many pictures sold . . . [He] thought David was more pleased with the public attendance to his Exhibition than the sale of the pictures – that they saw his work!!'[6] Though the reviews were largely enthusiastic, Hilton Kramer, in the *New York Times*, wrote that though he enjoyed the show enormously – 'Few contemporary painting exhibitions are more entertaining than David Hockney's. What fun they are to see!' – in the end he found the

* Hockney had originally bought his Powis Terrace studio from Melissa North.

paintings 'superficial and even reactionary . . . a kind of 19th century salon art refurbished from the stockroom of modernism'.[7]

Hockney was quite unperturbed by Kramer's review, cutting it out and sticking it up on the wall of his temporary studio, a description of which was given by Anthony Bailey in his *New Yorker* profile. 'The floor is bare parquet,' he wrote. 'On the walls Hockney has put up his own things: a Dry Dock Savings Bank calendar, for writing down engagements; a sheet of paper with the telephone numbers of close friends; five postcards of Egyptian Art in the Metropolitan Museum; color reproductions of a Whistler beachscape in the Frick Collection and of a St. Sebastian by Antonello, with arrow shafts sticking out of thigh and torso and his sole garment a pair of tight, surprisingly modern-looking briefs; a large plan and elevation of the Glyndebourne Stage; a clipping from the *New York Times* of a by no means wholehearted review by Hilton Kramer . . .; and a large piece of white paper in which he has written in red felt-tip the whereabouts of various scenes in "The Magic Flute" . . . On a marble mantelpiece . . . A dying yellow rose in a silver vase stands between some boxes of film or his four cameras and a framed eight by ten color photograph, taken frontally, of "Michael" wearing nothing . . .'[8]

Here Hockney and Maurice Payne lived for the next few months, and he put to use all the experience he had gained from working on *The Rake's Progress* to solve the very different problems presented by *The Magic Flute*, an opera filled with numerous and varied scene changes. 'There's a hell of a lot to learn about designing for the stage,' he wrote. 'Luckily Glyndebourne's a marvellous place to learn it. Down there they combine knowledge and professionalism with . . . a sort of cheerful helpfulness.'[9] At least it was an opera he knew quite well, having seen at least ten previous productions, including a marionette version in Salzburg, and his research was meticulous. Many and various were his sources of inspiration. He was particularly interested, for example, in the beasts of the forest that are charmed by the flute, wondering what Mozart himself might have thought they looked like. Before leaving London, he had discussed this with a friend of Ann Upton's, David Graves, who had immediately volunteered to go to the British Library to research some medieval bestiaries. 'I went to look through all these incredible books,' Graves recalls, 'travellers' tales illustrated by artists who'd never been to the places described, and filled with pictures of amazing beasts they had imagined.'[10]

Hockney himself had done some studies into eighteenth-century Masonic imagery in the British Museum, while in the National Gallery he was stimulated by his favourite Venetian and Florentine paintings, such as Uccello's *St George and the Dragon*, on whose winged monster he based the dragon which pursues Tamino in the opening scene. He even looked to contemporary advertising for a source, taking the colour for the waterfall in the second scene of Act Two from an advert for Kool menthol cigarettes. Having made the decision to locate the opera in his own version of its original setting of ancient Egypt, on his arrival in New York he spent many hours in the Metropolitan Museum looking at their Egyptian collections, and integrated many of the things he saw there into the design, such as a pair of jackal-headed deities which were to appear in the room in which Pamina is imprisoned by Monostatos. He based the Great Hall in the final scene on the museum's grand interior staircase.

Steeped in the culture of pantomime since childhood, when he used to go to the Bradford Alhambra, Hockney saw *The Magic Flute*, with its numerous and diverse short scenes, as a glorified panto and he settled on the old-fashioned device of using painted backdrops, which could be quickly changed, to drive the action along. 'Painted drops might seem old-fashioned,' he told the journalist Mark Amory, 'but I wanted to keep the performance flowing without pause and that is the most obvious way. And anyway I'm a painter, you see. Painting is what I do.'[11] Since the opera is one of dramatically changing moods, this also enabled him to quickly shift the atmosphere to go with the music. 'In *The Magic Flute*,' he noted, 'you have contrasts between comic bawdy entertainment like a pantomime and then rather solemn almost church-like music when of course you wouldn't want a comic setting behind it. That's the difficult part of doing it, you have to be able to combine these two things which you don't usually come across in a play. So I used the mood of the music for the scenes; depending on what was going on you'd then decide to make something jolly or something solemn . . .'[12]

John Cox managed to fit in a trip to New York to look at the sets, of which Hockney had done a number of versions. It was his first view of them, and his initial reaction was one of relief that the model was large-scale – the one for the *Rake* had been so small that the scene shop had had to scale it up before they could do anything with it. 'He had made versions of certain key scenes,' he recalls, 'and he said he didn't know which one he preferred, though I think he did . . . They were all pretty colourful and were modelled up in totally different ways, and in the end we chose the one with the widest palette. I remember he made a joke about it. Peter Hall and John Bury had just done *Don Giovanni* at Glyndebourne, which was very dour. It was a very restricted palette, almost black on black, and you felt that the rain in Spain was raining all the time. David said rather mischievously, while we were watching it, "I've had an idea for *The Magic Flute*. I think I'll restrict my palette to only the colours that Peter Hall *doesn't* use."'[13] It later got back to Hockney that the scene painters at Glyndebourne had said they needed to wear sunglasses to paint the set.[14]

Like an excited schoolboy, Hockney loved to make an event out of showing visitors his ideas. He would settle them down, turn down the lights and, with the help of Maurice Payne, make a theatrical presentation complete with music and model figures and animals created from plasticine which he would move around. Anthony Bailey was among the audience for one such show and wrote: 'He says "There are ten different scenes in Act II, all of which have to be changed very quickly. Here, with three palm-tree drops, you have a wide vista. Hey, presto – in five seconds a brick pyramid appears and there's no space at all. A pictorial opera! 3-D! Now, this is where the Queen of the Night lives, in this mountain." Hockney hangs a cloud or two from above, and the clouds swing back and forth for a moment. He goes to the stereo and puts on a record: A cracked bit; thunder; voices. In German "She comes! She comes!" Hockney runs back to the stage. Stars appear in the sky behind the mountain. The mountain opens. A strange blue figure stands there. Quite magical. He says "There'll also be stars inside the mountain." One is reminded of two boys making sand castles.'[15] For those of his friends who were subjected to repeat performances, the magic tended to wear off. 'I always made sure I stood at the back,' George Lawson says. 'After you'd seen it once, you had rather got the point.'[16]

Though work was Hockney's primary motivation, he allowed time to do the things that he had complained he couldn't do back home, namely eating and drinking late in bars and clubs. He liked the feeling that life was going on twenty-four hours a day. New York has always been 'the city that never sleeps', but this was particularly so in the late 1970s, when the disco craze was all the rage and Studio 54, a nightclub newly opened in a former CBS radio and television studio on West 54th Street, was making headlines. There was a buzz in the air, and at night crowds of young people, straight and gay, poured into the clubs, fuelled by drugs and pounding music, to dance and fuck their way into oblivion. Often in the company of Joe McDonald, the ever-curious Hockney enjoyed cruising gay clubs like the Ramrod on West Street. 'The sort of place,' he said, 'where you take all your clothes off and check them as you go in,' or the various bathhouses that flourished in the city.[17] One of his favourite haunts was the Gaiety Theatre, a male burlesque revue on West 46th Street. 'The Gaiety was a boys' strip club,' he recalls. 'It was on every Saturday, and actually it was rather seedy, but as you well know seedy and sexy can go together. The boys stripped and danced around. It was rather good and even if it wasn't that good, in your head afterwards you could make it better.'[18]

Hockney returned to England in time for Christmas, and on Boxing Day went with his whole family to the pantomime at the Bradford Alhambra, which reinforced his view that he had made the right decision regarding the design for *Flute*. On 11 January, Laura Hockney recorded in her diary, 'David has almost completed the sets for "Magic Flute" — now has costumes to start on.'[19] Much of her time in the following few weeks was spent in preparation for a trip to visit Philip in Australia, and her diary notes the usual ups and downs of life with Kenneth and her worries about how he will manage the journey. Among these entries is an amusing account of an expedition with him into Bradford to visit her sister, which perfectly demonstrates his eccentricities.

'We went together – he had his tangerine armbands on coat – also on raincoat – flying open over jacket, cardigan, waistcoat etc – all in view as he can't button up for the contents of his pockets. Carries his stick & a shopping bag. My pride has to be pocketed as I'm dressed up. He finds it difficult to walk – has dark glasses on – I offer my arm and we make our way to bus – he is grumbling all the time about cold, wet paths, just everything – we get on bus – Ken asks for two 9p tho' he knows the fares have gone up – I think it best to keep quiet!! No need for help now!! He jumps off bus in centre & is off – but stops in middle of road (how he needs the armbands) to say he will just go with me to meet Audrey. We meet in B.M's entrance & chat awhile – then off Ken goes – amid traffic – we watch to see him safely across – & then – just laugh – he really does look a character & cares not and there's nothing one can do.'[20]

Having spent so much time living in the Egypt of his imagination, when the sets and costumes for *The Magic Flute* were completed Hockney decided to make a return visit to the real Egypt, and gathered up Peter Schlesinger and Joe McDonald, one of the most successful male models in New York, and took them on a Bales Tour. 'It was like youth-hostelling,' he told Kitaj, '. . . three in a room. I could live in youth hostels the rest of my life, – with Peter on the left and Joe on the right . . .'[21] There were twenty-five other travellers, mostly Americans, and one Englishman, who was a pyramidologist. 'I knew nothing about Pyramidology,' wrote Hockney; 'it seemed to be a kind of pseudo-science to do with numbers and measurements of the pyramids . . . Some of the Americans in the group also turned out to be Pyramidologists; they were from Tennessee. Joe and Peter were a little snobbish about them; they thought they were hick Americans and that I shouldn't spend my time talking to them. But I told them, they're more interesting than you think. I was amused, actually, by all this Pyramidology, although I could see it was perhaps rather silly.'[22]

The pyramidologists got Hockney thinking about how extra-ordinary the ancient Egyptian civilisation was and, clutching his 1910 copy of the Baedeker guide, he wandered round the ruins of Karnak, dreaming of what it must have been like with golden gates and painted pillars. 'You start thinking of things like this in Egypt,' he wrote, 'because of the very long historical periods involved. I always find this stimulating to my imagination. I drew all the time I was there.'[23] The drawings included masterly pen-and-ink studies of the Sphinx and pyramids at Giza, coloured crayon drawings of the Old Winter Palace Hotel in Luxor and the Old Cataract Hotel in Aswan, and a crayon sketch of a restaurant in Luxor, which was later developed into a small oil painting, *Egyptian Café*. He also took many photographs with his Rolleiflex camera, usually early in the morning or at dusk – it was too bright in the daytime – but the camera turned out to be faulty and when he took the films to be printed back in London, he was told they were all ruined.

'If you've never been to Egypt,' he reflected, 'and you start reading about different dynasties it all seems a little boring; it doesn't seem alive, there's something missing. But the moment you're there it becomes vivid: Ramases II seems vivid, the Pharaohs come alive and you get carried away.'[24] On his return to England, a freshly inspired Hockney went straight down to Glyndebourne to discuss the lighting of the set with Robert Bryan, the lighting designer, who told him bluntly that it would be very difficult. 'We couldn't light it properly,' John Cox recalls, 'because it was very flat and two-dimensional, and by this time in the development of theatrical design, the material aspect of production had become very three-dimensional. So there just weren't the old-style lamps in the grid to just give a light wash to a two-dimensional coloured surface. It was all spot lamps and things like that, and that gave us a big problem. Also, because space was so restricted, we couldn't get lamps in because there was so much scenery. The result was that ironically we only really saw the *Flute* at its best later, when it went into bigger theatres.'[25]

The production opened the 1978 season at Glyndebourne on 28 May, and on this occasion Hockney's parents were not only in attendance, but were personal guests of the Christies'. It was a welcome break for Laura, whose sister Rebe had only recently died after a stroke. 'Went by train to Glyndebourne . . . stayed overnight in beautiful stately home,' she recorded. 'Thoroughly enjoyed opera – very successful in every way – artistes – orchestra – all on top scale. David was pleased with his work & so were we all. For the 2nd time – A day out of this world & one to remember.'[26] Once again there was perfect weather and the Christies, while not repeating the bacchanalian experience that was the first night of *The Rake's Progress*, still laid on an unforgettable occasion. 'On the first evening of the first performance of *The Magic Flute*,' wrote Stephen Spender, who was one of Hockney's guests, 'there was an outdoor party on the lawns after the performance, with food and drink served from long tables. There was something greenly, sumptuously English about seeing guests, performers, David Hockney and the director, John Cox, enjoying their triumph on that occasion, a *fête champêtre* at which one might have found Mozart and Stravinsky toasting one another and the artist and performers.'[27]

Critically the production was largely a resounding success. 'Magic blends mystery with spectacle,' wrote Desmond Shawe-Taylor in the *Sunday Times*. 'There is a hint of toy theatre in the succession of 36 drops constructed from Hockney's charming maquettes, with their clean, pure lines and bold, resonant colours that match the solemn or playful, but always crystal clear, Mozartian score. They work beautifully in the theatre.'[28] Though he voted the duo of Hockney and Cox 'a thoroughly reliable partnership', it was quite clear to the majority of the critics who the audience's applause was aimed at. For example, writing in the *Guardian*, Philip Hope-Wallace, who considered the production 'one of the most successful and strikingly different I could have ever imagined', wrote that 'the real champion of the evening is David Hockney who in scene after scene catches the true pictorial effect wanted by this piece'.[29] While William Mann, *The Times*'s redoubtable critic, noted that 'The distant prospect of Sarastro's Egyptian estate looked particularly spectacular and drew applause even though the orchestra was playing the sublime introduction to the first act's finale.' He added that even though he considered this a 'detestable practice', he 'could understand the motive'.[30] The only dissenting voice was Peter Conrad in the *New Statesman*, who considered Hockney's designs 'beautiful but irrelevant. Rather than explaining *Die Zauberflöte*, they annex it, assigning it a place in Hockney's private pictorial world and begging every question about character and meaning as they do so.' He finished his piece with the statement: '*Die Zauberflöte* is a comedy because it insists we are all victims of physical nature, until art or religion rescues us . . . it is not a panto for grown-ups, as the Glyndebourne staging implies.'[31]

In an interview he gave to William Green in British *Vogue,* Hockney admitted to having been stung by this criticism, in that it completely ignored the depths of research and thought that he had brought to the project. He had worked on it for six solid months, and that was on top of the time he had spent thinking about it beforehand. The English, he said, were 'ignorant, unaware and philistine', and he couldn't wait to get back to Los Angeles. 'You can feel energy there; there are lots of creative people doing all kinds of things . . . some of the great works of art of the C2oth were made there, if you think of Hollywood, of film – it's no hick place. Of course there's a hick side to it, but then there's a hick side to England which I'm fed up with.'[32] This included his current bugbear of the time, English closing time, which was very much on his mind since by the time the Glyndebourne opera was over, the local pubs were all closed. He would bang on about the subject to anyone who came within spitting distance. 'I like life to go on 24 hours a day,' he told Melvyn Bragg. '. . . in 99 per cent of Britain, you are not allowed to get a drink outside the hours they say you can drink. You're not allowed to enjoy yourself when you want to. I think you should be able to have an adventure a day if you feel like it . . . Even on television they say "Goodnight and turn off your sets". And that's generally before midnight!'[33]

But there were other reasons that he longed to get away, connected with his fame and the demands on his time that this brought, a problem largely caused by his inability to say no. 'David says yes to twenty-nine requests a day,' Paul Cornwall-Jones said at the time, 'and then blames Kasmin and me because he's under pressure.'[34] Many of these were favours for friends, such as designing book jackets for George Melly and David Plante, a Silver Jubilee party invitation for James Kirkman, and a drop curtain for a charity ballet for Wayne Sleep. He expressed his frustration in a letter to Henry Geldzahler, who had persuaded him to agree to illustrate a children's book, *The Dulcimer Boy*, for Tor Seidler, a mutual friend. 'Tor still wants me to work on his book,' he moaned; 'I think he feels let down, which makes me feel a heel. I have done a small drawing for the cover and the drawings of leaves inside — yet I can't get into it . . . I've tried to explain, I've tried hints, yet he wants me to do it and I just feel at the moment I cannot . . . I don't really know what to do, but I feel I must pass it all back to you. When my friends overload me like this I begin to feel terribly isolated and bitter . . . I try to keep my life simple. I'm very very fed up with being a very public "art celebrity" — and I must be serious. I think it's beginning to affect my own sanity.'[35]

There were also constant and numerous requests from newspapers, such as the *Sunday Times* asking him to go to China for them, or from art galleries around the world wanting information, almost all of which came via the telephone, as Hockney was incapable of keeping the number to himself. 'When he got back to London . . . from eighteen months in Paris,' wrote Anthony Bailey, 'he told his good friend, Ann Upton, "My new phone number is *highly* secret." A little while later she heard him giving it to someone he hardly knew.'[36] Since he tended to take all calls personally, this had obvious consequences. 'The most pictures I've ever done in a year,' he reflected, 'sixteen or seventeen, was when I was in California with Peter Schlesinger and we didn't have a telephone. There must be a link.'[37] He despaired when he received a call from Ray Stark, the Hollywood producer of films such as *The Night of the Iguana* and *Funny Girl*, asking if he would do some drawings for the credits on his Neil Simon movie, *California Suite*. 'My heart sank,' he told Geldzahler. 'I explained as politely as I could my desire to work in California quietly and without interruption on some paintings. It would break me if things started crowding in on me in LA like London.'[38]

On 11 July, Hockney wrote to Kitaj, 'I hope to leave England about August 16 for Los Angeles. Maurice is going next week to find a studio as well as the house . . . I long for peace and quiet and hope to get it in LA. *The Magic Flute* just dragged on too long . . . I don't want to do anything but paint for at least two years . . . If I stayed in England I'd get destroyed I'm sure, and in the end in California if you put someone off

they get the hint – in England they come back about a week later . . .
Henry says to me that I'm trying to recapture my happy days there with
Peter – wrong says I. I desperately just want to be alone here and just
paint – to be left alone so I can do anything I want on the canvas junk
– rubbish – without it being reproduced in the *Sunday Times* . . . The
thought of spending all my future days in Powis Terrace fills me with
horror, I would prefer a shack on Pico Blvd with beautiful flesh nearby.
I do feel the moment I start painting a lot will come out that's been
trapped for a while. The theatre is interesting to work in but frustrating
– waiting for this, adjusting that, compared to painting where you do
it all yourself . . .'[39]

When Hockney left London on 7 August, he closed the door on
Powis Terrace for the last time. He did so with a sense of relief, since
even in the new studio he had felt ill at ease. 'I hated that studio,' he said,
'I hated being back in that house . . . It was quite a beautiful studio, but
I felt cut off. In my old apartment downstairs my studio had looked out
over Powis Terrace so that if I was sitting at the table drawing I could see
what was going on in the street. I could see the people walking up and
down, ladies gossiping in the dry-cleaners; I had known everything that
was going on, and I missed that. When I walked out of Powis Terrace
and pulled the door to, I said to myself, I never want to come back again
while I own it.'[40] Before he departed, he posted cheques to his parents
for £500 each. This delighted Laura, who was able to buy a new three-
piece suite for the house as well as pay off any debts.

In the meantime Hockney had been waiting for the arrival of a
new California driving licence, his existing one having been mislaid. He
decided to fly to New York and stay for a while with Arthur Lambert
in the new house he and Henry Geldzahler had bought in Greenwich
Village on West 9th Street before joining Maurice Payne in LA and
starting again the painting that he was so desperate to get back to.
Instead something happened that completely distracted him from his
intentions. He came across a new technique of printing with which he
became, in true Hockney fashion, obsessed to the exclusion of all his
other plans.

One day he received a telephone call from his old friend Ken Tyler, 'the Master Printer of Los Angeles', who, after leaving Gemini, had set up his own printing business, Tyler Graphics, in Bedford Village, New York. Tyler was an extraordinary figure. The son of a Hungarian steelworker from East Chicago, he had worked as a set builder, an art teacher, a garage manager and a travelling salesman, before learning printing and setting up Gemini Publications at the back of a frame shop in LA. Hyperactive and aggressive, he was a man of boundless energy, a workaholic who had transformed the face of American printing, taking it from being the poor relation of painting and sculpture right into the mainstream, and in doing so forging working relationships with some of the greats of the post-war art world, such as Robert Rauschenberg, Jasper Johns, Frank Stella and Roy Lichtenstein. He was a true innovator, who liked to work with strong artists, and for some time he had been trying to lure Hockney to New York to come and see the things he was doing, at one point even sending him a large bronze apple to remind him of the city. He understood that it wasn't enough to invite an artist back just to make another lithograph or a silk screen; you had to keep giving them 'something new to chew on'.[41] Now that Hockney was actually in New York, it was difficult for him not to be intrigued by Tyler's exhortations, so he agreed to go out to the workshops to take a look, but with the express intention of not getting involved. 'I didn't want to do any kind of graphics work,' he wrote. '. . . I was a bit fed up with working always with other people and I just wanted to go off on my own and I wanted to paint . . . I went up to see him and to say this to him.'[42]

Tyler had been working on some large pieces by Ellsworth Kelly, for which they had set up their own paper mill. 'David came for dinner,' Tyler remembers, 'and he wanted to see the Kelly works, which were really quite brilliant, beautiful coloured pieces.'[43] What Tyler showed him were some works using a new technique he had devised with a papermaker, Lindsay Green, of printing colour into paper pulp. Hockney was astonished. 'They were stunningly beautiful,' he said, 'especially Ellsworth Kelly's. I thought they looked so good, and I responded. I said they are very, very good, beautiful, Ken, but I'm on my way to California.'[44] Tyler was persuasive, however. 'Because he was

David Hockney
working on *Paper
Pools* at Ken Tyler's
studio

so impressed,' Tyler recalls, 'I suggested that he should try his hand at it in the morning. So he stayed the night and in the morning we went out into the garage and made some paper.'[45]

What the process involved was making paper from scratch using rags, and adding dyes directly to the pulp, which created stronger and more vivid colours than if paint had been merely applied to the surface. 'Drawing' was done by creating an image and making a mould from it, like a cookie cutter, into which the coloured pulp was poured before being weighted down, under four thousand pounds of pressure, so that the final image was part of the actual paper, rather than just being painted on it. 'David was instantly attracted to it,' Tyler remembers. 'A new process for David is like everything. It's like an all-time high, and he was high. He moved into our studio apartment for forty-nine days.'[46]

Hockney was now hooked, and as he began to understand and work with this technique, he became as excited as a small child becomes when it is shown something new. 'We were making unique objects, not prints, and it was thrilling work,' he said. 'We worked long hours, but we liked it. Ken is incredibly energetic and inventive. In using this paper pulp technique, you had to be bold. It is the exact opposite of an etching needle . . . here line meant nothing. It couldn't be line; it had to be mass, it had to be colour.'[47] Reflecting his love of Van Gogh, the first pieces he made were of sunflowers, and as he worked on them he began to realise how different the process was from printing, where every print in an edition is exactly the same. In this case each image had to be individually made, which was a painstaking business. 'It was a workaholic kind of situation,' Tyler says, 'where you had to get up early and make paper, and it was like sixteen-hour days, and if you can work sixteen hours a day with David, you're in heaven and he's in heaven. He loves to work until he's so exhausted that it's his nervous energy that is keeping him going because his body has already caved in. At that moment he's making his discoveries and those are inspirational.'[48]

After making ten different versions of flowers, Hockney got bored with them and began to look for a more interesting subject, something that would allow him to create images in bold, simple colours. 'I have done about twelve large studies of water in a swimming pool,' he wrote to his mother on 19 September. 'Perhaps next year we'll show them in London. It's all been very exciting as I love new mediums to work with – they make me be inventive in the forms the pictures take. I don't know whether the enclosed pictures will mean anything to you, but they should give you a little idea.'[49]

'Paper Pools,' Tyler says, 'was really a new development for him and for the world. We had come close to making coloured paper pulp important with Kelly and Kenneth Nolan and Frank Stella, but we really didn't get to the moment where it had scale and painting presence until David came along. He was able to focus on the pool as a subject.'[50] One of the things that struck Hockney about the process of working with paper pulp was how much water was involved, so much that it was necessary for the participants to wear gum boots and rubber aprons, and therefore it seemed natural to look for a watery subject. It was staring him in the face. 'Ken had a swimming pool in the garden,' he wrote, 'and every day we would have lunch by the swimming pool, every lunch time I would have a swim. I kept looking at the swimming

pool; and it's a wonderful subject, water, the light on the water . . .
every time you look at the surface, you look through it, you look
under it. It dawned on me that the swimming pool was a much more
interesting subject.'[51] He began by studying the pool extensively at
different times of day and night and taking many Polaroid photographs,
at first of the pool on its own and later including Gregory Evans as a
model, posed in various positions both in and out of the water. He then
made line drawings to scale, small to begin with and then getting bigger
and bigger, and from these metal moulds were created into which the
coloured pulps were poured.

The more Hockney learned about and worked with the process,
the more excited he became. He loved the physicality of it, and became
increasingly inventive with the tools and techniques he was using,
employing instruments as diverse as dog combs, toothbrushes, fingers,
a garden hose and even natural rain, to obtain textural effects, while
the liquid dyes were applied with paintbrushes, an airbrush and turkey
basters. As he progressed he became bolder with the colours, and with
the size, creating beautiful fluid images of Gregory diving, and of the
pool at night, making the latter appear so mysterious that someone
commented that it looked as if it had come from *The Magic Flute*. 'The
result was these really marvellous images,' Henry Geldzahler said after
seeing the finished results, 'that are not quite paintings, not quite prints.
They are something that hasn't been seen before and they are, I think,
extremely beautiful.'[52]

All the time that he was creating this innovative series of images that
were later to be exhibited as *Paper Pools*, Hockney was also drawing all
the things that he was seeing going on around him, very bold drawings
done with a big reed pen of interiors of the studio, of Ken Tyler and
Lindsay Green carrying out the various processes of papermaking,
of them laying down the metal moulds outside, of Gregory in the
swimming pool and of the pool itself. Tyler had asked him to record
the whole process in photographs, but Hockney's reply was, 'That's a
real bore, to take photographs, when I'm an artist here: I'll draw them
myself . . . if Van Gogh were here, he'd draw them, wouldn't he?'[53]

So immersed did Hockney become in the whole project, he was

unable to stop. 'I was wondering should I leave or not. I had begun to get quite excited by the process and Ken himself was very excited . . . I have never worked with somebody with more energy; it was fantastic. He was willing to work any hours; it didn't matter. And if I was turned on, we would just work and work although it was a lot of very physical, very tiring work. In fact we worked for forty-five days and only took one day off in the end . . .'[54] But when it did end, it ended for good. 'We were terribly exhausted,' Tyler recalls, 'and we had done about thirty paper pools. They are unbelievably magnificent with all their exploratory areas of taking paper pulp and manipulating it, blending colours in such a way that was never seen before, on a scale that was never seen before, and imagery that he developed *with* the medium – he didn't develop it through drawings, he developed it in the medium. They had a certain Matissean quality that David loved. But after that was over with, it was over with. There was no way ever to get David back to do more.'[55]

While Hockney had been so engaged in the creation of *Paper Pools*, Maurice Payne had also been busy, sorting out a studio and accommodation ready for his eventual arrival in Los Angeles. He had succeeded in renting a small house on Miller Drive, off Sunset Boulevard, a stone's throw from the Chateau Marmont Hotel, and had located a studio in an abandoned warehouse, the former home of the Versailles Furniture Company, on Santa Monica Boulevard. With the completion of the *Paper Pools* project, Hockney finally travelled to California. He did so alone, as Gregory Evans had departed for Madrid to meet a boy with whom he had started a relationship while he was living in Paris. 'For at least 4 months I will let no one in,' Hockney told a friend, 'unless they are a model. (I do want to do some nudes of boys, – sensual + sexy like Renoirs. Renoir liked plump girls, – I like Californian boys) At times in London I'm very lonely yet I want to be more alone and I think only in Los Angeles can I succeed.'[56] Scarcely had he arrived in Los Angeles than he had to leave for San Francisco to fulfil a long-standing promise to do a week's teaching at the Art Institute. While working there he noticed that he had difficulty hearing the female students, who tended to speak in a softer tone than their male counterparts. 'There were

some seminars,' he recalled in an interview, 'where I found myself in
a room as big as this [his studio] or a bit bigger . . . and if it was a girl
talking I couldn't hear. And it was very embarrassing to keep doing this
[cupping his ears] all the time. And I had to say "I'm sorry, I can't hear;
I'll come to <u>you</u> though."'[57] Remembering his father's deafness, which
had begun to get progressively worse when he too was about forty,
Hockney was profoundly disturbed, not so much by the difficulties he
might face hearing people, but by the implications regarding his love
of music. 'My God,' he said, 'I couldn't bear a world without music!'[58]

As soon as he got back to Hollywood, he arranged an appointment
with a specialist, who told him that the problem was probably
hereditary, and that he hadn't particularly noticed it before because as
a painter he was normally just talking to one or two people. '"You've a
lot of difficulty hearing girls," he said. I said to him "Well I don't listen
to girls very much." He said "They speak at a slightly higher pitch and
you don't hear. You need this hearing aid for it." And when I told Henry
[Geldzahler] I'd need this hearing aid for girls, he said "Oh, well, you
can throw it away then!"'[59] The bottom line was that he had already
lost 25 per cent of his hearing, and that it would probably get worse. A
hearing aid was inevitable. 'I have noticed it a bit myself,' he wrote to
Kitaj, 'but other people have commented – that I played opera too loud
in my car and studio . . . I dread getting more and more like Kenneth,
so I will get the hearing aid next week and wear it. I shall just have to
readjust my persona as a slightly deaf person and paint the hearing aid
red and blue. I think it's better to try and make it a virtue than hide it
in my spectacles. I must admit the news depressed me a bit, but then
I thought "I can hear this news so it can't be too bad," – after all the
audiologist could have started hand signals to me and that would have
completely freaked me out. Anyway she said it should animate music
for me again so I'm looking forward to my new world . . .'[60]

The Hollywood to which Hockney returned was livelier than ever,
a fact perfectly embodied in the restoration of the famous Hollywood
sign that had sat on Mount Lee up in the hills since 1923, but which
had become increasingly dilapidated. On 14 November 1978, a new
version was unveiled before a TV audience of 60,000, the money

having come from donors as diverse as Hugh Hefner, Alice Cooper and Gene Autry. It beckoned people to come and partake of all the delights that the town had to offer. The movie *Saturday Night Fever* had come out the year before, and disco fever was at its height, with songs like Chic's 'Le Freak' and Donna Summer's 'MacArthur Park' topping the charts. Roller skating was all the rage in LA, a craze that was to be wholly symbolised by the opening the following year of Flipper's Roller Boogie Palace where, in a flashy purple-blue building on the corner of La Cienega and Santa Monica, disco and skating were combined.

None of this passed Hockney by. 'Hollywood Blvd is better than ever,' he described to Kitaj. 'Rollerskaters everywhere gliding silently along smooth pavements . . . they have wonderful sexy outfits, pretty boys and girls – yes, even you would love it. I stood outside Musso and Franks the other Friday watching it all, and suddenly thought – if Breughel came to LA – this is what he'd paint. The young and lithe gliding past the regular little Hollywood couples window shopping on the street as though it's Rodeo Drive.'[61] He told him that he was now convinced that his hunch to return to California had been correct. 'I love it all,' he enthused, 'and feel at home here, and what's more important to me I feel my activity painting in the studio has a lot to do with what's going on right outside the door. I never felt this in Powis Terrace. I think that's why I hated it. It was as though I was the Baron high up in the Castle having nothing in common with the peasants below – a horrible feeling to me for an artist.' Now he was working at street level, he felt in touch again with what was going on around him. 'It's a big turn on,' he wrote, 'and I know how I'm going to organise the next few months. I'm starting some big paintings of LA streets. Santa Monica Blvd is full of fresh-faced hustlers from Iowa and slightly tired Hollywood types driving round in circles – that's subject No. 1.'[62]

CHAPTER FOUR

SANTA MONICA BLVD.

In the late seventies, in spite of Hockney being so identified with California, there was in fact relatively little opportunity to see his work there. Though Nick Wilder was a friend and had mounted a drawing show in 1976, it had been difficult to get enough pictures, much to his chagrin. Part of the reason for this was that when Hockney had first come to the States, he had been represented by two New York dealers, Charles Allan and André Emmerich, the result being that most of his paintings went either to them or to Europe. One person who was determined to do something about Hockney's lack of exposure in California was Peter Goulds, a young Londoner who had graduated in Communication Design from Coventry School of Art, and had arrived in LA in 1972 to take up a position as a visiting lecturer at UCLA Video Workshop.

Goulds's initial plan had been to make a series of films on structuralism in twentieth-century art, but, after becoming immersed in the history of modern art as a result of his lectures, this idea had been shelved in favour of a new scheme that would engage him in art history on a full-time basis. In spite of having no experience or training as an art dealer, in January 1976 he had opened his own gallery on North Venice Boulevard, the LA Louver Gallery, named after the windows so favoured by southern Californians. In many ways this was a watershed time on the LA art scene. There was excitement in the air. 'The art school system in LA was expanding,' Goulds remembers. 'The dialogue in the studios of Venice became animated; artist-led meetings with collectors and curators were held in the studios of Robert Irwin, Larry Bell and Sam Francis . . . Los Angeles was growing up. From this heightening of energy, local collectors became confident to follow the advice of LA dealers and wanted to support the activities of their local galleries.'[1] People were even talking about the possibility of founding a Museum of Contemporary Art in LA.

Goulds had been a fan of Hockney ever since he had met him back in 1970, when he had come to lecture at Coventry School of Art, and Goulds's first big coup as a gallery owner had been to persuade the Hamburg dealer Hans Neuendorsell to sell him the large Hockney canvas *A Lawn Being Sprinkled*, which he had sold on for the then record price for the artist of $64,000. On seeing how little of Hockney's work was generally available, he decided to mount his own exhibition of his work. 'So I assembled a show,' he recalls, 'working very closely with publishers of his work. I borrowed from them, consigned from them, and purchased what I could and by October of 1978 I had one copy of everything he'd ever published, including some very rare things of which he'd only made one, like things from the Royal College. All the while I never met him and he didn't know me, other than the little encounter when he lectured at Coventry.'[2]

This was soon to change, however, for Hockney, having heard on the grapevine that Goulds was putting together an exhibition, called him up to arrange a meeting. 'He said he could come over in the afternoon,' Goulds says, 'so I delayed going to the framer's, and he came down and we spent the next two and a half hours reviewing all this work and it became clear to me that he had never done this before himself. He was enthralled and excited to see it all, and at the end he said, "What can I do to help you?" I had to think on my feet as I couldn't actually think of a single print I needed, but I had heard on the grapevine that he had been involving himself in line drawing, so I suggested that we should end the show by doing a salon hanging on one wall of some of his drawings. He told me to come up to his studio the next day at two o'clock when I could look through a print drawer full of drawings and I could make a selection. That night I was so excited I barely slept.'[3]

Hockney was equally excited by revisiting his entire catalogue of drawings, and the private view for *Drawings and Prints: 1961–1977*, which took place on 26 November, a Sunday afternoon, became like a 'Welcome back to town, David'. 'Everyone who was anyone in Hollywood was there,' Goulds says. 'He had a joyful afternoon. For some reason we did it on a Sunday and he was the first person to arrive. The most expensive print was $3,750, which was a lot of money then, and I had bought a load of cheaper prints for around $100 so there would be something for everyone. As it happened, all the expensive prints sold immediately and for years I was left with quite a number of the ones I had been out and bought! At the end David came up to me and did something no man had ever done to me. He kissed me right on my lips. Then he just said, "Thank you so much, love," and off he went.'[4]

If this was a watershed period as far as the LA art scene was concerned, so it was for Hockney's work, though it was not without struggle. However optimistic he may have seemed in his letter to Kitaj, and however determined he was to get seriously back into painting, he found he had great difficulty with it. It was a problem not unknown to him, as he had told the art critic Peter Fuller in an interview in *Art Monthly*: 'I see my own painting continually as a struggle. I do not think I've found any real solutions yet . . . I'm determined to try, but I keep going off on tangents that get nowhere.'[5] Initially there was excitement. He was back on his old stamping ground, surrounded by the hustle and bustle of LA street life, the tanned bodies and the blond hair, and he was excited by some new acrylic paints he had discovered. These were designed for film animation, being very finely ground and dense in pigment, and would enable him to use the bold colours that he knew would be perfect to depict the way life looked in the bright Californian light. He decided to test them, beginning by putting patches of colour on a canvas, and then gradually adding more, leaving it and going back to it, always testing different things. 'I kept moving down the painting,' he remembers, 'and then I kept thinking, "It's a lot more lively than I thought. It's got a lot of energy in it." And I thought it was strange the way it looked like a canyon. Then, with driving up and down Nichols Canyon every day I thought it was perhaps that that was reminding me of it.'[6] Thus what had initially begun as merely a test canvas became *Canyon Painting*, a picture with an abstract quality about it that suggested he was finally breaking away from those conventions of naturalism that he felt had held him back for so long. At first, however, he didn't take it seriously, regarding it merely as a technical experiment.

Instead he devoted his attention to the work he had described to Kitaj, a large painting depicting the life that was going on right outside the studio door. 'In this painting,' he wrote, 'I wanted to show the street life of Los Angeles and I began by taking a lot of photographs using a miniature Pentax Auto 110 camera so that people didn't know I was photographing them. Los Angeles streets are not like European streets; in Europe the streets are created with pedestrians in mind; in Los Angeles everything is built to be looked at from a slow-moving car.'[7] *Santa Monica Blvd.* was a work conceived on an enormous scale, twenty feet wide, and featured an architectural background of a parking lot, a shop with bright green shutters, and a section of an apartment building, while in the foreground five figures were engaged in various activities – a woman pulling a shopping trolley, a male hustler in tight shorts leaning against a lamp post, a woman walking past the shopfront, and another two hustlers, one hitching a lift, the other leaning against a doorway. All these people were taken from photographs he had snapped on the street, both of strangers and of friends like Don Cribb, which he had then pinned onto the canvas so that he could work directly from them. It differed from previous works in that it included more figures than he had ever used before, and they were engaged in everyday activities rather than being formally posed. 'Santa Monica Boulevard is all facades, painted bricks, painted crazy paving,' he observed. 'Nothing is what it seems to be. But what I love are the hustlers, they look like ordinary hitchhikers, but they are hustlers. And then there are these wonderful old ladies with their shopping bags, not noticing anything, smiling at the boys like their sons.'[8]

Hockney had all kinds of problems with this painting, many of which stemmed from just trying too hard, and it was a relief to get away from it on his annual trip home to Bradford for Christmas. This was one of the two constants in his life, along with the two dozen red roses he always sent his mother for her birthday on 9 December. This year he enjoyed two Christmas dinners, the first on Christmas Eve in Bradford with his brother Paul, and the second with his sister Margaret, who had moved to a job in Bedfordshire. 'Christmas Day,' Laura Hockney recorded in her diary, 'Ken, Margaret, David and I breakfast together. Ken and I went to Salvation Army.'[9] On Boxing Day they all went on a trip to Cambridge, 'but places closed', noted Laura. 'Took many photos with Ken's new automatic. Played Scrabble in evening. Left Margaret's 9.30am after lovely holiday.'[10]

The fact that everything in Cambridge was closed was not just because it was Boxing Day. These were lean times, and everybody in the UK had been living precariously for the previous few months. The Labour Prime Minister James Callaghan's reluctance to call an autumn general election, combined with the dissolution of the pact with the Liberal Party that had allowed him his majority, had given the trades unions the confidence to call a number of strikes over pay. Ford car workers had been the first to down tools, followed by bakers, *Times* journalists and lorry drivers, the latter causing particular chaos as petrol deliveries were soon affected, which led to the supply of essentials being put at risk. Just as the whole country appeared to be on the verge of grinding to a halt, the weather turned especially cold. On 31 December, Laura wrote, 'Very cold and 6′ snow,' and the next day she put, 'New Year started cold and with 4′ or more of snow.' In the days following, all her diary entries start with the words 'Bitterly cold', and on 16 January 1979, in bold capital letters she noted, 'NEWS IS STILL TERRIBLE – STRIKES FROM ALL SORTS OF WORK – BUSES – LORRY DRIVERS – RAIL etc etc. Ken very enraged . . .'[11] This was indeed the 'Winter of Discontent', as the press labelled it.

Throughout January, the weather got steadily worse and life in Bradford was hard for Hockney's parents, with icy pavements and deep snow making it difficult to go out to shop for basic supplies. 'What a morning!!' wrote Laura on 20 January. '12′ deep in snow & windblown drifts. Paul phoned – did we need anything? – he could not get car out. Decide to ask next door to bring me a loaf as they were going to shop . . . Later kind neighbour from No 8 came to ask if we needed anything & brought potatoes . . . I felt it was so kind as we have only passed time of day before. So here we are!! Warm cozy & enough food & no need to go in the deep snow. Traffic has been very disrupted. There are ten cars under snow in our terrace – The lovely upright evergreen which Stanley planted 25 years ago is actually bending with the weight of snow.'[12] Laura, who was suffering constantly from arthritis, mostly stayed home, though Kenneth did manage to get into Bradford one day, where he took a fall in the untended snow. He appeared no worse for wear, however, and on the evening of 27 January he attended his granddaughter Janine's twenty-first birthday party, at which, Laura noted, he 'joined in dancing with one of Janine's friends'.[13]

Two days later, Laura received a welcome message. 'Paul phoned – said David would be home in London on Sunday & would we like to see his exhibition – Of course we would please!'[14] Hockney returned to England at the weekend, arriving on the day that the gravediggers of Liverpool, who had also been on unofficial strike, returned to work. It was still snowing. He had come to London for the opening of a show of *Paper Pools.* Kasmin had arranged the exhibition in the Warehouse Gallery in Covent Garden, which had been opened in 1973 by the extraordinary Vera Russell, née Poliakoff, a Jewish-Russian émigré who had fled the revolution in 1917 and taken up residence in London. After a varied career as an actress, a radio commentator and an art critic, she had married her third husband, a fellow art critic, John Russell, and had become a leading figure in the London art world, dedicated to helping young artists. 'She was a rather terrifying woman,' George Lawson recalls. 'She was big in every sense. She had a huge head, a huge body, a loud voice and she loved to hold forth. She knew everybody and she was extremely hospitable.'[15] Russell ran her gallery as an artists' cooperative calling itself Artists' Market, with the idea of showing new work at reasonably affordable prices, and Hockney adored her. 'She's a wonderful woman,' he said, '. . . a real art groupie – she loves art and she loves artists. And I love her. A lot of people think she's a bit tough . . . but she's terrific. She ran that Artists' Market in a kind of strange way because she felt artists should sell their work to people who want it, people who like it.'[16] This was to be their last show, however, new and exorbitant rents in the up-and-coming Covent Garden area forcing them out after pleas for a rescue package from the Arts Council fell on deaf ears.

Hockney gave his parents a treat, putting them up at the Savoy, which was conveniently close to the gallery. 'Off to London,' wrote Laura, '. . . Paul & David met us at K.C. David took Dad to Gallery – Paul stayed at <u>Savoy</u> with me as I rest an hour. He gave me <u>Brandy</u>. First time ever!! Paul and I go to Exhibition – meet many friends old and new. Was pleased with Exhibition. Proceed to Kasmins . . . More prints & sketches.' After tea at Fortnum & Mason, they went to the London Palladium to see *Aladdin*, the annual Christmas pantomime. 'Meet Wayne Sleep & Danny La Rue, who are artistes. Met Ken Tyler & Lee his assistant from New York. Back to Savoy & beautiful flowers of welcome from Paul & David.' Unfortunately her enjoyment of the occasion was marred by her arthritis. 'Had a fair night but much pain. Paul phoned for H.W. Bottle which maid brought. What a lovely bathroom – Black & White & Grey – How I longed to use the shower – but daren't risk it. David, Paul, Ken and I had breakfast in the dining room downstairs – then made our way to Kings Cross and home-bound train.'[17]

Breakfast at the Savoy was to be the last occasion Hockney spent with his father. The day after his parents returned home, 9 February, he flew to New York for a short stay before he was due to return to LA. Laura recorded that particular day as having been 'very very cold'. She added, 'Ken persists in going out into Bradford & came home <u>very</u> cold . . . [He] really enjoyed his visit to London & told everyone he met today – also said how well he was! (until going out in the cold). He seems really ill now.'[18] Over the next couple of days Kenneth's condition deteriorated, not helped by Laura's inability to get him into hospital. 'I feel so helpless,' she wrote despairingly. 'If only the Ambulance men were not on strike, he would be in hospital. He is so poorly . . . Ken never been so long without hospital treatment.'[19]

The weather continued to get steadily worse, with six inches of snow falling on 12 February. Kenneth was very weak, and on 13 February his GP, Dr Manchester, rang to give the good news that he had managed to get him a bed in the hospital and that an ambulance was on its way. 'Only an hour, & lights flashing & struggling thro snow an ambulance arrived. The <u>first</u> time I did <u>not</u> accompany Ken in ambulance. I was not well & wondered how I would get back. Amb. Men said he <u>would be O.K.</u> – I <u>must not</u> go. In evening Paul and I visited – I felt so sick & wondered what to expect – but Ken was sitting up . . . Enjoyed his snack which he had whilst we were there & according to him he had eaten jam & bread 3 times since admittance.'[20] When Hockney telephoned from New York, she was able to reassure him that now his father was in hospital they would be able to get his blood sugar levels correctly balanced.

There was more snow the next day, and conditions were so bad that Kenneth called Laura from the hospital and told her not to try to come in. He would be quite happy to see her in the morning. 'I was sad but relieved,' she wrote; but the following day she woke up to 'Snow – snow – snow – I stayed put – There were terrible blizzards and buses stopped – Paul phoned, he was stranded in Bradford & did not know how we could visit. I phoned hospital – nurse said there were many phone calls from people who could not make it & she and two other nurses could not get home – so had to stay. Ken phoned Paul later – he had been up and walking about & asked how I was.'[21]

This was the last message that Laura had from Kenneth, who died suddenly, early next morning, on 16 February. 'At 7am whilst I was still in bed, Paul phoned. Dad on danger list! – would I get dressed slowly – he would call in 45 mins! He arrived at 8.30 am – I had things ready but Paul was so distressed – "Don't bother mum, he's gone."' Paul then took Laura back to his house, where he set about ringing round the family. 'His phone was hot all day,' she wrote.[22] 'The telephone rang at six in the morning,' Hockney recalled, 'and it was my brother. When I heard his voice I knew there was something wrong because my brother knows about the time difference. He told me my father had just died in hospital; he had had a heart attack, a big one, and just died. I put the phone down and burst into tears.'[23] At the time he was staying in Gregory Evans's apartment. 'David was with me when he got the call that his father had died,' Gregory remembers. 'He said to me, "My father's died and I have to go to England," and then he was making arrangements to fly over on the next Concorde, and then he was gone.'[24]

Hockney arrived in Bradford on the afternoon of 17 February. 'He was very shocked,' Laura commented. 'My mother said,' he later recalled, '"Oh, you've come back to a sad house." In a way, at first, I was thinking of my mother more. Suddenly a partner gone – they were about six months off their golden anniversary. My first feelings were to try and strengthen her . . . I thought she'd be very vulnerable then and I felt that my first duty was to the living.'[25] Ken's wishes that his body should be bequeathed to Leeds University for research could not be carried out, because there had been an autopsy, so after a family conference it was decided that the funeral, a cremation, should be held the following Wednesday, 21 February, in the small chapel at Eastbrook Hall. In former days, this had been the room in which the young Kenneth used to teach Sunday school. The hymns they chose for the service were 'O Love That Wilt Not Let Me Go' and 'God Be in My Head'. Remembering his father's habit of putting dayglo stickers all over his letters as a way of emphasising certain points, it was Hockney's idea to put them all round the funeral notice that was sent to family and friends. 'The funeral people thought that was a bit odd,' he said, 'but I thought it was in his spirit really.'[26]

When she was finally alone, Laura wrote, 'I can't imagine Ken doing nothing – I wonder what he will be given to do in the place prepared for him! Altho I have seen him change over many months – he never gave in & battled on just living in a world of his own.'[27] Paul and Margaret realised that one way in which they could help their mother was to try and introduce a sense of order to the chaos which Kenneth had created in the house. Paul started shifting things in the cellar, while Margaret soon made an impression in the attic. 'David interested – but not active,' Laura noted. What he did do was start drawing, experimenting with a new technique, using a reddish-brown ink and a reed pen, that was inspired by the drawings that Van Gogh had made when he was living in Arles, where he had discovered a particular type of reed that could be cut and turned into a pen. This was a method favoured by Japanese artists, prints of whose work Van Gogh collected, and whose draughtsmanship he greatly admired. 'The Japanese draws quickly,' he wrote, 'very quickly, like a flash of lightning, because his nerves are finer, his feeling

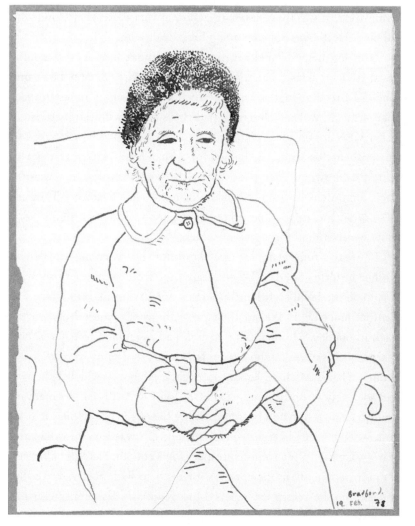

*Mother, Bradford,
19th Feb. 1978*

simpler.'[28] Similarly Hockney employed this technique to create a series
of poignant portraits of his mourning mother – sitting in a chair dressed
to go out, her coat still buckled, her hands gently crossed in her lap,
her eyes cast downward – which captured perfectly her sadness and
vulnerability. Looking at these drawings, the viewer also feels the artist's
own sense of loss. 'It was my way of sitting with her,' he explained. 'She
said "Oh, David, those drawings. I look so sad." And I said "Of course you
were sad. It was a very sad day."'[29] 'When my father died,' he told Marco

Livingstone, 'it was the first person who was very close, very close, who had died. Death was not something I had dealt with.'[30]

Drawing helped Hockney through the next few days. 'I sat for David after breakfast,' Laura wrote on 20 February, '& later Lisa came & he did two drawings of her.' Meanwhile the cleaning up continued. 'Margaret . . . worked all day & made bags of rubbish. (Unfortunately DUSTMEN are on strike) Nobody but Margaret could have worked so efficiently in that attic. Paul helped too & then he too sat for David who made two drawings.'[31] In the evening 'the whole family . . . – went to Harry Ramsdens for supper – table for ten & such a family – They are all so good and so sensible – how could one feel low-spirited – yet I know we all smiled through our sadness.'[32]

Kenneth's funeral took place the following morning, which was another bitterly cold day. 'David cleared the front steps etc of snow, & at 1pm all the family left Hutton Terrace for Eastbrook Hall. Here was comfort indeed – in the small chapel – the room where Ken used to teach in Sunday School about 100 folk had assembled to pay respects & share our sadness. John's friends Michael & Philip were there & Philip's friends Michael Jenkinson & Jack Nichol – which I thought was so lovely – representing Philip & John in Australia. So many of Paul's friends – our holiday group & my friends & neighbours & even some of Ken's clients & Peace News friends. It was very revealing and heart-warming to see so much respect for Kenneth. He will be missed as many people say in their letters for his help with posters etc & the sincerity he showed in his beliefs. Most realise he was a character but speak well of him.' Hockney, who up until this moment had thought he was being quite brave, found 'I couldn't speak or say anything. I just felt tears thinking about him.'[33]

The Bradford daily newspaper, the *Telegraph & Argus*, carried a sizeable obituary in which 'Mr K. Hockney' was remembered as being 'a passionate supporter of the Campaign for Nuclear Disarmament and an enthusiastic opponent of smoking' as well as being 'a kindly eccentric' who 'wore special orange arm-bands round his coat sleeves so he was more visible to traffic when he crossed the road and made his own garish ties complete with multi-coloured spots'.[34] They also published a letter from the head of Bradford CND, Alex Eaton, who praised him for having been 'a great and colourful Bradfordian'. 'Small in stature,' he continued, 'this incredible tenacious man will long remain dear to those who strive for an end to Britain's dependence upon the obscene weapons used at Hiroshima and Nagasaki. His courage and the vigour of his conscience drove him to campaign alone along the streets when there was no demonstration to join. Bird-like he was everywhere and his banners, ever-growing in number and size, shone forth his message of hope in luminous paint "A World without war".'[35]

With the funeral over, the family gathered together at Paul's for a cup of tea and a snack and a chance to share their memories. Hockney then left for London. In the following few days, Paul put on a slide show, and played some tapes he had made of his father singing hymns. 'Everyone is amused,' Laura noted, 'with Ken's tone deafness & each hymn the same tune. I find it sad!!' They swapped stories, recalling his eccentricities and his extraordinary stubbornness. 'He used to go on these holidays every year organised by the church,' Paul remembers, 'but he'd only be away for two days before they'd ring up and say he was in hospital, because he hadn't taken his medication and he'd been eating everything that he shouldn't. One year he went on a boat, and he was seasick and lost his teeth. So he rang me up and asked me to send him his spare ones. He said they were in a cabinet in his bedroom at the side of the wardrobe. Well, when I opened this cabinet, there were all these teeth, about twenty pairs and they were all labelled – "good for eating lettuce", "good for smiling", "good for eating meat" etc. – so I sent the "good for smiling"!'[36]

There were also endless letters to write and more sorting out of Kenneth's vast accumulated collections, the detritus of a man who was incapable of throwing anything away because he might need it one day. 'It is painful for me to sort out,' Laura wrote, 'and find so many things I never knew of. When my rooms are tidy, I shall be glad to leave attics & cellar to the family. I don't think they will be as hurt as I am.' Her final reflection in her diary on Kenneth was poignant. 'Ken was so outward looking. Thought he could put the world right – but I missed the love and understanding at home – and longed for companionship which was not there. God only knows our unusual partnership but it must have been for the best. Now I must live on & hope I will be given strength of mind & body to fulfil the purpose He has planned for me still to do.'[37]

A few days after writing this, she received a letter from David, who was by now back in LA. 'Dear Mum,' he wrote, 'It was a sad week in Bradford, but I hope we get over it quickly and try and think positively. I think you made a marvellous choice for a partner in life and I know in a way you are very proud of him. I know it must have been difficult at times but his motivations were like yours, always to kindness. His were more in the abstract (world problems etc) and yours much more personal – and I think the combination was wonderful. I think the record he has left of his life reflects a great deal of his character and personality and will always be with us. So keep cheerful and look to a few new adventures.'[38]

'I'm glad you think of our partnership in that way,' Laura replied. 'Being poor did not matter, we were always provided with meals. It took me a long time to accept that we were so different . . . but I believe our being together was ordained to create such a wonderful family . . . I seem to have been in a daze. He was so active and alive in his own way. I cannot imagine him dead, & feel sure he will be busy somewhere even now.'[39]

When Hockney departed for LA, he left behind not just his grieving family, but a veritable hornets' nest that he had stirred up in the art world. The *Paper Pools* show had been a triumph. 'Your exhibition continues to be an enormous success,' wrote Vera Russell. 'We had a thousand on the day you left and nearly two thousand yesterday, Saturday 24th. Peter and I do flag occasionally as we know the next morning we shall have to scrub the place out. But the beauty of your pictures and the joy it has brought the public makes up for everything, and every time we are tetchy we regret it – especially myself as I am going quite crazy describing the medium that you used to literally hundreds of people, who, in fact, don't understand in the end.'[40]

The critics were positive too, with Michael McNay in the *Guardian* calling it a 'joyful show'[41] and comparing the light, almost liquid, paintings to Monet's lily ponds, while William Feaver in the *Observer* loved the 'scintillating watery effects: shoals of green commas, coalescing blues, ribboning shadows under the diving boards, a freestyle swimmer dissolved into pink underwater blobules'.[42] It transpired, however, that these were not views shared by the director of the Tate, Sir Norman Reid, who turned down the opportunity to buy one of the double-sized pictures of Gregory Evans diving into a pool, for the greatly reduced sum of £6,000, a work which went instead to the Bradford City Art Gallery. This meant that the Tate, Britain's major modern art gallery, held in its possession only two paintings by Hockney, *The First Marriage* and *Mr and Mrs Clark and Percy.*

Hockney felt, with good reason, these two pictures were scarcely representative of his great output over the previous two decades, particularly in a year in which he was about to have his first solo exhibition at the Museum of Modern Art in New York, which was to open in April, as well as having two major touring exhibitions of prints and drawings on the go, one mounted by the Scottish Arts Council touring Britain and the other by the Yale Center for British Art touring America. Justifiably peeved, he decided to investigate their acquisitions policy, only to find that while they had been generous in their purchases of abstract paintings by artists such as Dick Smith, William Turnbull and Robyn Denny, owning a combined figure of thirty-three works, to his amazement they had not purchased in the previous fifteen years a single work by L. S. Lowry, Patrick Procktor, Euan Uglow, Allen Jones or David Oxtoby. That the work of the latter was not represented particularly surprised him, since the subject matter he touched on, rock 'n' roll, was of interest to so many people.

Hockney, never a man to avoid sounding off, decided first on the direct approach. 'I went to see them,' he recalled. 'I told Norman Reid he's just a pathetic little shit. I said it to his face actually, and I found myself enjoying it! Anyway, the moment I'd been, the word went round the Tate Gallery, people saying "Oh, we've had David for four hours lecturing us on this, that and the other."'[43] He followed this up with a public expression of his misgivings in an interview with Miriam Gross

which was published in the *Observer* on 4 March under the banner
headline 'NO JOY AT THE TATE'. 'The Tate has two functions,' he told
her. 'It is the major, State-supported museum both for British and for
foreign art of the past 100 years . . . In the case of foreign art they must
try to get the very best, in the case of modern British art they have an
additional responsibility; since it's a narrower area, they must be more
inclusive, act as a museum of record and try to cover the ground more
fully. That is their duty and their job. And it seems to me that it is a
job which in recent years they have been doing rather badly . . . We
know that art can be full of joy, and my criticism of the Tate's present
attitude is that it is so narrow, so biased in favour of joyless and soulless
and theoretical art.'[44] He laid the responsibility for this state of affairs
directly at the feet of Reid, citing a conversation he had had with a
Tate employee. 'When I asked one of the staff why they did not have
anything by Uglow . . . I was told: "Oh Norman is not too keen on
that kind of painting." Not too keen? If the Tate gallery is being run on
the personal whim and personal taste of Norman Reid, he should be
willing to debate his policy in public, willing to put forward his point
of view . . .'[45]

Sir Norman, known to readers of the satirical magazine *Private
Eye* as 'Norman Weed', was no stranger to controversy, having been
the cause of howls of outraged protest back in 1976 over his decision
to buy an untitled piece by the American sculptor Carl Andre which
consisted of a number of ready-made bricks. Hostility to the purchase
was pretty well universal, and jokes at his expense came thick and fast
– 'Art may come and art may go but a brick is a brick for ever,' wrote
Bernard Levin in *The Times*[46] – but Reid had stoutly defended himself
and his curators, though it was a scandal that haunted the rest of his
directorship, and even Hockney could not resist referring to it in the
interview, stating that 'they are a piece of art only within the context
of the Tate Gallery. If you put them outside in the street, they would
be stepped over.'[47] A figurative artist himself, Reid was particularly
distressed by what he saw as a personal attack on him by Hockney,
particularly since he had so stoutly defended him back in 1969 when
his collection of American 'beefcake' magazines had been confiscated

by customs at Heathrow Airport. In a mildly written rebuttal of the accusations, published in the *Observer* the following Sunday, he admitted that his taste and predilections shaped the collections, stating 'and it may well be that during the last fifteen years my particular love of abstract art has placed the main growth there'.[48] For this he made no apology. 'I feel sure,' he added, 'that the intensity of experience offered by a collection built up along lines of personal conviction is a benefit which outweighs the advantages a purely representative collection would give.'[49] Though he pointed out that over the previous seven years, the Tate had in fact bought a number of major works by contemporary British figurative artists, including Freud, Bacon, Kossoff, Kitaj, Hilton, Caulfield and Coldstream, Hockney was unappeased, prompting Reid to comment that he was glad he had already announced his intention to retire at the end of the year 'or it might have been thought that David Hockney's whiff of grapeshot had finally done the trick'.[50]

On his way out to California, Hockney stopped off for a few weeks at Ken Tyler's studio in Bedford Village, initially to complete some coloured lithographs he had been working on the year before, but also to experiment a bit and get himself back into the swing. 'At Ken's,' he wrote to Kitaj, 'I tried to discover lithographic techniques so as to be bolder and freer especially with colour. I have always thought my colour lithographs to be stiff and lacking in spontaneity and talking with Ken was very good. I did a lot of rubbish which will be thrown away but I learned a great deal.'[51] On his return to LA, he was relieved to be back in his Santa Monica Boulevard studio after the cold, sad days in Bradford. '. . . it's only now, in California,' he said at the time, 'that I feel I'm really painting again in a way that's fresher . . . I know that if I paint for six months I can do an awful lot of work, it just comes out because I'm finding ways again to do it like that . . . I enjoyed doing the theatre and it's another kind of inventiveness.'[52] Vera Russell believed that doing *The Magic Flute* had inspired him to use colour in a much bolder way, as was evident in the *Paper Pools*, *Canyon Painting* and the huge *Santa Monica Blvd.*, which was currently taking up much of the wall space in the studio. The latter was a painting that was to be a turning point in Hockney's work, not because of its success but because of its failure.

'I'd moved to Los Angeles and was working on a painting of the view outside my studio on Santa Monica Blvd,' he recalled. 'And it wasn't working. It was still stuffy, still asphyxiated by that sense of supposedly "real" perspective.'[53] He had taken hundreds of photographs for the picture, some of which were pinned directly onto the canvas, others onto the studio walls, and he struggled to get it to look real, in the course of which the whole process of painting had become laboured. 'I realised finally that I had probably painted about ten pictures on that canvas and I had kept taking them out, the picture had a horizontal format but the eye didn't move enough across it and the painting was too static. I wanted to get away from doing pictures in which the static element had become too dominant.'[54] In the end he came to the conclusion that it was photography that was the problem because it fixed perspective, in effect petrifying space. 'Perspective takes away the body of the viewer. You have a fixed point, you have no movement; in short, you are not there really. That is the problem . . . For something to be seen, it has to be looked at by somebody and any true and real depiction should be an account of the experience of that looking.'[55] Though *Santa Monica Blvd.* would eventually be abandoned, for Hockney it marked both a startling new use of colour and the end of the use of photographs in the composition of paintings.

When he felt things becoming laboured, he switched mediums and turned to drawing, making several large images of Celia Birtwell, who was visiting from London and who he was paying to model for him. 'I picked up a reed pen and started doing big drawings,' he wrote. 'These pens do not have a fine point and they make you draw a different way. Whatever your medium is you have to respond to it . . . I deliberately pick a medium which forces me to change direction.'[56] He also produced a series of lithographs, which were strongly influenced by his love for the work of early-twentieth-century French artists like Raoul Dufy and Henri Matisse, and which showed a tremendous freedom of technique, in particular those of Celia depicted in a variety of moods and stances,

Celia Elegant

such as *Celia Elegant*, *Celia Weary* and *Celia Inquiring*. Painted directly onto the plates using a large brush and liquid tusche, rather than drawn on with crayons, they are among his most vital and joyous portraits.

He never stopped experimenting, and when Ann Upton and her son, Byron, came out for ten days he did some lively drawings on plates of them. 'They were a marvellous subject,' he told Kitaj. 'The trouble

David Hockney
playing cards with
Ann and Byron
Upton, 1979

was I was trying to find ways of doing things, the same time as trying
to make a representation of them so a lot of zinc and time were wasted
for them – but not for me.'[57] Charles Ingham, a postgraduate student
who was conducting a lengthy interview with Hockney at the time,
described two new paintings, of Ann Upton and Peter Schlesinger, as
being 'completely fresh, and an apparently new departure for Hockney.
Strong, moody colours, very expressionistic. Ann combing her hair
before a mirror, Peter sitting beside a small table and leaning forward,
arms outstretched, to adjust a bottle on the table. We talk about his
use of colour here, and Hockney notes that he had used a lot of yellow
for the first time. He admits that, in fact, previously, "Colour hadn't
seemed that important to me in painting."'[58]

Among other lithographs he completed during this period was one
of Jerry Sohn, an assistant of the artist Sam Francis and a mutual friend
of Jean Léger and Alexis Vidal. After meeting Hockney at an opening
at LA Louver, Sohn had written asking if he needed any occasional

help in the studio. The letter had arrived at an opportune moment as Hockney's relationship with Maurice Payne had recently become somewhat strained. There were various reasons for this, beginning with the fact that this was not a particularly happy time emotionally for him: he had lost his father; he had difficulty accepting that his relationship with Gregory, with whom he was quite in love, was not exclusive, so that he was often lonely, while being wary of having his heart broken for a second time; he wasn't yet 100 per cent certain that he'd done the right thing in moving back to LA; and he was struggling somewhat with the direction in which he was moving as an artist. At the same time, Maurice was also going through a difficult time, having separated from his wife Sarah, of whom Hockney was particularly fond.

'My relationship with David just got harder and harder,' Payne recalls. 'It was partly "log cabin blues", and it was also a changing period for him and probably for me too. I split up from Sarah, and I think he was pissed off with me and thought I was making a stupid move. I had a girlfriend who used to come and visit, and he didn't really like that. She got in the way. I just misread the situation. For me in a professional sense, it was probably a missed opportunity because I should have been really focused. I should have taken on more of the role of a dogsbody, and done more organisation for him, so that he could get on with his work, which was really what he was looking for. He wanted somebody to be organised and get him organised and do things for him, and I wasn't up to it. It wasn't a good period and it took a long while to get over that. The job of being an assistant to an artist like David is a complicated one because you don't know if you're really a friend or you are just there in a professional capacity. I mean, if you're a writer and you have a secretary it's quite defined. Had I been older, I would have had it more defined.'[59] After endless arguments, things came to a head when Hockney told Payne, 'Your ego is as big as mine. It's time we parted.'[60] Fortunately Jerry Sohn was able to step in and help out on a part-time basis, something he was only too happy to do.

*

Laura Hockney
watching her son at
work on a painting
of her, 1979

At the end of February 1979, Laura Hockney wrote in her diary, 'Family want me to go to Australia!! I just don't know if I should. Margaret has left & David gone back & the clearing up is overwhelming. What should I do?' The next day she noted, 'David phones & urges I should go & then fly on to Los Angeles & return to London with him on April 19.'[61] Following much indecision, she eventually went along with her children's wishes and, after visiting Philip and John in Australia, she found herself spending Easter Day in California. 'David, Celia and I went to Disneyland. It was a beautiful sunny day. Crowds of people – strange way to spend Easter for me. Later invited to neighbour of David's for tea and met a score of actors & actresses & famous folk – most of whom I did not know. Rock Hudson was one of them.'[62] It was Laura's first visit to LA, where she was mystified by the fact that, as she told David, 'with all this sunshine, it's wonderful drying weather, but nobody ever seems to hang their washing out'.[63]

After Easter, Hockney took his mother back to Bradford. He then spent three weeks in London before returning in late May, bringing with him Don Bachardy. Such visits kept her spirits up. 'Had meal ready for David & Don at 5pm,' Laura recorded on 21 May, 'but they arrived at 7.30pm . . . a beautiful grey evening – we drove to Ilkley via Baildon Moor & Bolton Abbey – The sky was light tho cloudy till well after 10pm & the views were beautiful. Don was fascinated – did not know England was like that – only thought of it as murky & dirty smoky mills. Called at Paul's & had a cup of tea after fish and chips (outside) on way home. Don's first time & he thought them delicious.' The tour continued the next day with a trip to Fountains Abbey, and finished on 23 May when 'David took Don & I round the Industrial parts of Bradford, Halifax, Queensbury etc. Called at Paul's & home for a fish & chip lunch before they left for London.'[64]

Back in town, Hockney met up with his old friend Peter Adam, now a writer and documentary film-maker, who had asked him to appear in a short film he was making for the BBC as part of a series they were running called *One Hundred Great Paintings*. The particular work he had chosen was Van Gogh's *Café Terrace at Night in Arles*, and they flew together to Holland for a recce in the Kröller-Müller Museum at Otterlo near Arnhem. This was to be Hockney's first experience as a television presenter and the eventual film, shot in the autumn and broadcast the following June, showed how comfortably he slipped into the role. Dressed in baggy trousers, a white shirt and striped tie, and sporting trainers, he engaged the audience straight away by referring to the artist by his Christian name. 'I'll try and remember,' he told the audience, 'to refer to him as Vincent, because even I have trouble pronouncing the name. I always say "Van Goff", the Americans say "Van Go", and the Dutch say "Van Goch", which I can't say, so I'll try and call him Vincent.'[65]

In the ten minutes the film lasted, Hockney managed to illuminate the painting in the manner that only a really good teacher can do. He explained how it came about as a result of Van Gogh's fascination with the artificial light of a little town at night, pointing out that it is a study in the contrast between two colours – yellow and blue. He talked about the speed at which he worked, how spare he could be with his brushstrokes, and his ingenious use of perspective. The work was, he said, 'a wonderful masterpiece and very, very clever in the best sense of the word in painting'. He enchanted the viewer with his boundless enthusiasm, laying the foundations for further excursions into television at a later date. His final observation, something that had stirred him emotionally, was addressed directly to the viewer. 'The other thing I should tell you,' he said, 'what I think is quite remarkable, and has moved me more, is that probably for eight years, the last of his life, we have more evidence of his existence than almost any human being of the nineteenth century. He made eight hundred paintings in ten years . . . he made thousands of drawings and then he wrote all those letters so the twenty-four hours of each day are probably accounted for . . . He would get up early in the morning, he would go out to paint, he would come back, he would eat with a few friends in the cafe, clean his equipment and write his letters. After he's done that, there's nothing left but to go to sleep . . . I think very, very few people can account for their experience in that way. It's very vivid and it's been left to us in a very vivid and generous way.'[66]

Van Gogh's influence on Hockney can be seen in many pictures from this period, such as *Looking at Pictures on a Screen* in which he actually reproduces the artist's *Sunflowers*, and *The Conversation*, with its bright yellow screen framing the figures of Henry Geldzahler and his new lover, the editor and publisher Raymond Foye. He began to use colour at full strength, and apply the paint in a much bolder fashion, making his brushstrokes more obvious, all of which is already apparent in *Canyon Painting* and *Santa Monica Blvd.* 'I now realise,' he reflected at the time, 'sometimes I've been labouring over things, therefore not being expressive enough. And in drawing, the drawings rarely get laboured because they're always done with some speed. And I think they're fresher than the paintings. Although it's harder to paint. Now what I always longed to do was to be able to paint like I can draw, most artists would tell you that, they would all like to paint like they can draw. But in California, I am beginning to find the way.'[67]

Perhaps the best example of Hockney's new-found freedom was his portrait of the outrageous drag artist Divine. In the summer of 1979, Divine, whose real name was Harris Glenn Milstead, was at the height of his fame, having appeared in a number of films directed by John Waters, the most notorious of which was *Pink Flamingos*, in which he played the character of Babs Johnson, 'the filthiest person alive', who in one scene was obliged to eat dog excrement in order to prove her right to the title. In those days, that was the price of fame. He was also an integral part of Andy Warhol's inner circle, and was introduced to Hockney by Don Bachardy, who was painting him at the time. In the way that Hockney placed him right in the centre of the canvas, using strong colours and contrasting patterns, the painting has echoes of Matisse's wonderful series of *Odalisques*.

'I introduced Divine to David,' Bachardy recalls, 'because when he was sitting for me he said it was the dream of his life to meet him, and, hope of hope, he might draw him or even paint him. So I invited David down to one of my sittings with Divine, and he made a date with him then and there. He also invited me to come and participate in the sitting. So I gave them a good hour and a half's start before I turned up. And how did Divine handle the great goal of his life? I arrived at around 11.30 in the morning, and there was Divine sitting in a chair on the dais absolutely dead asleep. And I saw David sighing and raising his eyebrows. Of course he had a camera and he did finish the painting entirely from photographs. I sat there for a good forty-five minutes and nothing would rouse Divine until suddenly he woke up with a start and said, "Potatoes!" He had smelled a stand round the corner frying potatoes, and instead of saying, "Oh gosh, I'm so sorry, I've been asleep,"

he just got up and made a dash for the potatoes.'[68] Whatever difficulties
he may have had with his larger-than-life subject, this portrait proved
to be a watershed for Hockney in that he finally achieved something
that he had always wanted, which was to translate the freshness of his
drawing style into paint.

CHAPTER FIVE

MULHOLLAND DRIVE

In the summer of 1979, Hockney moved from the small and rather cramped rental he had been living in on Miller Drive, to a house on Montcalm Avenue, high up in the Hollywood Hills. It was a decision that was to have a profound influence on his work. This neighbourhood, which is situated in the south-eastern part of the Santa Monica Mountains, is a far cry from the sprawling suburbs that lie beneath it, with narrow roads climbing steeply through canyons that are abundant with flora and whose natural streams run down into the Los Angeles River, attracting a variety of fauna, such as coyotes, raccoons, possum and deer. Here Gregory had found for rent a cluster of small, unpretentious bungalow-type houses surrounded by hanging gardens and situated towards the end of a 'no-through' road. It was a property that belonged to the actor Anthony Perkins. Since Hockney was still working in his studio on Santa Monica Boulevard, this necessitated a long and complicated drive there and back, often twice a day. Driving across West Sunset to Hollywood Boulevard was easy, as it was all on the flat, but the route then took him onto Nichols Canyon Road, and he was soon in another world, snaking his way up a steep, twisty road into the hills below Mulholland Drive. From there he would take Woodrow Wilson Drive, following its tortuous route round sharp bends and up precipitous stretches till it finally reached Montcalm.

Within a few days of moving into the new house, Hockney was writing to Kitaj, 'It's a big house really . . . Over half of it we have ripped up the carpet, and will work on three operas and some etchings.'[1] The operas were to be for the Metropolitan Opera House in New York, and had come about as a result of a letter he had received the previous September from its then Director of Productions, John Dexter. Like Hockney, Dexter was from the north of England, having been born and brought up in Derby. His father was a plumber and an amateur artist who believed strongly in self-improvement and had instilled in his son a love of music and theatre. After an erratic school life, which included much truancy, and a period in the army, Dexter tried his hand as an actor in rep before discovering that his real talent lay in directing. He worked his way up, producing and directing shows for various repertory companies, and in 1957 joined the English Stage Company as an associate director, before being employed by the National Theatre in a similar capacity in 1964. Here he shone, directing such distinguished productions as *The Royal Hunt of the Sun*, *Othello* and *Equus*. He had joined the Met as Director of Productions in 1974 and had worked hard to try and drag what was then an inefficient and old-fashioned opera house into the twentieth century. He had all the charisma and energy to do it, combined with a bullying streak that could prove useful in an impasse. 'When he was high in his cleverness, his skill, his imagination,' wrote the playwright Arnold Wesker, who had worked with him on *The Kitchen*, 'when he buzzed with elation from an inspired day's work, he was electrifying in a way that few other directors I know have been, and it communicated itself to the cast who would then give him their all.'[2]

Dexter knew Hockney's work, and had crossed paths with him briefly. 'I'd met him once at the Royal Court, when he was doing *Ubu Roi*,' he recalled, 'and had seen all his work from the very beginning, because I used to putter around the galleries . . . *Ubu Roi* had some of the madness I was looking for – so many parts of it had so much, especially the Polish Army scene. His work also had the sense of movement and colour I thought I could translate directly to theatre. But we'd never really met although we come from within thirty miles of each other and in England everyone used to say we had a lot in common.'[3] Only someone who could seduce Hockney would have been able to persuade him to return to designing opera at this particular time when he was trying so hard to get back into painting, and Dexter certainly had the right attributes. He was charming, witty, knowledgeable and scholarly in spite of his erratic education.

'It was very good to see you, finally, at the Metropolitan the other night,' he had written to Hockney in September 1978. 'Ever since I saw the possibility of helping to jerk the place into the 20th century, I have been trying one way or the other to seduce you into the house.' He told him that he had discussed some possibilities with their mutual friend John Cox, who had suggested that they might share a production of Rossini's *The Barber of Seville*, an idea that did not appeal to him. In his mind he wanted something that would attract schools and might also possibly bring in a new audience, productions that might also tour. 'In the 1980/81 season,' he continued, 'I hope to celebrate this jump into another area of the opera house with a parade of all the things which have never normally been permitted in that august establishment. I have sent to James Levine and Tony Bliss[4] my thoughts on the triple bill, which I hope will not seem too cut and dried a concept for you to join. Let me promise you that it is only six months old, fraught with dangers and can change in any direction, subject to an exciting battle of tastes and theatrical instincts between ourselves. Such a collision I look forward to with an excitement I hope Fokine felt on meeting Bakst, or, better than that, Ravel on meeting Satie.'[5]

Such words were music to Hockney's ears. Moreover he was immediately excited when he read of the proposed programme, a triple bill of early-twentieth-century French music – two operas, *Les Mamelles de Tirésias* by Poulenc to open the programme and *L'Enfant et les Sortilèges* by Ravel to finish, with a ballet, Satie's *Parade*, in the middle. He was particularly enthusiastic because he knew that none other than his great hero Picasso had designed the first production of *Parade* in 1917. 'I loved his idea,' Hockney recalled; 'it was a fresh approach to do a triple bill . . . I had heard the Poulenc piece on records, and *Parade*, but I did not know the Ravel opera and when I listened to it and read the story it greatly appealed to me.'[6] He was also inspired by Dexter's chutzpah. It was well known that while triple bills might work for ballet, they had a notorious failure rate at the opera, and Dexter had had to battle with the Met to get his idea accepted. His argument was that the three works were related, not just nationalistically, but by the fact that their stories were all conceived during the First World War when the Germans were about thirty miles from Paris, a time when the French were made only too aware of the mentality of war, the waste of it and the mindlessness of it. 'The theme of the evening,' wrote Dexter, 'hopefully has a gentle reminder throughout of how wildly and weirdly the arts survived in a time of world chaos.'[7]

It was a meeting of minds. As a confirmed pacifist, Hockney loved the concept, and he also admired Dexter's ambition 'to make . . . a full-scale display of the kind of totally theatrical illusionist theatre to which I believe opera belongs'.[8] They also shared a similar work ethic. 'Whenever [John] came for three or four days,' Hockney recalled, 'we did an amazing amount of work; we'd work twelve hours a day . . . I had never worked with him before, but I'd seen things he'd done on the stage, and we saw eye to eye.'[9] A number of his friends tried to warn him off the commission, suggesting that neither the Ravel nor the Poulenc would work on a stage as vast as that of the Met since they required a much more intimate setting. After spending time at the Met to master its geography, however, and making numerous drawings of the stage from every possible angle, he disagreed. 'I felt you could do anything you wanted in that theatre,' he remarked, 'if you didn't think about its space in conventional ways. I must admit though, every time I was away from the Met, it grew bigger whenever I thought about it.'[10]

When Hockney began work on the triple bill in earnest, he realised that with Maurice Payne gone, he would need someone else to help him, and the obvious person was Gregory Evans. 'I had moved from Madrid to New York,' Evans remembers, 'and during that period I would go and see David in LA. Then he was offered to design the French triple bill by John Dexter, so he asked if I would come out to LA and help him with that, and find him a house. I found Montcalm, and I put that together for him. I ran the house and I was his assistant, so I guess I was the assistant housewife!'[11] With work piling up, having Evans back on a full-time basis was an extremely positive move for Hockney, as he wrote to Kitaj: 'Gregory is very good at organising things, he's much more confident than Maurice in dealing on the phone with people, and at long last I think something will work. I'm not assuming it will but I think there's a serious side to Gregory that is coming out in organising talents.'[12]

As usual Hockney started with a period of research into the

history of the three works. The original production of Satie's *Parade*, which had been created for Diaghilev's Ballets Russes, had opened in 1917, and had been a collaboration between some of the hottest talents of the day. As well as the set by Picasso, the scenario, a parade in which three groups of circus artists try to attract an audience to an indoor performance, was by Jean Cocteau, and the choreographer and principal dancer was Léonide Massine. Poulenc's *Les Mamelles de Tirésias* is a surrealist two-act 'opera bouffe' based on the play of the same name by Guillaume Apollinaire, which was also first performed in 1917. Set in the fictional town of Zanzibar on the French Riviera, it has as its theme the replacement of all the children killed in the First World War, and features a man in drag who gives birth to 40,049 children in a single day. The final piece, Ravel's *L'Enfant et les Sortilèges*, written between 1917 and 1925, is a one-act opera based on a story by Colette in which a naughty schoolboy rips up his workbooks, smashes some crockery, tears the wallpaper from the wall and is cruel to his cat, all of which then come to life to haunt him with his misdeeds.

After the research Hockney immersed himself in the music, and taking inspiration from the French artists of the period, began work on a series of sketches of his ideas. 'The first drawings I made for the triple bill,' he wrote, 'I called "French Marks" because, listening to that French music by Satie, Poulenc and Ravel, I thought the one thing the French were marvellous at, the great French painters, was making beautiful marks: Picasso can't make a bad mark, Dufy makes beautiful marks, Matisse makes beautiful marks. So I did a number of drawings using brushes, letting my arm flow free, exploring ways of bringing together French painting and music.'[13] But when Dexter saw the drawings on one of his first visits to Hockney's LA studio, it immediately struck him how difficult it would be to arrive at a design merely from sketches. He told him that he must work from a model and offered to have a quarter-inch scale one made. When Hockney replied that he couldn't possibly work from something so small, Dexter arranged for the construction of a large and complex working model of the Metropolitan Opera stage, complete with fly gallery and miniature lighting system. This wonderful new toy brought out the child in Hockney, whose favourite of the operas was *L'Enfant et les Sortilèges*. 'I guess Ravel and I are children at heart,' he told his friend Peter Adam, 'and we both believe the world can be transformed by childlike wonder.'[14]

He decided to get inspiration by looking at toy shops and, on a whim, bought a set of child's building blocks from a store on Hollywood Boulevard, along with some small dolls and a little clockwork plastic squirrel. 'I put the building blocks on the model stage to spell Ravel,' he wrote. 'I didn't quite know what to do but I thought there was perhaps an idea there.'[15] Dexter loved the concept that Hockney eventually came up with of using the building blocks as a visual theme to help relate the three works. 'We decided on how many we would need to spell Maurice Ravel,' he recalled, 'then decided to carry the motif through the whole evening, also spelling Satie's and Poulenc's names. Thus the blocks became a device that would begin the evening and that people would still find acceptable by the time we got to *L'Enfant*. I then suggested it might be interesting to use the other sides of the blocks to make up the furniture – the armchair, fireplace and other objects in the room – and he said, well it would take a bit of working out. So we sat down and worked it out.'[16]

Though they largely worked well together, Dexter was not an easy man, and there were times when Hockney found him exasperating. 'He was his own worst enemy,' he says. 'He used to shout a lot. He would shout at me and treat me like a schoolboy, so I started treating him like the headmaster. I didn't mind because I kept thinking, "Well, when I've done this, I don't need to do another one. I can just go back to painting."'[17] Max Charruyer, an assistant of Dexter's, recounted how Hockney would sometimes hand Dexter a piece of paper on which he had elaborately drawn his ideas for a blocking or an angle, and if Dexter didn't like it he would simply tear it in two and chuck it in the waste bin, much to the astonishment of any onlookers.[18] At times, Dexter was also exasperated by Hockney, especially in the way that his enthusiasm could take him off on a tangent. He soon learned, however, how to get him back to specifics. 'Whenever he goes off into an area which is absolutely irrelevant,' he wrote, 'or repeats himself for the 199th time and goes on with the same point, you just say, "Yes, David, yes" . . . and let him go on till he's talked himself out. And I wait for a moment till I'm sure, and say yes, that's what we agreed on two days ago. Now we can get back to work.'[19]

In September 1979, Hockney travelled to Bradford to attend his niece Janine's wedding. It took place on 22 September, a warm, sunny day after weeks of cold weather, and was tinged with sadness for his mother, who, if his father had survived, would have celebrated her golden wedding anniversary only a fortnight earlier. Hockney's arrival cheered her up, however, and he also brought Henry Geldzahler to stay, to whose charm she was greatly susceptible. After taking Geldzahler and Raymond Foye on a 'Mr Whiz Tour' of Scotland for two days, where he sang the praises of the Scots for their liberal attitude to opening hours, Hockney returned to Bradford for some more Yorkshire sightseeing, driving them and his mother to Ponden Hall. All this lightened Laura's mood, and after they had left for London, she wrote in her diary, 'How hectic but happy it has all been.'[20]

Hockney returned to Los Angeles in late October to attend the opening of a show in which he was exhibiting, put on by his new dealer, Peter Goulds. Titled *This Knot of Life*, it was inspired by an exhibition called *The Human Clay* that Kitaj had organised at the Hayward Gallery in 1976. While that was a huge salon-type show of mostly prints and drawings by artists who worked figuratively, the new show at the LA Louver was a much smaller and focused celebration of English figurative painting. It had proved a difficult exhibition to pull together, works by Bacon and Freud having been particularly hard to secure, but with Hockney's help Goulds had eventually pulled it off, his own contributions being a painting of Ann Upton called *Ann Upton Combing Her Hair* and the recently completed *Divine*.

Among the ten artists represented were Howard Hodgkin and Peter Blake, two good friends of Hockney's, who made the decision to travel over for the opening and stay with him at Montcalm Avenue. While they were there, Hodgkin, who was on his first visit to LA, kept a diary, extracts from which provide an entertaining account of the trip

as well as a snapshot of Hockney's life. They arrived the evening of the
opening, 22 October. 'Arrive to sunset and hot breathing winds and
palm trees on the front at Venice,' he recorded. 'I said to P. "Fuck India."
Little light left; boys pumping iron and exercising; roller-skating round
deserted tennis courts. To the gallery when still just light outside. *Very*
white room immaculately hung. Large DH portrait of Divine. Am given
most of a wall . . . C. Isherwood and Don Bachardy (the colour of
cocoa). Very white light, very aware of the surfaces of skin and hair, most
people of all ages looking appallingly bright-eyed and healthy. Outside
the night is like dusk – very formally people say: "I like your pictures
Mr Hodgkin." Squeezed in to DH's car . . . home up switch-back road
through Laurel Canyon to D's house – an instant home, the kidney-
shaped pool seen through Kotah palms shimmers in the moonlight.'[21]

*Mo and Lisa
McDermott*

One of the people Hodgkin noted seeing on this first evening
was Mo McDermott. 'Opposite Mo at dinner, who looks wonderful
and young,' he wrote, 'we pay each other silly compliments.'[22] There
were reasons for Mo's glowing appearance other than that he was,
temporarily at least, off the drugs. He had recently got married to Lisa
Lombardi, a wealthy girl from San Francisco, who Hockney used to
refer to as a 'California Hooray'. It seemed an excellent match in that,
being strong and tall, she fulfilled Mo's ideal of the perfect woman,
while she in turn had a penchant for Englishmen. She was also artistic,
and had encouraged him to go back to making his cut-out trees. 'She
was handsome and rather beautiful,' Celia Birtwell remembers, 'and
they were creative together. They went to live in a house in Echo Park,
with a workshop in the back garden where they made three-dimensional
sculptures.'[23] Mo seemed finally to have become independent.

The following morning, Blake was hung-over and remained by the
pool, while Hockney took Hodgkin to look at his studio. 'D and I go
for a drive around town,' wrote Hodgkin, 'as romantic and artificial as
I had hoped and then to his studio in the Versailles Furniture Company.
A shop with white washed windows on to the street but with empty
transoms through which you can see bits of buildings, the sky, part
of a neon sign which says "NUDE". A smallish room with a balcony,
a Matisse bergère, and many more or less finished paintings in a style

which, among others, contains elements of Fauvism and Camden Town and is relentlessly bright in colour.'[24] He then turned his attention to *Santa Monica Blvd.*, with which he could see his friend was struggling. 'On the wall a *very* large painting of a street,' he noted, 'which suffers, as all such compositions must, from the fact that the horizontals, of the street, buildings, etc, are all parallel with the top and bottom of the long canvas on which it is painted. Sadly this is an almost unbreakable situation but DH is obviously determined to win.' They spent the afternoon round the swimming pool, eating salami and listening to Ian Dury's 'Reasons to be Cheerful', before Paul Cornwall-Jones, one of Hockney's publishers, picked them up and drove them down to look at the Gemini print workshops, which Hodgkin found 'elegant, functional and obsessive'. In the evening they enjoyed 'The Prime Rib Experience' at one of Hockney's favourite restaurants, Lawry's in Beverly Hills. 'Dinner at Laury's [*sic*],' wrote Hodgkin. 'Instant England with panelling, family portraits, Margheritas, long wait, waitresses in mini-skirts; Tate Gallery, Norman Reid, Arts Council, James Callaghan, Tony Benn and wicked Trustees as conversation. Largest plates of roast beef. Exhausted.'[25]

Apart from an interview Hodgkin and Blake had to do with a journalist from the *Los Angeles Times*, their days passed in a delightful haze of sunshine, sightseeing, eating, drinking, and completely falling under the spell of LA. They sat round the pool with Hockney. 'DH swims. We drink tea out of cobalt mugs . . . the gardeners have come walking along the flat roof with pots of plants, talking about design . . . The sun is bright so that the blue pool and transparent yellow umbrella are strictly art. As is the garden, full of trees that must have arrived in middle age and ground cover so elaborate that even the grass when you look closely isn't; just some miniature kind of creeping clover; the house, so simple and austere, looks almost too perfectly like DH paintings.' They went to Venice and walked on the beach, and revisited the gallery 'where the show seems so much less resonant than the street outside the open door'. In Palm Springs they watched 'the golf carts come and go. Buildings no higher than a tall bungalow, gardens like liquorice all-sorts in shades of green.' One night they were taken to the Back Lot, which Blake described as 'a semi-gay disco'. Hodgkin wrote that it was 'Huge, brilliantly stroboscopically lit, and as clean and wholesome as a nursery school. Everyone of all ages looked as if they lived on cornflakes.' After their interview, they lunched at the Sidewalk Café on Venice Beach 'under a convincing Venetian arcade with cast iron columns. We both ate omelettes, PB's a Jack Kerouac, mine was a Gertrude Stein. Both revolting, but the scene of people gliding by on roller skates (pushing prams and carrying shopping) or playing frisbee or running was amazing and the hot sun delirious . . .' Snoozing all the way on lunchtime Bloody Marys, they then went to Disneyland, where they were impressed by Hockney's personal favourite ride, Pirates of the Caribbean, and were disappointed by the Life of Snow White, 'described by P.B as an early work'.[26]

On their last day they were taken to lunch with Billy Wilder at LA's most famous restaurant, Ma Maison on Melrose Avenue, a favourite haunt of movie stars like Orson Welles who came to savour the rich French dishes prepared by its celebrated chef, Wolfgang Puck. Wilder, a friend and hero of Hockney's, regaled them with stories of the film business, including one about his attempt to sell a movie about the life of Nijinsky to Sam Goldwyn. '. . . he suggested [it] as the answer to "Gone with the Wind" and having taken SG through it all with homosexuality, passion and madness till he ends in a Swiss asylum thinking he's a horse, against mounting doubts says, "If you want a happy ending have him win the Kentucky Derby."'[27]

Returning home, Blake and Hodgkin agreed that the trip had been so memorable that they should work on a joint exhibition about it. Though this never materialised, both artists produced paintings inspired by the visit, the best known of which is Blake's *The Meeting or Have a Nice Day, Mr Hockney*, showing him and Hodgkin, rather formally dressed in sports jackets and trousers, meeting a very casually dressed Hockney, against a background of billboards, palm trees and beautiful roller skaters. The painting was a witty take on Gustave Courbet's *The Meeting or Bonjour, Monsieur Courbet*.

*

Christmas 1979 was one of the very few that Hockney did not spend in Bradford. Realising that his mother might find Christmas at home something of an ordeal, it being her first without Ken, he invited her and a friend out to LA. 'My Mother and Paul's mother-in-law came for Christmas with my younger brother John from Australia,' he wrote to Kitaj and others. '. . . Christmas in Hollywood was strange (very warm), only my second away from Yorkshire and my mother's first. Everywhere we went, if asked her name, my mother's friend said "Mrs Rushworth". Of course nobody in California calls themselves Mrs anything, so it was amusing. We met George Cukor who was very charmed by them instantly recognising them as provincial unsophisticated English ladies with wide eyes everywhere. It was delightful and not in any way a chore . . . "The time of my life", said Mrs Rushworth, and I think it was. We played Scrabble about 30 times. I got quite good at the end but my mother won most games. They became experts on two or three letter words which a non Scrabble player rarely thinks of.'[28]

Laura was delighted both by her trip and her son. 'I don't know how to say a big enough thank-you for all the love you showed to Annie & I,' she wrote to him. 'You gave so much of your time and thoughtfulness to our enjoyment. I'm so proud to have a son who not only shares his material things but the more precious one of friends & love. It's no use wishing I was younger – but I do wish I was not quite so disabled – it is so frustrating when one has always been active – but I must not complain – I have eyes & ears & found great pleasure in your lovely home & meeting your friends. I was most impressed by their kindness & welcome everywhere & the feeling of goodwill to us & amongst themselves. It was a very kind consideration on your part when you invited a companion for me. Imagine me on stilts in your kitchen or dropping the frying-pan.'[29]

The letter that Kitaj received was a round robin sent out by Hockney to all his close friends. 'I miss you a great deal,' he told them. 'I don't miss London, only my friends there and there are melancholic moments when I think of Europe . . . Somehow I'm calmer here, more unhurried, even more contemplative and I think it suits me . . . I'm working away on quite a few paintings, in fact it's a long time since I had so much going in a painting studio. Gregory has been marvellous at helping to organise it all and things run reasonably smooth hence the work. Paul (CJ) and Paul H have been here for about ten days seeing accountants etc. Business is a bore to me although I know it has to be done, and really for the first time in many years I feel in control a bit . . . my painting is exciting me again.'

The catalyst for this was undoubtedly working on the designs for the operas, which by January 1980 were well on their way to completion. Dexter and Hockney had proved to be a formidable team, bouncing ideas off one another and unafraid to take a free-form approach to the production. For example, they had been discussing the best way to treat the sixty-strong chorus, who, from the conductor's point of view, needed to be in the middle. Hockney therefore thought they should look neutral and be dressed in black tie. One morning Dexter called him and told him to look in the *New York Times*, at a photograph that might provide the solution for the chorus. 'He didn't even say what the picture was,' Hockney recalled. I put the phone down and went to get a copy. I looked through and there was a review by Hilton Kramer of a show of the drawings of Giovanni Domenico Tiepolo, illustrated with a drawing of Punchinello being carried by his friends. It was the Punchinello! I called John back and I said . . . I'd go right away to New York to see it.'

Hockney was mesmerised by the exhibition, and immediately agreed with Dexter that the Punchinellos would be perfect for the chorus. He had only ever seen two of these Tiepolo drawings, and those were in books. Here were fifty-one of the originals showing the extravagant figure of Punchinello in his tall cylindrical hat, with beaked nose and bulging belly, depicted in an immense variety of dramatic situations, from scenes of courtship and marriage to work and play, games and entertainments, and crime and punishment. It was Punchinello as Everyman. 'The titles of the drawings are marvellous,' he wrote: "Baby Punchinello Being Entertained by a Caged Bird", "Punchinellos Picking Fruit and Quarrelling", etc. One day in New York, when I was with John in a taxi, we started inventing Punchinello names. We just looked along the street: Punchinello selling hot dogs; Punchinello being arrested;

Punchinello as a policeman.' When it came to the actual production, even the stagehands donned Punchinello costumes. 'When they got dressed it was marvellous,' Hockney remembered. 'Each one looked like a different character. One of them had a slouch and a beer belly and didn't like wearing the costume, but the way he walked out on the stage, he looked like Punchinello as a weary stagehand. It was a brilliant idea because everything fitted. It was as though a troupe of actors had come to do the whole evening.'[30]

Originally the ballet, *Parade*, was to be sandwiched in the middle of the triple bill, acting as an entr'acte between the two operas. Hockney, however, had another idea. 'I suggested to John,' he recalled, 'that we treat it as a little overture to what would follow. That seemed like a good idea, because in French "parade" does not mean a parade. It means a sideshow with a barker in front of a curtain trying to get people into the theatre – a very old technique that is still used in travelling theatres, carnivals and fairgrounds. That way, I thought, there were all sorts of things we could do with it.'[31] He had not, however, reckoned with the third creative force involved in the production, and that was Rudolf Nureyev, who the Metropolitan Opera Board had insisted Dexter should hire to choreograph *Parade*, feeling that such a risky venture would benefit from having a star name attached to it. To begin with, Dexter had welcomed the idea, though he had expressed his misgivings to Hockney about the logistics involved. 'God knows,' he wrote to him, 'how I will bring you, Rudy and myself together as we all three seem to be travelling around the world in ever decreasing circles, gradually disappearing up some orifice or other not visible, I trust, to the naked eye. However I don't think it's beyond the bounds of possibility . . .'[32]

After being approached by Dexter and having researched the project a little, Nureyev had decided to make the emphasis of the ballet the creation of the original 1917 production and the artistic differences between Cocteau, Picasso and Satie that grew out of this. 'He saw it very differently,' Hockney told the *New York Times*. 'The spirit of Satie seemed miles away.'[33] Unfortunately there was also a certain lack of communication between him and his collaborators. 'David and I,' wrote Dexter, '. . . locked into gear at our first meeting and we really didn't have any problems. It was just a question of the right order or technical problems. By the time Rudolf Nureyev was suggested by the management, and by the time we got hold of him, David and I were forging ahead. Because we were unable to have much contact with Nureyev, we found ourselves on divergent paths. It was a very unfortunate and time-wasting procedure.'[34] It is a measure of how bad things were that Dexter wrote in his diary on 10 March 1980: 'The problem is to prevent the Russian cuckoo throwing the English golden eggs out of the nest!'[35]

The headache that Nureyev was causing was partly the reason that Hockney decided to turn down a request from John Cox to design *The Barber of Seville* for the 1981 season at Glyndebourne. His letter announcing his decision gives a good account of the pressure he would have been under had his answer been yes. 'This is what my timetable would be like,' he explained to Cox. 'For the next two months in California I'm going to teach one day a week at U.C.L.A. During this time I want to paint, but I will also be refining the triple bill. With every meeting with John D. we work out more things and I refine the concepts, sets or costumes . . . In June I am coming to England, – to help relight the flute and see my mother in Bradford. I would then return to California to paint for July + August. In mid-Sept. I was going to China with Stephen Spender, returning near the end of October. If I did the *Barber* I would then have to begin work almost immediately and leave it with you for Christmas. Then I would be in N.Y to stage the triple bill for Feb 21st. Then perhaps a trip to England to check on *Barber* set progress, and then June in England working on it. As you can see it is a heavy commitment to the Theatre for someone very eager to paint and draw in quiet isolation for a while . . . Meanwhile I must say I get more excited by the triple bill, although working with Nureyev has not been too exciting yet, – he still isolates his contribution for *Parade* as a single work unrelated to the other parts of the evening, when we have found so many threads running through the works as to give the whole evening much more unity than I ever thought was there when we began.'

The problems with Nureyev came to a head in the early summer when the whole team had assembled in London, and he had reached an impasse with Hockney and Dexter as to how to move forward. Dexter then told Hockney that *he* had to fire him. 'So Nureyev came over to Pembroke Studios,' David Graves recalls, 'and sat down on the big leather sofa there, and David said, "Well, Rudi, it's obvious that we are not going to be able to work together, so I'm afraid it's all finished." Nureyev looked completely shocked. He sat there for a few minutes in silence and then got up and left.'[36]

'David Hockney from 1–4pm,' Dexter noted in his diary on 21 June. 'Rudi 1 hour late, walks out after 15 minutes, dresses for 20 and finally walks out. Let us hope for good. Work recommences on *Parade*. Outline finished 8.30.'[37] A week later, on 29 June, he wrote, '*Parade* meeting AT LAST. Rudi walked away reasonably quietly if all people say is true. But on the evidence of my eyes and ears, he is a stupid cunt.'[38] The following day, he added this note: 'There was nothing in it he could not have done if only he had done as he was told. Unfortunately, however, he may have been the grit in the Margarita. I suppose Anthony Bliss would have preferred the pearl. Well he will have to make do with the healthy oyster.'[39]

And the oyster really was healthy. Hockney had not felt so charged in years. On his way over to London, he had stopped in New York to see the great Picasso retrospective that had opened at the Museum of Modern Art and been described by John Russell in the *New York Times* as being 'one of the most remarkable exhibitions that ever got hung on the wall'.[40] Other than the ground-breaking Jackson Pollock show he had seen at the Whitechapel Gallery back in December 1958, no show had ever excited Hockney so much. '. . . it's like the National Gallery all painted by one man,' he wrote to Kitaj. 'Totally incredible . . . no artist ever left such incredible evidence of his experience before; it's like Rembrandt, Piero, Van Gogh and Degas all in one . . . you really <u>must</u> see it. You'll thank me for nattering you. If you were 25 you wouldn't think twice about braving snow, sleet, three hour queues and hot bad breath to see it.'[41]

The show filled forty-eight rooms of the museum and brought together the known work from all over the world, including the most substantial loans ever made from the Picasso Museum in Barcelona, with the unknown, in the form of a huge body of work that had been accepted by the French government after the artist's death, and it had a powerful effect on Hockney. '. . . it made me just want to paint,' he wrote. 'I still had to do things for *Parade*, but the exhibition affected me so much I thought, God, if you want to paint, just paint. I thought, if Picasso was here, what he would do would be to make paintings of the sets instead of doing them as gouache – so that's what I did.'[42] The result was a burst of energy unprecedented in his work for more than ten years, during which, in the space of a two-month stay in London, he completed a series of sixteen paintings on the theme of music and dance. None of them took more than a few days to paint, and they were freely drawn using bold colours and simple forms. He told Marco Livingstone, 'The Picasso exhibition made me realise that sometimes just getting it down quickly, what you get down is often more your thinking than when you coldly plan it. Henry [Geldzahler] used to say to me, "The real bit of Puritanism you have left is that you think if you've spent three months on a painting it's forced to be good, and if you've spent two days on a painting, it's nothing. Often when you just spent two days on it something came out that doesn't come out in the others."'[43]

As well as painting, Hockney also threw himself into the social life of London, arriving with Gregory at the beginning of June, and immediately taking up with the old gang where he had left off. George Lawson's diaries record them being out on the town most nights, dining, going to the theatre and opera, and to the occasional nightclub. On 2 June, for example, they were at Langan's with Wayne Sleep; on 7 June at Il Passetto with Celia, Jane Kasmin and Eugene Lamb; 14 June found them at Glyndebourne for a revival of *The Magic Flute*; while on 18 June it was Ronnie Scott's followed by the Markham Arms and the Chelsea Arts Club. Hockney also revived his tea parties, one of which Lawson attended on 28 June. 'Hockney's tea – Richard Hamilton, Sandra Fisher, Tullio Brunt, Angus O'Neil, Gregory. Then the Kebab and Humous in Charlotte St, then Heaven.'[44]

Once again there was the usual stream of people passing through

Hockney's studio on a daily basis. His friend Peter Adam, who was discussing making a film about him, was nevertheless impressed by how much better he seemed to deal with the constant interruptions. 'He seemed not to be distracted by the endless cups of tea and the casual chat which filled his studio,' he wrote, 'and would manage to finish a new canvas in between friends' visits . . . As so often, working in one medium had spilled into another. Every corner of his studio was now filled with exuberant new paintings on the theme of dance and music. From the small gallery hung *Ravel's Garden*, *Waltz*, an adaptation of Picasso's original curtain for *Parade* and a large *Harlequin* doing a handstand. The boldness of the design and the brilliant colours of no less than sixteen new paintings filled the room.'[45] 'I'm painting a new picture every few days,' Hockney told Peter Webb, 'plundering Picasso and Matisse and loving every moment.'[46]

Though most of the designs for *Parade* were complete, he still had concerns about the lighting, and had asked for help from David Graves, who had assisted him with researching the animals in *The Magic Flute*. Graves, who worked as a paper restorer for Paul Cornwall-Jones at Petersburg Press, had originally trained as an architect, so was able to build a quarter-inch scale model of the set. 'I then got a friend of mine to come up with someone who knew about electronics,' he recalls, 'and crude though they were by today's standards, we built a lighting kit. We used the bulbs from Jaguar headlights, which were dipped into different colours, and we made a handset like a TV controller on which you could control three different sets of lights, so you could bring the red down and the blue up etc. David'd work out all the cues in his head so that when it came to the time that someone had to put those lighting cues into a score, he could do the performance for them and they could make the notations. It was really very impressive. There were always people dropping in, and he could never resist putting on a "Show and Tell" for them.'[47] It being midsummer, to get the best out of the lighting, these performances often took place at eleven o'clock at night. Of the three pieces, Hockney's undoubted favourite was *L'Enfant et les Sortilèges*, which also had the advantage of being only forty-five minutes long, so he could perform the whole piece. He would invite people to sit around the model, turn down the lights and lose himself in the performance, telling the story as he went along, his Yorkshire accent giving it added charm. 'A little boy says, "I'm fed up with being good. I want to be wicked!" So he picks up the poker from the fireplace, he runs around the room, he smashes the teapot, he breaks the cup. The teapot and the cup do a dance. Naturally, the teapot being a black Wedgewood teapot, he sings in English, and naturally the china cup sings in Chinese. He says, "Oh, I'm fed up and bored with books!" and a little old man comes out of the book followed by a lot of numbers, and all the numbers start running around. Then a cat comes in the room, and the cat leads him into the garden, and the music as he goes into the garden is just fabulous. It is full of childlike wonderment. In the garden is a great big tree, and the great big tree sings and says, "You wretched boy! You stuck a penknife in my side and the sap is still coming out." Then a dragonfly comes up and says, "You shouldn't behave like that." They're all running around the garden and as they run around they tread on a squirrel and they damage his foot. And the little boy sees this and takes off his tie and bandages up the squirrel. And then they say, "Well, perhaps he is not too bad after all." And the last words are "Maman" as he calls for his mother as if it's all been a dream.'[48]

Martin Friedman, the then director of the Walker Art Center in Minneapolis, was in the audience at one such presentation. 'Once the lush Ravel tape was running, he was both commentator and performer, giving voice to the various roles in his unique *Sprechstimme*. He hummed along with the chorus and danced about while raising and lowering the painted flats. In his presentation of *L'Enfant*, he was the incorrigible little boy, soon destined to see the error of his ways. For the lucky visitors, Hockney's one-man opera performances were superb show-business. For Hockney, they were rapturous self-hypnosis.'[49] As Friedman left the studio, he told Hockney, 'It won't be better than that on the real night!'[50] Laura Hockney also loved 'the tiny miniature theatre for the opera'. For her it was 'a proof of the hard work you have given through mind & hands'.[51]

*

The film that Peter Adam had been discussing making with Hockney was to be an hour-long documentary for television as part of a series he was making on artists at work for the BBC's *Omnibus* programme. So far, he had filmed the composer Hans Werner Henze, the novelist Lawrence Durrell, the film director Luchino Visconti, the playwrights Lillian Hellman and Edward Albee, and the actresses Lotte Lenya and Jeanne Moreau. Hockney was to be the first painter. Knowing how wounded his would-be subject had felt after his experience with Jack Hazan, when what he had believed would be a documentary about his work turned out to be a feature film about his private life, Adam had been especially sensitive in his approach. He made it absolutely clear that he would be concentrating not on the personal details of Hockney's life, but on his working methods and the different mediums he employed, namely painting, drawing, printing, photography and set design.

Having secured his agreement, he had the perfect place to start the film – in London at the Tate, where a major show of Hockney's prints and drawings, *Travels with Pen, Pencil and Ink*, had opened on 1 July with a party attended by, among others, Christopher Isherwood, Don Bachardy and Henry Geldzahler, followed by a dinner at the home of Kasmin's business partner, Sheridan Dufferin. Geldzahler was in buoyant mood and as a tease, after the odd line of cocaine, to which he was not averse, and no doubt egged on by some of the gang, scribbled down on a scrap of paper 'The Faults and Failings of D. Hockney'. These were, he opined,

1. STUBBORN
2. HARD OF HEARING
3. UNINTENTIONALLY RUDE
4. SUFFERS FOOLS GLADLY
5. GENEROUS TO A FAULT
6. EMOTIONAL IN THE GUISE OF REASON
7. OFTEN OVER-HEARTY (WALKING AND BATHING)

He signed the list 'H. GELDZAHLER "THE HORRIBLE"'.

The Tate exhibition, which had originated at the Yale Center for British Art and had been travelling round America for the previous two years, was well received, with John Russell Taylor writing in *The Times* that though the new show was 'deliberately lightweight . . . what we do have . . . is ample evidence of Hockney's sheer brilliance as a draughtsman, his sharp and quizzical eye for the character of a person or a place'.[52] And Hockney must have taken the greatest satisfaction from the comment of Michael McNay writing in the *Guardian* that 'his sheer skill with line in some of the ink portraits of such friends as Mo McDermott and Peter Schlesinger is reminiscent of the Picasso drawing of Diaghilev'.[53] Bernard Levin felt that Hockney must be 'inexhaustible, that before the last of the 150 pictures was hung, he had already made a dozen experiments in a dozen entirely new areas, styles or methods. The energy that comes off the walls is very remarkable; it is not too much to say that it is the same feeling that we get, at its most intense, in a room full of Picassos, and it leaves the spectator in no doubt that Hockney's creative spring will go on gushing in a powerful and sparkling torrent for a very long time indeed.'[54]

As Peter Adam and his camera crew followed Hockney round the exhibition, he once again revealed his great skill as a teacher and communicator, analysing his own work in simple comprehensive terms, and drawing in the viewer to his own creative process. 'Hockney was undeterred, even excited,' Adam recalled, 'by the presence of the camera; he walked through the rooms, pausing here and there, commenting, discovering, delighting as always in his own work, the portraits, the swimming-pools, the vases of flowers, an amiable clown in funny baggy trousers and colourful cap. "I like flowers," he suddenly said, "they are very difficult to paint. In the old hierarchy of skills, faces are the most difficult, hands are next, feet, the human body, and after that flowers. Not that I can do them well, but that's the way it was."'[55] Looking long and hard at the portraits of Celia Birtwell and Henry Geldzahler, he commented, 'I think the line drawings are the most difficult to do because a tension is building up inside you as you go on looking for things and you have to go on doing it, to be able to draw well, to reduce everything to a line. It is not just an outline, it's different textures, different surfaces.'[56]

*

Towards the end of August, Hockney headed back to California, but
not without paying another visit to the Picasso show in New York for
further inspiration, writing once again to Kitaj to encourage him to see
it. 'How many times,' he asked him, 'have you seen 48 rooms of pictures
representing 75 years of a man's life? All painting is autobiographical.
It's amazing how the history of modern Europe is reflected in his
feelings depicted on the walls – how after the tumult of the late thirties
and the austerity of the war years, and then joyous fun with the peace
of the fifties . . . It truly is thrilling.'[57] He finally arrived back in LA,
charged with energy and inspired to paint in a new way, both by the
work he had done on the operas and by the example of Picasso. After
the hectic two months he had spent in London, however, it took him
a while to readjust to the Californian life. 'It seems strange after being
in London so long and seeing lots of theatre and music,' he told Kitaj.
'There seems little to do here in the evenings by comparison and it's
only when I motor on Santa Monica Boulevard and see the boys that I
remember why I came back.'[58] Then disaster struck.

A labour dispute at the Met between the musicians and the management, which had been quietly simmering for weeks, blew up into a
full-scale strike and the 1980–81 season was indefinitely postponed.
Such disputes had a long and acrimonious tradition at the Metropolitan
Opera, a previous one in 1969, for example, having led to a three-and-
a-half-month shutdown of the house. On that occasion, the lawyer for
the musicians had emerged from one meeting to state that the biggest
impediment to a settlement was 'the wave of hate blowing across that
table'.[59] At the root of the problem was the strongly held belief of the
musicians that over the years they had not been treated as the talented,
educated craftsmen and artists they were, and as a result had had to
put up with short seasons, low pay and no vacations. One orchestra
representative put it this way: 'The Met was founded in the 1880s
by robber barons as their plaything. The attitude has persisted that
everybody who walks through the door is a servant.'[60] They were now
asking for a four-performance week and their pay and conditions to be
on a par with those of the major symphony orchestras.

The effect of the strike on Hockney was drastic, casting him from a state of euphoria into a deep depression. 'I had put in an awful lot of effort,' he wrote, 'and . . . I was confident it would be really good. Having already done two operas, I knew well enough how the models would translate on the stage and I was convinced it would work as exciting theatre. I kept going to New York. The costume department carried on, but I kept asking, "Are they really going to cancel it?" I got so depressed; I thought all that I've done will be wasted.'[61] His health suffered too, and Ken Tyler, who was clearly worried about his appearance, encouraged him to go for a check-up. 'I took his advice,' he recalled. 'I tend to avoid doctors usually. So I went for this check-up and they thought there was something wrong with my heart. For about three weeks I heard every single heartbeat. I had more tests at UCLA and the man said "Have you had a heart attack?" I said, "No, I haven't." He said, "I don't know what you're doing here then, everything seems fine to me." I never went back, and, frankly, I'm sure my heart was affected because of the strike at the Met.'[62]

When Peter Adam flew to LA to continue filming in October, Hockney was in New York, having forgotten the arrangement in the drama of the strike. Adam, however, being used to waiting around, often for days, to film the great and the good, was undaunted and decided to make the best use of the spare time, and drink in the tackiness of West Hollywood. 'A friend of mine,' he wrote, 'had lent me his flat in "boys town", as it was called. The flat was right above that of Betty [sic] Davis, whom I watched daily watering the plants on her terrace. She was terribly proprietary about the building and had sent her secretary down to inquire about the stranger swimming in the pool. There was a manager who never stopped boasting about the filmstars he "made". He ended up showing me what one can do on a waterbed, "which a few days earlier was graced by the body of Sylvia Kristel, of *Emmanuelle* fame", he bragged. She was also living in the same house. Everything was so deliciously unreal and tacky.'[63] Eventually, with still no sign of Hockney, he decided to start filming without him and drove around taking shots of little colourful houses with palm trees, the manicured lawns and grass sprinklers, and the occasional skyscraper. He also got hold of a couple of Hockney's friends, Mark and Sam, and filmed them diving into a swimming pool, in a re-creation of one of the pool paintings. Finally a call came from Hockney to say he was on his way from New York. 'I went to fetch him from the airport. He and Gregory were loaded down with books and paintings. He was very apologetic and we drove up to his house on Montcalm Avenue, nestling on the hills over Los Angeles which spread like a twinkling carpet underneath. It was a lovely unpretentious house in a garden with a swimming-pool, a warm welcoming place humming with attractive and ineffectual creatures, eloquent and charming. The large living-room gave out onto a wooden terrace. On the wall among Hockney's own drawings was a painting of Laurel and Hardy by his father. Mark brought in a huge pile of mail, which David shoved into a drawer already full of unopened letters.'[64]

The following day they went location-hunting. 'David drove us in his open sports car around town,' Adam recalled, 'the radio blaring Mozart . . . We drove to the sea, and on to Little Venice. The Bohemian section was full of people on roller skates and a steel band played on the lawn. "It's a bit like Europe in a sense," David rambled on enthusiastically, "a sunny, naked version of Portobello Road . . . It is always sunny. It's got the energy of the United States with the Mediterranean thrown in, which I think is a wonderful combination."'[65] On their return home, Adam filmed some of the boys diving in and out of the pool while Hockney took photographs of them, and talked excitedly about his fascination with water. '"I can't describe it with words," he said, "it's so elusive. It's a subject that has a lot of richness in it. Strange changing surfaces I find fascinating. When you look at a floor your eyes stop on the floor. With water you can look at the reflection, or you can look through it . . . the interesting thing about water is something you can't quite define, it's unclear yet clear."'[66]

Adam was impressed by the meticulous order that Hockney kept in his studio, with his clean brushes all tidily standing in large glass jars or pots, and the thick tubes of paint lined up in neat rows. The painting that still dominated the space was *Santa Monica Blvd.*, about which Hockney was refreshingly honest. 'This is an unfinished picture that I keep struggling with,' he admitted, standing on a stepladder and drawing in the shapes of little flags that he had seen earlier decorating a second-hand-car dealer's showroom. 'I thought it was an interesting subject and I liked the idea that it was just outside the door. But I think the picture's a bit of a mess. I don't really mind spending three or four years on it. I keep going back to it, altering it. Sometimes the more I work on pictures, the worse they can get. You can kill it. It can just die off, but you can bring them back to life if you get going on it.'[67] In fact, after Adam had returned to London, Hockney finally decided to abandon the painting, considering it ponderous and overworked.

Having come to this momentous decision, which went right against the stubborn side of his nature, he felt a huge sense of release. His depression lifted, and he resolved to use the strike at the Met as an excuse to work on some new paintings. 'He was really excited,' Gregory Evans recalled. 'He was turned on by the idea of producing a series of images of Los Angeles viewed in a new way altogether, and he worked really fast that Autumn.'[68] Driving had always been an important part of Hockney's life, and it was the daily drive from the Hollywood Hills down to Santa Monica Boulevard and back again that was the inspiration for Hockney's next work, which took him in a completely new direction. 'I had never lived up here before,' he wrote, 'I had never even been up here much. I didn't know many people who lived in the Hills and if you don't know people in this area you don't come up because it's easy to get lost. The roads aren't straight and you don't know which one goes down the hill and which doesn't . . . But the moment you live up here, you get a different view of Los Angeles. First of all these wiggly lines seem to enter your life, and they entered the paintings.'[69]

He had intended *Santa Monica Blvd.* to be a 'journey' painting in which the eye of the viewer would move across the canvas as if they were walking down the street, but in the end, probably because he had spent too long on it, it was too static, too tightly drawn and fragmented to have any flow. It was also painted from photographs. For his first new painting, *Nichols Canyon*, Hockney went back into his imagination, working entirely from memory. 'The first thing I drew was this line,' he recalled. 'It went all over the place at first, but then I kept taking things out and putting them back. With driving up and down in a little open

car, you sensed how it was big, how it was above you, how you were
small and it zoomed up on either side. This painting really came out
of *Canyon Painting*, which was done a year earlier and which I just left
around and didn't really regard as a picture at all.'[70] For Hockney, this
was a new perception of Los Angeles, a new experience of a city that is
laid out in straight lines and cubes. Suddenly he found himself painting
a picture that conveyed sensation rather than literal appearance, and
it made him happy. 'I came back here in 1978,' he told James Teel, a
journalist from *After Dark* magazine, 'and I wanted to paint LA a bit
differently – I wanted a fresher look at it . . . It took me two years to
find it.'[71]

Though Hockney had in fact instructed Jerry Sohn to destroy *Santa
Monica Blvd.*, keeping only a couple of fragments that pleased him,
Sohn merely tacked a new piece of canvas, eight by twenty feet, over it,
and later rolled up the abandoned canvas and put it into storage. (This
turned out to be a smart move as, more than a decade later, Hockney
was surprised to rediscover it, and allowed it to go on tour in Japan as
part of an exhibition called *Hockney in California*.) A witness to what
happened next was Bing McGilvray, a young art student from Seattle,
who had met and become friends with Hockney after writing him a
fan letter. 'One day, perhaps my second visit to his tiny little studio,' he
remembers, 'I was admiring a large colourful painting of Santa Monica
Boulevard, which took up most of the room, when David instructed
his assistant to cover it up immediately with a blank canvas. There was a
certain tone in his voice that indicated he had become very dissatisfied
with the picture. Once a long blank canvas had covered it, he took
a black crayon and drew a wavy line along the length of it. "That's
Mulholland Drive," he said assuredly.'[72]

In the canon of Hockney's work, this new painting was to be quite
revolutionary. 'This is not one of the "splash" paintings that characterized
Hockney's work in the 1960s and 70s,' wrote James Teel. 'The angular
swimming pools are gone, the ram-rod straight palm trees are gone, the
cubic architecture is gone. In their place is a swirl of hills and trees and
winding roads.'[73] He named the painting, which depicts the main road
from Montcalm Avenue down to his studio on Santa Monica Boulevard,

Mulholland Drive: The Road to the Studio, intending that people should read the word 'drive' as a verb. '"You drive around the painting, or your eye does," he said, "and the speed it goes at is about the speed of the car going along the road. That's the way you experience it."'[74]

Painted in acrylic, and like *Nichols Canyon* entirely from memory, the picture is a blaze of colour, a sweeping panoramic view of the extended landscape, with the winding road running along the top of it, while beyond, the grid-like pattern of the San Fernando Valley communities of Burbank and Studio City stretches into the distance. As the viewer's eye follows the road, it is drawn into a series of details, flashes of memory of things seen out of the car window: vegetation of various kinds, trees, pylons, the roofs of houses, some tennis courts, and in the bottom left-hand corner the ubiquitous swimming pool complete with more wiggly lines. 'It was all about movement and shifting views,' he explained. 'What I was learning was amazing to me. I realised more and more what you could do, how you could chop up space, how you could play inside the space, that only by playing could you make it come alive, and that it only became real when it came to life.'[75]

While Hockney was working on the new painting, Norman Rosenthal, the Exhibitions Secretary of the Royal Academy, flew out from London to see him, in an attempt to get him to complete it so that it could be included in a survey exhibition at the RA called *A New Spirit in Painting*, which was to open in January 1981. '*New Spirit* sounded to me like a new kind of turpentine,' he said. 'I wasn't that interested in it.'[76] However, he did complete it in three weeks, and it was then rolled up and sent to London in time for the show. It amused and pleased him when someone saw the new picture for the first time, and commented, 'You wouldn't know that was painted by David Hockney.' 'I thought that was exciting,' he recalled. 'Picasso didn't care if things didn't look like Picasso.'[77] The show opened to mixed reviews, with Marina Vaizey in the *Sunday Times* referring to his work looking like 'demented needlework',[78] while Lynda Morris in the *Listener*, though acknowledging his 'enormous energy, great sense of joy and good humour', felt that with his many references to Matisse and Picasso he had opted for 'short cuts to good painting'.[79] John Russell Taylor, however, in *The Times* wrote that 'the new Hockneys, very large, very brightly coloured, do mark a promising new departure and confirm Hockney's continuing ability to break out of the constrictions his familiar manner might seem to impose'.[80] Talking about this change of direction, Hockney told Peter Adam, 'I've never really found it easy, but you don't want to find it easy, and you often deliberately make things difficult for yourself. Certain things I could do easily. I mean, I could paint ten pictures of swimming pools and make them look rather nice, but I don't want to do that. It would bore me, which I don't want to do. I don't mind boring you, but I don't want to bore myself.'[81]

Hockney's love of Los Angeles and his intention to continue being its Piranesi was reaffirmed in these new paintings. 'The longer you stay here the more fascinating it becomes to you,' he explained to James Teel. 'I think visually it's a stunning city. Wherever you drive, it's interesting . . . Even in the suburbs. Even when you get into east L.A. there's variety in the streets.' He told him that in Bradford 'It's always dark, it's always raining, the buildings are black, the climate is cold. So when you come to L.A., by comparison it looks like a sunny Paradise. And you see a lot of colour here . . . I wanted to put colour in my pictures, so I think you have to go to a place where you feel it . . . And the Californian architecture, it does continue to glorify that unique Southern Californian sun. People are more physical here because in the sun you're more aware of your own body. You wear less clothing, therefore you make the body look nice. In a cold place like Bradford you hardly see anybody without their clothes on.'[82]

CHAPTER SIX

PARADE

On 30 October 1980, Hockney received a letter from Ann Upton, who had been worried about his health ever since hearing of his heart problems. 'Just a little note hoping you and Greggermuffin are back to your old selves,' she wrote. 'Here is some advice from a mother – Don't worry doctors with the loss of iron and get pills and shots, just eat <u>sensibly</u>! Eat more <u>fruit</u> and fresh and lightly cooked vegetables. Meat is not the whole answer. Oranges enable you to absorb iron as well as being a rich source of Vitamin C. Parsley is rich in iron. Eat plenty of garlic! Don't get into the American way of eating things in tablet and juice form. Eat the original with as little cooking as possible. Don't take it seriously, just be sensible.' She added, 'I see in the paper yesterday the "Met" have settled . . .'

This referred to the good news that the Metropolitan Opera musicians had resolved their differences with the management and that the season was back on again, even if in reality it was only a half-season. It opened on 9 December with a ceremonial performance of Mahler's *Resurrection Symphony*, and a promise from the Musicians' Union of a four-year truce. The first night of Hockney's triple bill, under the overall title *Parade*, named after the opening ballet by Satie, was scheduled for 20 February 1981, and he and Gregory went to New York for a whole month before the opening. Hockney and Dexter knew just how risky the venture was, not just because triple bills were so difficult to sell, but because two of the pieces, the Ravel and the Poulenc, were normally staged in houses where, as John Russell wrote in the *New York Times*, 'every wink can be seen and every last consonant can be heard'.[1] The Metropolitan was not such a house.

Hockney based himself at the Mayflower Hotel on Central Park West, conveniently placed for the opera house, and turned up each day at the Met in varying stylish outfits. 'Mr Hockney cuts an unusual figure backstage,' wrote John Rockwell in the *New York Times*. 'One day recently he was wearing a red and white baseball cap over his blond hair, dark baggy pants and jacket, a yellow and red striped shirt with a white collar and dark striped tie, a yellow watchband, white sneakers and a white handkerchief in his breast pocket.'[2] He threw himself into the work. 'I was excited,' he recalled. 'Nevertheless there was the hard work of actually getting it onto the stage.'[3] This was compounded by the shortened rehearsal times owing to the strike. 'The actual rehearsing of *Parade* was more hair-raising than anything I have experienced in years,' wrote John Dexter to his friend, the playwright Peter Shaffer. 'Having intended to begin with the children in September and work through gently ('No DEAR, you do not put your block down on Miss Harris's* foot, that's not stylish DEAR'), unfortunately the reasoned approach had to be abandoned as we only had four weeks in which to put the piece on the stage. So one was reduced to the usual screaming, storming and, in one case, bodily throwing a child out of the rehearsal room. Plus ca change, etc.'[4]

One of the most important aspects of the production was getting the lighting right. Dexter had originally wanted white light on the set, but Hockney had persuaded him to think again. 'When I said we should use red and blue lights on it,' he said, 'I must admit he showed little interest, yet I felt that was how we were going to get visual equivalents of the music. He used to joke about "your coloured lights", and I said, "Well, to my eye, it expresses the music." When you see that colour, with the blue light on the huge blue mass of the tree foliage, I think you physically take the colour into your body as you take in the music . . . A physical colour is a physical thrill.'[5] The children certainly thought so. During the rehearsals, one ten-year-old whispered aloud to another, 'Did you see that tree and that sky? The tree is blue.' 'That's nothing,' said the second boy. 'You should see the designer.'[6]

At the end of January, Hockney received an encouraging letter from Mo McDermott, who, in spite of his life having seemingly taken

---

* Hilda Harris, who was playing the Princess in *L'Enfant et les Sortilèges*.

an upward turn since his marriage, had started drinking again. 'To begin with we were all so pleased that he had found someone,' Gregory Evans recalls. 'Lisa took Mo away and was able to take care of him, as she had a little money. The problem was, they both liked drinking, and it's only fair to say that they were horrible drunks. You would see their feet up at the gate and you would immediately turn off the lights, because if they came over, you couldn't get rid of them for two or three days. They wouldn't leave till they were finished with you.'[7] In spite of this, because he loved Mo, Hockney had given them a loan to buy an apartment, which seemed to have made them re-evaluate their lives. 'Thank you so much for the loan,' Mo wrote. 'We are moving to Los Feliz, Monday, 2 Feb. It's a very beautiful apartment built in the 1930s, great old kitchen & Bath tiled, and has a wonderful Banana Tree garden, inner courtyard out front and a little garden out back. We have joined A.A and been to eight consecutive meetings. It actually works and is good live Theatre as well. Every year of Sobriety one gets a cake with a candle. We feel so much better and it's FOREVER . . .'[8] This was a promise Hockney suspected he should take with a pinch of salt.

Though there was very limited spare time away from rehearsals, Hockney still managed the occasional night off to cruise the nightlife of the city, often in the company of his close friend Joe McDonald. McDonald loved the bathhouses, which had been a tradition in New York since the mid-nineteenth century when Turkish, Jewish and Russian establishments had sprung up all over the city. These were mostly straight, and though they did occasionally tip over into a gay clientele, it was in 1888 that the first bathhouse opened that would eventually cater predominately for gay men. This was the Everard, later nicknamed the Everhard, which was converted from a church on 28 West 28th street by the financier James Everard. Along with the Lafayette Baths on Lafayette Street, managed by George and Ira Gershwin, and the Penn Post Baths on West 31st Street, in the 1920s it became a popular haunt for homosexuals, though there was some risk attached to visiting these places, subject as they were to periodic raids by the police.

Then, in the 1960s, the Club Baths, a chain from Miami, purchased a town house on First Avenue near Houston Street and opened the first gay-owned and gay-operated bathhouse in New York City, cleverly getting round the problem of police raids by making the admission price a private membership. This was the top end of the market, a place that had all the required accoutrements – the steam rooms, the showers, the hot tubs and the obligatory 'orgy room' – but done with taste and comfort, with carpets, soft piped-in music and subtle lighting. 'All over the bath-house,' wrote Erik Mitchell, a regular customer in the 1970s, 'you could cruise at will, approach whoever interested you, handle their goods, then go to your room with that person, followed immediately after by a shower and sauna. On the main floor, there was a very comfortable and almost elegant lounge with sofas, armchairs, and a big TV, a perfect place to get to know someone you just had pleasurable sex with.'[9] Another popular bathhouse was the St Mark's Baths on St Mark's Place in the East Village, which described itself as the largest bathhouse in the country. If its heyday and that of the other bathhouses was in the late seventies, little did any of their customers suspect that 1981 was to be their swansong.

On his trips to the bathhouses, Hockney was less the participant and more the voyeur. 'Joe was the most promiscuous person I'd ever met, and he couldn't keep away from the baths,' he remembers. 'I knew that, and I'd occasionally go with him. They were a bit seedy, but nobody cared. They were a bit like a kind of democratic brothel – everybody was a whore and everybody was a client. I did point out once that if you didn't know whether this was heaven or hell, it was probably hell. There was something so mad about them. I mean ten people could fuck Joe in a night, and if you wanted to do something like that at home, it would need a lot of organisation. When I was working at the Met, I would go over to Joe's and we would have dinner somewhere till about one o'clock and I would say, "Tomorrow morning I have to be on duty to work at 10 a.m., so I think I shall go home," and Joe would then go out to the baths again.'[10]

One night, on a visit to Henry Geldzahler, now living down on West 9th Street with Raymond Foye, Hockney made the acquaintance of a young boy called Ian Falconer, the Connecticut-born son of an architect and a fashion designer, who was an art student studying at the Parsons School of Design. With his blond hair and angelic looks he had one night caught the eye of Geldzahler, who was drinking in the Ninth Circle, a gay bar on 10th street, off Greenwich Avenue. 'It was around 1978,' Falconer recalls, 'that wonderful period when everybody from uptown and downtown were all getting together. Henry was sitting in the corner with Jerome Robbins, and a friend of mine introduced us. He was very sweet to me and I ended up sleeping on the sofa in his apartment for about six months. At one point there was Chris Scott living in the back room with his boyfriend, and Raymond and Henry living upstairs, and me on the sofa. Life was much looser then. There were people draped all over the furniture.'[11]

Ian Falconer

The night they met, Falconer remembers Hockney as wearing a Marylebone Cricket Club cap and being 'terribly shy. Eventually he asked me if I'd like to go uptown with him and watch a rehearsal of *Parade*. We went up to the Met, and after the rehearsal there was a blackout. There were no trains or buses, and you couldn't get a taxi, so we had to walk all the way downtown. David had one of the very first Walkmen, and he had two sets of headphones for it, so we walked all the way down to 9th Street listening to *The Barber of Seville*. I remember it was a terrific recording with Beverly Sills, and it was a revelation to hear that kind of sound on this tiny machine. At that point I didn't really know who he was as he wasn't yet famous in New York.'[12] It was the beginning of what was to be a lifelong friendship.

*

As the first night of the triple bill approached, the tension at the Met was palpable. It was a difficult enough production anyway without the added setback of such drastically reduced rehearsal time. Dexter fretted about the children's chorus, Hockney fretted about the lighting, Gray Veredon, the New Zealand-born choreographer who had replaced Nureyev, fretted about whether his choreography would live up to that of the original by Massine, while the veteran conductor, Manuel Rosenthal, who had actually been a student of Ravel's and had conducted the piece many times, had doubts that it might be too French for New York and that if it failed it would ruin French music there for years to come. At the same time, rumours were also rife among New York opera-goers that it wasn't going to be any good. 'You say to yourself,' Dexter told John Rockwell of the *New York Times*, 'Jesus, if this doesn't work what happens to what we've planned for the next few years?'[13]

The dress rehearsal took place on 19 February. '. . . it all worked very well,' Hockney recalled, '. . . and the Met people were pleased. They said to me afterwards that they thought it was wonderful, but they wondered what the critics would think. And I said, Frankly I don't care, it's what I think that counts, and as far as I'm concerned, it works wonderfully as theatre . . . If the critics don't like it, too bad for them.'[14] It opened the following night and was a resounding success with the audience, who 'roared with delight'[15] at the end of the performance. Hockney, wearing a white suit, sat in the front stalls with Divine, who was in full drag. Though he could not be persuaded to go up onstage to take a curtain call, he acknowledged the rapturous cheering from his seat. The following morning, before a single review had been posted, the box office sold five thousand tickets on word of mouth.

And the critics loved it, the *New York Times* calling it 'the most brilliantly captivating affair that the Met has offered us in a long time', and passing out medals of honour – to Dexter for directing 'with unending inventiveness', to Hockney for his 'dazzling poster-art sets and witty costumes', and to Rosenthal for his 'authority and style'.[16] It was Hockney's work, however, wrote Dale Harris in the *Guardian*, that was 'the undisputed hit of the evening'. 'As a result,' he continued, 'the name of David Hockney, already well known in the New York art world, has suddenly become as famous as that of a Broadway star.' He picked out the climax of *L'Enfant et les Sortilèges* for special praise. 'In the enchanted garden at the end of the opera, the entire universe is transformed by childlike wonder. To this conception David Hockney rises with the mastery of a born theatrical genius.'[17] Perhaps the greatest compliment paid to Hockney about the production was by Manuel Rosenthal in person: 'Ravel would have loved it.'[18]

Among the audience were Hockney's mother, his brother Paul and family, and his brother John, who had come from Australia as a special surprise for Laura. 'Thank you for a most wonderful holiday,' she wrote on her return home, 'meeting you & John & Paul & Jean, having the family and grandchildren around, The Beautiful Opera, The kind & happy friends, The highlights & skyscrapers of N. York, The comfort of Hotels, The meals together & just everything which will return to mind many times a day . . . Much love to an honourable son from his Mother.'[19]

During one of the technical rehearsals for *Parade*, Dexter suggested to Hockney that he work with him on another triple bill, three works by Stravinsky – *Le Sacre du Printemps*, *Le Rossignol* and *Oedipus Rex* – which were to be put on at the Met to mark the hundredth anniversary of the composer's birth. Even though this was to open as soon as December 1981, meaning that he would have to throw himself into it straight away, and much against the advice of friends like Henry Geldzahler, who told him that he'd be unlikely to pull off the success of *Parade* twice, Hockney decided to accept the invitation. 'All the work I have done in the theatre has been useful to me,' he wrote, 'and I have never regretted any time spent on it. What is most important is using real space. You begin to think spatially much more . . . I thought to myself, you shouldn't be frightened off . . .'[20]

He began work on the most charming of the three works, *Le Rossignol*, which was based on a story by Hans Christian Andersen. The fairy-tale story and atmosphere of enchantment was perfectly suited to his turn of mind, telling as it does the story of a nightingale who is invited to sing for the Emperor of China. 'The Emperor's palace,' ran the story, 'was the most splendid in the world; it was made entirely of porcelain, very costly, but so delicate and brittle that one had to take care how one touched it.' While spending Christmas with his family back in England, Hockney made a visit to one of his old haunts, just round the corner from the Royal College of Art, the Victoria and Albert Museum, which housed a wonderful collection of Chinese porcelain. 'I remembered those collections from my art school days,' he recalled, 'and though I hadn't actually visited them for some fifteen years, I went straight to the gallery where they were installed and took about one hundred and fifty photographs, I really started scrutinising those pieces, something I'd never done before . . . I eventually settled on the early C18th blue and white pieces, because they were covered with wonderful representations of the sea, mountains and buildings.'[21] With John Dexter he also paid a visit to Chatsworth in Derbyshire, which had a large amount of porcelain. 'We wandered around,' said Dexter, 'under the eyes of God knows how many curators photographing stuff there. The Emperor's palace was there and so was the special opalescent quality of the porcelain glaze.'[22]

Though Hockney based his designs for *Le Rossignol* on early Chinese porcelain on view in England, he was actually about to make his first visit to China to work on a project that had been in the pipeline for over a year. This had been dreamt up by Nikos Stangos, his friend and editor at Thames & Hudson, and was to be a collaboration with Stephen Spender on a diary of a trip to China. Stangos was interested to see what Hockney would make of the country, both artistically and photographically, while he considered Spender, with his leanings towards communism, the perfect companion to write the words. Hockney, who invited Gregory Evans to accompany them, was keen to go so long as they did not take it too seriously, and looked upon it as 'a little personal trip' they made together. 'I think the book should be in that sense a bit bitty – like life – patched up in some way, as if made by three schoolboys on a tour of a continent for the first time.'[23]

In 1981, China was in a state of transition under the leadership of Deng Xiaoping, who had outmanoeuvred his rivals in the power struggle after the death of Mao Zedong in 1976. A vocal critic of the Cultural Revolution, under which he had twice been purged, he had embarked

Mulholland Drive: The Road to the Studio, 1980. Acrylic on Canvas, 86 × 243″

Harlequin, 1980. Oil on Canvas, 48 × 36″

The Set for Parade, from Parade Triple Bill, **1980.** Oil on Canvas, 60 × 60″

Child with Books, Cup and Teapot, 1980 from L'Enfant et Les Sortilèges. Gouache on Paper, 14 × 17″

Hollywood Hills House, 1981–82. Oil, Charcoal and Collage on Canvas, 60 × 120″

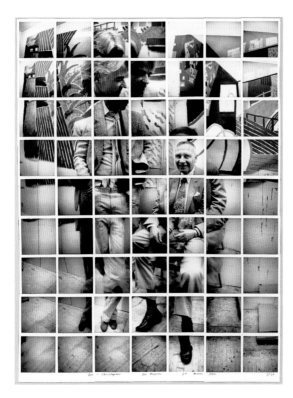

Don + Christopher, Los Angeles, 6th March 1982. Composite Polaroid, 31 ½ × 23 ¼″

My House, Montcalm Avenue, Los Angeles, Friday, February 26th 1982. Composite Polaroid, 11 × 34″

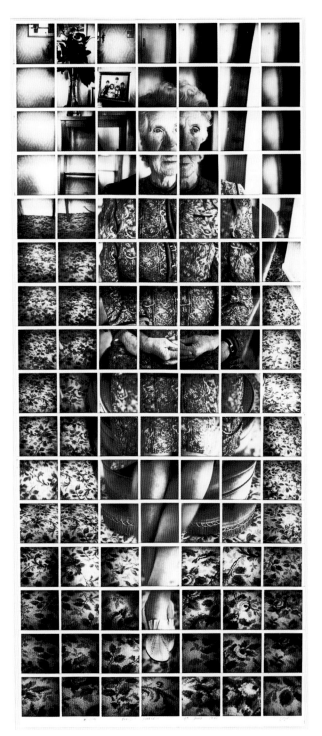

Mother, Bradford, Yorkshire, 4th May 1982.
Composite Polaroid, 56 × 23 ½"

The Scrabble Game, Jan. 1, 1983. Photographic Collage, edition of 20

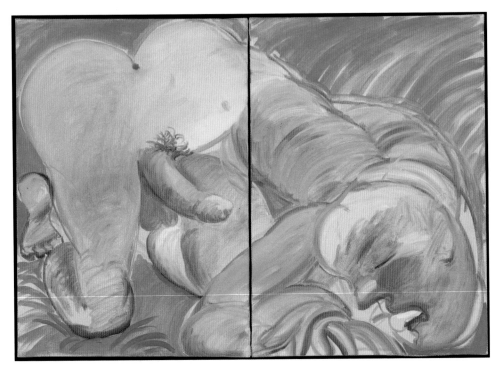

Nude Self-Portrait*, 1983. Acrylic on 2 Canvases, 26 × 36″

Large-Scale Painted Environment with Separate Elements Based on Hockney's Design for Poulenc's Opera Les Mamelles de Tirésias, 1983. Oil on Canvas, 134 × 288 × 120″

on a programme of economic and social reforms, gradually dismantling the commune system and opening up the economy to foreign trade. It was the first time that tourism was encouraged, and Stangos's motley crew were in the vanguard. Before leaving, Hockney had sounded out two of his friends for advice. Christopher Isherwood warned him about travelling with Spender, saying, "'He'll be wanting to go to the British Ambassador's and Consulates and stuff like that." And I said "Oh, thank you for that tip, because I wasn't too keen to do that, I thought we were going to see China . . . I didn't want to go halfway round the world and spend my time in English houses in Peking."'[24] Tony Richardson's recommendation, given on the eve of their departure while dining at Lawry's Prime Rib in Beverly Hills, was, wherever possible, to ignore the instructions of their guide and do their own thing.

Uncertain as to what he might be able to buy in China in the way of materials, Hockney decided to take everything he needed with him. He took paper, ink, watercolours, two Pentax cameras and film, and, on the advice of Richardson, who had told them that there was nothing the Chinese liked better than Polaroid photographs of themselves, a Polaroid Land camera. They left Los Angeles on 19 May, travelling via Tokyo and Hong Kong, 'perhaps', wrote Spender in his diary, 'because some official had decided that we should have the opportunity of comparing the corruption of the British Colony with the purity of the Chinese People's Republic'.[25] On the plane, Hockney listened to the score of the Stravinsky triple bill on his Walkman, while Spender read the speeches of Chairman Mao, and pondered on how their group appeared to their hosts.

'David wore a white flat peaked cap and a striped jersey,' he recorded, 'Gregory a yellow Robin-Hoodish kind of jerkin, canary-coloured, I a fawn-coloured camel-hair jacket and dark-blue trousers. David, from the intensity of looking through his gold-rimmed spectacles, has, when drawing or taking photographs, a pursed-up expression, his features focusing on some target of his attention. Gregory resembles one of the group of young Florentine nobles standing in the foreground of Botticelli's *Adoration of the Magi* . . . I must have looked very much the odd man out compared with my two younger companions. It is obvious though that all three of us must have looked comical to the Chinese and this should be remembered because those observed are themselves observers of the observers and sometimes cannot prevent themselves laughing at them. We looked a bit absurd, especially me with my big feet.'[26]

They spent one night in Hong Kong, where they stayed at the Peninsular Hotel in large luxurious suites with doors padded on the outside with leather – 'inside-out padded cells for millionaires', noted Spender – then had a whistle-stop tour of the waterfront the following morning, which elicited the opinion from Hockney that the view across the harbour was even more beautiful than the spectacular view of the Manhattan skyline from the Staten Island Ferry. From Hong Kong they boarded a Chinese Airways (CAAC) plane to Beijing, which 'seemed like a school bus in comparison with the Boeing 747 we had been in before'.[27] What struck them all was the number of American tourists on board, mostly women. This was a legacy both of President Nixon's visit to China in 1972, which healed the long breach between the two countries, and Deng's further opening-up of relations. 'These American tourists,' wrote Spender, 'seemed all set on loving China and atoning for the years of division which had poisoned Sino-American relations. To many Americans China is a love-object, once tended by American missionaries, teachers and doctors, many of whom spent their lives in Chinese villages or slums and worked to help people there.'[28]

After his experiences with Gregory on their package tour to Egypt, and anticipating that they would be part of this large group, as they had been then, Hockney had done his best to reassure Spender that 'tourists looking at things are just as interesting as the things they are looking at'. In the event, on their arrival in Beijing, they were directed to a small Toyota minibus of their own, while their fellow tourists were herded aboard a large charabanc. The instigators of this pleasant surprise were the two guides who had been assigned to them, 'Mr Lin Hua – who for the next three weeks,' wrote Spender, 'was to be Virgil to our threesome Dante – and Miss Li. Mr Lin was rotund, smiling with commanding, intelligent features – so there was some affinity in his appearance to those photographs of Mao Tse-tung which one sees everywhere in China . . . Miss Li had features that looked prettily carved from wood.'[29] From that moment on, wherever the threesome went, Mr Lin went with them, always accompanied by a different local guide who would spring up in whatever location they found themselves, and invariably appeared scared stiff – not, they presumed, of them, but of Mr Lin, who was obviously some kind of important official. If there was anything significant to be said, it was Mr Lin who imparted it. Miss Li and the other local guides were only there to spout statistics.

On the way from the airport to their hotel in Beijing, Hockney made a schematic drawing showing the straight road, first with rows of trees on either side, then with high tenement blocks which were described by Miss Li as 'housing for the people'. He also included the rows of bicycles which were such a vital part of the people's lives, though they were surprised to learn that only a third of the inhabitants of the city owned one. This turned out to be one of relatively few drawings Hockney made in China, many being done later from memory. 'It was hard to keep drawing all the time,' he told Spender. 'The difficulty I had, as we rushed round to so many places, so many things, was that I never realised quite the speed with which we would travel. If I had known that, or if we made the journey again, I would have adapted myself to very speedy drawing, which I never got round to because it would have taken another week to re-invent another style of doing it.'[30]

They were housed in the Beijing Hotel, a massive Soviet-style building, seventeen storeys high, which had been built in 1900 and was reserved for foreign tourists and official guests. It had a vast lobby on the ground floor, and banqueting rooms and a dining room on the first floor, in which they had their own small table for four. No sooner had they deposited their bags than Mr Lin marshalled them back into the bus and took them to a local restaurant, the Kau Ru Ji, where they were to dine with the British Council Representative, Keith Hunter, and his wife. They ate outside on a balcony overlooking the Shichahai Lake, which left Hockney resolutely unimpressed. 'I sat looking at the park, facing outwards and, to me, it was like the lake in Peel Park, Bradford; nothing very beautiful compared to, say, a European spa; it seemed dusty and grubby.'[31] Afterwards they went to the Hunters' apartment where

Mrs Hunter grew bonsai trees in a very English room with armchairs and sofas and pictures of English scenes on the walls.

As Hockney stretched himself out in one of the comfortable chairs, Mrs Hunter commented on the fact that he was wearing odd-coloured socks, one blue and one canary yellow. 'David said yes, when he was twelve years old and living at his parents' home in Bradford,' Spender recorded, 'he read Robert Herrick's poem 'Delight in Disorder'.

> A sweet disorder in the dress
> Kindles in clothes a wantonness

He said that when he first read these lines he had thought, "Well, that's perfectly true, there must be something good about poetry if poets say things like that", and continued to read poetry ever after while exemplifying in his attire Herrick's lines.'[32]

Their days were rigorously organised: they got up at 6 a.m., breakfasted, and then went out all day, under the ever-watchful eye of their guide. 'Mr Lin is quite the disciplinarian,' wrote Spender. 'He tells us when we should appear in the lobby; and outdoors when we are in the streets he rattles out commands – "Come here!", "Don't go there!", "Hurry up!" These we know to be necessary in our case (because each of us is liable to go wandering off by himself, escaping from Mr Lin and Miss Li). So we docilely breakfast each morning at exactly ten minutes after the time that on the previous evening he has told us we must get up, and are always punctual in getting down to the hotel lobby where he and Miss Li disentangle us from the other tourists, and lead us to our private minibus.' Their only time alone together was at dinner, when they would swap impressions of the country and talk about Mr Lin.

In Beijing, they took in all the tourist sites – the Summer Palace, Tiananmen Square and the Imperial City, the Eastern Tombs, the Ming Tombs and the Great Wall – as well as engaging in a number of visits that had been arranged specially for them, such as a meeting with a group of artists, and another with some poets. In spite of Mr Lin's enthusiastic guiding, however, Hockney was resolutely unimpressed by the city, finding it 'dusty and grubby'. 'By the time we had been there three days,' he wrote, 'you felt a certain deadness; everybody seemed docile. We mentioned this to the British Ambassador . . . and he said to me, this isn't China; you just wait, it will be a lot more exciting. He was right.'[33]

Things did pick up for Hockney when they left Beijing on 26 May to fly to Xian, though it was an uncomfortable flight on a packed Russian turbo-prop Ilyushin. It was hotter down south, and to Spender was reminiscent of the Middle East. On arrival they barely had time to check into their hotel before Mr Lin had them piling into cars to drive to Panpo, the site of a Neolithic settlement, followed by a visit to the Giant Wild Goose Pagoda. 'We passed through a gate which led to a large courtyard,' Spender recorded, 'at the end of which, against a hedge, with the stone-coloured pagoda towering rather gloomy in the distance, there was a table with a vase of flowers and a solitary chair about a foot away, to one side. The top of the hedge was a light-yellowish green, with shadow below that. David took a photograph of what seemed very much a David Hockney arrangement.'[34]

Wherever they went, this happy band of travellers attracted attention, particularly when Hockney was seen drawing. After a visit to the Terracotta Army of the Emperor Shih Huang-ti, for example, they stopped for lunch at a large and airy restaurant reserved for foreigners, when their local guide, a pretty young girl, asked him to sketch her. As soon as he started, their waiter downed tools to watch, and was soon followed by the other waiters in the room, happily abandoning their tables, and then the chef, who appeared sweating and smiling out of the kitchen. Hockney also saw this as a perfect opportunity to show off his Polaroid camera, and took photographs of the guide and the chef and his assistants, all of whom were riveted watching their images slowly appear on the small square prints as if by magic. 'After this,' wrote Spender, 'even outside the restaurant in the street, where there was a small crowd awaiting us, the citizens of Sian seemed particularly friendly, as though we were three goons arrived there. We did look rather funny: David with the flat cap he nearly always wears, even indoors, his shirt with horizontal red stripes and his different coloured socks; Gregory with his Robin Hood jerkin with a kind of cape at the back; and me with my enormous feet. The Chinese, I noticed, were always looking at my feet and politely concealing their smiles.'[35]

Hockney's drawing style was to be greatly influenced by what he experienced on this trip. He absorbed everything he was introduced to in the way of Chinese art. In Nanking, the old southern capital where the group were much taken with the wide tree-lined avenues, he spent a morning at the Nanking Institute of Calligraphy and Painting, watching a dozen, mostly quite elderly, artists practise their skills. Though he was feeling too ill from an attack of the 'runs' to participate, he asked many questions about the various tools of their trade and looked on intently as they painted a picture for him. 'David watched closely the way in which they used their brushes,' Spender noted, 'with little medium on them and making marks which imprint on the paper the part of the brush used . . . Each brush had as it were its vocabulary of signs it could employ. They painted themes that seemed a bit predictable: the falling straight and curved lines of water, the rocks from which it falls, trees on either side, the irregular platform-like landscape in the foreground, hits, etc. That was the picture for David . . .'[36] What also struck Spender at the time was that despite Hockney feeling too off colour to join in, there appeared to be some deep-rooted, almost spiritual communication between him and his fellow artists.

Further south in Hangchow, a city of canals and lakes on the Yangtze River Delta, they visited, first, a lacquer factory where dozens of young apprentices were hunched over tables, cutting intricate designs into lacquer. As Hockney observed them working with the utmost concentration, he was reminded of his father drawing the straight lines along the metal tubes of his bicycle frames. '. . . he asked one of the apprentices,' wrote Spender, 'what he did if he made a mistake when cutting a line through a surface which was one of the hundred or so layers of paint from which the lacquer was built up. The boy delighted him by answering that the situation did not arise. No one ever did make a mistake here. David said his father would have made the same reply.'[37]

The following afternoon found them in the Hangchow art school, where the director offered to paint them any subject of their choosing. Hockney asked for leaves and watched with fascination as, with speed and economy of brushstrokes, he produced a picture of leaves on a branch. He then told the director that he had never used Chinese brushes and paints before and would like to have a go. 'Paper, brushes and paints were brought,' Spender recorded. 'Asked what subject he intended to paint, David said he would do a portrait of the director. The director promptly seated himself at the end of the table and kept prodigiously still . . . David made a few enquiries about the materials that were set before him. He dipped his brush first in the water and then in the saucer of black paint and began to draw lines across the paper. He used the brush as a pointed pencilling instrument, not as the impress of different stylised marks on the paper . . .'[38] The director was pleased with his portrait, and later that day Hockney went out and bought Chinese brushes and paints and wrote postcards to his friends in imitation Chinese calligraphy.

The new materials were put to good effect when they arrived a few days later in Kweilin, a city in the far south that sits on the west bank of the Li River, and is famous for the dramatic scenery of tall limestone hills that surrounds it. 'I had no idea it was such a magical, beautiful place,' he recalled. 'We saw an extraordinary landscape from the plane and we were thrilled. Our hotel – actually a big house – had lovely rooms . . . Immediately I got out brown ink and paper and made some big blobs that were the mountains I'd just seen. On the trip down the river . . . you float through the most magical, beautiful landscape. It is as though children had drawn the mountains . . .'[39] Coincidentally, it was a child who had the most profound effect on Hockney above anything else on the entire trip.

They were told one morning that they were to be taken to meet a young artist, an eight-year-old prodigy called Tang A-hsi. Though naturally sceptical, Hockney was eager to go, as it would be their first visit to a private Chinese home. The Tang family lived in a modest house on the edge of a small lake outside Kweilin, where the child's father, also an artist, turned out pretty landscapes of the area for the tourist market. The floors of the house were bare concrete, and the front room was lit by two naked bulbs hanging from wires in the ceiling. Beneath these, the young boy sat at a table consisting of a board supported on two packing cases. The bare walls were livened up by some of his work, paintings mostly of cats, or of the limestone hills rising up from the river. To begin with he sat there sulkily, refusing to cooperate, in spite of his father having placed a large sheet of paper in front of him, and his mother standing close by murmuring encouragement. '. . . they said,' Hockney recalled, '"Oh, he's very tired." I thought, no, he's not very tired; he's sick to death of them bringing people like us here; he just doesn't want to do it.'[40]

As it happened, Hockney had brought with him a large box of crayons that included ones that could be used with water, as well as a couple of different kinds of sketchbook. He gave the box to the little boy, who smiled and began to count the crayons. There were thirty altogether. Hockney showed him how they could first be used like pencils, then how the marks made could be turned into a wash with the use of a water-loaded brush. He superimposed colour washes one over the other, and demonstrated how, using a penknife, he could scratch lines into the layers of paint once they were dry and hard. He then drew a picture of the boy's bicycle, which was leaning against the fence opposite the window, using every technique he could think of. 'The moment I began drawing,' Hockney remembered, 'he grabbed my hand. He realised I was an artist as well, who had come to see him, not just a tourist. He was dying to get his hands on the crayons and Mr Lin told him I was going to give them to him. I was speaking in English about what you could do with these crayons and he just kept nodding, meaning, whatever you're saying, I understand what you're doing . . . And then he drew pictures for us, cats, done in the Chinese manner with brushes, which were stunning. Watching him do them was something: the way they were placed on the paper. Everything about them was terrific; he was like a little Picasso . . .'[41]

When the group were ready to leave, and Hockney had taken many Polaroid photographs to give the family, Tang A-hsi took his hand and walked with him back to the car. 'It was very touching,' Hockney recalled. 'I felt we had communicated without the interpreter . . . Any artist who watched him would have been thrilled, anybody who liked painting or brushwork . . . The boy's work made me realise all the

beautiful things one could do with the brush, what the brush does; it was his work that made me look at Chinese things with new eyes.'[42] The Chinese method of painting also had a profound influence on his drawing style in that it loosened him up, freeing him both from worries about what was expected of him and from his hang-ups about watercolour. Having little time to paint on the move, he was forced into making quick sketches from memory, experimenting with the techniques he had seen to create a series of watercolours that were deceptive in their simplicity, their few bold brushstrokes confidently bringing to life landscapes that had been only briefly glimpsed.

Sketches from China Notebook

With the Stravinsky triple bill opening in December, and *Le Rossignol* already designed, Hockney's priority on his return from China was to complete his ideas for the two remaining pieces, the ballet *Le Sacre de Printemps,* and the opera *Oedipus Rex.* 'The three works were distinctive, one from the other,' he wrote. '*Sacre* was extremely kinetic, with dancers rushing around. *Rossignol* was more like conventional opera, with people moving about on stage. In contrast to both, *Oedipus* was a static narrative with music.'[43] Dexter had established only one rule about the theme of the evening – that it was to be all about circles and masks. For *Oedipus* they decided on the classic Greek half-mask. For *Sacre*, the masks were painted on in a very primitive style, while for *Rossignol* they used Chinese round masks that were held above the heads of the performers.

Oedipus Rex was the very opposite of *Rossignol*, relentless in its gravity, and a virtually actionless performance in which an enthroned narrator intones the plot, while the protagonists, seated on a raised dais, rise in turn to sing the words. But however foreign it may have at first seemed to Hockney's sensibilities, he took inspiration from both the powerful story and the music. 'I had a recording of *Oedipus* in London,' he wrote, 'which I hadn't played for a long time. It has an amazing feeling of solidity – it's like granite. I had never seen it performed in the theatre, only in a concert hall. My problem was to make one strong image fit this spoken drama.'[44] He achieved this by presenting it as a heroic tableau, with the orchestra at ground level, the seated narrator above them, then the chorus above him, and the principal singers at the top, giving the whole design the appearance of a monumental staircase. To break down the feeling of separation between audience and stage, he made the proscenium arch and the curving shape of the auditorium part of the design. 'Because I wanted to destroy the proscenium,' he explained, 'I thought of the simple device of projecting lines of light on its sides so they would look like Greek columns. The shapes and colours on stage echoed what you saw in the auditorium; the large red circle on the dais was the colour of the carpet; the chorus in black tie becomes part of the black and white pattern of the orchestra below it. On opening night the audience was also in black tie, so everything blended and the whole theatre was engulfed in the work.'[45]

Of the three works, Hockney found *Sacre* the most time-consuming. '*Sacre* took me longer to design than the operas,' he recalled, 'which is crazy. After all, a ballet set doesn't even take up the stage; you leave most of it bare for dancing.'[46] The reason for this was his natural desire to inject as much theatricality into it as he could, mostly by use of clever lighting. 'I did about twenty-five models for the *Sacre* set and I would light each one to see the effect of colour on it, while playing the music again and again. When I thought I had finished, I went off to a little spa in Germany, supposedly to relax, but I took the tape along and listened to it on my Sony Walkman. As I kept playing it, I realised my design wasn't quite right . . . I went back to London and worked on it some more, eventually getting something that was more satisfactory to my eye and ear.'[47] The final design, striking in its simplicity, consisted of two giant discs, one suspended, the other on the floor, the purpose of each of them being to function symbolically, suggesting images of the Earth and the cosmos.

At the end of August, exhausted by the pressure of getting the designs ready for the December opening, Hockney and Gregory took a holiday with Celia Birtwell and her two sons, Albert and George, aged twelve and ten respectively, and always referred to by Hockney as 'the fighting boys' owing to their incessant squabbling. 'I rented an R.V,' he wrote to Kitaj, 'which is a contemporary Californian equivalent of the Gypsy caravan. It was supposed to sleep six and had a cooker, fridge, shower, toilet and two dining tables. Naturally it was big and I've never really driven a truck before, but I thought it might be exciting. Our original plan was to go to Zion and Bryce Canyons in Utah and then over to Yosemite and back home, but when I went to pick it up I noticed it was a bit bashed in and had already done 68,000 miles.'[48] When he got the RV back to Montcalm Avenue, he was so worried that it might break down during their travels that he persuaded Jerry Sohn to follow them in his Oldsmobile station wagon as an emergency backup. His hunch turned out to be right, as it broke down several times.

'The first place,' he told Henry Geldzahler, 'was just near a hot spring in a river. I remembered it from 1966, so while we waited for the R.V to calm down, we went swimming in it. Celia thought it was heaven. The River itself is very warm with little pools of hot water on the banks. They had also built a swimming pool (temp 100 degrees) with concrete walls around it about 8ft high. On this was painted a rocky landscape, and above the wall you saw a real rocky landscape.

Quite beautiful. I photographed it, but unfortunately then something went wrong with the Rolleiflex – a sign from the muse to get me drawing again.'[49] However, scarcely had they got the RV started again than 'it conked out right outside the R.V campground at Zion Canyon so we had it towed in and wired it up. You plug in for electricity and water and attach the lavatory hose to a sewer. Unfortunately the air-conditioning then broke down and it was very hot. Celia, Gregory and the boys slept in it for one night, and then they moved across the road to join Jerry & me in the luxurious motel (Double rooms $22). It did seem luxurious after the R.V, flushing toilets, large showers, real beds etc. Naturally we kept cursing the Dinnasor [sic] we'd had to drag along. "Never again" etc, etc. then we'd relent and go and cook in it, or light a fire outside and enjoy all the other campers. It was right next to a river where the kids went down the rapids on old inner tubes.'[50]

They eventually got the RV going again, but it then broke down in the desert, leaving them with little to do except laugh. 'I think if it had blown up,' he told Kitaj, 'we would have had a whole day of laughter.'[51] After this, their third breakdown, 'I drove straight back to L.A,' he wrote, 'abandoning the trip to Yosemite. As I drove, Celia made cups of tea – Typhoo, much superior to what you could buy on the road. The food in restaurants in Utah is meant to make you drive right through the state. I think Wigan in 1937 would have had better food (at least it would have had tripe). I'm back putting the finishing touches to the Stravinsky triple bill and then will begin painting.'[52]

Passing through New York in October, John Cox found Hockney 'on top of the world and enjoying the Met very much'.[53] He was trying to persuade him to take on The Ring cycle for Scottish Opera. 'I didn't launch into any discussion about The Ring,' Cox wrote on his return home, 'because you've got too much on your mind with Stravinsky and I know how worried you can get, and rightly, about neglecting your easel. This is just to say that I'm still very keen on the idea of our doing it together and hope that you feel able to make . . . a commitment in principle to it. We are in any case talking about a date far in the future – namely Winter of 1985, or even later that season, just for the first two parts, then completing the following season . . . I'm getting my bid in early as pressure on you to design can only increase.'[54] It was a project that was never to come to fruition.

Opening night for the Stravinsky centenary tribute was 3 December, and with principals like Natalia Makarova and Anthony Dowell, and choreography by Frederick Ashton, it was a stellar occasion. If the Met were hoping to strike gold for a second time, however, with the same team of Dexter, Hockney and Levine, they were to be disappointed. The reviews were mixed. Though Peter Davis in *New York Magazine* loved the 'magical effects' and gave the opinion that 'More than Dexter's, this is Hockney's show',[55] the *New York Times* critic, Donal Henahan, considered that only *Le Rossignol* succeeded with its striking blue and white design 'that ranged from Wedgwood to swimming-pool hues'. The rest, he felt, did not live up to what had made his *Parade* such a triumph. *Le Sacre* 'dragged on and on', and its sets and costumes, along with those of *Oedipus Rex,* were below his usual standard, as though Hockney had concentrated on *Le Rossignol* at the expense of the better-known operas.[56]

When Hockney returned to England, to spend a week in London before travelling to Bradford for Christmas with his family, it was to find the country in the grip of one of the coldest and snowiest Decembers of the century. Twenty-five to thirty centimetres of snow fell in London the night of 11 December, and the following day temperatures plunged to below -18°C in many parts of the country. To cheer himself up in cold, grey London, Hockney decided to paint from memory a picture of his house on Montcalm Avenue, which would be a nostalgic evocation of the open-plan living and warm sunshine that define California. He called the painting *Hollywood Hills House* and, as Henry Geldzahler described, it was intended to be read as a guided tour of the house. 'At the extreme left the visitor descends the steps through the garden, and enters by the kitchen table, above which hangs a portrait of Laurel and Hardy, painted by Kenneth Hockney. A cozy fire burns in the hearth, lit by a gas jet that can be turned on and off and lit with a single match, thus doing away with smoke and ashes (a feature highly prized by the artist's eighty-four-year-old mother). Above the hearth, Hockney sketchily indicates the many clippings he keeps on his visual bulletin board, as well as an actual postcard of a Renaissance portrait which Hockney has glued onto the canvas. Conspicuously displayed in the foreground are two working models for the opera stage . . . reminding us of the prominence the stage has played in the artist's creative life. The living room opens onto a patio with its red floorboards. Finally, in the far right panel, we glimpse the pool, the brick wall, the exterior of the rest of the house, and the balcony to David's bedroom.'[57]

As the painting occupied three canvases, the eye of the viewer was forced to keep moving, scanning the surface of the picture as if their body were moving in space. It foreshadowed the way Hockney's conception of space was to change radically as he sought to dispel the 'lie' of one-point perspective, which he saw as cutting the viewer off from the world. The way he was about to do this was through photography.

CHAPTER SEVEN

DRAWING
WITH A CAMERA

During the latter half of 1981, Hockney had been seeing more and more of Ian Falconer, the result of which was an ever-deepening friendship. He saw in this charming and attractive young man the same qualities he had first noticed in Peter Schlesinger. He was intelligent and interested in the arts, so they could enjoy long conversations, and was a talented and bright student who was happy to accompany him round the New York galleries and museums, and was only too ready to learn from the master. Since any hint of the master–pupil dynamic had long since disappeared from Hockney's relationship with Gregory Evans, he was only too keen to find somebody new to love and admire him, and with this in mind, at the end of 1981, he suggested to Falconer that he should leave Parsons School of Design in New York and move to Los Angeles to attend its sister school there, the Otis Art Institute.

'David also told me he could give me some work,' Falconer recalls, 'so I transferred. When I started off at the school, it was the period when art schools were not teaching you technique, but were teaching you how to make "art". It didn't take me long to realise that I was learning a lot more working in David's studio. He would tell me, "Don't mix white in with your colours. It makes them flat and dead. Just use them as glaze and build up the glazes." He taught me about different kinds of pencils and what they each can do. He was terrific in the way he encouraged me. He'd come in and look at my stuff and say, "Very good, very good, love."'[1]

Hockney was thrilled by the new arrival, and they soon became lovers. He told Peter Adam, 'I need someone sexy around me and anything with Ian was a tremendous turn-on, just looking at him.'[2] He celebrated by repainting the house. 'The new mood,' wrote Adam, 'may best be described by the fact that the houses were suddenly repainted in bright colours inside and outside. It was like a children's playground; one wall was green with a pink edge and there was a lot of red and blue and some bright yellow. Even the furniture did not escape, nor did the bottom of the pool. It was just like living inside a Matisse painting – or a Hockney!'[3] One night, when they were both thoroughly stoned, they created an 'aquarium' by hanging cut-outs of fish from the branches of a tree outside one of the picture windows. 'We got a couple of cans of fluorescent spray paint,' Falconer says, 'and sprayed the fish so when you lit them up at night, it looked just like an aquarium. It wasn't an art piece, it was just kidding around.'[4]

For Falconer, LA was an eye-opener. 'It was great fun for me,' he remembers. 'I was twenty-two and in full stride, and Los Angeles was in a great place then. All the old stars were still alive, and the new stars were all coming along and they all mixed. I loved old movies, so for me meeting people like Cary Grant was amazing. We used to see a lot of these people at Chris and Don's where we'd go regularly to dinner. Billy and Audrey Wilder used to come over a lot, and I used to love to listen to his stories. I remember him telling me that he'd had to sell a lot of his art collection to buy his wife a Rolls-Royce. "Well, she has a showgirl mentality," he said.'[5]

The situation that now existed in the house was not easy for Evans, who, gentle soul that he was, had been finding himself increasingly in danger of becoming subsumed. He had moved downstairs and, in order to cope, was relying more and more on drugs and alcohol. 'The atmosphere was quite fraught,' Falconer says, 'because Gregory was drinking heavily and there was a lot of cocaine around. He was in bad shape when I arrived and would start the morning off with a great big highball glass of vodka on the rocks.'[6] The drinking was a symptom of the trouble, not its cause. 'I realised that I could not submit any more,' Evans later admitted. 'There was no room for me to grow. His idea of growth and mine were different. In his world there is no compromise, and it has to be his world. He does not realise that you have to be present to have a relationship, you have to give something of yourself.

He always wanted what Christopher Isherwood had, but failed to realise that Chris was emotionally available to Don.'[7]

At this point, Hockney simply ignored the situation, burying his emotions in work, while Evans locked himself in his room downstairs and drank. There was no one to help him. 'Nobody in that house wanted me to go to treatment,' he recalls. 'They might have wanted me to lighten up a bit, but that was all. I wasn't the only person in the house on drugs, but for me it was a problem, and it was a problem I wanted to deal with.'[8] In the end help came from an unexpected quarter, in the form of Mo and Lisa McDermott, who, having gone into rehab, had turned their lives around. 'They were actually my inspiration for getting sober,' Evans says, 'because they really did pull their lives together. They moved into a charming house in Echo Park, and they suddenly became very productive. I then checked myself into a place called the Beverly Glen, and after that I went to AA.'[9]

In the meantime, Hockney was heading off in a new direction. 'When I arrived,' Falconer remembers, 'he had a half-finished painting of Henry and Raymond Foye that he was getting fed up with and never completed. At times like this he likes to fix on something, and often I think it's to relieve his own anxiety.'[10] The perfect subject came about as a result of an approach from Alan Sayag, the curator of the Pompidou Centre in Paris. Since he had bought his first large green photograph album from Harrods back in 1967, Hockney had filled over a hundred of them with thousands of snapshots, creating in the process an extraordinary visual diary of the previous fifteen years. As he hadn't owned a proper camera till then, other people had taken the majority of the photographs in the first volume. After that, he had bought himself a 35mm Pentax and had begun to photograph in earnest and, from then on, each subsequent year would require four or five albums. The photos he stuck in recorded every detail of his daily life: portraits of his family and friends, his partners asleep in bed, views from car windows, endless landscapes, weddings, still lifes, scenes on the beach, architecture, pretty boys, not to mention the many references for his paintings, iconic works like *American Collectors*, *Christopher Isherwood and Don Bachardy*, *Portrait of Nick Wilder* and *Beverly Hills Housewife*.

Word soon got around about Hockney's photo albums, which by
1981 comprised about twenty thousand photos, at a time when Alain
Sayag was launching a series of exhibitions of photography by painters
such as Man Ray and Robert Rauschenberg. 'The Pompidou Centre
kept nattering away at me . . . to do a show of the photos,' Hockney
recalled, 'and I kept putting them off. I wasn't interested: most photo
shows are boring, always the same scale, the same texture. But they
kept insisting – they said they wanted to do it *because* I was a painter,
and so forth. Finally in 1981, I gave in, but I told them they'd have to
come and make the selection themselves because I didn't have a clue.'[11]

Sayag arrived at Montcalm Avenue early in 1982, and spent four
days browsing through the albums, making his choice for the show.
In the evenings he sat around being lectured by Hockney, who at that
time had gone cold on photography. 'We'd sit by the plastic fire,' he
recalled, 'and I'd tell him why I thought photography was not really
a good medium for an artist. The main aspect, it seemed to me, was
this lack of time in the photograph. I'd become very, very aware of this
frozen moment, that was very unreal to me. Photography didn't really
have life in the way a drawing or painting did, and I realised it couldn't,
because of what it is. Compared to Rembrandt looking at himself for
hours and hours and scrutinising his face, and putting all these hours
into the picture that you're going to look at, naturally there's many
more hours there than you can give it. A photograph is the other way
round. It's the fraction of a second, frozen, so the moment you've
looked at it for even four seconds, you've looked at it for longer than
the camera did. It dawned on me that this was visible, actually, and the
more you become aware of it, the more this is a terrible weakness.
Drawings and paintings do not have this.'[12] Because of this perceived
weakness, he had come to the decision that the best use of a camera was
for photographing other pictures. 'It is the only time it can be true to its
medium,' he wrote, 'in the sense that it's real. This is the only way that
you can take a photograph that could be described as having a strong
illusion of reality. Because on the flat surface of the photograph is simply
reproduced another flat surface, a painting. In any other photograph,
it's not reproducing a flat surface.'[13]

Having made his initial choice of a hundred or so images, Sayag found himself with a problem. The uncatalogued negatives were stored in dozens of boxes, and there was no way that they were going to be able to locate them before he had to return to Paris. Their solution was to go to the local photographic store and buy up as much Polaroid SX-70 film as they could find, $12,000 worth, and simply photograph the prints he had selected, so he would have something to work with to prepare the show. In the meantime, Gregory Evans would search for the original negatives. In spite of having made two sets of each picture, after Sayag had departed Hockney still found himself left with a large quantity of unused Polaroid film, and, ever the innovator, he began to experiment with it.

He started by attempting to replicate photographically the free-form painting he had made in London of his house. He moved through the rooms, from the entrance to the deck, snapping a series of details, of the walls, the floor, the ceiling, the furniture, the plants, the pool, which he then laid side by side on the ground, working them slowly into some kind of composition. This differed from his earlier 'joiners', such as the one of Peter Schlesinger, composed for *Portrait of an Artist*, in that those were taken essentially from one point of view. The result of this new attempt at a photographic 'painting' was a rectangular panel of thirty Polaroid prints of fragments of the house taken in succession at different angles, laid out on a grid pattern, ten across and three down, without any attempt to effect an exact matching between them, which conveyed to the viewer the experience of walking through the house and out into the garden. Across the white borders of the bottom prints, he wrote the title, *My House, Montcalm Avenue, Los Angeles, Friday, February 26, 1982*. As he did so, he felt the blood tingling in his veins. 'I pinned it on the wall,' he recalled, 'and I kept going back to it. Even in the middle of the night! It was different somehow. It was a narrative, a story, you moved, the viewer's body moved through the house. But the main point was that you read it differently. It wasn't just a photograph. It was abstracted, stylised: the ideas were based on Cubism in the way that it filters things down to an essence . . . it worked so well that I couldn't believe what was happening when I looked at it. I saw all these different spaces, and I thought: my God! I've never seen *anything* like this in photography.'[14]

True to form, having made a new discovery, there was no holding him back, and like a schoolboy with a new craze, Hockney threw himself into exploring every possible avenue that the medium might open up. 'I started to play with the Polaroid camera,' he wrote, 'and began making collages. Within a week, very quickly, I made them quite complex. This intrigued me and I became quite obsessed with it. I made about 150 collages with Polaroids. I went on until I felt I had exhausted the idea.'[15] Though his first effort contained no people, two days later he had done a portrait of Maurice Payne reading the *New York Times Magazine*, followed by another of him seated in a chair looking out of the window towards the swimming pool, and these were followed by collages of Ian Falconer painting a self-portrait, and *Ian and Me Watching a Fred Astaire Movie on Television*.

Once he had included people in the collages, they became Hockney's preferred subject, and all his friends and workers were dragged into an orgy of picture-making, his subjects including David Graves, Gregory Evans, the Gemini printers, Celia Birtwell, Stephen Spender, Billy and Audrey Wilder, Henry Geldzahler, and Elsa Duarte, his housekeeper, and her family. As he explained to the writer Lawrence Weschler, 'There are some lines in Auden's "Letter to Lord Byron" which I've always particularly fancied.

> To me art's subject is the human clay,
> Landscape but a background to a torso.
> All of Cézanne's apples I would give away,
> For a small Goya or a Daumier.

I mean I don't know about those particular apples – Cézanne's apples are lovely and very special – but what can finally compare to the image of another human being?'[16]

In those first weeks Hockney was like a man possessed, driving himself on with barely any sleep, and becoming, in the eyes of his friends, like a child, playing for hours on end and then just suddenly conking out. 'So there'd be these late nights with strange boys wandering around in jockstraps,' Falconer remembers, 'which I suppose you'd expect with David Hockney. He would sleep for two hours, and then get up and do stuff and then sleep for another two hours. You could never be sure of a good night's sleep because David would always be bursting into your room in the middle of the night, shouting, "Lovey, you must come and look!" Then you'd probably hear his Picasso lecture for the eighty-fifth time. He'd wake up in the night with an idea and then come down and ruin everyone else's night and then go back up to sleep. He was disciplined in his way. He went to bed early and got up early. It was an eccentric discipline that didn't take anyone else's life into account. It wasn't so much self-obsession as the optimum way of getting his work done.'[17]

As he progressed, the works got bigger and more complex and more difficult to create. 'These photographs took a long time to make,' he recalled. 'Some of them took about four or five hours . . . Just to describe how one was taken, for instance, I portrayed Christopher Isherwood and Don Bachardy; I got them to pose against a wall in the studio, and began, as I do in a drawing, with the eyes, then the head, then the figures. At first they were both looking at me, but as the picture took such a long time, they relaxed into a more natural pose. I realised after a while Don kept looking down rather protectively at Christopher, so I altered the picture to include this, re-photographing parts of Don when he thought I'd done that bit. I thought . . . this is not like an ordinary photograph. It's really about drawing . . . In this way I got a more interesting picture, altering it as I went along.'[18] The complications of working with the Polaroid camera stemmed from the fact that it had a fixed lens, so to get a close-up, the photographer had to *go* close up, and vice versa for a wider-angle shot. There was therefore much moving around. 'It took me over two hours to make that collage,' Hockney said. 'I'd snap my details, spread them out on the floor while they developed and go back for more. Christopher said I was behaving like a mad scientist, and there was something mad about the whole enterprise. Looking back at the completed grid, it seems as if each shot were taken from one vantage point . . . but if you look more closely you can see that I was moving about all the time.'[19]

As Hockney proceeded with his experiments, losing himself more and more in the medium, he was struck with a singular notion – that in creating these images, accuracy had taken a back seat, while the relative importance of objects in the scene was stressed. Thus in a portrait of Kasmin sitting in a blue chair, 'I kept having to re-photograph the chair to get it right,' he said. 'As it turned out, the chair looks much larger than it actually is, but that's because it seemed that way with Kas sitting in it.'[20] Similarly in an image of Stephen Spender, there is a tropical plant beside him that, again, appears much bigger than it was in real life, because it happened to seem interesting at the time. It then occurred to him that the whole process was exactly like drawing. 'The camera is a *medium* is what I suddenly realised,' he explained. 'It's neither an art, a technique, a craft, nor a hobby – it's a tool. It's an extraordinary drawing tool. It's as if I, like most ordinary photographers, had previously been taking part in some long-established culture in which pencils were used only for making dots – there's an obvious sense of liberation that comes when you realise that you can make lines!'[21]

In April he made a trip to England where he created more Polaroid portraits of, among others, his mother, David Graves, Bill Brandt, Vera Russell, and George Lawson and Wayne Sleep. 'I had to stare at Wayne's right tit for what seemed like forever,' Lawson recalls. 'Having it done was quite frightening in a way because sometimes he would come very close with his camera. Then the Polaroids would emerge and he would put them on the ground and look at them. There was a great skill in the way he knew exactly from what point he had taken them so that they would all match up.'[22]

While Hockney was in London, the Falklands War broke out, an event which, predictably, upset him. 'I couldn't help but be affected by the Falklands crisis,' he told Stephen Spender, ' – a horrible mess caused by stubborn stupid people. I suggested to my friends + Ann that they should drop thousands of books on Matisse everywhere to remind people of the beauty of life. She was the only one who thought this was a good idea.'[23]

Spender cheered him up by showing him the proofs of *China Diary*. 'I really wanted to say how much I enjoyed the shape of the China book,' Hockney later wrote. 'I think it is a very enjoyable read and look, and was to me of course very vivid. I loved the way it reflected our experiences, not just of the monuments but of our oscillating thoughts, doubts, loves and confusions. I hope Mr Lin is not too upset when he reads it. I don't think he should be, he comes across as a real person slightly shocked by us really but eventually admitting "I really liked you people."'[24]

Hockney was pleased with the trip home, reflecting on his return, 'Coming back here after being in Yorkshire for a few days is always a bit of a shock for me. They might be unsophisticated in Bradford, but they're not daft.'[25] He threw himself back into the intense outburst of photographic work that had resulted in the production of nearly 150 Polaroid collages in a short period of three months, and had reawakened in him his interest in cubism and in Picasso's ideas in general, and made him think anew about the cubist ways of seeing. 'I quickly aligned my new photographs to ideas of Cubism,' he wrote. 'I made a kind of pastiche Cubist still life. I borrowed a guitar and put in the traditional still life motifs, and it looked rather amazingly like a Braque or a Picasso. It looks more real than if I had taken only one photo. This technique quickly developed into many areas, among them some very elaborate portraits.'[26] A good example was a portrait of Celia in languorous pose, looking both in profile and straight on, with three eyes, two mouths and two noses, which was a homage to one of Picasso's most celebrated series of portraits. 'People complained about Picasso,' he commented, 'how he distorted the human face. I don't think there are any distortions at all. For instance those marvellous portraits of his love Marie-Thérèse Walter which he made during the thirties; he must have spent hours with her in bed, very close, looking at her face. A face looked at like that *does* look different from one seen at five or six feet. Strange things begin to happen to the eyes, the cheeks, the nose – wonderful inversions and repetitions.'[27]

Word of his frantic activity soon leaked out and André Emmerich dispatched Nathan Kolodner to find out what all the fuss was about. Kolodner, a young protégé of Emmerich's who handled Hockney's work for the Emmerich Gallery, was immediately excited by the new compositions and decided to mount a show of them straight away, though Hockney made the decision not to allow any of them to go on sale. Since they were unique objects, there being no negatives involved in the Polaroid process, he was not ready to say goodbye to them, needing them to be around for further study. The show opened in early June, with the title *Drawing with a Camera*. In some ways, this exhibition might have been seen as a risky venture since Hockney was by no means the first artist to have experimented with a Polaroid. Lucas Samaras had been producing his self-portraits since the mid-1970s, while Joyce Neimanas and Robert Heinecken were both artists who were well known for their work in the medium of photographic collage. The Belgian artist Stefan de Jaeger, who had been creating what he called 'Polaroid Friezes' since the late 1970s, even went so far as to accuse Hockney of plagiarism, a charge he vigorously renounced, denying all knowledge of ever having seen de Jaeger's work. On the whole, however, the critics were largely impressed. 'Other photographers may have probed somewhat the same ground,' wrote Andy Grundberg in the *New York Times*. 'Nevertheless Hockney manages – with customary alacrity – to give his work an originality and authority that is unimpeachable.'[28] While John Russell Taylor asked and answered the question 'Why should someone who draws as brilliantly as Hockney, be messing about with Polaroids, "drawing with a camera", whatever that means? . . . the whole pictorial point of these pieces is to reopen the great Cubist question, re-creating space through fragmentation and re-synthesis . . . And always the result is unmistake-able Hockney.'[29]

After the opening, Hockney returned to California, where *The Rake's Progress* was about to be put on by San Francisco Opera. He travelled alone, while Falconer stayed behind to visit his father, who had been diagnosed with pancreatic cancer. After a few days back in the Hollywood Hills, Hockney wrote expressing his feelings about the previous few months. 'It's been very calm up at the Mont for the last few days, – two days completely alone here (very nice) . . . I must admit I enjoyed having you here these months, they were stimulating for me as I'm sure they were for you. I'm sorry I didn't just "draw + paint" for you here, but the track my mind went off on was just as interesting if not more so. I don't think I'll give up the camera as a small medium so easily, – but just add it to my list of materials. Nevertheless on my return from Europe I do want to concentrate on some painted pictures, especially again portraits – double portraits in this environment I have made or am making, so if you wish to come back and study later you are more than welcome – the teacher always learns from the bright pupil, and I'm sure the odd relationship here between the three of us is still workable.'[30]

The trip to Europe he spoke of was for the opening of the photographic show in Paris. He had invited Falconer to accompany him, and afterwards they would travel to London. 'I look forward to our trip to dear old England,' he wrote. 'I'm sure you will like its tacky and grand charm and its vast difference in Mood from N.Y. It's not better or worse, just wonderfully different. It's always contrasts that make for excitement.' He finished the letter on a wistful note: 'I miss you not being here, it's as though some kind of strange mirrors have been taken away.'[31]

Hockney's plan had been to meet up with Falconer in New York and fly from there to Paris, but the trip started on an unhappy note. It had been his routine to speak regularly on the phone to his old friend Joe McDonald, and always to visit him whenever he was in New York. 'One day I rang and there was no reply,' he recalled; 'I assumed he'd gone away. Eventually his mother called me and said he was in hospital with pneumonia. I thought, pneumonia's not that serious; it's a curable thing.'[32] He arranged to go and visit him before they left for Paris. 'We went over to St Vincent's Hospital,' Falconer recalls, 'and David went in to see Joe, and I was behind him, and I saw Joe looking up from his bed and making frantic signs to me not to come in. I got a shock because I'd known Joe as this strapping all-American boy and there he seemed to have shrunk to nothing.'[33] It was an ominous moment.

In July, Hockney and Falconer travelled to Paris for the opening of *David Hockney, Photographe* at the Pompidou Centre. Though the show had originally been conceived as an exhibition of prints taken from his collection of photograph albums, Hockney wanted people to see the new direction he was heading in, so he had insisted that there should be something new on display, and had included three of his Polaroid compositions: *Ian and Me Watching a Fred Astaire Movie on Television*, *A Little More Rain on the Pool* and *David Graves, Pembroke Studios*. Sayag was excited enough about being the first person to have been granted access to the Hockney albums, but he was particularly thrilled by the new Polaroids. 'The best illustration,' he enthused, 'of the complex connections that exist in David Hockney's photographic oeuvre is without doubt his latest works in Polaroid. They have provided him occasion to push his photographic experiments beyond his daily practice to become the object itself of his search, allowing us to make the leap forward from a "monocular vision" of the world, to one regarded subjectively. These are no longer just photographs, but [to quote Hockney] "ideas about perception" that allow us to "represent on a flat surface the lovely and wonderful experience of looking".'[34]

The last of the Polaroid joiners were done later in July when the pair passed through London, and included one of Henry Moore in his studio in Much Hadham. Though he was very frail at the time, and was walking with two canes, Hockney watched as he made several drawings, and the inspiration he took by looking at the sculptor's hands was reflected in the subsequent work, in which they are repeated six times. 'I thought his hands were quite marvellous,' he remembered, 'and he tends himself to draw marvellous hands, so I put in a lot of his hands.'[35] At Pembroke Studios he started painting again, beginning work on an eight-panel portrait of four of his friends that was entirely influenced by his excursion into photography. 'I started some portraits in London,' he told Kitaj, 'using ideas from the photographs – not the photographs themselves but what they had taught me about looking. I did Ian, Celia, Stephen Buckley, and two of David Graves. Ian has three legs – or should I say two legs with one of them viewed twice, and David G, who finished up with four arms. I was surprised how quickly I got into them, also I expected them to be more Picassoesque than they are. I can't wait to get back to LA and lock myself up with some models-friends.'[36] In the portraits, he twisted round the bodies, gave them heads that looked both frontal and in profile, and several eyes and hands, 'and yet they don't read as monsters. They're clearly and simply individuals in the midst of living. I've made something of a leap here: never again will anyone I'm painting have to "sit" for me, in the traditional sense – frozen still for hours. I can deal now with their liveliness.'[37] He felt he'd made a real breakthrough.

At the very time that things were beginning to be so exciting for Hockney, a dark cloud loomed on the horizon. On his return from London, and after spending some time with his old friend Dagny Corcoran on Martha's Vineyard, he passed through New York and was shocked by the deterioration in the health of Joe McDonald. 'I hated New York on my few days through there,' he told Kitaj. 'I went to see . . . Joe McDonald who is very seriously ill with what is referred to as the "Gay Cancer", which seems to be some kind of sexually transmitted form of cancer . . . He looks extremely thin, pale and very slow like an old man, and as I left his apartment the image of him decaying seemed to emphasise the decay you see in the streets. A lot of my friends there seem gripped by fear, and I'm told the bath-houses and other extremes of New York are not doing as well. Somehow it all seemed rotten to me and I was very glad to leave.'[38]

People had been talking about a 'Gay Cancer' since the summer of 1981, when the New York Times published an account of a rare and often rapidly fatal form of cancer that was being seen in gay men specifically in New York and the San Francisco Bay area of California. At that point forty-one cases had been diagnosed of whom eight had died within two years. 'The cause of the outbreak is unknown,' wrote the Times correspondent, 'and there is as yet no evidence of contagion. But the doctors who have made the diagnoses . . . are alerting other physicians who treat large numbers of homosexual men to the problem in an effort to help identify more cases.'[39] The cancer, which appeared in the form of one or more violet-coloured spots anywhere on the body, was eventually identified as 'Kaposi's sarcoma', named after the Hungarian dermatologist who first described it in 1872, and a disease that had been almost entirely associated with men older than fifty. Now, however, doctors in New York and California were beginning to see it in younger men, all of whom were homosexual.

Like many gay men, Joe McDonald had embraced the sexual freedom that New York had offered in the 1970s, where men could walk freely hand in hand, and the bathhouses offered a multitude of sexual partners and experiences. 'He was completely promiscuous,' Hockney told Stephen Spender. 'He'd go with people five or six times a day.'[40] It was not unusual for people to have had hundreds of partners, even a thousand or more, but though this relentless sexual activity satisfied both a physical need and a desperate seeking-out of companionship, the unfortunate consequences now began to be seen, as increasingly large numbers of young men were reporting to their doctors with feelings of fatigue and swollen glands, to be told that they were 'immune-deficient', a condition their physicians were finding hard to understand.

Ignorance and fear were to stalk the streets of New York for many years to come. In an attempt to combat this, one of the original investigators into the disease, Dr Alvin E. Friedman-Kien of New York University Medical Center, did his best to educate some of the city's gay community. 'Larry Kramer, a screenwriter and producer and novelist, convened a meeting of gay men,' the writer Edmund White remembered, 'in his Fifth Avenue apartment overlooking Washington Square. We were addressed by Dr Friedman-Kien, who'd studied several cases of Kaposi's Sarcoma [which] was showing up in young gay men, as was an unusual and virulent form of pneumonia . . . Dr Friedman-Kien said to us that he thought we should give up sex altogether until researchers understood a little more about how the disease was transmitted. We looked at him as if he were mad. Just as the Crash of 1929 ended the Roaring Twenties, so the AIDS epidemic of 1981 ended the sexy seventies.'[41] White felt thoroughly depressed by this and began to have the same feelings about New York that Hockney had experienced. 'New York didn't change right away,' he wrote, 'but a feeling of dread was now in every embrace . . . What had seemed innocent revels now felt like the manoeuvres of a death squad.'[42]

The fact that he too might be in danger cannot have escaped

Hockney, which makes it somewhat ironic that he should have returned to LA to find a letter from his mother in which for the first time she openly addressed his homosexuality.

> My dear David, once more you have been home & gone again. I so very much enjoyed your company . . . looking – talking – driving – living with – sharing your very wide & deep loving kindness – but – now you are gone again – there still remains with me my lack of understanding of a problem. Yet I have to wonder if it is a problem! I don't really look upon it as such – but I do retreat, because my last wish is to hurt or embarrass you. We all shared in Paul's marriage & Philip's & John's. God has created us, & we all differ & yet we need to be fulfilled & to enjoy life. I think you have a marvellous outlook on life & believe it is to enjoy . . .
>
> I must admit that I have spent much time & thought about you – because – & only so – I was not asked – or maybe you knew <u>I would not have been able to help you when you were in need of love and understanding</u> in the early days when this "homosexuality" was hush-hush to the public, you bravely & openly went on and sorted yourself out.
>
> I first heard of it on Radio from Rev. L. Barnett who wrote a book which I bought & read – but for so long did not understand. There was no one to talk to & Ken did not share with me. You know I have always been rather naive, but I've always trusted and believed in you – no matter what was said – you were my boy! When these things were televised – talked of in news etc etc. I still believed in you & was emphatic of your honour – attached no shame & loved you with all my heart – but was helpless to understand & you did not seek our confidence. I'm sure it was because you realised <u>we</u> did not understand . . .
>
> From my searchings I have wondered if this particular creation has anything to do with parents – if so, David, you have never shown any resentment – & now it is out! You know what my deepest thoughts & prayers have been for you (& myself). I love you so very much & your whole being tells me you love me. I

have never ever met anyone who carries love & caring on their
person as you do – even as a child.

I just believe God is the Great Potter. He makes & moulds us
after his own will & we are supple in his hands.

Please forgive me if this is a revelation to you – it has been hard
to write . . . I do not wish to probe – only you are part of me!
There are many things I shall never know in this life. The world
changes every day – but I'll be modern where I can – God bless
you my own dear boy . . .[43]

While staying with Dagny Corcoran on Martha's Vineyard, Hockney
had concentrated on sketching, but he had also taken with him a Pentax
110, a miniature camera, made by the Ashai Optical Company, which
was the smallest interchangeable-lens SLR on the market, not much
bigger than a packet of cigarettes. Though he only used it to take a
series of snapshots of a tour round his bedroom, when he finally laid
out the processed prints in some kind of order, it struck him that the
lack of a grid formed by the white borders of the Polaroid prints could
prove to be an advantage. The spatial flow of the images would be
uninterrupted. He first of all decided to do some more experiments at
home, making, for example, a portrait of a swimmer in his pool, and
another of his assistant, Jerry Sohn, on the terrace, before setting off
on a road trip to the south-west. He had David Graves and Ann Upton
staying and it seemed like a good opportunity to try out some ideas,
while simultaneously showing Ann's son, Byron, something of the Wild
West. Bing McGilvray also accompanied them. 'The trip was more of a
vacation than anything else,' Bing recalls. 'David doted on Byron, and I
had been showing him the sights, taking him to a gig by the Go-Go's at
some local bar, and down for a day at the beach. Then David decided he
wanted to show him the American West. He loved that part of America.
We went to the Hot Springs, and the crazy Calico Ghost Town, and
stayed in a hotel on the North Rim of the Grand Canyon.'[44] On this
trip, Hockney took relatively few photographs. He didn't really know
what he was doing yet, and it was only when he got back home and

started playing with the pictures that he began to get really excited. 'Well, I'm actually back at Mont Hysterical,' he wrote to Kitaj. 'I got back last week . . . I took a 76 section joining photograph of the Grand Canyon with the small Pentax and I have just glued it together. I'm quite pleased with it.'[45]

These early expeditions were entirely experimental. With the Polaroids he could see straight away how the picture was developing. Using negative film, however, he would have no idea how the finished image was going to look until the film was all processed. Thus intense concentration was required to remember the exact point from which each shot was taken so that the next one would fit alongside it. 'These early collages were really more like studies,' he wrote: 'you did them, just as you do a drawing sometimes, to teach yourself something; it doesn't matter what they look like when you're finished, that's not why they were made. In this case, in retrospect, I realise I was training my visual memory, and this took a lot of time.'[46]

As soon as he returned home, the rolls of film were taken to the nearest lab where he could get them developed. In 1981 a new era in photographic development had been ushered in with the invention by a French company called KIS of the first photo mini-lab, which reduced the time of processing a roll of film, right through to the print stage, to one hour. Within a year places like Benny's Speed Cleaning and One-Hour Processing, which was a combined dry-cleaner's and photo processor's in Hollywood, had sprung up all over the world. Benny's had no idea who Hockney was, and sent the prints back complete with standardised notices explaining all the mistakes he was making, such as failing to centre the camera on the subject or focus on the background. 'It took me a long time,' he recalled, 'to convince them that I truly wanted them to "print regardless".'[47] When he began to put the uncropped prints together into a collage, he realised he was on to something: a way of showing the grandeur and awesomeness of these landscapes, which he had always experienced but which photography, it seemed to him, had never been able to show. 'I've always loved the wide-open spaces of the American West,' he wrote. 'But I was never able to capture them in photography, to convey the sense of what it's actually like to be there, facing that expanse – that incredible sense of spaciousness, which is somehow as elusive to ordinary photography as time is. I thought that among other things, this new kind of photography might be able to capture that sense of vast extent.'[48] In a fever of excitement, he couldn't wait to get back on the road again.

When Hockney was on a high, it was to the exclusion of everything. Most of his friends simply accepted this as being par for the course of friendship with an artist. Those who were as egotistical as him had a bigger problem. Henry Geldzahler, for example, chose this very time to bid for sympathy, and it did not go well. Having worked for five years for Mayor Koch as New York City's Commissioner for Cultural Affairs, a difficult and stressful job at which he had excelled, he had decided to resign, citing worries about his health. He suffered from high blood pressure and had recently been hospitalised with diverticulitis. 'The only times I have been sick in my life,' he told the *New York Times*, 'have been during my five years as commissioner. The schedule is hectic. There are difficult situations. My health is good now. It is restored. But if I did this indefinitely, I wouldn't be fine.'[49]

It was Geldzahler's intention to write books and do some art consulting, but the loss of his $62,000-a-year salary brought a financial problem which, together with worries about his health, required a sympathetic ear, together with, perhaps, the possibility of a loan, or even a picture to sell, in this case the portrait titled *The Conversation*, of himself and Raymond Foye. With these things in mind, he paid a visit to 'Mont Hysterical' to bend the ear of his old friend. His old friend, however, was in no mood for listening. All he wanted to do was to regale Geldzahler with the brilliance of what he was doing, and listen in return to his praise and amazement, none of which was forthcoming. Eventually Geldzahler left in a huff, penning a letter to Hockney as soon as he got home that was tinged with sarcasm.

'This is one way to communicate with the non-hearing,' he wrote. 'It seems to me that when you need my support you expect and get it. I have been trying to talk <u>to</u> you (not through you or around you) for the past three weeks about my life and the need to change it to save it . . . However when I mention a step you might take to help me realize my dream – the four or five minutes of freedom from stress and agitation that I need to clear the board – moving the portrait of Raymond and me from storage to studio so <u>you</u> can decide <u>if</u> it can be split and saved, you make me feel like some lower form of hanger-on – as if you had to drop the work you're involved in and move the picture yourself . . . I understand your priorities and respect them, but at least give me the consideration of listening to the vulnerable quaver in my voice. The medication I am on is depressive so please excuse the anger and self-pity, the tone of this missive. I am hurt and at your mercy and that is a most uncomfortable feeling.'[50]

Hockney did, however, have pangs of guilt, and wrote to him, 'I understand you were (and are) worried about your health. I also understand your sense of insecurity in giving up your job . . . I now understand you were too much concerned with your problems to engross yourself in what I was doing here. I understand now, but at the time I felt you had just come to get a painting or some money and not to be friends and discuss ideas. It got me down but sitting alone afterwards at the Grand Canyon I began to think I was being very selfish looking at it that way. Selfishness though is a common enough vice in artists especially when they are engrossed in some new and exciting project as they see it. Well, when I heard you'd resigned, I was pleased, and proud of you. A sign of strength had been shown that can only be good. Of course I will help you, although I don't think I am quite as rich (financially) as you think . . .'[51]

In the same letter, Hockney admitted to having 'gone mad with the photographs (if that's what they are) since you left, and there are now about 34 large ones. (The largest contains 168 separate pictures).'[52] Over a period of a few weeks, he took thousands of photographs. His method was to snap dozens of pictures at a particular site, using different lenses for the varying perspectives. Then, he related, 'once I've got the prints, I start building the collages, keeping to one strict rule: I never crop the prints. Somehow this seems more important to the integrity of the enterprise: the evenness of time seems to be tied up with a regularity in the print size, and things would get all messed up whenever I trimmed the prints. This, in turn, forces me to be aware of how I'm framing the shots as I take them: in effect I end up "drawing" the collages twice.'[53]

Hockney's intention was to train his eye to look with great care at, say, a landscape and then construct as true as possible a documentation of that look. He wanted each photo-collage to reflect, as accurately as possible, human perception, the way our eyes move about and the many moments and points of focus they take in. The breakthrough came when he discovered that it was not necessary to restrict himself with edges, or by stopping at some arbitrary middle distance. He had to bring the picture right up to the viewer, beginning with his own feet and the ground in front of him, before taking it to the view beyond. 'Cubism, I realised during those days,' he said, 'is about our own bodily presence in the world. It's about the world, yes, but ultimately about where we are in it, *how* we are in it. It's about the kind of perception a human being can have in the midst of living.'[54] Though he did some huge and spectacular views of the Grand Canyon incorporating these ideas, some of which have an almost vertiginous sense of depth, leading *Vanity Fair* magazine to describe them as a blending of 'NASA spaceship photography with Cubism',[55] perhaps the most radical of all these images was *Telephone Pole, Los Angeles*, in which the eye is simultaneously led up to the very top of the pole as well as down the steps beside the house into the valley below, providing the viewer with an extraordinary sensation. 'For years I've thought my eyes are funny, or something,' he wrote. 'I kept thinking how much can you really see and what is it you really take in as your eye moves about focusing. As your eye moves in space it tells you about it. The space between you and what you see is very important. In my new photographs I deal with all the ground from under my feet on into deep space.'[56]

Hockney had scarcely returned home from his trip to the Grand Canyon when he received some devastating news. Byron Upton, Ann's much loved only child, had been killed in a terrible accident. 'I was with David when he got the phone call,' Ian Falconer remembers. 'We were sitting in the little room between his bedroom and the living room. It was unbelievably horrible. Byron was such a beautiful sweet boy, Italian-looking and very cocky as sixteen-year-old boys are. Ann doted on him.'[57] He had also recently been the subject of one of Hockney's Polaroid joiners, *Ann + Byron Upton, Pembroke Studios, May 6th 1982,* in which he was lying on the ground behind his mother, who was seated in a basketwork chair, wearing a blue polka-dot dress and looking serene and happy. Apparently he and a friend had been eating 'magic mushrooms', which produce hallucinogenic effects similar to LSD, and which were then a legal 'high'. They had tried to take the Tube home and, at some point, Byron had either missed the train, or had got off at the wrong station, and had attempted to get from one station to the next by walking along the tracks. He was struck by a train and killed.

'I'm just leaving for London and its sadness,' Hockney wrote to Geldzahler, 'but I think Ann needs me very much. She sounds devastated. I know what a loss it must be although I don't think any male can quite understand what it must be like for a woman to grow a little child, bring him up and then have him torn away. I think she will come back here with David for a while, he was coming anyway to do the photographs . . . I think they will enjoy it here more than Colville Square.'[58] He flew straight to London to be with his old friend, who was inconsolable. The funeral took place a week later, on 11 November. 'At 3.30 drove to Kensal Green cemetery,' wrote Ossie Clark in his diary. 'Cold, damp day. Muddy underfoot. Bit of sunshine. Quite a crowd of sombre people gathered. I shuffled into church. Stood at the side. Saw Hockney and Mike Upton arrive. Felt terribly sad, everyone so quiet. A priest said how popular etc. Reggae music and prayers. I threw earth on the coffin and walked away crying. Home, tea and sympathy with Ann.' She told Clark, 'I just hope some good will come of it.'[59] It was then decided that, as soon as it was feasible, she and David should fly out to LA, where he had lots of work, and stay there for the foreseeable future.

Hockney also took the opportunity to visit his mother, and perhaps it was because he had death on his mind that he chose to make a photo-collage of her seated among the tombstones of Bolton Abbey, the place where she had become engaged to his father. In an interview with the *Listener,* however, published at the beginning of November, he did admit that while he loved the sun, and the Mediterranean aspect of California, 'I also do like Gothic gloom . . . and I've a weakness for it and I assume that's Bradford in a sense. Bradford makes me think of fairytales, Grimm's fairytales – that's the Gothic gloom side and when you think of all that neo-Gothic architecture of Northern England or even the ruined abbeys of Yorkshire . . . I can always remember as a child on rainy days how black they were then and it's rather an affectionate image.'[60]

In London he photographed David Graves looking wistfully out of the window of his Bayswater flat, the grim street beyond the balcony, with its shabby houses covered with scaffolding, somehow echoing his feelings of sadness, and at Pembroke Studios he also made a photo-collage of his old friend from Bradford, Norman Stevens. Soon after, he was visited there by his biographer, Peter Webb, who described finding him 'crouching on the floor beside a large sheet of grey cardboard. David Graves had just come back from the local chemist's shop with the latest batch of photographs of the interior of the studio, and Hockney was checking whether his memory had served him well since he had had to work without the advantage of the immediacy of the Polaroids. He very rapidly fitted the new photographs into the collage . . . all the time giving me a running commentary on how anyone could do the same with a little imagination, since it did not require expensive equipment or specialist knowledge.'[61]

Before returning to LA, Hockney passed through New York, where John Dexter was rehearsing the revival of *Parade*, which was to open at the Met in early December. He too became the subject of a photo-collage, seated in the stalls of the opera house, with the set of *Les Mamelles de Tirésias* unfolding onstage. Joe McDonald, now out of hospital, was also photographed, standing in the doorway of his apartment, looking gaunt and old beyond his years, the walls hung with memories of their long friendship: a poster of *Parade*, one of the *Paper Pools* series, a large lithograph of him and a friend, and, the most recent, a touching drawing of two trees and a lawn, bearing the hopeful message 'Dearest Joe, get well soon'. By now, though ignorance about the illness was still rife, it was common knowledge that he was suffering from AIDS, as Ossie Clark noted in his diary: 'Poor beautiful man is dying from a sexually transmitted disease, AIDS, which breaks down the body's natural defence system. It's too sad and apparently quite ghastly.' [62]

On 25 November, Ann Upton flew out to LA to join David Graves, the idea being that they would join the household at Montcalm Avenue while they looked for a place of their own. As soon as she arrived, she telephoned Ossie Clark. 'Ann Upton has gone to Los Angeles,' he recorded. 'She phoned later and wept when she heard of George's birthday party. I do feel for her so much.'[63] Laura Hockney joined them for Christmas, and helped try to keep Ann's mind off Byron during what would be a particularly sad time for her. Christmas Day went smoothly. 'Anne & I & David G's help make Yorkshire dinner,' she wrote in her diary. 'Roast beef & trimmings. Mo & Lisa arrive for dinner. Very successful meal. Gave Mo T-Shirt which had bought for David G's but sure it would not suit. Mo delighted – will give D.G. Token. My Christmas cake appreciated for afternoon tea.'[64] In the evening they all went out to a party at Tony Richardson's. 'Always a happy gathering,' Laura commented. 'His two daughters – Natasha & Joely – by Vanessa Redgrave are very attractive – Natasha had spent 3 days preparing for today's banquet . . . The round table is always gay with crackers, silver candlesticks & red candles. I sat between Tony & an Englishman, Kenneth, who had been married 3 times and had 3 stepdaughters with him . . . Christopher & Don were guests too – they turn up like children to all the parties. David & David G played like children with a child's toy which, filled with play dough, grew hair from the top of its head.'[65]

On Boxing Day, Hockney took Ann and Laura to Santa Monica. 'We spent a glorious morning on the pier,' she wrote. 'Passed thro the old town with dear little wooden houses in such individual styles & past the gracious & portly houses of the very rich in Beverly Hills. Afternoon went to Samantha Eggar's (ex-film star) party – had Punch – cheese rolls and vegetarian pie. Played Scrabble in the evening.'[66] This was the first of several games of Scrabble to be played over the next few days, all of which were photographed in detail for a new collage. 'David G. & David ever busy with the photo pictures. They are a completely different technique from David's other works & paintings. It is a slow and tedious process – but very satisfying and interesting. I feel almost as thrilled as David — he only stops clicking his camera when he is putting the jigsaw together (or thinking out the next one).'[67]

The Scrabble Game was Hockney's most complex work yet. 'My eyes seem to be changing or something is happening to them,' he told Henry Geldzahler. 'I have been pushing photography for a year now, but I must admit to making some strange discoveries . . . I've even formulated new theories of modern art from the ideas . . . here's my present theory. The reason artists did not take off from Cubism into a strong depiction of the visible world, and took what looked like the exciting road to abstraction, was that another invention at about the same time looked as though it depicted reality with even more vividness — the movie. Perhaps we have forgotten what the "moving" picture must have been like to people, how incredible it must have been. Nevertheless it's a backwards step from Cubism and it has slowly dawned on me in my experiment how limited it is . . . I've some very interesting experiments in "looking" to show you . . . and they are still going in weird directions that somehow we hadn't thought about. It seems to open up new pictorial areas and makes me ask questions I for one had never thought about.'[68]

With its asymmetrical margins and overlapping layers, *The Scrabble Game* sprawls across the mount, virtually encompassing a 360-degree view, and, with its clear depiction of the letters on the board and the facial expressions of all the participants, invites the viewer to participate. In fact it is almost impossible for any lover of the game not to want to join in. In the foreground, Hockney's own hands hover over his stand of seven letters that read, from left to right, LQUIREU. Seated to his right, his mother looks pensive, her five-times-repeated face giving little away as she rests her chin on her hands or scratches her nose, her right hand eventually poised over the word 'VEX', which, encompassing a double word square, would net her a score of twenty-six points. She gives off every indication of being an expert. Ann, on the other hand, seated to her right, looks anything but, obviously struggling to find a word and finally grinning with pleasure at managing 'NET', giving her a pathetic score of three. Next to her, David Graves, keeping the score, just laughs, while in the far left-hand margin of the picture a bored cat cleans its face. 'I couldn't concentrate much on the game,' Hockney later wrote, 'because I was taking the pictures. It was while I was doing this piece that I saw that I was using narrative for the first time, using a new dimension of time.'[69] When Ann Upton saw the completed collage, she commented, 'It's better than a movie.'[70]

'I enjoyed more than 1 hour looking at the "pictures from photographs" with D.G.,' Laura wrote on 29 December. 'They are so large & should be a most interesting exhibition which I look forward to – each picture framed to its own shape & with such a vast expanse yet intimate viewing.'[71] It was Graves's job to stick them down, which was a time-consuming and often tedious procedure, but he had been working on a method of simplifying the process. 'David would have the photographs out loosely,' he recalls, 'laying them down how he thought they should be, and the early ones were just tacked together. Then I had this idea of getting little blocks of Perspex made, with which I could weigh down the prints and be able to see through them, then when they were perfectly placed you would lift up an edge and get a bit of glue in.'[72]

Laura's steady presence was a support to Ann Upton. They went shopping together, saw *Gandhi* at the cinema, ate French toast with maple syrup and whipped butter at Schwab's Hollywood Drugstore, and toured the Bel Air Community, which particularly impressed Laura for having its own armed guard. When Ann was feeling down, Laura was there to talk to and lean on. 'David G., Anne & I went to Santa Monica,' she wrote on 30 December. 'Walked along the cliff top & saw a most wonderful sunset. I have never seen the sun "drop" down in one big ball just lessening & all the horizon aflame. I've seen many sunsets – but this was a most memorable one. Returning we saw the moon rise, a lovely round full moon low in the sky. Later as we went to Imperial Gardens (Jap. Restaurant) for dinner, it was high & bright & beautiful. Ann was very upset for a few minutes. She always thinks how Byron would have enjoyed it.'[73]

With New Year approaching, the next couple of days were difficult ones for Ann, and everyone rallied round. Because the weather had been unseasonably cold, Hockney decided to raise everyone's spirits with a trip to Palm Springs, a two-hour drive south of LA. 'Our first stop at the Spa,' Laura recorded, 'where D & J left Anne & I, where we had a wonderful experience of a hot mineral bath. It was a lovely glowing feeling of massage & warmth. I was a little scared I could not hold on to grip the rail, but the attendant stayed with me & helped. Both Anne & I felt refreshed – Anne quite uplifted.' Unfortunately the long drive back left them both feeling tired and a little sick and in no mood for a New Year's Eve party at the home of one of Hockney's former students. 'At 9pm,' she wrote, 'we all leave for "Salome's". Anne & I not feeling our best. Arrive to find many guests seated & waiting for a very homely musical evening. Salome's husband & another string player, violin & cello & piano formed a very good band. The house was very beautiful & full of pictures & antiques but large enough to be well displayed & most attractive. Poor Anne could not face the company & the evening of this passing year & had to be taken home within ½ hour of our arrival – I wanted to go with her but realised she may feel better with D. Graves – so I stayed with David – after all I was treated as an honoured guest & did not want to let David down.'[74]

When Laura flew back to England a couple of days later, Hockney and Ian Falconer went with her, leaving Upton and Graves to get on with the business of moving into a flat they had rented in the Martel Apartments just off Sunset Boulevard. They travelled to Yorkshire, Falconer's first visit there. 'Yorkshire was the greenest place I'd ever been,' he recalls. 'The stone walls were green as well as the fields, like Ireland. It was entirely beautiful. He took me to Fountains Abbey and Bolton Abbey, and all the ruins, and we went up to Howarth and saw the Parsonage. It was a perfect day, one of those with sideways rain and I laughed to think of this poor coughing girl in this tiny little place, coming up with those stories. We spent a night at Ponden Hall too. That was the first place I'd ever seen ice on the *inside* of the window before, in the bathroom as I was trying to wash!'[75]

At Fountains Abbey, Hockney took many photographs for a photo-collage of Falconer standing in the ruins, and on his return to London worked on portraits of Celia and her children, and one of Sir Frederick Ashton. Ashton, who had choreographed Stravinsky's *Le Rossignol* for the John Dexter triple bill in 1981, had been invited by the Met to mount a production of *Varii Capricci*, a ballet he had created to music by William Walton, as part of 'Britain Salutes New York', a festival of art, drama, music and dance that was to take place there in April. He had in mind a backdrop that would evoke 'La Mortella', Walton's garden on the island of Ischia, which had been transformed from what Laurence Olivier once referred to as 'nothing but a quarry' into a tropical paradise full of exotic trees, rare ferns, camellias, fountains and a beautiful swimming pool with views across to Vesuvius. It had occurred to him that Hockney would be the perfect person to ask to design it, a commission that came along at the very moment that another theatrical project was about to take shape.

CHAPTER EIGHT

HOCKNEY
PAINTS THE STAGE

In 1981, while Hockney was working on the Stravinsky triple bill, he was approached by Martin Friedman, the director of the Walker Art Center in Minneapolis, who asked him if he might consider doing an exhibition there of all his theatre work. They had known each other since 1965 when the Walker had been one of the first galleries in the US to show Hockney's work, in an exhibition called *London: The New Scene*. Friedman was a legend in the art world, a museum director who had created a cultural mecca in an unlikely part of the country. He liked to hang out with artists and was devoted to helping them achieve projects, however improbable they might have been. During the 1960s and 70s he would make regular visits to New York to check out the scene. 'He wanted to know what was going on and what we thought,' recalled Chuck Close, whose *Big Self-Portrait* had been bought by Friedman in 1969 for $1,300, the first of his pictures to be sold to a museum. 'None of us had any money. He would say "Let's go to Chinatown and have Chinese food", and then we would just collect every artist we saw while we were walking. We'd start out with two or three and by the time we got there we would have 20, and he'd happily pick up the check.'[1] In return for dinner they would pass on tips on which artists to visit and whose work to buy, artists like Richard Serra and Keith Sonnier. From visiting artists' studios, Friedman learned the kind of space they required, and in 1971, only ten years into his tenure, having seen some of the challenging, large-scale pieces then being made, he had added a new column-free warehouse-like wing to the museum to display such works. He saw the space as being perfect for a show of theatre sets.

To begin with, Hockney was not convinced. 'I didn't think showing theatre drawings was that interesting,' he wrote. 'They're often no more than diagrams to show people how to make a costume or something. I had always thought exhibitions of theatre designs were a bit dull really, and I told Martin this. I said, I'm not sure there's that much material; there are the models, I know, but they're not that big and I don't know how interesting they are to people who have not seen the opera.'[2] But Friedman had bigger ideas than this and was suggesting that they could include in the show some of the real sets. 'I pointed out they'd be far too big to put in a museum; they're meant to be seen from some distance, they're crudely painted. But he persuaded me we could reinterpret them for a show.'[3]

When, two years later, he finally allowed himself to be talked round, Hockney had only the faintest idea of what he had let himself in for, and at a time when he was about to be busier than ever. Notwithstanding the work he had agreed to do for Frederick Ashton, he was still heavily engaged with the photo-collages, which he had agreed to put in a number of shows, as well as permitting limited editions of some of them to be made for sale. There were to be forty-two in editions of about fifteen, and these were to be published under the imprint of Petersburg Press, and sold through a few galleries, namely André Emmerich in New York, LA Louver in Los Angeles, Richard Gray in Chicago, Nishimura Gallery in Tokyo, Knoedler/Emmerich in Zurich and Kasmin in London. It was a project that presented huge technical problems, and David Graves was put in charge of bringing it to fruition. In spite of the fact that he was a trained architect, had designed houses, laid out interiors, and charted wiring and plumbing and stress calculations for big building projects, he later admitted that the photo-collages were the most elaborate, intricate enterprise he'd ever been involved in.

The first thing he did was to hire someone who understood photographic printing on an industrial scale. Richard Schmidt was a young photography graduate from Minneapolis who had been working at a one-hour photo company called Fromex, as a trainer and insurance photographer. While in graduate school, he had also worked in an industrial lab doing colour printing, so he was an ideal candidate for the job. Once hired, he advised Graves on the right equipment to buy, essentially a Photo-Mat machine of the same kind that was used in Hockney's local photo-processing shop, Benny's, and together they duplicated a one-hour lab on the upper floor of the Santa Monica Boulevard studio. Here, Schmidt and another trained operator, James Franklin, processed the hundreds of thousands of prints that would go into the finished works, a job that required the machine to be working day and night. Franklin worked the day shift, Schmidt the nights. 'Once you had the correct colours figured,' Schmidt recalls, 'you could just leave the machine to print them.'[4]

The main difficulty in the production lay in the complex nature of the collages and the fact that each number in an edition had to be identical to the one before and after it. The procedure was that once the machine had produced the photographic prints, they all had to be trimmed to exactly the same size as the originals. Using an adjustable contact adhesive, so they could be stuck down lightly, these were then positioned onto a piece of archival museum card, mounted on a stretcher frame to keep it rigid, which had been silk-screened with the outlines of all the photographs, and a sequence worked out so they went down with all the same overlaps. The last part of the process was making any necessary tiny adjustments, and then a roller was pushed over the whole piece by hand so that the glue could really take effect. Finally Hockney would come down to review the finished panels and, if he was happy with them, handwrite the title and sign them ready for the framer.

There was one concern, which was whether or not the colour prints might fade, even though they were using a new Ektacolor print process that was supposedly guaranteed to remain fast for at least fifty years. 'Of course they'll fade over the very long run,' said Hockney. 'But then artists' reputations fade too, and there's no protection against that. Anyway these are much more about line – about drawing – than they are about colour. Still, a lot of people don't see it that way, so I've had a rubber stamp made up which says, "Not recommended for investment. Buy for pleasure only."'[5] Over four hundred of these photo-collages were made for sale. 'It was a mad time,' David Graves recalls, 'particularly for me. I was given the nickname "Leadfoot" because my foot was constantly on the accelerator of the car, dashing backwards and forwards between Santa Monica Boulevard and Montcalm Avenue several times a day, bringing David trial proofs and helping him with new pieces. From start to finish, between December and April, we had built a darkroom, bought the equipment, hired the staff, of whom there were ten in addition to me, and produced enough editions for five shows on in three countries.'[6]

All the time that this hive of activity was taking place in the Santa Monica Boulevard studio, Hockney was also working on new and progressively complicated pictures, such as a series he made during a trip to Japan in February 1983. He had gone with Gregory Evans and Paul Cornwall-Jones to give a lecture at a paper conference on the use of paper as a medium. From Kyoto he wrote to Kitaj: 'I'm excited about my work. I've been pushing photography into realms I never thought possible, especially into areas of narrative that are very exciting. I'll show them in N.Y in May . . . Photographers are a bit freaked out by them but oddly enough film makers are not and have gotten the point . . .'[7] One of these narrative pictures was of a lunch party at the British Embassy, hosted by the ambassador, Sir Hugh Cortazzi, and his wife. Cortazzi was a scholar and an expert on Japanese history and culture, and one can only imagine his surprise at the behaviour of his guest of honour, who spent the whole time jumping up and down, taking hundreds of photographs. Like *The Scrabble Game*, the resulting *Luncheon at the British Embassy* intimately involved the viewer in the event, as if they were a guest at the party seated in Hockney's chair, even taking in the servant preparing a tray of liqueurs in his peripheral vision. 'There's a circular motion in this,' said Hockney. 'Once you start to look, it's hard to stop. You can just go on and on . . . It's the most complicated one I've done yet.'[8]

Because he had decided not to get any of the film he had shot developed in Japan, Hockney methodically kept notes every time he took photographs for a new collage, making detailed diagrams of how they would be laid out. These were of particular use when it came to assembling the shots he had taken of the Zen Garden at the Ryoanji

Temple in Kyoto. Created in the fifteenth century, this *karesansui,* or Japanese rock garden, is considered to be one of the finest examples of its kind in Japan. It consists of a large rectangular field covered with perfectly raked white pebbles, and punctuated by fifteen stones of various sizes which sit in pools of green moss. Only fourteen of the boulders can be seen at once from the designated viewing spot, and it is believed that solely through attaining enlightenment may the viewer see all fifteen at once. 'The garden at Ryoanji does not symbolise anything,' wrote the German garden historian Günter Nitschke, '. . . nor does it have the value of reproducing a natural beauty that one can find in the real or mythical world. I consider it to be an abstract composition of "natural" objects in space, a composition whose function is to incite meditation.'[9]

In order to try to symbolise movement, Hockney took each series of shots of the garden from a different vantage point, moving from one side of the garden to the other one pace at a time, stopping with each step to take a column of photographs extending from the border in the foreground to the wall in the distance. To underline his movement, he included shots of his feet in the foreground. Consisting as it did of dozens of photographs of pebbles laboriously fitted together, he admitted that it was 'a real headache' to put together. 'When I was first laying it out,' he wrote, 'I got them all mixed up and I had to have them all printed again so that I could put the pebbles in the right place . . . The pebbles had to be in the right place for it to work. I had to count and really look at those pebbles to link one with another.'[10] Much to his surprise, when it was finished, he appeared to have made a photograph without perspective. 'What really excited me was when I pieced together the Zen Garden in Kyoto . . . it was then and really only then that I began to realise that one of the areas I was really examining was perspective, that this was what you could alter in photography. I had not realised this until then, not fully . . . To do it in photography was, in a sense, quite an achievement because photography is the picture-making process totally dominated by perspective.'[11]

Hockney's excitement was soon tempered on his return home by news that Joe McDonald was back in hospital. 'Joe McDonald is very

seriously ill,' he wrote to Kitaj. 'I flew to NY last week with Anne U
to see him. At first he hardly knew we were there, but the second day
his spirits had lifted a little, but he is very weak and his mother sits in
the room all the time. You have to wear a mask and rubber gloves etc to
go in. I was so depressed after the first visit, the decaying City of New
York just seemed horrible . . . Nevertheless the knowledge that our
visits cheered him up pleased us a little and made it a bit more bearable
– it makes everything else seem a bit trivial.'[12] News that McDonald
had AIDS had spread like wildfire through the modelling community,
infecting the gay men with the fear that they would soon suffer a similar
fate, and the women with the terror that they might somehow catch it
from them. Ignorance fanned the flames. Some models refused to use
brushes belonging to gay make-up artists; others would wash out their
mouths if kissed on the lips by a gay man.

Nor was the fear restricted to the modelling community. Employees
at a Wall Street firm refused to work with a colleague who had AIDS.
On Long Island, parents would not allow their children to play with
the daughter of a woman whose husband was infected, and put pressure
on her to take her daughter out of school. The sanitation department
refused to collect her garbage. In Manhattan, a health fair that planned
to offer examinations for AIDS was bounced at the last minute from
Public School 41 when the school-district superintendent expressed
fears that the cafeteria would be contaminated. The fair opened at a
local community centre instead. One woman came in and asked if her
daughter was in danger of getting AIDS by attending a synagogue with
homosexuals. 'At the Zoli modeling agency, on East 56th Street,' wrote
Michael Daly in the *New Yorker*, 'and in the cubicles of the Everard
Spa, on West 28th Street. Backstage at the Metropolitan Opera and
in the locker room of the 6th Precinct station house. At an advertising
agency off Eleventh Avenue and in the cellblocks at Auburn prison.
Everywhere, talk of AIDS is erupting into conversations. One moment
there is idle chatter about the Yankees or the new Lucas film. And then,
suddenly, fear and reason are grappling with the specter of this fatal
illness for which there is yet no cure.'[13]

On 30 March, Ossie Clark recorded in his diary: 'I phoned David

Hockney in LA. When David got on the phone I said "What's the matter? You sound distant." He answered "do I?" He has got to go to NY tomorrow to see Joe McDonald, who is definitely near death in hospital, and he's not looking forward to it at all – "I think it will be pretty awful" he said.'[14] And so it was. He spent the next week with him, visiting three times a day in the hospital. He was shocked by what he found. McDonald was completely emaciated, his face sunken in like a skull so he looked about ninety. He'd lost all his hair and could barely speak. 'You could not kiss him,' Hockney told Stephen Spender. 'He was resigned to the idea of dying at the end. He said he did not regret his life but felt he had wasted a lot of time.'[15] '. . . sorry about your friend Jo being so ill,' wrote Laura Hockney. 'Hope he is improving – He would be so glad to see you & know you had kindly travelled to N.Y. to see him.'[16] McDonald died on 7 April, the day her letter was written, the first of Hockney's friends to succumb to AIDS, though he was to be by no means the last.

Hockney was deeply affected by the death of Joe McDonald, a man of great charm and gentleness who was loved by all who knew him. 'I thank you for introducing me to him,' Ann Upton later wrote to Hockney. 'I loved his kind naughty personality. I found it intensely appealing. I think of him every day. He understood you very well and loved your quirky foibles. He was proud and happy for your talent and humour. It was a great privilege for me to kiss him goodbye.'[17] After the funeral, Hockney remained in town to attend the rehearsals of *Varii Capricci*, which featured two of the Royal Ballet's star dancers, Antoinette Sibley and Anthony Dowell, he playing Lo Straniero, a strutting young gigolo, she La Capricciosa, the elegant mistress of an Italian villa with whom he flirts during a poolside party. It was being premiered on 19 April, and he had designed the backdrop, while Ossie Clark, at Hockney's suggestion to Ashton, had designed the costumes. In spite of the ups and downs in their relationship over the years, Hockney remained loyal to Clark, who was about to file for bankruptcy over a £14,000 tax bill. Clark flew in from London for the dress rehearsal, which took place on the same day as Joe McDonald's memorial service, and found Hockney in a black mood. 'David very morose about the Joe McDonald memorial service,' he recorded. '[I] was late for the Dress Rehearsal at the Metropolitan Opera House. "Well, you've missed it," said David in a fury. "Where were you? Just tell me what period this is supposed to be?" I felt very hurt with David's non-appreciation, but shrugged it off when Sir Fred came over, obviously very pleased. I told him DH wasn't thrilled with my costumes and he just shrugged his shoulders as though to say, "Well I'm very happy and that's all that matters." Fuck her dear, which is just what I thought – Poor David had made a little speech at Joe's memorial and was choked up.'[18]

Varii Capricci was a wild success, the *New York Times* critic Anna Kisselgoff describing it as 'a Carnaby Street ballet' that came as something of a surprise to the audience. She called the set, with its bright blue and orange colours, 'spectacular', and loved the 'tacky' costumes designed by Clark. But she also felt that the ballet showed a new side to Frederick Ashton, for though his genius and sense of humour were well known, his outlandish interpretation of the lead roles, which included dressing up Anthony Dowell as a gigolo in sunglasses, was a revelation.[19]

After the opening, Hockney took Clark back to LA for a few days to see Ann, who was struggling to cope with her life away from London. A big problem for her was that she couldn't drive, which made living in the vast sprawling suburb of Los Angeles very difficult. 'She had an awful lot of lessons,' David Graves remembers, 'and she had two driving instructors. The first was called Axle, and she took the test once or twice under his tutelage, but that failed. Then the driving school gave her Greg, an instructor who had two specialities – police chase and pursuit, and teaching nuns to drive. He tried to take her in hand, but she still failed. When it came to taking the test she just went all to pieces.'[20] So to keep busy, and for its Zen-like qualities, she had taken up the pastime of knotting and hooking rugs, and became the subject of another photo-collage, of Ian Falconer drawing her while she was engaged in this hobby. His face appears eight times in a state of intense concentration as he kneels over the paper on which he is drawing. He couldn't get her mouth right. 'It's the mouth that's really difficult, said DH,' wrote Clark in his diary. 'It's hard to get her to keep it still, said Ian.'[21]

At some point, Graves and Upton had made the decision that they should stay in California. This would not have been a problem for Graves, who had a working visa, but it would have presented difficulties for Upton as they were not married. 'We'd already been living together for a long time, but had never thought about doing it properly. So we'd been debating how we could get married in a wacky way, which is not difficult to do in America.' After months of gruelling work, both Graves and Hockney were ready for a holiday, so they decided to travel with Upton and Falconer to Kauai, an island in the Hawaiian archipelago, and stay at the Cocoa Palms Resort, made famous by the Elvis Presley movie *Paradise, Hawaiian Style*. On their first night there, they saw a notice advertising weddings in the 'Fern Grotto', a fern-covered lava rock grotto on the Wailua River. 'That sounded perfect for us,' Graves recalls, 'though we had to have a syphilis test first as Hawaii is so full of sailors.'[22]

Upton bought herself a special Hawaiian wrap dress for the ceremony, and on their wedding day they boarded a boat to take them upriver to the grotto and waterfall. 'There was a Hawaiian preacher there, non-denominational, wearing a wonderful Hawaiian mud-print blazer,' Falconer remembers, 'and he married them. And as he slightly dramatically intoned "and by the power that's invested in me", the background noise was the clicking of David's Pentax camera as he took literally hundreds of photographs of the ceremony. The whole thing reminded me of Evelyn Waugh's *The Loved One* in that it had the efficiency of an American funeral. In the evening we went back to the hotel which had a Tiki Tiki show in a big coconut grove, with all these guys dressed as Hawaiian natives with grass skirts and hula hoops, and it was all lit by kerosene lamps made out of old coffee tins. It was very charming and very pretty.'[23]

The Marriage in Hawaii of David and Ann became the last major photo-collage to be made by Hockney during this period, and he couldn't wait for people to see them, a sentiment shared by his mother. 'I think I have an obsession like you,' she wrote, 'to see these new pictures exhibited. I know I treasure and admire your pictures & hope you will do more – but these are artistic but so different and exciting.'[24] The first showing of the photo-collages took place at the André Emmerich Gallery in New York at the end of May, under the title *New Works with a Camera*. Among those attending the opening was Ren Weschler, a staff writer at the *New Yorker* who had recently become friends with Hockney, after being invited to tea to discuss his newly published book on the Californian artist Robert Irwin. On the way into the gallery on 57th Street, Weschler ran into a friend who was on the way out. 'I asked how she liked the show,' he recalled. 'You want to know the truth?' she replied. 'At first I was really liking it a whole lot but within about ten minutes I ended up fleeing in terror: it was too much like being inside somebody's eyeballs.'[25] Later, while discussing one of the new works with Hockney, a conversation piece featuring Christopher Isherwood and Don Bachardy, which he said made the photographic studies he'd done of them in 1968 look like they'd been taken in 1868, a first-year art student came up to him and gushed enthusiastically, 'You know what I like about these things? I've always been fascinated by insects' eyes . . . This is what the world must look like to a fly!'[26]

Critical appraisal for the collages was muted, with many reviewers not quite certain how to place them. Andy Grundberg in the *New York Times*, for example, devoted only three sentences to the exhibition, telling the readers that in the new works 'Mr Hockney . . . liberates photographic perspective from the tyranny of the lens',[27] while Christopher Knight, writing in the *L.A. Herald Examiner*, claimed 'Hockney's latest photomontages expose the limits of the medium'.[28] In London, where the show opened at Kasmin's in the week of Hockney's forty-sixth birthday, it went virtually unnoticed, with brief listings in *Time Out* and *The Times*, and a short paragraph by Waldemar Januszczak in the *Guardian* stating only 'This photographic cubism is rather effective'.[29] As for professional photographers, they were in disagreement as to the validity of the works. Although Henri Cartier-Bresson wrote to say how wonderful he thought the photographs were, David Bailey told *The Times* journalist Michael Young, 'It is nothing but rubbish, unoriginal and executed without any real understanding of what's going on.'[30]

This was a view that did not sit comfortably with Hockney's own opinion, given to Melvyn Bragg, the presenter of the flagship arts programme *The South Bank Show*, that what he was doing with photography might be considered more important than what he was doing as a painter. Bragg was intrigued enough to take a team out to California to film the creation of one of the photo-collages that Hockney used to refer to as 'joiners'. The subject was Ann Upton sitting by the pool, crocheting a rug, while a friend, Fredda, brings cups of tea. To try and prove that his joiner would give a more 'real' impression of the scene than a movie could, Hockney first filmed it using a 16mm cine camera, and then photographed the identical actions with a still camera, which took 160 different shots of the scene. He then took the film to Holloway Cleaners and 1Hr Processing where he gave them instructions to print everything, but unfortunately they rang an hour later to say that two of the rolls of film had been ruined in the processing. Undeterred, Hockney set about building up the picture using what was left. While doing so he found a note from the shop which read: 'Mr Hockney, I'm very, very sorry, very sorry about the two rolls of film. It was an accident. I thought I had pushed the button hard enough, but I didn't. I was trying to get your film done and I thought the machine was finished, but it never got started and I exposed it to light. I'm very, very sorry. I know it's not enough, but I didn't know what else I can do. Sorry again, Tom.' Typically unfazed by this setback, Hockney simply decided to incorporate both the note and some of the ruined roll into the work, which he titled *Fredda Bringing Ann and Me a Cup of Tea*.

Most interestingly, in the second half of the programme, he extended the idea of the joiner, attempting to make a movie joiner for *The South Bank Show* using their cine cameras. Shooting in London, at Pembroke Studios, he filmed the same scene nine times, each time covering a different part of the scene with the camera. When the nine separate films were processed, he would arrange them just as in a still joiner, and have them processed together in that shape. No one knew what the experiment would look like, and though the result was primitive, it was prophetic and showed that there was an unexpected richness to be found in the medium. 'The cinema needs cubifying, I'm

convinced,' he told an interviewer for *The Face*. 'A cubist revolution
has to come. Steven Spielberg knows what I mean. I think the time has
come when the artist has to deal with these things.'[31]

Photography had virtually taken Hockney away from the canvas for two
years, and in spite of the importance he felt of what he was doing,
there was a part of him that was beginning to grow weary of it. After
the opening of the Emmerich exhibition, walking with Ren Weschler
a few blocks from the gallery to the Museum of Modern Art, he stood
in front of a few favourite paintings. 'Immediately before us,' Weschler
remembered, 'were some Cézanne landscapes, and to the side a Picasso
and a Braque. Hockney was suddenly struck speechless. "Oh dear," he
sighed finally, taking a deep breath, "I truly must get back to painting."'[32]
He had the perfect excuse to do so, as Martin Friedman's show, which
was to be called *Hockney Paints the Stage*, was scheduled to open in
Minneapolis in the autumn.

Having carefully considered Friedman's suggestion that they might
include some of the original sets in the exhibition, Hockney had come
up with the idea of creating new works that would consist of a number
of specially made tableaux which would in effect be reinterpretations
of the original sets. Since these would be on quite a monumental scale,
neither the Santa Monica Boulevard studio, which was now anyway
taken up with photographic equipment, nor the front-room studio
at Montcalm Avenue would be big enough spaces in which to work
on them. As it happened, the solution was already in the pipeline: a
new studio, to be built on the site of a former paddle tennis court that
stood next to the house. Initially Hockney consulted the architect
Frank Gehry about the design, who told him that so long as he knew
what he wanted, he would only need an engineer rather than an
architect. In the end, the influential LA architect Carl Maston, a
specialist in garden-apartment design, created for him a large studio
with good northern light. 'It was terrific for him having the new
studio,' Ian Falconer remembers, 'because it had skylights, and both
incandescent and fluorescent lighting, the latter creating a daylight

effect at night. Before that, all the painting was done in the living room.'[33]

By the time the studio was completed and Hockney had finally got to work on his ideas, the opening of *Hockney Paints the Stage* was only a few months away. David Graves was roped in to help, and the Walker Art Center sent their own man, Ron Elliot, as an extra assistant. Because he was very big and wore shorts all the time, he was given the nickname 'Mountain Man'. 'He was terrific,' wrote Hockney, 'a very nice person . . . and wonderful to work with. He always knew when to leave me alone and when to help. When things needed cutting out he was good with the saw and he did all the measuring needed to make sure that what we did would fit in the gallery. But he also knew I needed quite a lot of time on my own when I just sat and worked things out and did them. He would then leave me alone . . .'[34] Elliot was equally impressed by Hockney, of whom he had previously had a rather different image. 'He told me afterwards,' Hockney said, 'he didn't know I *worked*. It was just life round the pool. Drugs and boys.'[35]

The exhibition was to open in November, and Friedman got more and more nervous until Hockney started work. He had already arranged for the show to travel to various other museums and galleries, so he wanted to make sure there were new things in it, and had decided that paintings should also be included. Hockney had thought that his idea of creating a series of tableaux would be relatively easy, since all he was doing was variations on the original sets, but, he realised, 'I had to animate them somehow. I'd pointed out to Martin that you couldn't just put a set in the exhibition, because sets are not designed to be just looked at, there are almost always people in them. He mentioned that there was somebody in Minneapolis who made stuffed animals.'[36] Since peopling the tableaux with stuffed animals was hardly the answer, Hockney came up with an idea that had its origins directly in the joiner photographs he had been making.

A few years previously Jerry Sohn had come across a large consignment of very small canvases in Paris, which he had bought for Hockney in the belief that one day they might come in useful, and these were all lying about in Los Angeles. While working on the first tableau for *Les Mamelles de Tirésias*, Hockney was struggling to find a way to do the figures, when he was struck by the concept of using the little canvases to build them up – one for the head, others for the torso, another for the legs, etc. 'I picked them up and started painting faces on them,' he wrote, 'and I realised immediately that I could use these to build up the figures for, say, the husband swapping into the role of the wife by swapping the canvases over. I did the figures in segments and I thought it was a good solution and that it looked good. Immediately I could see that my photo-collages were offering me some solutions to this.'[37] The next tableau, the Bedlam scene from *The Rake's Progress*, presented less of a problem because all the figures had masks. These were made out of styrofoam coated in plaster of Paris and mounted on poles which were then set into the original boxes from the Glyndebourne design.

For *The Magic Flute* he began by painting, on a massive forty-foot by ten-foot canvas suspended from the new studio wall, a backdrop based on a design for a desert garden in Sarastro's kingdom. Bright colours were applied using long-handled brushes. The cut-out animals were like sculptures. 'I decided I would cut out the figures from Styrofoam board,' he recalled, 'and break them up to show them moving, and I started fragmenting. This too came from the photography, and it turned out to be an interesting solution, much more interesting than stuffed animals. As you walked past them they all seemed to move – you, the viewer, were, in a sense, making them move. Once I'd discovered this, I got very excited.'[38] There was a sense of movement too in the set he made for *Le Rossignol*, made up as it was from numerous small canvases painted in shades of blue and white, which allowed the story to unfold as the viewer went by.

All this was an incredible workload, and Hockney threw himself into it with his customary vigour, creating seven huge pieces in a period of three months. 'It never ceased to amaze me,' David Graves recalls, 'the amount of energy he seemed to be able to pull out of the bag. It made me tired looking at him sometimes.'[39] But work was more than just fulfilling his artistic drive; it was also a way of escaping from the worries that were besetting him. The death of Joe McDonald had left him feeling empty, and sick with anxiety, a not uncommon feeling among the gay community in those days, and, even though he was still only forty-six, it had also made him confront for the first time his feelings about growing old. These concerns were compounded by his poor hearing, which was steadily deteriorating. '. . . my deafness is getting worse,' he had written to Kitaj from Kyoto, 'and with it my hatred of the telephone . . . that awful, noisy instrument.'[40] This often made him feel isolated and depressed. 'We lunched with Henry Geldzahler and his friend Raymond at the Century Club,' Stephen Spender had recorded in his diary of 5 May. 'In their – and my – company David became almost silent. Geldzahler made some conversational opening to him and David only murmured an inaudible reply. Henry said "Your attention span seems to be diminishing even further than before, David." I said, in an aside, to Henry – "Sometimes David does not hear what one says." . . . Owing to David's refusal to make any real effort – in effect to treat us as though we were scarcely there – the meal was boring and a bit embarrassing . . .'[41]

Hockney's deafness meant that he didn't want to go out in the way that he used to. 'I avoid large gatherings,' he said. 'I don't want to go, whereas before I might have enjoyed chatting away to people here and there. I can't do it now . . . I would rather stay at home and have two or three people for dinner than go out to a restaurant.'[42] He was also suffering from a general anxiety about his health, in particular his heart, from which he had suffered problems in the past, so he had put himself on a salt-free diet. 'Gregory thinks I am getting to be an old home-body,' he told Kitaj, 'but I don't mind that. I do want to stay home more. I do like sitting by the plastic fire up in the hills and reading. I care less about going out to restaurants, indeed with the salt-free diet I seem to have lost interest in food and there seem so few salt-free movies on TV, so I stick to the old low-sodium English literature.'[43]

None of this was much fun for Falconer, who at twenty-four was in full stride and loving the LA life, and was in no way ready to settle down and read by the plastic fire each evening. The inequalities of their relationship were beautifully demonstrated in *Waking Up*, a series of emotionally raw drawings that showed Hockney making attempts to persuade his lover to indulge in a bout of morning lovemaking after he

had been out on a night on the tiles. 'We were never really successful as sexual lovers,' Falconer recalls, 'because David is a voyeur. He likes exhibitionists who like to show off, and I was very embarrassed about my skinny little body. He thought it was beautiful, but I didn't, so it never really quite worked. And I liked to sleep late and he was always pestering me in the morning. He used to get frisky, and I was always saying "Leave me alone, for God's sake!" That's what the series *Waking Up* is all about, with me poking at his eye. I was quite irritated by the drawings at first and used to ask him, "Was I that mean to you?" But I'd often been out carousing the night before with my much younger friends from art school. They tell the story of the pretty boy with the older man.'[44] Hockney also transferred his deepest feelings to canvas in an extraordinarily personal *Nude Self-Portrait*, which brings to mind Egon Schiele's paintings of himself masturbating. On two small canvases that joined together, he portrayed himself naked on all fours on a bed, sporting a large erection, his body twisted round, his eyes closed and mouth open, his face simultaneously expressing both pain and lust.

Things came to a head in September in London where Hockney was overseeing the Covent Garden production of *L'Enfant et les Sortilèges*, on which both Evans and Falconer were assisting him. Stephen Spender attended the dress rehearsal, and found the production a great improvement on the one he had seen at the Met. 'In the Met it was certainly very beautiful,' he noted in his diary, 'but though I had a seat in the stalls, one had a bit the feeling that it was an "event" looked down on from a height . . . Here it looked like a stain-glass window in which figures and colours changed constantly as in a kaleidoscope which one was looking at from the nave of a cathedral. The music also seemed to fill the theatre and come from every direction . . .'[45] After the rehearsal, he lunched with Hockney and Evans at Bertorelli's restaurant, across from the opera house. 'David quite different,' he wrote, 'from the rather irritable brushing-off monologuising David I had been with a few months ago in New York . . . he didn't seem even physically deaf, and he seemed entirely at ease with others and himself. Gregory too was sensationally changed: thinner, younger-looking, fresh-complexioned, wide-eyed, short-haired, rather beautiful . . . Gregory said he had drunk no alcohol for a year. He also said that Ian had been thrown out by David in London. He has a funny way of talking about the discomfiture of his rivals, curiously without malice but with distinct pleasure and a gurgling amusement.'[46]

Hockney had no illusions about the effect the age difference had had on his relationship with Falconer, and it made him look at himself. In September he began work on a series of self-portraits, completing one each day. 'Every morning, before we started,' David Graves remembers, 'he'd do a charcoal self-portrait; chipper one day, gloomy the next, smoking, smiling, drawing. It was like a form of limbering up.'[47] This was something out of the ordinary for an artist who had previously shown himself to be quite unwilling to examine himself too closely. 'They were drawn mostly early in the morning,' Hockney recalled. 'I noticed if you did this they were always different: Not only did you have different expressions, you also had totally different moods and feelings, and that affects your mind. I realised that your mood is reflected in the way you draw the lines and marks. You also try to pick up the mood of the sitter, so in a portrait of someone else there are two moods. In a

*Self-Portrait with
Cigarette*, 1983

self-portrait it is the same mood . . . the self-portraits do reflect the fact
that even I was beginning to panic a little bit about the massive amount
of work I had taken on. I'm not a panicky sort of person – I keep very
cool; but I realised that I had to cover a lot of canvas and that I still had
to invent some of them. That is probably reflected in *Self-Portrait with
Cigarette, 1983*, a somewhat anguished look. I'm not panicking; if I was
panicking, I wouldn't even have drawn myself.'[48]

In these drawings he wiped away the public persona of the
gregarious, always cheerful, witty Yorkshireman, and replaced it with

the many and varying moods of what he saw as the real him. 'One of the most moving aspects of this series,' Marco Livingstone commented, 'is the honesty with which he represents his own occasional bouts of depression, as in the dejected expression of his *Self-Portrait with Cigarette* or the *Self-Portrait with Finger Behind Glasses*. It is curiously comforting to know that even someone with such a sunny disposition sometimes experiences such moods . . . What I value above all in these drawings is Hockney's avowal of our common humanity, his readiness to depict himself with the same honesty and casual forthrightness that has always marked his portrait of others.'[49]

Hockney's personal problems were compounded at this time by a major professional one. For the previous few years, Paul Cornwall-Jones, whose Petersburg Press was publishing the editions of the photo-collages, had in effect been acting as his business manager, with offices in London and New York working entirely on his behalf. 'David has a big ego, and he needs people to help him who understand him and are sympathetic to his foibles,' said Cornwall-Jones. 'He needed people to do things for him and he needed a constant income, without the pressure to produce work for sale. We diverted our energies into looking after him without being fully paid for our time and energy.'[50] Projects such as the one Cornwall-Jones and his team were currently working on were immensely expensive to run, and it was normal practice to fund the new project with the profits from the previous ones. In this case all the money that had been coming in had been diverted not just into paying the mounting bills, but into expanding the company, and when that started to run short, he had approached Hockney's dealers for further help.

'Paul Cornwall-Jones, unbeknownst to us, had got himself in a jam,' Peter Goulds recalls, 'and he didn't tell anyone about it. He came to each of the dealers individually to offer us the opportunity to expand our percentages by becoming in effect investors with him, according to how much we wanted to put up. Naturally, as we all represented David, we presumed that this was with David's knowledge. The dealers were Kasmin, Emmerich, Richard Gray and LA Louver. So to varying degrees we each became involved. But Paul was using the project to solve a larger problem. We all simply presumed that this was an incredibly expensive undertaking, which it was, going way beyond the normal scope of a publisher's reach. As it turned out, his problems were much larger, and he found himself in a financial jam, such that it called into question whether he could even complete the project, which in the end he couldn't.'[51] The result was that Petersburg Press declared themselves bankrupt, leaving the whole photo-collage project high and dry. In order to complete it himself, Hockney was eventually forced to sell work he had wanted to keep, something about which he felt extremely bitter.

With all this going on, and with only six weeks to go to the opening of *Hockney Paints the Stage*, Hockney still had two major pieces to finish, so under pressure from Friedman he decided to ship everything to Minneapolis. Once there, he started work first on the auction scene from *The Rake's Progress*, complete with all the objects in Baba's collection, the Egyptian mummies, the stuffed fish and alligators, hanging from the ceiling, and then on the garden from *L'Enfant et les Sortilèges*. Friedman may have been in a panic, but he had reckoned without the extraordinary energy of the artist and his team. 'All this was massive new work,' wrote Hockney, 'quite experimental in a way; it was thrilling to do because I didn't repeat much; I get bored just doing something over again . . . We worked seven days a week, twelve hours a day. The moment I'd done one of those tableaux, I realised how long they were going to take to work out, especially as I wanted to paint them all myself.'[52] And on top of this, he was still drawing a portrait every morning.

The show that finally opened in Minneapolis on 20 November 1983 was far removed from what Martin Friedman had originally envisaged. Hockney had taken it to a new level. '. . . the more he worked on the re-creation,' said Friedman, 'the more free-form it became. The set for *Le Rossignol* is close to total abstraction. It no longer looks exactly like the performed version; it now consists of a series, a big series of paintings, in which the elements appear almost montage-fashion — and it's much, much more interesting.'[53] Altogether he produced seven gallery-scale models of the Glyndebourne and Metropolitan productions that were in effect a series of installations, huge three-dimensional paintings, complete with lighting and sound, and populated with his first 'sculptures', made up of different-sized canvases, that represented the characters in the operas and ballets. For the spectator it was like moving through a series of enchanted grottos, each one conjuring up a different image and tone, culminating in the *pièce de résistance*, which was a room built around the idea of the ghostly garden in *L'Enfant et les Sortilèges*. Here the viewer walked into a complete environment that rethought the idea and, with the help of Ravel's music, re-created the atmosphere in a way that could never have been done in the theatre, but which constituted a vivid equivalent to the theatrical experience.

'One comes away,' wrote John Russell Taylor, after seeing the exhibition later at the Hayward Gallery in London, 'with an intense awareness of Hockney as a wholly practical man of the theatre, with no nonsense and no side. No hint of the dilettante here: brilliant and unflagging inventiveness to be sure, but also every evidence of the blood, sweat and tears which must have gone into the creation of these apparently effortless delights.'[54] The Minneapolis show opened to great acclaim, and was immensely popular, both there and at the six venues to which it travelled, bringing escalating fame to Hockney, along with the ever-increasing pressure on him that that entailed. It was the beginning of a period in which Hockney, driven by a combination of extreme creativity and emotional unrest, was to push himself to the limits, a situation that would ultimately lead to ill health. For the next few years, it was, says David Graves, 'production, production, production'.[55]

CHAPTER NINE

A WALK ROUND THE HOTEL COURTYARD, ACATLAN

Hockney's first paintings on his return to LA showed the direct influence of the 'sculptures' he had created for the Minneapolis exhibition. They were made up of more of the separate small canvases procured by Jerry Sohn, and included a self-portrait in five parts – one for the hair, two for the face, another one for the upper torso in a red-striped shirt, and the last for the lower torso and legs. There was also a two-panel portrait of Ian Falconer, and an eight-panel one of Peter Langan, who was in California to open a Los Angeles branch of his brasserie, a project that was doomed to failure owing to a combination of its location in Century City and Langan's almost permanently inebriated state. 'Forms have a way of transferring,' Martin Friedman told Paul Froiland in an interview for the arts magazine *Horizon* in November 1983. 'There was the transfer from painting to theatre design, and now, really, the transfer back from theatre design to painting, because as a result of this exhibition, David Hockney is now on another great journey.'[1] It was a journey towards what he was to call a 'new Cubism', a technique based on ideas gleaned from a variety of sources, predominately the work of Picasso, a newly discovered fascination with Chinese scrolls, and an interest in quantum physics that came from reading New Age books like *The Dancing Wu Li Masters* by Gary Zukav. 'I never thought I'd read a book like that,' he recalled. 'But once I did, I started making connections, and found myself in a deeply fascinating subject. I realised that Cubism is very deeply related to recent scientific ideas, with physics, with the idea that we can't separate ourselves from the world.'[2]

This is specifically what the Chinese artists had discovered, a fact that was revealed to him while browsing in the bookshop at the Walker Art Center. 'I came upon a book called *The Principles of Chinese Painting*,' Hockney remembered. '. . . I thought "Well, most Chinese painting looks the same to me." But I opened it, noticed the chapter headings, and one of them was called "Moving Focus." So I started to read it, bought the book, brought it back to the hotel, and got more and more excited.'[3] The reason he became so excited was that he realised that the book was an attack on perspective, because Chinese painting was all about the spectator being *in* the picture, not outside it. The way they had mastered this was by the form of the scroll. The artist painted his picture on a long and continuous piece of rectangular paper which was then rolled up, between two staffs of wood. It was designed to be slowly unfurled by the viewer from right to left, loosening one side and picking up the slack with the other, until they had 'walked' right through the landscape. 'In my own photo-collages,' Hockney continued, 'some of the ones I'd done on my trip to Japan . . . I'd been pushing the notion of the observer's head swiveling about in a world which was moving in time, but I'd really only just begun to try and deal with how to portray movement of the observer's whole body across space. And that's precisely what the Chinese landscape artists had mastered.'[4]

On a trip to London shortly afterwards, Hockney visited the Department of Asia at the British Museum to look at some rarely exhibited scrolls, and, later, passing through New York to see Ken Tyler, he contacted Mike Hearn, a curator of Asian art at the Metropolitan Museum, who was assigned to show him some of their collection, including the extraordinary seventy-foot-long *A Day on the Grand Canal with the Emperor of China*, commissioned by the Emperor in 1690. This probably took about a year to paint, and was only seen once by the Emperor before being rolled up and kept in the map archive in Beijing. Looking at it was a profound experience for Hockney. 'It was open on the floor,' he recalled, 'and I spent four hours looking at it on my knees, and it was one of the most thrilling afternoons I'd ever had. It was a marvellous work of art, totally unknown to me.'[5]

Over the next few weeks, Hearn showed Hockney thirty or

forty different Chinese scrolls, and his excitement at seeing them was infectious, especially to the other staff at the museum who were overjoyed to find a contemporary artist taking such a strong interest in what they considered their rather arcane discipline. The inspiration he took from them was put to good use on his return to California, starting with *A Visit with Mo and Lisa*, a five-foot by sixteen-foot gouache of the Echo Park home of Mo and Lisa McDermott, a charming little house with a lush garden and a workshop in the backyard. In this picture, which portrays both the interior and the exterior of the house, the constantly shifting focus carries the eye from point to point, through the rooms and in and out of the patio in a more or less horizontal path that is not dissimilar to a scroll painting.

Hockney considered this gouache somewhat crude compared to his next work, which stands out as one of the major paintings of the period. He had been spending a lot of time with Christopher Isherwood and Don Bachardy, as he was thinking of doing a new picture of them, and had actually started work on a portrait of the former, who had recently been diagnosed with prostate cancer. 'For a week I had gone down every morning,' he wrote to Stephen Spender, 'just to get a feel of them in their house in the day time – I'm so used to it at night. Each morning I'd sit and have tea with them, but Christopher didn't really sit down (I think it was just too painful for him) and he just stood around in his blue bath robe, his hands were almost always clenched, and that is how I am painting him. I have made the hands much bigger than they should be to emphasise the clenching which I assumed was to contain the pain. I noticed my father doing that a lot the last time I was with him.'[6]

The new painting that emerged from these visits, *A Visit with Christopher and Don, Santa Monica Canyon, 1984*, was a far cry from the cool, studied portrait he did of them in 1968. The symmetry and precision of the former had given way to an intricate system of cubist perspective shifts designed to take the viewer on a journey through the house and its surroundings. 'I was trying to create a painting,' he said, 'where the viewer's eye could be made to move in certain ways, stop in certain places, move on, and in so doing reconstruct the space across time for itself. I was combining lessons from both the Chinese scrolls and my study of Cubism . . . This sense of multiple simultaneous perspectives was something I'd of course honed during my work on the photocollages.'[7] It was an enormous work, twenty feet in width, and was intended to be read from left to right. The fact that he had placed Bachardy and Isherwood at opposite ends of the canvas demanded that the spectator make the journey from Bachardy's studio to Isherwood's study, taking them down steps into the living room, through the dining room and bedrooms, past the windows with their views of cliffs and the ocean, upstairs and downstairs. It was, he commented, 'the most complicated painting I've ever done'.[8] In this work, space and time merge and all the themes that characterise Hockney's pictures – portrait, landscape and domestic interior – are integrated.

The creation of shifting-focus images became Hockney's new obsession and he found inspiration in the unlikeliest of sources. After Minneapolis, Martin Friedman had arranged with its director, Robert Littman, for *Hockney Paints the Stage* to move to the Museo Tamayo in Mexico City. Designed by the architects Abraham Zabludovsky and Teodoro González de León, and inaugurated in 1981, the museum had been built to house the collection of the Mexican artist Rufino Tamayo. For Hockney, Mexico was new territory, his experience of the country being limited to a visit to some border towns, and before he went he read as much as possible about its history, including William H. Prescott's *The History of the Conquest of Mexico*, whose insights into the Aztec practice of human sacrifice both horrified and fascinated him. He drove down for the 19 February opening with Gregory Evans and David Graves. 'Mexico was wonderful,' Evans recalls, 'and it was a discovery for all of us. There was a lively arts scene in Mexico City, which we didn't know about. We had a fantastic time there.'[9]

With its bright colours, sculptural figures, and abundance of birds and animals, the exhibition was made for Mexico. 'The Mexicans loved it,' wrote Hockney. 'I worried a bit that if they did not know the operas it would not mean much to them. I think what attracted them was the hand-done look it had, the colour. Mexicans love colour, and they're good with their hands. In some ways they're very close to art . . .'[10]

After the show had opened, Hockney, Evans and Graves drove from Mexico City to Oaxaca and on the way the car broke down in Acatlán, a small town in the Mexican state of Hidalgo. 'We stayed in what seemed to be a funky little hotel,' Evans remembers. 'The beds were old and it was a little bit run-down and dusty. You wouldn't necessarily have wanted to live there, but it was charming.'[11]

The name of the hotel was the Hotel Romano Angeles. It had rooms arranged around a central courtyard, which had exotic trees and plants growing in it, and a central well, and this courtyard became the inspiration for a number of sketches with a view to a painting. The group were there for the best part of a week, much to the chagrin of Evans and Graves. 'There was nothing to do in Acatlán for the rest of us!' recalls Evans. 'But David was happy and that's all that mattered.'[12] He was in fact ecstatic, mesmerised by what he saw as the 'wonderful space' within the courtyard. When he returned to LA he immediately set to work on a three-foot by ten-foot painting on two canvases, in which he showed the garden viewed from inside the covered terrace, but used reverse perspective so that the straight lines of the terrace became curved as the eye scanned the scene. Excitedly he bent the ears of anyone who would listen about the magic of the hotel in Acatlán.

'I am now doing a painting of a courtyard of a Mexican hotel,' he wrote to Kitaj. 'I loved the space of it when I first discovered it, and went back to stay for five days. It has so many different perspectives that you are forced to move your eye constantly over the surface of the canvas. It is a totally impossible view from one point, yet there is a clarity and order about the picture. The effect of the space is extremely strong, yet it is not an illusion you want to walk in to, – because you are already in the picture and walking round – every viewer so far feels this. This also has the effect of seeming to soften the edges of the canvas – you are not looking through a hole. The effect is, as I've said, very powerful indeed, and one seems to want to go on looking and looking at it. Like the photographs, there is no way it can all be seen easily or at once, yet it is always recognisable as a courtyard. In short the only way it can be seen all at once is as an abstraction, which is what it is, as are all things on a flat surface.'[13]

He also got back in touch with Ken Tyler. Tyler was more than keen to collaborate on a new project with Hockney, though he knew that getting him to commit was always fraught with difficulty. 'Each time was a rite of fire to get permission to get going,' he remembers. 'I was working on expensive projects and funding the new ones with the profits of the previous ones. So whenever David would call, or it looked like there might be an opening, I had to measure whether I could leave the project I was working on and go to David and have a project, or maybe not.'[14] At this time, Tyler was particularly excited because he had recently devised a new technique for printing, on which he had been working for the previous two years. It was called the Mylar technique. Mylar was a stretched sheet of very thin plastic, which even when coated and frosted was still semi-transparent, and could then be drawn on. It was like drawing on acetate, and because you could see through it, it was possible to make multiple drawings, using a different colour each time, in perfect registration. This solved the perennial problem when making colour lithography or coloured etching of registrating whatever you were drawing onto whatever you had drawn before.

After enthusiastically describing the Mylar technique over the telephone, Tyler was invited to LA to give a demonstration. He took with him a special sketchbook he had made up with transparent Mylar and acetate sheets, and crayons custom-made for the project. The separate transparent sheets gave Hockney the ability to isolate each of his colours, thereby simulating the colour separation process of lithography, so that as he worked on his initial sketches he was able to visualise the final prints. 'He told me it was fantastic,' Tyler recalls, 'and asked if he could draw any size he wanted. So on my next trip I brought another bigger book with me, and he said, "Let's go back to the Hotel Acatlán." So I called up the hotel and told them I wanted two suites. When I told him what I'd done, he chuckled, and I thought, "Ha ha, he obviously knows something I don't." Well, when we got to the hotel I found out that it hadn't got any suites, just little monks' cells which consisted of a bed and a little open stall, and each morning the maid would come in and throw a bucket of disinfected water into the stall, and that was the shower, the john and everything else!'[15]

David Hockney registering a prepared Mylar sheet for his 16-colour *Views of Hotel Well I*

The return trip to Acatlán with Tyler and Evans marked the beginning of an intense period of work that was to last the better part of a year, during which Hockney further explored the subjects of space, movement and time in painting. It started with the week spent at the Hotel Romano Angeles, where Hockney made numerous drawings of the courtyard using the Mylar sketchbooks. Tyler himself did not share his romantic view of the surroundings. 'The garden that David loved so much in the courtyard was all fakery,' he says, 'like something that a poor Latino family might have created in Los Angeles in their backyard, but he thought it was wonderful and it turned him on. So with his magical mind he created this luscious thing from something that was not luscious at all, but really quite barren.'

When the week was over, Tyler returned to Bedford Village to proof all the sketches, while Hockney returned to California where he had to put the finishing touches to an upcoming show that was to take place in October at the Emmerich Gallery, as well as travelling to the openings of *Hockney Paints the Stage* in both Ontario and Chicago. It was while attending the latter, at Chicago's Museum of Contemporary Art, that a momentous decision was made relating to the sale of his works. In his role as his brother's accountant, Paul Hockney called together all the dealers who handled his work, namely John Kasmin, André Emmerich, Richard Gray and Peter Goulds, and made an announcement. 'I told them, "He isn't giving any of you anything exclusive any more. He'll give you things when he wants to." They didn't like that particularly, but they had to accept it. They were all nattering him for exhibitions and he was saying to me, "I don't really want to give them anything particularly." In the end he said, "You can have exhibitions but I'll do it in my time, not yours. That really did take the pressure off him."'[16] For Hockney, still smarting from the collapse of Petersburg Press, this was a watershed moment. 'The resolution that came out of that meeting,' Peter Goulds remembers, 'was that from then on David would look after his own affairs and look after his own work, and we would all work through him, and what became the studio. From that point on he was controlling his own destiny.'[17]

Hockney was the talk of the town the week that the Emmerich show opened in New York, coinciding as it did with a new book of his photography, *Cameraworks*, being published by Alfred A. Knopf, the first commercial showing in the US of *A Bigger Splash,* opening at the Guild's Embassy 72nd Street Theatre, and his appearance at the Guggenheim Museum in a charity production of Picasso's play, *Le Désir attrapé par la queue,* in which he read the part of Swell Foot, alongside fellow performers who included Louise Bourgeois, Larry Rivers, Marisol and Philippine de Rothschild. The show was of particular importance for Hockney, as it was his first exhibition of new paintings for two years and was to establish him as an artist who could now command significantly high prices. It also demonstrated how productive he had been during the previous year. The influence of Picasso was clear, in images of Christopher Isherwood with and without glasses, three luscious portraits of Celia Birtwell, and the full-length painting of Peter Langan in which his body, seen from different angles, was split cubistically over eight canvases. The two large panoramas, *A Visit with Mo and Lisa* and *A Visit with Christopher and Don*, were also on show, though the latter was not for sale. The response to the exhibition 'both critically and financially', wrote Nathan Kolodner, from the André Emmerich Gallery, was 'no less than spectacular'. *Celia with her Foot on a Chair*, a small painting, fetched $50,000, the huge vista of the McDermotts' house in Echo Park went for the enormous sum of $240,000, while a large print of the McDermotts' backyard fetched $100,000, a record for a work on paper. 'We are delighted with the great success of this show,' Kolodner continued, 'but most of all it was such a joy to live with this exceptional body of work for the last few weeks.'[18]

Among the works on display were a number of the photo-collages, including a new one, made in June, which was a spectacular pastiche of the famous nude calendar shot of Marilyn Monroe, reprised by the actress Theresa Russell. Unusually, *Nude, London 1984* was a commission, from her husband, the film director Nicolas Roeg, who wanted to use it in his new film, *Insignificance*, a comedy-drama that featured the characters of Monroe, Joe DiMaggio, Joe McCarthy and Albert Einstein. Hockney saw this as an excuse to find a way of pushing the boundaries of erotic photography. 'Only erotic photographs inspire you immediately to look for more than 30 seconds,' he commented, 'and my pin-up requires you to look very slowly, you are forced to move over every inch of her body which makes it more interesting, more erotic. It was the most complicated photo collage I had attempted, because I wanted to push my ideas further. Every one of the 170 photographs is taken from a different position. It is really just like drawing – I could do whatever I wanted.'[19] It was a remarkably sexy image, which he put to good use when Ian Falconer's father was in hospital, mortally ill with pancreatic cancer. Hockney made several visits to see him. 'One time he came,' Falconer remembers, 'and he brought with him the large photo-collage of Theresa Russell as Marilyn Monroe, and took down all the pictures on the wall of the hospital room and put this up in their place. So my father had this great nude to look at.'[20]

With the Emmerich show out of the way, Hockney moved up to Bedford Village to work with Ken Tyler, primarily on the lithographs that had come about from the trip to the hotel in Acatlán. But like all projects in which he became involved, as his interest increased, the whole thing became much bigger. Initially it was his excitement with the new process that got his blood up. 'This Mylar technique was really quick,' Ken Tyler explains, 'so we could get proofs to him within an hour or so. You didn't have to wait days for plates to be processed. David loved that. He loved seeing the results quickly. He loved having many possibilities on the wall before he went to bed, and he loved getting up in the night to go and visit them, and he loved getting up in the morning and having three thousand questions for me. He was able to push things because they were quick and they were matching his restlessness.'[21] In the lithographs of the hotel courtyard, the eye of the viewer was forced to move rapidly round the picture in order to take in all its elements. He employed multiple perspectives, and, to further activate the eye, used vibrant colours, vivid reds, yellows and blues, to bring to life the courtyard lit by the bright Mexican sun.

After spending the Christmas break with his mother, and some time in London, where he made preparatory sketches for a series of lithographs of his rooms in Pembroke Studios, Hockney went with Celia Birtwell to Paris, where the spectre of AIDS had raised its ugly head again in the person of his old friend Jean Léger, who had been given only a short time to live and in whose honour friends were throwing a party. Though the trip was a sad one, and Léger died a few weeks later, Hockney did take back from Paris ideas that were to prove useful. On their arrival, he and Birtwell had visited the Grand Palais to look at a major exhibition of paintings by Watteau. 'There was a little painting of a woman being powdered by her servant,' wrote Hockney. 'It's called *La Toilette Intime* – very pretty, a charming picture, beautifully painted. You feel the skin and the softness. Well, next day we went to the Beaubourg . . . and there was a little Picasso in which you could see the front and the back of a girl. Now, if you can see the front and the back, it means that you, the viewer, are in the picture. You weren't in the Watteau, you were a voyeur, looking from a distance. Picasso has done something more complex. He's made us not voyeurs, but participants. And that seems to me to be an incredible achievement . . .

It's more exciting and it makes the world more intimate by drawing us into it.'[22]

The painting, *Sleeping Woman*, was a nude study of Picasso's mistress and model Marie-Thérèse Walter, and with it fresh in his mind, on his return to Ken Tyler's he embarked on a whole series of what might be termed 'Picassoid' portraits, such as a life-size painting of Gregory Evans in two halves, with his face seen from different angles and his hands in two positions, and a number of images of Birtwell, culminating in the complicated *An Image of Celia*, which was worked on over the next two years, and which required thirty-five different colours in the final proof. Not content with merely making these prints, Hockney also designed and painted frames for them, which were made up by a framer in LA, rekindling the interest in frames he had shown in his first set of lithographs, *A Hollywood Collection*, back in 1965. Though many critics were only too ready to attach the label of 'pastiche' to these works, Tyler was quick to defend them. 'I think it's unfair to use that word about David's work that was influenced by Picasso,' he says. 'I think he was trying to come up with another language, a language that did have its roots in Picasso, but so what? Artists have always copied other artists. What David did with it was he moved his drawing style to another level of boldness. The drawings he did with the moving focus are a tougher stroke. They're more theatrical.'[23]

Hockney brought back for Tyler to proof cubist-inspired sketches of his mother, and a series of his rooms in Pembroke Studios, the most complicated of which, *Walking Past Two Chairs*, required twenty-one printings. He also began work on a four-panel screen printed with scenes taken from the sketchbook he had kept on trips to the Caribbean island of Mustique with Nathan Kolodner. These were holidays which demonstrated just how far up in the world Hockney had come, renting the grand villa of Lord and Lady Glenconner, hanging out with Princess Margaret, and even, much to the amusement of Gregory Evans, playing cricket for a team organised by the photographer Lord Lichfield. He started work on the screen, titled *Caribbean Teatime*, in 1985 but did not complete it for another two years. 'Screens were very much part of the art world at that time,' Ken Tyler recalls. 'We'd been working on a Helen

Frankenthaler screen, and there was a big Chinese study of screens at the Met. It was the only one David made, though we had talked about making the *Paper Pools* into screens, but had never got round to it.'[24]

The final work connected with this period was made back at the studio in Montcalm Avenue, and was of the hotel courtyard in Acatlán. It was a huge oil painting, on two canvases that measured six foot by twenty foot, in which the eye was literally made to take a walk round the picture, hence the title, *A Walk Around the Hotel Courtyard, Acatlán*. It was a picture not about a hotel but about an attitude to space. 'Some people have observed,' Hockney wrote, 'that, since about 1980, the human figure is absent from my work. The main reason for that is that I have wanted the viewer to become the figure. The figure is still there but in another way entirely: not depicted, it is meant to be felt. That was a conscious decision. The human *clay* is not there, literally, not in the same way as before, but the *mind* is.'[25]

Hockney believed there was also another element at work in his growing fascination with space and perspective, and that was connected to his increasing deafness. 'My mad theories seem to be working and where they are leading is exciting and unknown,' he told Kitaj. 'Let me begin by making one observation that only hit me very recently. About a month ago I got another hearing aid for my left ear. The effect is amazing. Music is more alive again (I hear the treble notes) and sound seems spatial, and made me think that over the last years to compensate for my muffled ears I developed a strong visual space sense. I say this because I'm very aware I seem to see in another way that has to do with noticing movement of the eye (time) and perception of space. A blind man develops his hearing to define his space; could not a deaf person develop his sight? No one of course would know this unless the person was an artist who was expressing (like the blind man who is a piano tuner). Anyway there's no doubt that either from the theatre or somewhere else I became more aware of space and time. All the photography is to do with it, and all the subsequent paintings, and something is happening in the paintings that seems like a new kind of pictorial space to me.'[26]

*

While this frantic amount of work was ongoing, there were the usual turbulent goings-on in Hockney's personal life. The death of Jean Léger had brought AIDS back to the fore. Falconer had moved out, and Evans was hitting the bottle again. 'Phone David Hockney in LA,' Ossie Clark noted in his diary at the beginning of April. 'He also incredibly depressed. Poor David H. Gregory's drinking will just about finish him off . . . he sounded so low. "Don't think of coming here just yet," he moaned. "Let me sort this lot out first." . . . Poor David. Despite all his riches, he sounds worse off than I do.' Evans's drinking had repercussions for everybody, and caused huge tension at work. 'It was not an easy time,' Tyler recalled, 'because the problems with Gregory caused constant interruptions. When he came to visit, it was sometimes ok and then not ok. It's important to say this, because those were quite serious interruptions. If David was worried about Gregory and Gregory was there posing, David might make a sketch or two and then get terribly involved with Gregory and then disappear for a couple of hours and then he'd come down and there'd be no finished drawing, so we might have to wait another two or three days before we'd see another Gregory drawing, and then it would be done, and would be full of the fantastic emotion and feeling he had for Gregory in it, and then we'd quickly print it.'[27]

It didn't help either that Montcalm Avenue was upside down, with the interior being revamped and enlarged, while David and Ann Graves had decided to return to London the previous year, for reasons that Graves laid out in a letter. 'Ann and I came back to London,' he wrote, 'for the simple reason that neither of us felt comfortable with Los Angeles as a place to live, and we both knew that we would not be able to do so indefinitely. That is something that is unlikely to change, as you probably realise. Home, as they say, is where the heart is and, unfortunately for me, my heart is in London.'[28] They had stayed for about fifteen months before coming to their decision, which they were certain was the right one. 'I remember when we landed in London,' Graves says, 'I felt like kissing the tarmac.'[29]

Their decision was not without its regrets, however, even though they knew it was the right one, as Ann wrote to Hockney. '. . . if it hadn't been for you last year, I don't think I would have got through. Even as I am now, which we both know is not the same as before, or perhaps I seem the same to others, I think you know different. I have to admit life has been pretty unbearable. I've settled down to a slow "jog trot" of sorrow in which I "try" to count my blessings which my reason tells me are many – especially you and David. Of course I miss California. I miss you and seeing what you are up to. I didn't realise how much it would mean to me giving up my front seat in the stalls. I miss lots of the general daftness, and I know you won't mind me admitting I miss our little friend Ian who I have to say was a big help to me . . . despite all this I am better here – I suppose like a fish in its own pond. You are unusual in that way. Although you love human companionship – in essence you are an island. You don't need outside stimulation to make you tick. Your mechanism is self-winding. In my experience this is most unusual. You just have a little thought for most of us who are not like that even if you despise it a little.'[30]

The arrangement was that David Graves would continue working for Hockney from London, occasionally helping with the odd project in LA. He worked on the Mylar prints at Ken Tyler's, before returning to London to prepare for Hockney's visit there in the summer for the opening of two exhibitions – *Hockney Paints the Stage* at the Hayward Gallery, and *Wider Perspectives Are Needed Now*, a show at Kasmin's of some of the completed Ken Tyler prints and the large painting *A Walk Around the Hotel Courtyard, Acatlán*. On Hockney's arrival in England at the beginning of July, in the middle of a heatwave, Graves accompanied him to Bradford to help with the creation of a panoramic photo-collage showing the National Museum of Film and Photography in Bradford, complete with its 'horrible walkways' and the statue of Queen Victoria opposite. Crowds of locals turned out to watch the artist at work, and the local paper, the *Telegraph & Argus*, even inveigled his brother Paul to create his own photo-collage showing himself and Hockney sitting at a table that was laden with beer cans.

On his return to London, *The Times* interviewed Hockney. 'Now 48,' wrote their correspondent, 'the Bradford boy wonder still sports a jaunty cheese-cutter hat and peroxide hair, but the years have given his face the look of Mr Punch and he has exchanged his Sony Walkman for a pair of pink hearing-aids. Judging from the way listeners to his recent theories on perspective go blank and shift in their seats, the general opinion is that he has gone a little mad.'[31] He certainly bent the ear of anyone within reach, be it a journalist or his oldest friend. 'Went unwashed . . . to see DH,' wrote Ossie Clark in his diary on 23 July. 'We had tea, and I sat reading in the garden, in beautiful sunlight . . . He asked me how I am, but he is hardly interested and soon changed the subject to his own work . . . He showed off his recent work of which he is very proud. How we need reverse perspective to put us back in the real world and in touch with God.'[32]

Hockney also discussed Gregory Evans with Clark, his worsening condition being a constant cause for concern, and, wrote Clark, 'we, or rather he, brought up the subject of AIDS'. This was brought on by the fact that the news had just come through that Rock Hudson, Hockney's friend and neighbour in LA, had been identified as a sufferer and was seriously ill in a hospital in Paris. After some discussion of the subject and of their various friends who had recently been diagnosed, such as Kasmin's former business partner Sheridan Dufferin, they went their separate ways. 'Before he left,' noted Clark, 'he said "Cheer up, Ossie, it could be worse." "I know", I replied. "I could have AIDS," which made him laugh – or rather brought a smile to his lips. He seems quite happy. Pleased with his work, I expect.'[33]

Clark had put his finger right on the button. Whatever else was going on around him, if his work was going well, Hockney was happy and always ready to share that happiness and enthusiasm. Marina Vaizey, writing in the *Sunday Times*, referred to 'the magic of Hockney's enthusiastic delight . . . [He] is a proselytiser, giving interviews, sell-out lectures, making not only his art but his views – on the primacy of drawing for example – widely accessible . . . On press day at the Hayward, interviewers were lined up three deep, and the artist took many a photocall.'[34] *Hockney Paints the Stage* opened on 1 August, preceded by the usual week of lunches and dinners and private views, attended by a mixture of the art world, socialites, personal friends and family, and the occasional cluster of what Ossie Clark referred to as 'gushing sycophants'.[35]

There were mixed reviews for the show. Vaizey called it 'absolutely delightful and exceptionally instructive',[36] and Richard Cork, writing in the *Listener*, said it was 'a spectacular delight'.[37] While these were opinions largely shared by the public, who flocked to see it, Hockney did have his share of detractors. 'The emphasis is entirely on fun, fun, fun,' wrote Waldemar Januszczak in the *Guardian*. 'The result is a completely vacuous, cardboard exhibition.'[38] Tim Hilton, writing in the *Observer*, considered that Hockney's 'implied connections with Picasso do not indicate much self-knowledge. One would like to see painting by Hockney that is sincerely without quirks, mannerisms or pastiche.'[39] One person who viewed it without criticism was Laura Hockney, whose three days in London for the private view had been a treat. 'I could just say a big "THANK YOU" & stop there!' she wrote to him. 'But I do want you to know how very much I enjoyed our time together. It was so full . . . I can't count the friends who remember me "by my picture" – those whom I remembered & was so happy to meet – and those whom we rarely meet but feel almost intimate with. I am so thrilled that your work brings such pleasure . . . to so many people. God Bless you my dear son.'[40]

With the London opening at the Hayward behind him, Hockney set off for France, to give a lecture at the prestigious Rencontres Internationales de la Photographie, a summer festival of photography that took place annually in the south in Arles. Founded in 1970 by the photographer Lucien Clergue, the author Michel Tournier and the historian Jean-Maurice Rouquette, its aim was to show almost exclusively new work by both established and up-and-coming photographers, in a variety of interesting architectural sites. In that summer of 1985, Hockney found himself lecturing and showing his work alongside, among others, Sebastião Salgado, Robert Capa, Eugene Richards and Fritz Gruber. The title of his lecture was 'On a besoin de plus grandes perspectives'.* Among those attending the festival was Paul Wagner, the art director

* 'Wider perspectives are needed'.

of French *Vogue*, who had flown down from Paris to invite Hockney to produce a feature for their upcoming December issue. Special Christmas issues were something of a tradition for the magazine, and artists who had previously been involved included Salvador Dalí, who had edited and illustrated the December 1971 issue, Joan Miró, who had done a special issue in December 1979, and Franco Zeffirelli, whose *La Traviata* had featured on the cover of the 1984 Christmas issue. 'When they first asked me, I refused,' Hockney recalled. 'I didn't know enough about fashion, and I was not interested in it anyway. Then they said it didn't need to be about fashion, it could be about anything. I thought, If it can be about anything, then I'll do it. I thought we could make my kind of photo-collages work on the page . . . and show therefore, that it's possible to break photography up, change it, provided it worked on the printed page. After all, forty pages in the middle of *VOGUE* is forty pages in the middle of pictures which make use of one-point perspective, because all the rest of the photographs in the magazine are made in the conventional way. I wanted to show how photography could be done differently.'[41]

Typically, in asking Hockney to edit a whole section of pages for them, *Vogue* got a great deal more than they bargained for. They had asked him to deliver his layouts by the beginning of October, a relatively short time, but they had thought they would be getting reproductions of his existing work, chosen and laid out by him, to be accompanied with a text by a writer of their own choosing. He didn't want to do that, seeing the whole exercise instead as an opportunity to test his recent ideas about photography. 'I realised,' he wrote, 'that the whole section in *Vogue* was a work by me, not comment on my work by *Vogue*, it was my work deliberately made for the magazine. I designed the pages, I did the layout, I did everything. I said I wanted to control every square centimetre of those pages from beginning to end, even the way they put the numbers on the page. And so the whole section became the work.'[42]

Returning to Los Angeles with David Graves, he pinned a number of blank sheets of paper up on the studio wall and began work on the layouts, which were to include not just reproductions of work he had already made, such as a portrait of Gregory Evans and a view of the courtyard of the hotel in Acatlán, reproduced in a four-page fold-out, but a number of complicated new photo-collages, both of American subjects such as Mo and Lisa McDermott in their house in Echo Park, and a Hollywood hustler hitchhiking, and of French ones, represented by views of the Place Furstenberg and the Luxembourg Gardens. These, he had established with the art department, would bleed to the edge of the magazine's page. 'I told them I wanted no borders around the photographs and no internal borders, which would mean more edges.'[43]

Hockney devised his pages to be a lesson on perspective, beginning with the words, all handwritten with pen or brush. 'The Chinese landscape painting is a walk through a landscape, the spectator is involved and surrounded and participates in nature. The static viewpoint is avoided.' He followed this with the statement 'Here are some pictures and thoughts on Time; Space; Illusion; Seeing; Drawing; Colour; Surface; Collage; Printing; Perception; Suggestion; Perspective; Photography; and Magazines', before devoting the rest of the section to 'The Perspective Lesson'. The most complicated part of the exercise was getting the photo-collages to fit the shape of the pages. 'We started working on the photo-pieces, but making them into a rectangle was not easy, because the way I had pieced things together up to then, none of them ever became rectangles. Making them into a rectangle was much more complex; it meant you had to be moving about.'[44]

The final two weeks were spent in Paris where he and David Graves worked in their hotel room. 'When he was doing the Place Furstenberg collage,' Graves remembers, 'and it was all laid out on the floor of our hotel room, Guy Bourdin came to visit. He stood looking at it, never taking off his sunglasses in spite of the fact that it was quite dark in the room. And he said, "I would love to be able to draw. Why on earth are you doing photographs?" He could hardly bear to look at it.'[45]

The last step was to decide what he was going to use as a cover image. Knowing that this was usually the face of a beautiful woman, he decided to paint a special picture for it, of his long-time muse Celia Birtwell. To make sure that the magazine would really stand out on the Paris news-stands, he painted her with heavy mascara and make-up, as a cover girl would normally be wearing, and in the style of Picasso. Later he was to include this image in the completed lithograph, *An Image of Celia*. Hockney was delighted with the final result. 'I am reaching a much wider audience than the readership of *Arts Review* or *Artscribe*,' he said at the time. 'There's nothing wrong with being associated with a magazine like *Vogue* whose accent is on fashion and commercialism. They will sell 120,000 copies, half of them abroad, and each will be seen by more than one person. I'm reaching a quarter of a million people with my ideas . . . I'm not that concerned with art world criticism and opinion of my work. I know I'm keeping Modernism alive with my ideas about seeing and depicting.'[46]

When Hockney got back to America in October, he found the country gripped by a wave of Anglomania brought on by the imminent arrival, on an official visit, of the Prince and Princess of Wales. Moreover, he found a number of messages from the White House to say that President and Mrs Reagan wished him to attend the gala dinner they were giving for the royal couple. Though his initial inclination was to refuse, he was eventually persuaded by his friends, most of whom would have given their eye teeth to have gone, that it would be rude not to attend, so he accepted and booked himself into the Hay Adams Hotel, across from the White House. After donning his black tie, he decided to walk to the dinner, only to be told on his arrival at the gates that he could only enter by car. He walked back to the hotel, where a limousine duly collected him and delivered him to the front door.

By now Hockney was dreading the whole event, but was a little cheered up when he went in and met two friends, the photographer Norman Parkinson and the philanthropist Drue Heinz. After talking to them for a while, he was given his table card, secretly hoping that it would be a corner table somewhere so that he could leave early without any difficulty, only to find out to his horror that he was seated at the President's table, along with Princess Diana, Mrs Walter Annenberg, Leontyne Price, Jacques Cousteau, Dorothy Hamill and Mikhail Baryshnikov. Reagan had a table plan beside him so he could remember

who everyone was, and Hockney soon realised, from the way he could
see him reading lips, that Reagan was very deaf. Since he was the only
person at the table who Reagan didn't know, whenever he spoke to him
he would use his name, such as, 'The wines are from California, David.'
They dined on lobster mousseline, spicy glazed chicken and peach
sorbet. Then, when the coffee was being served and Reagan got up
to speak, just before Princess Diana took to the dance floor with John
Travolta, he made a toast to 'Prince Charles and Princess David'. It was
a story Hockney would dine out on for weeks to come.

Back in LA, Gregory Evans had reached rock bottom. 'By the end
of 1985,' Hockney recalls, 'Gregory's drinking was completely out of
control. Mo had a nickname for him – Grogory. I knew it was very bad
when one time I went to collect him from New York and he drank about
six rums on the plane and was still able to just walk off. He had become
abusive to me all the time, but I always thought he was worth saving,
because he's a person of some depth, not a shallow person at all.'[47]
Watching this happen to perhaps his closest companion was devastating.
'It was absolutely terrible,' he told Peter Webb. 'I didn't understand. I'd
say "Why don't you just stop drinking and taking drugs, what are you
doing to yourself?" Slowly I realised how serious it was, how deeply
alcohol affects people. I had to put up with it. Then eventually I got him
into a hospital and he hated me for it.'[48]

After spending two months in the Beverly Glen Treatment Program
on Beverly Drive, and then attending AA meetings, Evans came to a
realisation. 'I knew then,' he says, 'that in order for me to stay sober,
I had to keep away from Montcalm Avenue, as it was no longer a safe
environment for me. So I got my own place in Echo Park. David didn't
like this, and he made it quite clear that if I wasn't living with him, then
he didn't want me working for him any more.'[49] At the end of January
1986, he received a letter from Paul Hockney that made the separation
official. 'I am sorry to be writing this letter to you, but I do feel the
situation between David and yourself has now become untenable,
which is affecting both David's health and work . . . we have therefore
reluctantly decided to relinquish your services as from today's date.'[50]
He was allowed to keep his VW Rabbit, but had to hand over the keys

to the studio and house, all joint credit cards, and was additionally expected to repay a loan of $9,000 for hospital expenses. It was the beginning of a long period of estrangement between them, until a significant event in Hockney's life would bring Evans back into the fold.

CHAPTER TEN

PEARBLOSSOM HWY.

Laura Hockney was used to receiving two dozen red roses each birthday from David, but on 10 December 1985 he surprised her with a trip to Paris to attend the opening at the Galerie Claude Bernard of *David Hockney: Images et Pensées pour la Magazine Vogue*, a show devoted to his work on the Christmas issue. The editor of *Vogue*, Francine Crescent, also gave a grand lunch to celebrate the occasion. 'French *Vogue* held a lunch in a very smart restaurant in celebration of David,' Celia Birtwell recalled, 'and his mother was there. It was very glamorous. I wore a beautiful Ossie black velvet and lace dress. And there was a celebration cake iced with a very impressive copy of that *Vogue* cover portrait of me.'[1] Laura thoroughly enjoyed herself. 'I thought I would say a very big thank-you to you,' she wrote on her return, 'for the gay – happy but hectic time in Paris. It is so good to see lovely buildings around and the beauty of the city, which make Bradford seem a slum with all its ugly flats & buildings pulled down to rubble which take so long to replace. Thank you for my birthday surprise. Each year seems to get better with all the caring which surrounds me. What a lovely Christmas we all shared – such a happy togetherness.'[2]

For Hockney, the only dark shadow on the horizon was the ever-looming presence of AIDS, in this case in the person of Alexis Vidal (the former partner of Jean Léger), whom he visited in the Paris hospital where his life was ebbing away. He died three weeks later. Death now never seemed far away. Soon after Hockney had returned to LA after Christmas, he found that his old friend Christopher Isherwood, who was suffering from prostate cancer, had no more than a few days to live. 'I . . . went straight down to see him,' Hockney wrote to Stephen

Spender. 'I think he only just recognised me, and didn't really speak, but the previous visit he <u>had</u> asked me if you were in the other room. He did say "Where is Stephen?"' Isherwood died on 4 January, leaving a huge gap in Hockney's life. 'I shall miss him a great deal,' he told Spender. 'I felt very close to him. I have dug out an unfinished portrait of him in his bathrobe, and begun work on it.'[3]

As usual when depression hovered, Hockney buried himself in his work, the excitement this time coming from the discovery of new technologies. The first of these was connected to the rapid advances in computer technology that characterised the 1980s. While in London before Christmas, he had been approached by the film producer Michael Deakin to try out the Paintbox, a computer that had been developed by Quantel back in 1981 for the production of TV graphics, since when it had been widely used by broadcasters to produce their weather maps, graphs and on-screen titles. 'Nobody had ever seen anything like it,' Deakin recalled, 'and every TV station had to have one. You could mix colours on a palette and use different thicknesses of brush, just like conventional painting. Nowadays everybody can do all the same things on a Mac. Before then it was lettraset and glue.'[4] Inspired by Henri-Georges Clouzot's film *Le Mystère Picasso*, in which Picasso paints onto a giant translucent canvas with a camera behind it, so that the work appears to evolve upon the screen, Deakin had the idea of making a series of programmes for television in which different artists would use the Paintbox as a tool for producing works of art.

At first, Hockney, whom Deakin had known through Mark Glazebrook and Editions Alecto since *A Rake's Progress* was published, was sceptical, telling him that he considered video art to be boring. Deakin, however, not being a man to take no for an answer, persevered and persuaded him to try it out, the result being that Hockney was almost immediately won over to its possibilities and agreed to be the first artist to be filmed using it, the others being Howard Hodgkin, along with Richard Hamilton, Sidney Nolan, Larry Rivers and Jennifer Bartlett. The way it worked was that the artist drew directly onto a plain screen using an electronic pen, enabling him or her to summon up at will palettes of colour, varying textures and different widths of brush by making a brisk downstroke of the stylus. Hockney saw immediately that the Paintbox was much more than just a tool for designing graphics. In effect, it was a new medium that gave the artist the facility of literally painting with light. No sooner was he seated in front of it, his microphone attached and the camera crew ready, than he became deeply absorbed in its workings, completely oblivious to the crew and lights, a state in which he remained for nearly eight hours.

To begin with he was finding his way, painting a series of shapes that developed into a landscape with some trees and a bit of a brick wall. The colours he was getting, and the way they seemed to come to life, immediately intrigued him. 'The only equivalent where you would get colours like this,' he commented, 'is in stained glass itself, which is using colour and glass and where you can get a richness of colour that even paint doesn't give. It has . . . almost a neon glow.'[5] As he became more skilful with his use of the stylus, he became increasingly aware of the possibilities that the Paintbox offered. 'The thing you can do on this which you can't do with paint,' he continued, 'is you can put on a colour like a very brilliant blue and you can draw on it with a very brilliant red. In paint, if you put the red on top of the blue – even if you used thick red on thin blue – you're going to make the red slightly into purple. That doesn't happen here whether you put it on thin or thick. In a sense you could go on forever, drawing with each one of these colours because you can just go on changing it, while if this was on paper there's a limit to what you can do. If you put two colours down on top of one another and then a third, you're going to get mud really, nothing would glow.'[6]

When the landscape was completed, he attempted a portrait from memory. 'I was trying to draw Francis Bacon,' he said, 'who I'd seen on television the night before saying he was an optimist about nothing, which amused me because I thought you could be a pessimist about nothing as well.' This was a failure and ended up as a portrait of David Graves, who happened to be in the room. The experiment ended with a view of the interior of Pembroke Studios, which included a tortoise, a cat, a galloping horse and two seated women. 'So there you've got a rather mad, silly picture,' he said, 'but you did watch it being made and you weren't looking over my shoulder.'[7]

Working on the Paintbox unleashed a spurt of creativity in Hockney that found another outlet in a piece of technology that was by 1986 common to every office: the photocopier. 'I happened to have a Canon Copier at home,' Jerry Sohn remembers, 'which one day David started fooling around with. He immediately saw the possibilities of using it in a democratic way, that he could produce things that anyone could have, that weren't necessarily something that were just for rich people. So he started experimenting with my copier, which could both reduce and enlarge, but also had different colours, so you could put in a brown cartridge, or a blue cartridge, or a red cartridge. You had to do the colours one at a time and pass the print through just like you would with a lithograph.'[8]

Hockney was immediately fascinated with the Canon. 'I just started playing with it,' he recalled. 'One of the first things I did was to use the reduction feature. I did a drawing and then reduced it. Every time I reduced it, I added to the drawing. Something that began big eventually became tiny and was placed off in the corner of the paper. I thought that was amusing. And then when I found out you could swap the colour about I started playing with that. I then realised how the machine sees.'[9] Stimulated by the experience of working once again in a completely new medium, Hockney went home and bought one, a Canon P.C.25, soon to be followed by two more elaborate machines, the Canon N.P.3525 and the Kodak Ektaprint 225F. 'Within three weeks,' he wrote, 'I realised that nobody had really explored them very much when compared to what I was getting out of them. The xerox machine is really fascinating . . . because I realise it's a camera and a printing machine. [It] opened up an amazing area that I certainly didn't think was there. Nobody else did, I don't think. It's a totally new kind of printing that is very beautiful if you know about it, if you know what to do.'[10]

Photocopiers printed from paper to paper, they printed totally dry, and the 'ink' was put on electronically, features which offered new areas and possibilities. The first was that printing directly onto paper meant that the artist's original marks were made on the same kind of paper that was used for the printing, thereby removing the

layers that exist in lithography, namely the need to use a plate, stone
or Mylar as an intermediary. Secondly, the fact that they printed
dry had tremendous advantages: '. . . you can print again and again,
immediately, immediately, immediately,' Hockney explained. 'With no
other printing can you do that. In, say, lithography, you might get two
colours on top of one another, but if you start doing three or four, they
start . . . coming off again, because it's not dry. It takes at least three or
four hours to dry. This dries instantly. Some of the pieces went through
twelve times.'[11] Lastly, the blacks produced on a copier tended to be
much denser. In lithography the printing ink was made by mixing up
the pigment with oil, which always left a slight reflection on the surface
that was especially noticeable with black. Copier 'inks', however, were
not ink in the normal sense but a powder – called a toner – that was
fused onto the paper by a heat process, leaving no reflective surface. 'I
noticed how beautiful and dense the black was,' Hockney commented,
'especially on the larger Kodak machine. It seemed to me that it was the
blackest and most beautiful black I had ever seen on paper. It seemed to
have no reflection whatsoever, giving it a richness and mystery almost
like a "void".' [12]

Hockney realised that all these features taken together gave back
to the artist the ability to become his own craftsman. 'Over the years,'
he said, 'I've made a lot of prints working in several different master
printshops. It's an exciting process, but I've always been bothered by the
lack of spontaneity: how it takes hours and hours, working alongside
several master craftsmen, to generate an image. How you're continually
having to interrupt the process of creation from one moment to the
next for technical reasons. But with these copying machines, I can
work by myself – indeed you virtually have to work by yourself; there's
nothing for anyone else to do – and I can work with great speed and
responsiveness. In fact, this is the closest I've ever come in printing to
what it's like to paint: I can put something down, evaluate it, alter it,
revise it, reexamine it, all in a matter of seconds.'[13]

So began a period, treated, to begin with, with some suspicion by
friends and business colleagues alike, of making what he termed his
'Home Made Prints', made entirely by him without any outside help.

Their size was necessarily limited to the size of paper that could be accommodated by the office copier, though he did make a number of composite images consisting of several sheets of paper pasted together. Nor did he stop at producing simple drawn images. Because he understood that the copier was also a camera, he spent hours exploring how the machine *saw* different things, photocopying leaves, wood, shirts, towels, maps, grass, etc., at various settings and in various colours, and incorporating them into many of the works. To create a print, he made a single image on a piece of paper, inserted a colour cartridge and ran it through the copier, sometimes four or five times to build up the pigment. He then superimposed another image on the already printed paper and ran it through again. By this collage process, and by the intense colour that the machine is capable of producing, he made his prints.

Paul Joyce, the writer and documentary-maker, who watched him working flat out on a complex six-part photocopied piece, described it thus: 'He began by sketching the design across six separate sheets of A4-sized paper, then he concentrated on one of these, using the basic design as a "master" and feeding additions through the Canon photocopier so that the original was gradually overlaid. Thus a design was built up through a number of different "states", not unlike conventional work on a lithographic plate, but at a hugely increased speed. He worked from 10.00am till 6.00pm without a break, finishing each master design to his satisfaction, then doing an edition of sixty from each sheet. Three hundred and sixty original Hockneys, designed and printed in one day!'[14]

As was the norm for Hockney, once he started on the process, he found it difficult to stop. 'I was very, very excited,' he wrote. 'I felt it was, in fact, the most spontaneous way you could make prints. Never before could you have been that quick doing it, and I galloped away making all kinds of things in rather a short period of time. Most of those that I call Home Made Prints were done in a period of about six months and they developed from very simple things to very complex prints.'[15] Never one to do anything by halves, Hockney did not stint on the production costs. He used Arches paper, made in France, which is the finest and most durable paper for watercolours, and had it cut to the right shapes. He then put it through a series of tests to make sure that it would be archivally safe. A certain number of the prints, for example, were put out in the Californian sun, the same number being shaded, to see how they might fade. In this case, he preferred the ones that had been in the sun, because the toner was plastic-based, and it got baked into the paper, giving a rich finish.

The Home Made Prints were to be sold at what might be considered a reasonable price, which was on average between $2,000 and $3,000. Editioning them, however, was not so simple, as the layering process was complicated and could only be done by the artist himself, which in itself constituted a staggering amount of work. 'Nobody else can do it for you,' he explained in an interview when a selection of them were shown at the André Emmerich Gallery in December 1986, 'because how it looks depends which way you put the layers on. I attempted to see what would happen if I printed some: Could I go back with the plates to do some more? But they're never quite the same, so I realised that's not possible. It's not really an edition because it's altered. The whole point of an edition is that it's reasonably identical. For me, it was thrilling. It seemed to me a totally new print medium because it's a totally new way of printing. I think it's a very genuine method of making what you would call an artist's print, just as much as etching, lithography, linocuts or anything. Things, to be art, don't have to be made of gold.'[16]

It might be said that the Home Made Prints evolved out of necessity, in that this was one of the few short periods in Hockney's life when he was pretty much on his own. Gregory was gone, Ian had by now moved out and was living down the hill with a new boyfriend, an actor called Butch Kirby, always known as 'Butchie', and their dachshund Heinz, and David Graves was back in London, where his future was under review, part of an economic tightening-up campaign inaugurated by Paul Hockney. This involved a reassessment of whether or not a London office was required, rather than just running everything from LA. Things were, however, hotting up again for Hockney, with an approach from Peter Hemmings, the general director of Los Angeles Opera, to design a new production of *Tristan und Isolde*, along with the planning of a major retrospective of his work that was to open at the Los Angeles County Museum of Art in the autumn of 1988. With all this on the horizon, he engaged a new assistant, and it was agreed that David Graves should fly over in April to help settle him in.

Charlie Scheips was a gay 25-year-old who had been born in New York and grown up in Connecticut, where his father worked as an industrial psychologist. After graduating from Ripon College in Wisconsin as a double major in art history and painting, he went to work as assistant director of public relations for the Museum of Contemporary Art in Chicago. This was a vibrant, exciting place, which was then located on Ontario Street, a block east of Michigan Avenue, in the centre of Miracle Mile. In 1984 their big autumn show had been *Hockney Paints the Stage*, and Scheips was in charge of organising the press for the opening, as well as making sure that Hockney's own party were taken care of. On the day of his scheduled arrival, Hockney turned up in the company of Cary Grant and his wife Barbara, friends of his from LA. Grant had come to Chicago to cut the ribbon for the opening of the thousandth store of Walgreens, the largest drug retailing company in the US. Their arrival caused something of a stir. 'Even the most radical lesbian on our staff,' Scheips recalls, 'who was not interested in anything commercial, had a reason to be in the galleries when Cary Grant was there.'[17]

Hockney and Scheips immediately clicked. 'He had to sign all the catalogues for the museum directors and as he did it we talked,' Scheips says. 'He asked me what I was interested in and I told him about my interest in Picasso and cubism. There was a show of the photo-collages on at the same time at the Richard Gray Gallery, and the next day David left a copy of the *Cameraworks* book for me, signed to "Charles the Cubist" as he couldn't remember my last name, together with an invitation to the opening that night.'[18] Over the next few days, the two of them spent a lot of time together discussing all Hockney's favourite subjects. 'At times, I felt the powers of the MCA were a bit perturbed by our mutual infatuation with one another, so I had to excuse myself from a few of his invitations for fear of possibly losing my job.'[19]

Charlie Scheips,
1986

A year and a half later, in January 1986, Scheips flew to LA to interview for a job at the Getty Museum in Malibu. 'I left a sub-zero Chicago for Burbank on January 15,' he recalled, 'where David picked me up and drove me back to his house in the Hollywood Hills. After a dinner he cooked of chicken and sautéed peppers, he took me up to his bedroom where we watched some videos of drawings he had made directly using the television screen monitor. The next day we got into his red Mercedes convertible sports car and he drove me to my interview. I stayed in LA for a week and at no time did David ever discuss a job with me although he had a lot of pending projects coming up and was worried about all he had to accomplish. I flew back to Chicago and the next day he called me and said he had been thinking that I seemed to understand his ideas and like the projects he was working on, and what would I think about coming to work for him?'[20]

When Charlie Scheips arrived at Montcalm Avenue, on April Fool's Day 1986, David Graves was there to show him the ropes. There was a lot to take in, as in addition to the upcoming *Tristan und Isolde* and the LACMA retrospective, there was a restaging of *The Magic Flute* for San Francisco Opera and a big show of photo-collages at the International Center of Photography in New York. One of the first projects on which he was asked to help was something of a curiosity, and was a perfect example of Hockney's inability at that time to say no to anything. It was a commission from the Austrian artist and actor André Heller, to design a pavilion for his Luna Luna Park, 'A Fairground of the Visual Arts' in which all the rides and attractions were the work of famous artists. Thus Salvador Dalí, Jean Tinguely, Jim Whiting and Roy Lichtenstein all created special installations, while Jean-Michel Basquiat, Keith Haring and Kenny Scharf, along with several German neo-expressionist painters, such as Joseph Beuys, decorated children's rides. Hockney's contribution was an enchanted tree painted in red, blue and green, inspired by his 'Ravel's Garden' designs. Heller led the artists to believe that his fair was to open in Paris, London, New York and Vienna, only for them to eventually find out that the one city where he could find the necessary funding of £4 million was Hamburg. On the opening night, the clouds parted and the rain poured down. '. . . thousands of guests had to shelter under golf umbrellas,' wrote the correspondent for the *Guardian*, 'and tip-toe through puddles to reach the Dali restaurant or the big wheel designed by Jean Michel Basquiat . . . They played delightedly with the musical sculpture, showed what a good shot they were in the shooting booth designed by Jörg Immendorff, and waltzed to Strauss inside the soothing Tree of Wishes by David Hockney.'[21]

Next came an urgent commission from *Vanity Fair*, then the hottest magazine in America, after being revamped by Condé Nast in 1983 under the editorship of the British journalist Tina Brown. They had seen what Hockney had done for French *Vogue*, and had asked if he could do something in the same vein for them, illustrating a story by Gregor von Rezzori, the Austrian-born author of *Memoirs of an Anti-Semite*. To commemorate the thirtieth anniversary of the publication of Nabokov's *Lolita,* they had engaged von Rezzori to retrace the steps of the novel's central character, Humbert Humbert, across America. Loving the American West as he did, Hockney was immediately intrigued and agreed to take on the commission, though without first finding out exactly what *Vanity Fair* had in mind.

Since the article was primarily about driving, Hockney decided that he, Scheips and Graves should immediately embark on a road trip, beginning by driving up to Death Valley in the Mojave Desert to spend a night at the Furnace Creek Inn, a remote ranch where in 1913 the hottest temperature ever on earth was recorded at 134 degrees Fahrenheit. They set off in mid-April, driving a charcoal-grey Audi station wagon which Hockney had recently bought from Robert Motherwell, and no sooner had they arrived at Furnace Creek than a storm brewed up and it began to pour with rain. The following day they drove fifteen miles south to Dante's View, where Hockney took a few photographs before telling Graves to drive back the way they had come as he was interested in a crossroads they had passed the day before. Eventually, after the occasional stop to take pictures of various road signs, they found the place, the crossing where the Pearblossom Highway meets the California State Route 138.

'The spot was beautifully desolate,' Scheips remembers, 'with the perfectly straight roads convening in the midst of a landscape of scrub brush, Joshua trees and roadside trash. In the distance the snow-sprinkled Angeles Crest Mountains stretched across the horizon. On the road's shoulder four signs signalling the intersection – a yellow, black and red "Stop Ahead"; the green and white "California 138" sign with its arrow pointing left and right; and at the intersection the hexagonal red stop sign and the street sign marking Pearblossom Highway to its right. Painted on the road in large blocky white letters was another admonition to "Stop Ahead" as well as the double yellow painted median lines. On the left side, power lines stretched into the distance. The sandy embankment on the roadside was strewn with soda and beer bottles and other trash.'[22] Hockney was excited and took photographs, before considering that since they were only an hour from home, they should drive back to fetch all the equipment he needed, and return.

Once the skeleton of the new collage was laid down, Hockney decided they should locate a one-hour processing lab in nearby Palmdale, and book a motel to use as a temporary studio. After he had photographed a number of road signs from up a ladder, the film was taken to the lab and they whiled away the time in a diner while the pictures were processed and printed. 'An hour later we picked up the film and headed over to the motel,' Scheips recalls. 'The motel clerk acted strange as we three men checked into the room – explaining that we were only going to use it for the day. The manager, who I think suspected we might be filming a porno movie – later visited us in the room. The motel room, to our delight, was a very tacky seventyish room with twin beds and some real "motel art" signed hilariously by an artist named Van Guard. We laid the matte board on one of the twin beds and David began again to sort out the latest shots, organising them around the margins of the board. Fairly soon it was clear that David had made complex mini-collages of the various road signs. The choice photos were secured down and we discussed what needed to be done next. Before leaving, David also suddenly decided that the motel room itself might be a good subject for illustrating the *Lolita* story and so he took several rolls of film of the room taken from the feet of the two beds and featuring Mr Van Guard's pair of colour-coordinated paintings above each bed.'[23]

Hockney spent a week in the creation of *Pearblossom Hwy.*, which he felt took his ideas about perspective further than he had taken them before. 'This picture is a big advance on the "Place Furstenburg" [*sic*] picture in *Vogue*,' he wrote to Stephen Spender. 'I moved around an enormous amount, but right in the centre is one "ordinary picture" of a road disappearing into the distance. It is the only picture that attempts to depict space, every other picture is about a surface – road signs, the road itself, shrubs, Joshua trees and garbage at the side of the road. The parallels with the Xerox machine struck me forcibly. I constructed my picture with pictures of surfaces and the "space" then is made in the mind, perhaps the only place it actually exists.'[24]

The time came when Wayne Lawson and Ruth Ansell, respectively literary editor and art director of *Vanity Fair*, were coming to check on Hockney's progress, but he felt the piece was still missing something, a crescendo. Remembering the pages in French *Vogue* where a drawing of a hand opening a page had actually opened out into a gatefold of the

David Hockney
with *Pearblossom
Hwy.*

hotel courtyard in Acatlán, he came up with the idea of a fold-out like the maps that were often included in copies of the *National Geographic* magazine. He designed a spread that began with a crayon drawing of a map, opening to a collage of a cylindrical gas pump and finally to a large reproduction of the *Pearblossom Hwy.* collage. He pasted this fold-out into a recent copy of the magazine, and then was ready for the arrival of the *Vanity Fair* editors.

Ansell and Lawson were suitably impressed and took the artwork back to New York to show to Tina Brown and Alex Liberman, an artist who knew Hockney as they shared a dealer in André Emmerich. Liberman also happened to be the editorial director of Condé Nast, and as such was the most powerful man in the company. 'A day later,' Scheips says, 'we were told that Brown and Liberman wanted to schedule a conference call with us to discuss David's design. David, who was even then very hard of hearing, had a small den on the first floor of his house where he could best hear the speakerphone. I recall the phone call being scheduled about 11 a.m., with the two in New York at Condé Nast headquarters at 350 Madison Avenue. They cut quickly to the chase: "We love what you did, David – it's fantastic! But we couldn't possibly afford to insert the folding piece in the magazine," Brown said. Liberman added there was no way it could happen given the production and distribution cost. They suggested that they would redesign the article using the individual elements Hockney had created and would send out a mock-up for David's approval. As we hunched over the phone, Hockney began to stare at me with his eyes getting angrier and angrier. He finally blew his top and explained that he had thought that they had understood what he was going to do after he did the French *Vogue* six months before. He said, "You should use it as I designed it or not at all!"'[25]

No amount of persuasion could convince Hockney to change his mind. He got Scheips to retrieve the mock-up and arranged to pay back any money that he had been given already by Condé Nast to cover costs. Von Rezzori's story ran as scheduled in the magazine, but was accompanied by some photographs of the American West by the film director Wim Wenders. In spite of his initial anger at what he considered cowardice by Condé Nast, Hockney considered the project had been more than worthwhile, as he had got such good work out of it. 'It was my last photo-collage and the most painterly,' he wrote. 'I see it as a panoramic assault on Renaissance one-point perspective.'[26] Scheips organised a frame for the piece and it was hung up in the studio, where it became the focal point for all visitors in the ensuing months. He was so pleased with it that he eventually decided to make a much larger version using 6"x 4" prints rather than the standard 3½"x 5"ones, and *Pearblossom Hwy. #2* became the culminating work in his autumn show at New York's Center of Photography.

Scheips's baptism of fire stood him in good stead, and by the time Graves returned to England, he was well settled in, with a good team around him. Jerry Sohn was there on and off, doing what he did best, which was to source materials. 'He was brilliant at finding things,' Scheips remembers. 'If David needed a certain kind of brush or a special canvas, he could source it. Like it might be a special brush that makes the effect of wood veneer, that is only made by one guy in Paris, and he's only open on Wednesdays from three till four. Jerry would know about him.'[27] Jimmy Swinea, a young friend of Hockney's who had appeared in the swimming-pool sequence of *A Bigger Splash*, was hired as an extra studio assistant, while Karen Kuhlman ran the office and storage on Santa Monica Boulevard. With the Home Made Prints still going at full tilt, the studio was buzzing again. Paul Joyce, who spent a few evenings there, noted, 'During my visit I saw his studio turn into an artist's impression of one of those large copy-shops, with people running around at breakneck speed as if trapped in an old silent movie.'[28]

Slowly Hockney adjusted to the new set-up. 'Life goes on here,' he wrote to Stephen Spender in April. 'Gregory has moved out and is devoting himself to A.A. (Alcoholics Anonymous not the Auto Club) I understand this, that he has to do it, but I miss him. I've got a new assistant, a bright boy called Charlie Scheips. I met him in Chicago where he worked at the Museum, and supported me intelligently in some arguments about Cubism . . . He seems to like California, so I'm getting myself organized a bit better. The last year with Gregory was very difficult with drink + drugs, but he's fine now – indeed he looks about 20 again with fresh sparkling eyes. I know you have a soft spot for him.'[29] For the time being, Evans had only one thing on his mind, which was to keep up his attendance at AA meetings and try to stay sober.

To consolidate an increasing desire to nest, as well as to provide a useful guest house for visiting friends, Hockney bought the next-door house, number 2921 Montcalm Avenue, which had recently come up for sale. While it was being fumigated, to clear it of termites and vermin, he headed off to Ken Tyler's for a week to work on some prints, leaving Scheips there alone with his brother Paul, who was visiting from England. Scheips was a city boy who still found living in the Hollywood Hills a little creepy, being unused to the strange night-time noises, and the coyotes and raccoons that used to gather in the garden. 'One night I got up in the middle of the night to visit the water fountain we had in the kitchen,' he recalls. 'I didn't have my contact lenses in and I didn't turn on the lights because I knew exactly where I was going. I had just got my glass of water, when I heard these odd noises. I suddenly looked with my very blind eyes to the bookshelves where we kept all our art catalogues, and there were thirty or forty rats scampering along them. I let out this primal scream, and Paul Hockney came out with a baseball bat! It was just like a scene out of the movie *Willard*. I had noticed when I was cooking that the air vents above the grill top never really worked very well, and it turned out that when they had redone the kitchen, they hadn't properly screwed on the outside vent grill and it had fallen off. Then they had tented the house next door to make it liveable, and all the rats had moved out of there into our house. I had an army of exterminators up there the next morning!'[30]

As the new team grew stronger, David Graves's place in the set-up became less certain. In spite of the fact that Graves had worked closely with him for so long and contributed so much, Hockney began to believe that with such a quantity of work in the pipeline, he needed to be either on the spot or not there at all. Though Graves had hoped that he might be able to stay on in a self-employed situation, working on exhibition projects in Europe and making the occasional trip to help out in LA, this was not what his employer had in mind. Hockney considered that total loyalty meant total commitment, and if that meant making sacrifices, then so be it. He did his utmost to persuade him to rethink his decision to return to live in London, making it quite clear that his future employment depended on it, but to no avail. 'In case there is any further confusion,' Graves wrote, 'I must tell you categorically that I will not come to live in California. This was a decision I made when I came back to England in 1984 . . . It would cause too much unhappiness and this would probably sour our working relationship and, in the end, our friendship.' It was, for the time being, the end of what had been a very fruitful association.

Graves's contribution had in fact been much more than just artistic. He had taken on a lot of clerical responsibilities with the express idea of allowing Hockney more time to concentrate on his creative work. Now that he was gone, Hockney was only too aware of the dangers of being sucked deeper and deeper back into the enormous volume of administrative work that went with being an artist who involved himself in so many different projects, and it caused him enormous anxiety. 'This was a very dense, giant creative period,' Scheips recalls. 'There was so much going on at the same time . . . Loads of stuff and David was really nervous about all of it.'[31]

This was hardly surprising considering that the preparations for the show of Home Made Prints alone was a huge volume of work. There were to be thirty-three different prints exhibited, each one in an edition that varied from twenty-five to sixty, adding up to 1,556 different printings. In addition to preparing these, there was the New York show which was to feature many of his largest photo-collages, including *The Scrabble Game*, *Luncheon at the British Embassy*, *The Marriage in Hawaii of David and Ann* and *Pearblossom Highway #2*. There was the restaging of *The Magic Flute* for San Francisco Opera. There was the major retrospective of his life's work due to open in 1988 at LACMA; and on top of all this he had agreed to do another opera.

LA Opera was brand new, started in 1984, when Peter Hemmings, an Englishman who was the general manager of the London Symphony Orchestra, was hired to create a local opera company in Los Angeles, which was keen to shed its reputation as being the only major city in the West not to have an opera company of its own. There had been numerous attempts to do this over the years, all of which had failed for reasons that included the far-flung dispersal of residential living in the city, or '27 cities joined by freeways' as it was once described, a Hollywood-spawned preoccupation with 'stars' at the expense of more lasting values, and political and social in-fighting among potential sponsors. Hemmings, who had an annual budget of $5 million, had the brainwave of bringing in Placido Domingo as artistic consultant, and on 7 October 1986 he opened the very first season, singing the title role in Verdi's *Otello*. The venue was the Dorothy Chandler Pavilion, home since 1969 of the Academy Awards ceremony, which the opera shared with the Los Angeles Philharmonic.

The inaugural performance came close to being a disaster. '. . . the gala audience,' wrote the *Guardian* correspondent, 'made up of the glamorous and the good, the stars and the benefactors gathered together to see the curtain rise on the ambitions of all new opera companies, witnessed an historic technical hitch. Lawrence Foster raised his baton to start the first act of Otello, the curtain rose a few feet, and it stuck there. The pit lighting failed to go up too and, as the stage staff struggled with the curtain and the orchestra plunged into Verdi in the dark, the conductor had to decide whether to stop the performance or not.'[32] And as if this were not enough, the lead soprano, Rosalind Plowright, booked to sing the role of Desdemona on the opening night, had to drop out owing to problems with her pregnancy, while her replacement, Daniella Dessi, was suddenly taken ill and also had to bow out at the last moment. In the end the performance did go ahead, and Domingo saved the night.

When Hockney was approached by Peter Hemmings to design *Tristan und Isolde*, it never occurred to him to turn it down because he had too many other commitments. He loved Wagner and had been twice to Bayreuth to see *The Ring*, conducted by Horst Stein in 1974, and by Pierre Boulez in 1978. He had also seen a number of productions of *Tristan*. 'I was deeply interested in the piece,' he wrote. 'I felt it was the kind of music that I would choose to work with in the theatre . . . *Tristan und Isolde* is a pretty static drama; it's essentially an internal drama. It takes place entirely out of doors, and nature, in a sense, is part of it. I thought this too was interesting because the problem of putting nature on the stage is a challenge.'[33]

It was Hemmings' idea to pair up Hockney with another Englishman, Jonathan Miller, who, along with Peter Cook, Dudley Moore and Alan Bennett, had been one of the stars of the Cambridge Footlights satirical show *Beyond the Fringe*, which had catapulted them all to fame. Beyond that, Miller had forged a successful career as a wit and polymath, writing books, directing films and plays, presenting television programmes, and latterly working in opera. Before *Tristan*, he had already directed a number of successful productions at the English National Opera, of which he was an associate director, including *The Turn of the Screw*, *Otello*, *Don Giovanni* and, in particular, a *Rigoletto*, set not in nineteenth-century Italy but among the Mafia in 1950s New York. At the time, he was about to have another huge hit on his hands with a Grand Hotel setting of *The Mikado*, again at the ENO.

Though it had seemed to Hemmings such a good idea to employ two giants of theatre and art to design and direct a Wagner opera, things did not go the way he had hoped. Hockney himself was surprised to be asked to work with Miller, because he considered him to be a strong visual director who really designed things himself. When they initially met, Miller's approach to the project differed from Hockney's, and this rankled him. In Hockney's telling of it, Miller refused his suggestion that they take a drive from LA to north of Santa Barbara, a four-and-a-half-hour trip, so that they could listen to the music together on the car stereo. And then, according to Falconer, 'When they were sitting around discussing how to approach *Tristan* Jonathan Miller said, "Well, the music is awful and the plot is ridiculous, but let's try and make this work somehow." David was appalled because he thought the music was magnificent.'[34] Hockney commented that he found this 'amazing. Because the story isn't the words – though the librettos are what most directors seem to spend most of their time mucking about with, plumbing them for motivation and so forth – *it's the music*. It's *in* the music. When I start work on an opera, I maybe read the libretto once, but then I set it aside and hardly ever go back to it: I just listen to the music over and over and over again. And the story *Tristan*'s music tells is anything but silly. It's overwhelmingly moving really. It's ravishing.'[35] He later said that Miller was the only director with whom he had not sat down to listen together to the music.

Miller no doubt had his own views on Hockney's ideas for *Tristan*. He had involved himself over the years in many successful theatrical productions, and took a far less abstract approach than Hockney. Moreover his designs tended to be filmic, and he favoured muted colours. Had Hemmings thought about these different styles, he might have seen that it was an arranged marriage not necessarily made in heaven.

It was five years since Hockney had last designed an opera, and he was thrilled to be working on his first piece by Wagner. He remembered the experience of watching *Rheingold* in Bayreuth, directed by the composer's descendant Wolfgang Wagner. 'I was excited to be there,' he recalled, 'sitting on those rather uncomfortable little wooden seats.

As *Rheingold* began, and the lights went out and the theatre was very dark, as that long opening chord began, slowly a deep blue appeared – beautiful I thought. I was very thrilled by the use of colour and realised that because the theatre was totally dark, colour could have more power.'[36] Hockney had been told that this production was to use the Los Angeles Philharmonic Orchestra, conducted by Zubin Mehta, the principal conductor of the New York Philharmonic, so he was determined to meet the challenge. 'It seemed to me with Wagner,' he told John Cox, 'what could be offered new was the addition of the plastic arts to Wagner's music, meaning the grammar of the plastic, space, real and illusionary, line, colour, mass, light to be used not just to suggest a place, but to enhance the whole dramatic musical and theatrical effects, to make such a unity with it that one doesn't isolate the visual from the aurel [*sic*].'[37]

As was his usual modus operandi, Hockney began by obsessively listening to the music until he knew every note, and the more he listened, the more he felt that colour was the key to the design. This association of music with colour is not uncommon to artists, the most famous example being Van Gogh, who, according to one of his pupils, Anton Kerssemakers, 'was always comparing painting with music and so as to get a better understanding of the gradation of tones, he started to take piano lessons with an old music teacher . . . This didn't last long, though, because during the lessons Van Gogh kept comparing the notes of the piano with Prussian blue and dark green or dark ochre to bright cadmium, and so the poor man thought he must be dealing with a madman and became so afraid of him that he stopped the lessons.'[38] Van Gogh later wrote to his brother Theo that he strongly felt 'the connections there are between our colour and Wagner's music'.[39]

Initially Hockney had two people helping him with *Tristan*: Ian Falconer, on the costumes, and Richard Schmidt, on the lighting and other technical aspects. The first step was to build the model, which was on a scale of one inch to a foot, twice the size of a normal set model, with a 12-volt lighting system, complete with all the necessary coloured filters to test the effects of the lighting on the painted scenery. The finished model took up so much space in the studio, there was

barely any room left in which to paint. To begin with, since the light
in the studio was too bright and he had no way of blocking off the
windows, he had to work a lot at night. 'I listened to the music,' he
recalled, 'over and over again, night after night. I loved sitting there
with the model . . . through the long hours, because, after all, if you
want to hear the whole piece in one evening, it's three and a half hours
of music. I did that on many evenings, listening, very carefully, trying
to find things in the music.'[40] To solve the light problem, Hockney
eventually had to hire a lightproof tent so that he could work on the
model in daytime as well as at night.

Drawing on the lessons he had learned from his photographic
experiments, in particular *Pearblossom Hwy.*, Hockney decided to try
out different methods of using perspective as a way of drawing the
audience into the action. The first act takes place entirely on a ship,
and he wanted the audience to feel they were actually aboard that
ship. 'I never made drawings,' he wrote, 'but kept cutting out shapes,
placing them in space, then lighting it, all the while playing the music
and realising what marvellously different effects you could get from
the use of the sails, how you could make it feel as though the ship were
on an open sea, how you could suddenly make it feel as if you were
close up on the deck. The sails were painted with a very bold texture,
which if you lit it in a certain way looked as though your face were right
next to the mast. Devices like this pulled you into the scene, called the
audience into the space of the drama.'[41]

These effects were all brilliantly realised by the lighting, an achievement only made possible by the use of a revolutionary new automated
variable-colour lighting set-up called Vari-Lite, which had been
developed in the early eighties for use by the rock band Genesis. LA
Opera was the first opera production company to take up the system, at
that time used mainly for stadium concerts, allowing an unprecedented
play of light and shadow on the stage. The only downside was that the
technology was very loud. This wasn't a problem on the rock concert
stage, but it was a different story with opera, and it amused Hockney to
point out that when Tristan in the last act sang, 'Hör' ich das Licht?' ('Is
it the light I hear?'), the reference was all too literal. Though the Vari-

Lite technicians did their best to quieten down the lights, there were still complaints from the singers. 'I had to give a little talk to Martti Talvela, who sang Tristan,' Hockney said, 'and convince him that the noise was just part of a long tradition of suffering in Wagnerian performances.'[42]

Hockney gave Mo McDermott some work assisting him on *Tristan*, as his life had once again taken a downturn. Celia Birtwell, who had visited Hockney in August, had reported back to Ossie Clark that 'Mo is thin and drinking again'.[43] 'One day I drove him to see this specialist and he had all these things wrong with him,' she remembers. 'He had liver problems, and something wrong with his testicles, and within ten minutes he had this doctor laughing because he amused him so much. He couldn't pronounce testicles, for example. This doctor told him that he could recover if he stopped drinking right away.'[44] He seemed incapable of giving up, however, and one day while visiting Montcalm Avenue he went into a hepatic coma. 'He was at my house when he collapsed,' Hockney recalls. 'I got him into hospital. When he came out of intensive care, he came back to me and when I tried to help him he just started attacking me, which is annoying when you're trying to save someone.'[45]

He then went back to his wife, although their marriage was on the rocks. 'They had started to fight a lot,' Birtwell says. 'I remember we were sitting around at David's house and Lisa was sitting in a rocking chair, and she suddenly stood up and she let out this extraordinary laugh and said, "Look what Mo's done to me now," and she bent her head so that we could see she had a bald patch where Mo had pulled her hair out. It was a fiery relationship.'[46] In October, Ossie Clark noted in his diary, 'Mo's in a bad way. It's over with Lisa . . .'[47] She had run off with the artist Adrian George, and he had gone to pieces and started drinking again. Two months later, Clark was writing, 'Isn't it awful about Mo? He's in prison for beating up Lisa.'[48] He was released just after Christmas. 'He's out of prison, in a new flat overlooking the lake in Echo Park, working for DH. Wept on the phone to Celia on Christmas Day. Poor Mo. I was so looking forward to seeing him. He's really determined to stop drinking otherwise he will be dead in a year.'[49]

By now diagnosed with acute liver problems, McDermott went

into a downward spiral, rescued only by Hockney getting him into hospital, and threatening, after the usual relapses, to cut him out of his life, something McDermott could not contemplate. 'Dear David, Please Please Let's Tick Again,' he pleaded. 'My heart will break if we cannot — we've been friends for such a Long-Long Time, and been through so much together. I apologise for being over sensitif [*sic*] but I'm still on the mend, and you are worn out with all the work you have been doing. We are both under different pressures, and it's still just the beginning of a Brand New Year. I'd like for us to still be friends, to have that Love and Trust we've carried with us from England. Forgive me, I need so much to be alone to sort myself out. They said I was a feisty Bugger in the hospital, and I know and you do that maybe that's what Pulled me through. Let's meet and talk soon. Love you: Mo. I really miss you.'[50] Celia Birtwell came to visit Hockney in March and they went to see McDermott in the Schick Shadel Addiction Center in Santa Barbara. 'I am well on the way now,' he wrote to them after. 'Smell-Sip-Swill-Throw 2 times a day, as well as sleep therapy every other day. The Tapes are marvellous. No wonder they call it the truth drug!! . . . your visit meant a lot to me.'[51]

When McDermott left Santa Barbara, Hockney thought it best that he come to live for a while at Montcalm Avenue where at least there were people to keep an eye on him. In order to boost his confidence, he gave him a little work in the studio and also asked him to undertake some redecoration of the house. 'I spoke to Mo,' wrote Ann Graves, soon after he'd moved into Montcalm Avenue. 'He sounded in a much better frame of mind. He loves being creative at home (it's his life's blood). I know you will give him his head. You can't go wrong there as you will have the prettiest home and he will be pleased.'[52] David Graves added, 'I hope he's on the mend and isn't exerting himself too much redecorating your house. I visualise you coming down from the studio for lunch to find he's marbled three rooms.'[53] In the beginning he certainly seemed to thrive in his new environment. 'Mo was wonderful arranging flowers, lighting candles around and making things pretty,' Charlie Scheips recalls. 'I remember many an evening when I was helping get the dinner set up for people coming over, and Mo chatting away with me, and he was very, very funny. He had gone to David's doctor, Dr Wilbur, who told him that if he drank any more he was going to die of liver failure, so David had got the cook to make no-salt dishes and other special meals that were right for his health condition, and for a while he flourished in some way.'[54]

But fitting into the new set-up at Montcalm Avenue was difficult for McDermott, since his role was never clearly defined, and there were times when he seemed to be able to do no right. 'I would like to apologise for the fuck up at the airport,' he wrote in one note to Hockney. 'It won't happen again I promise because a) either I won't go to meet you accompanied or b) I'll just get a cab there . . . and we'll get another one back. My problem is (if it's a problem at all) I really don't quite know what my role here (at Montcalm) is – ?? Unless I have your permission I cannot really tell <u>anyone</u> what I think you want – or how things should be done, or at least sett [sic] about getting things accomplished. I do know that after 20 ?? or so years of knowing you and working with & for you that I do know a little more than most people what you would feel is right or wrong. You brought that home to me coming home last night from LAX. "Fuck the Flowers and the Fridge . . . Just be there before the plane gets in!!" SO will you just sit down with me sometime this week or so and tell me what I can do and then let the others know that I am only acting on your behalf. I don't want to upset any apple carts or steal anyone's job . . . I do know that I feel very happy being here . . . and if there's anything you don't like tell me if it's me that's doing things wrong.'[55]

With the pressure building up all around him, there were times when Hockney felt both at his wits' end and alone. He now tried to persuade Celia Birtwell, who was selling her Linden Gardens flat to move somewhere bigger, to up sticks and come to California to live next door at 2921. 'Your life in California is wonderful,' she wrote in reply, 'and you have created quite a little Paradise which for me is a great treat whenever I come + visit. At the present time you are living with quite a lot of very serious problems. I have enormous sympathy with you David and I can see how it would get one down . . . I do have to live in London David I think it would be most unfair to uproot Albert

+ George at this moment in time – in fact unthinkable. Teenagers are quite complex + complicated beings as we all can remember and I am trying my best to be an understanding parent. I also have my mother to consider who like yours is now on her own and is finding it quite lonely without my Dad.'[56] Ossie Clark did not take kindly to Hockney's suggestion. 'Selfish cunt,'[57] he noted in his diary.

Hockney was hard at work on the *Tristan* designs while all this was going on. When Paul Joyce visited him in March, he wrote, 'I was used to finding organised chaos within the Hockney home. When I arrived, David was sitting in a small lightproof tent in a corner of his vast studio with a scale model of his sets . . . frantically fiddling with a miniature lighting rig. Jonathan Miller, the opera's director, and the conductor, Zubin Mehta, were due in the next day . . . Soon after Mehta and Miller's arrival, all three of them retired into a tent for hours on end, and cigarette smoke billowed through the cracks and settled along the studio floor, reminding me of a Hollywood "haunted house" set.'[58] Mehta would come up regularly to the studio and they would run through the opera with the model and talk about the music, which would give Hockney useful insights.

Occasionally there would be dinners when Hockney would present one of his opera performances with the model, and he would invite friends like Don Bachardy or the Wilders. When they, or anyone else, visited the studio at this time, they would have noticed the walls densely hung with small canvases painted with almost childish sketches of little scenes from the opera. These were paintings done quickly and out of practicality, so that he could try to picture the drama with the characters from the opera in it, something that was difficult to do from the model, as the figures in it were so small. He then placed the paintings all around to bring the characters to life. 'That's what the paintings were doing for me,' he recalled. 'In a sense the paintings [were] close-ups of what I thought the drama was going to look like . . . I did the paintings to provide my own atmosphere.'[59]

There were other things happening too. When his *Home Made Prints* show had opened at the André Emmerich Gallery in December 1986, Hockney had given an interview to Andy Warhol's magazine,

Interview, in which he had stated that he considered the whole process of producing prints with a copier to be very subversive, in that it undermined the traditional idea of reproduction, with its reliance on outside craftsmen to do the work. To prove his point he invited the magazine to print its own original 'Hockney', providing them with the specifications and separations – the mechanics of the artistic process – to do so. The result was a lithograph of a plant in a pot with the words of the title of the work, *Peace on Earth*, inscribed around them. 'A print by David Hockney appears on the following two pages,' proclaimed the magazine. 'It is not a reproduction: it is an original work of art from a highly original artist.'[60]

While home in England for Christmas, he agreed to repeat this exercise to help promote his home town of Bradford, which in the previous decade had suffered from a number of setbacks, starting with the general depression in the area caused by the loss of manufacturing industries during the 1970s. The Yorkshire Ripper, who killed three of his victims in Bradford, did little to help the city's reputation, and in May 1985 a terrible fire had swept through one of the stands at the Valley Parade football stadium, killing fifty-six people and injuring hundreds of others. In an effort to rebuild Bradford's image, an energetic member of the city council, Gordon Moore, came up with the idea of a campaign called 'Bradford's Bouncing Back'. When asked for a contribution to this, Hockney suggested an original print be given away with the local paper, the *Telegraph & Argus*. As with the *Interview* piece, he sent them the wherewithal to make an original print, in this case four sheets of card, each with one colour of a design, from which they could make their printing plates. The finished work, *Bradford Bounce*, showed a ball bouncing back and forth across the page. 'It is not a reproduction in the normal sense,' he stressed in a letter. ' – the only way your image exists is on your page. There is no such thing as bad printing or poor printing. Any printing process has its own beauty that can be used.'[61]

The 100,000 readers of the *Telegraph & Argus* were each able to buy an original print of his for eighteen pence, giving Hockney the idea that he could use this as a riposte to criticism that had been levelled at him the previous summer after he had submitted three of his Acatlàn hotel lithographs to the Royal Academy Summer Exhibition at what were considered vastly inflated prices. 'Forget the old phrase about a licence to print money,' commented Pendennis sarcastically in the *Observer*; 'now there's a new one – a licence to etch money . . . Amid all the £40, £50 and £100 tags, the catalogue suddenly says "Lithograph, edition of 98: £10,925 each". There are three Hockney collections, 98 at the price just quoted, 75 at £12,075 each, and 80 at £10,925 each. Pulling out my trusty calculator I found that Mr Hockney, anxious not to suffer for his art, is asking for £2,850,275. Other people at the exhibition seemed very angry and were muttering "rip-off", believed to be a term of artistic criticism.'[62] Hockney was furious about this, claiming ignorance and laying the blame squarely at the feet of David Graves for setting the prices.

So, for the 1987 Summer Exhibition, he entered only one piece, *Bradford Bounce*, his brother Paul having persuaded the *Telegraph & Argus* to run off another 10,000 copies, and selling the print for the same price of 18p. 'Nobody can deny that . . . 18p is a snip for an "original" Hockney,' wrote Michael Davie in the *Observer*. 'Behind the scenes I learned that the Academicians have not been too sure what to make of Hockney's submission . . . One of the jolliest RAs, John Ward, has suggested that Hockney might have had in mind an old rhyme as follows,

> *Polly Collins had no sense,*
> *Bared her bum for eighteen pence,*
> *But for those with more to pay,*
> *She turned round the other way.*'[63]

Davie suggested that since newsprint, if untreated, soon became brittle and brown, the owner of a print who could be bothered to treat it with magnesium methoxide might find that in a few years' time it had become extremely valuable as the only survivor of the run. In the *Guardian*, Waldemar Januszczak wrote: 'Best of all, both picture and price-tag challenge the view that the artist's job is to make exclusive knick-knacks for the living rooms of the well-to-do. Thus this tiny 18p print challenges the very foundations on which the Royal Academy Summer Show is built.'[64]

Hockney's interest in the latest technology had not escaped the attention of its manufacturers. Canon had just developed the first digital full-colour copying machine, the CLC-1, and people were soon asking the head technicians whether or not they had demonstrated the machine to him. 'Canon in Los Angeles had asked whether I would like to come and see this new printing machine, a laser photocopier,' he recalled. 'Richard Schmidt and I went and the man said he had written to me because so many people had asked him, Has David Hockney seen this machine? He didn't know who I was. He gave us a demonstration and we were very impressed. We had taken one or two pictures along and we made a few copies and the colour copy of a photograph was quite amazing.'[65] Schmidt, however, who had seen the pleasure that Hockney had been getting from painting again, felt that this was what he should now be concentrating on, rather than continuing to play with machines, and he did his best to dissuade him from buying it, especially as it came with a hefty price tag of $40,000. But the more he thought about it, the more Hockney was convinced that the machine might have a function that no one else had investigated, something that the technician had been unable to show them because he didn't know about it.

'I said, "I think we should play with it,"' he recalled; 'I got it finally. I had just finished a portrait of Henry Geldzahler on a square canvas and the moment the machine arrived I put the portrait on it and made a copy. And immediately I knew my hunch was right. This was something new . . .'[66] The laser copier had produced the most vivid reproduction of a painting he had ever seen. 'In a more standard reproduction, say of the *Mona Lisa*,' he declared, 'what happens is that the photographer stands five feet away from the painting, snaps his picture, and produces a negative from which the reproduction is then derived. But the point is, you can *see* the intervening five feet of air *in* the reproduction: the image seems to hang back, to exist below or behind the surface of the page. It seems to withhold itself. Whereas with the laser copier, I'm able to put the image directly on the camera's lens, with the result that the image almost seems to hover *above* the surface of the page. It can get to be incredibly lifelike.'[67]

One month from his fiftieth birthday, it was a smart move for Hockney to remind people that he still had the capacity to be a trouble-maker. 'I'm deeply interested in subversion,' he told the writer and journalist Gordon Burn. 'I know radical art cannot happen in an art gallery any more. It can't. It won't do anything there. It has to happen on these new surfaces, the TV screen and the pages of newspapers and magazines. I do think we're moving into a new age now. New technology's going to do far more than they think it is. Far, far more. And I intend to do my bit to push things.'[68]

CHAPTER ELEVEN

THE ROAD TO MALIBU

Hockney's boyish looks, his round glasses, his mop of dyed blond hair, his odd-coloured socks, now colour-coordinated with his twin hearing aids, his loose-fitting suits and baseball caps all belied the fact that he was entering his sixth decade. Increasingly, however, his lifestyle did not, as his encroaching deafness made him more and more unwilling to go out. This was much to the chagrin of the younger members of 'the Circus', as Henry Geldzahler used to refer to Hockney's entourage, who all enjoyed the trips to the fashionable restaurants of the day such as the Bistro Garden on Canon Drive, Chasen's on Beverly Boulevard, the Musso and Frank Grill on Hollywood Boulevard, and Spago on Sunset Strip. At the latter, Charlie Scheips remembers, 'We used to drive Wolfgang Puck crazy because we always sat in Siberia where David could hear better, as it was too loud at the front.'[1] One place he did like was the Imperial Gardens, a Chinese restaurant on Sunset that was beyond dullness it was so quiet, which was why he liked it. 'Every time he said he wanted to go there, when we wanted to go to Spago, our hearts would sink because every one of his friends really hated it, but they would never admit it!'[2]

Having tried and failed to persuade first Celia Birtwell and then Scheips and his boyfriend Tom to move into the next-door house, Hockney had offered it to Ian Falconer and his new lover Butchie. This helped alleviate the feelings of loneliness he occasionally suffered from, as did the arrival of a new companion, a dachshund puppy he got through Falconer, named Stanley after Stan Laurel. 'I had always had dachshunds all my life,' says Falconer, 'and my boyfriend Butch and I got one which we named after the cute boy Heinz in Christopher Isherwood's book *Christopher and His Kind*. David had always said to me that he wasn't a dog person, but when he met Heinz, he completely

David Hockney
with Stanley

fell in love with him, so we took him to the breeder and he picked out Stanley.'[3]

Knowing him to be such a peripatetic person, Hockney's friends were astonished when they heard he was getting a dog. He did, after all, live like a gypsy, and he certainly wouldn't be able to take it in and out of England. He brushed all these worries aside, however, suddenly seeing Stanley as a reason to stay in one place. 'I've got an excuse to people,' he said. 'Stanley is here. I can't possibly leave Stanley. And . . . I've got a lot to do. There are a hundred things I want to be doing. I'm going back into painting; I can feel it coming on strong. I want to stay in one place now.'[4] It wasn't long before Stanley was ruling the roost. 'When [Hockney] isn't fielding phonecalls and queries,' wrote Gordon Burn, 'he is curled up on the carpet nuzzling his constant companion, Stanley. He throws plastic waffles and squeaky toys for Stanley, and holds Stanley so that his little pink tongue flickers in and out of his nostrils. Hockney is besotted with Stanley . . . and the feeling seems mutual . . . "One of the main reasons I used to travel was to get away from all the nattering," Hockney is quoted as saying. "But I don't have to worry about the natterers any more. Stanley's going to growl at them when they come to the door."[5]

Stanley's arrival, followed soon after by another dachshund puppy, Rupert, created a happy dachshundland, which increased Hockney's desire to stay at home. 'I go to really lousy restaurants,' he told Waldemar Januszczak, 'because there's hardly anybody there. Actually I stay in most of the time.' '. . . from my experience of a long warm afternoon in the Hockney household,' wrote Januszczak, 'the whole world comes to see him. The phone never stops ringing. An assortment of males, young and old, secretaries, workmen, assistants, biographers, hangers-on, visitors from abroad, people doing books, people who make the tea, people who look after Hockney's two noisy little dachshunds, gardeners, college friends from Bradford, and me, all of us buzz around the lopsided house clinging to a hillside like drones around a hive.'[6] Though Scheips was happy to do a lot of cooking himself, as Hockney increasingly wanted to stay in, he eventually persuaded him to hire a full-time chef to come and work for him. He was a young gay guy who was known simply as 'Mike the Chef'. 'When David was doing *Tristan* and had the model up at the studio,' Scheips remembers, 'we had a lot of dinner parties at the house where David would give a performance with the model. The world came up to Montcalm Avenue.'[7]

Among the guests who frequently graced Hockney's table were Morris and Rita Pynoos. Morris Pynoos, 'Morrie' to his friends, was an aeronautical engineer who had worked during the war for Curtiss-Wright, Lockheed and Hughes Aircraft and had designed the original nail gun specifically to help build Hughes's famous Spruce Goose. After the war he had started his own company, Morris S. Pynoos Co., and had made a fortune building innovative and custom-built homes and public buildings designed by famous architects. Together with his wife, he had become a collector of both art and artists, many of whom became close friends, and they were known for their generosity and their numerous parties. 'Rita was always bringing up soup for David,' Scheips recalls, 'and bringing catered lunches, and they doted on Celia and Ann. They bought things for people all the time, and were always trying to have a party or a dinner.' On 9 July 1987, they hosted Hockney's fiftieth birthday party at their house in Beverly Hills, a lavish buffet dinner complete with a huge birthday cake decorated with an icing-sugar portrait of the artist holding Stanley.

Laura Hockney was unable to attend the Pynooses' party as she had been suffering badly from arthritis, and had also recently had an operation to remove cataracts from her eyes. Hockney, however, made time in his increasingly busy schedule to go and visit her, which cheered her up immensely. '. . . how great it was to see you,' she wrote to him later, '& share your being here & your fun & good company . . . it is worth more – much more than medicine. It is not very thrilling to be on one's own & have no one to converse with . . . but to have you right here with me & near me was wonderful . . . Thank you especially my dear for your hard earnings which have given me my sight again to see the beauties of the earth & faces of people.'[8]

It was a flying visit, for not only was there *Tristan und Isolde* to finish, but the LACMA retrospective was due to open only two months afterwards and Hockney was involved in a major argument with the museum over a film he had made on the subject of Chinese scroll painting, which they wanted him to cut from its original forty-five-minute length to fifteen. Kasmin used to say, 'He's always got a bee in his bonnet, that boy,'[9] and this was the latest. A year earlier, LACMA had been over the moon when the American TV network NBC had expressed interest in making an hour-long documentary about Hockney to air around the opening of the retrospective. Hockney, who had already seen his life stripped bare in *A Bigger Splash*, refused to go along with it, but said he would make his own film instead. 'I didn't want them to do it at all,' he recalled, 'so I put them off. The museum didn't like it, but I did. I pointed out that my work was moving towards showing that there was something wrong with the television screen. Why, therefore, should I go along with them and pretend that there wasn't? . . . and in the end we've done this other film which, frankly, I think is far more interesting.'[10]

The film, *A Day on the Grand Canal with the Emperor of China*, was made with the American artist and film-maker Philip Haas, and explored Hockney's thoughts on perspective. In it, he stands in what looks like the storeroom of a museum and slowly unrolls an ancient Chinese scroll painting on a velvet-covered table. It is a simple film in which he talks directly to camera about what is revealed, and the camera moves between shots of the scroll and medium close-ups of him. 'Not exactly Kenneth Clark,' he said of himself on-screen. The final sequence of the film features Hockney, chalk in hand and with a ragged hole in the sleeve of his pale blue sweater, standing in front of a blackboard and lecturing the viewer. 'I would like to now explain,' he states in schoolmasterly fashion, ready to draw a diagram, 'just about the perspectives used in the pictures . . . You will notice that in the first scroll, the lines are always parallel that way or that way . . . etc, etc.'[11] It is understandable that it was not quite what the museum had in mind. Hockney, needless to say, would not budge on the cutting, and the film was eventually shown in its entirety.

Meanwhile, Jonathan Miller had long since given up on having the kind of input he would normally have had in an opera he was directing. From the very start, seeing how Hockney was lionised not just by the LA Opera but by everyone around him, it was clear to him that they regarded this *Tristan und Isolde* as a David Hockney production. 'When Jonathan Miller said: "It's your show," he shocked me,' Hockney, somewhat ironically, later recalled. 'I told him, "I always thought it was the singer, and the composer, a lot more than you or I."'[12] Miller was right, of course, and soon found out that AT&T, the telecommunications company that was sponsoring the production, were advertising it nationally as *Tristan and Isolde and David*. Possibly as a result of this, and certainly bearing in mind his numerous other commitments, Miller seemed less involved than he might have been. Until rehearsals began he often remained in London, where he was working on *The Mikado*, and had also been appointed artistic director of the Old Vic. According to Hockney, the fact that he had taken on so much 'made it very hard and long' for him.[13]

When rehearsals started, Zubin Mehta commented, 'It was a tug of war! They didn't get along . . . At one rehearsal, I suddenly heard

Jonathan saying, "That looks like a nightclub in Beirut."[14] This remark came at a moment when Hockney was experimenting with the Vari-Lites, trying out different colours. 'I don't think Hockney's approach was wrong,' Miller recalled. 'It was like a pop-up book, thunderously over-coloured, and it had nothing to do with me.'[15] In the end, he said, 'I was just a real estate agent showing people round the premises.'[16] It was a view largely confirmed by the critics at its premiere, who judged 6 December 1987 to be Hockney's night. Gerald Larner wrote in the *Guardian* that the first set of *Tristan und Isolde* was 'one of the most beautiful and original ever inspired by a Wagner opera', comparing it with Alfred Moller's designs for Mahler's production eighty years earlier, but asserting that 'Hockney's vision is entirely his own and his technique absolutely new . . . A producer evidently can do very little on such an elaborately pre-painted stage. Jonathan Miller's hand, in his first approach to Wagner, is nowhere recognisable . . . Perhaps the best that can be said of Miller's production is that he lets his designer get on with it.'[17]

The audience too saw it as Hockney's night, and when the curtain rose on Act Three, revealing a vertical cliff face falling towards an unseen sea, they broke into spontaneous applause. John Walsh, the director of the Getty Museum, spoke for them when he wrote, 'We were just breathless at the magical way you manipulated the stage-space with light in <u>Tristan</u> (deep one minute, then shrinking and flat the next). And we never saw anything as subtle as the changes of color and angle and intensity you got (especially in Act III): it was as close to Wagner's music as anything visual is going to get, and nearly subliminal – <u>not</u> obtrusive, tricksy, look-at-me effects, but the opposite, <u>functional</u> . . . It will open up stage and lighting design in a thrilling way.'[18]

In the final scene, when Isolde sings the 'Liebestod' before falling dead upon the body of Tristan, Hockney used his painterly skills to play to the crowd. As she sang the moving aria, the stage grew darker and darker and a mass of stars began to emerge in the night sky, which, on the final notes of her song, began to turn into dawn. 'The transcendental dawn,' Hockney called it, 'that last chord, despite the bodies' lying there littered all about the stage, the music somehow lifts you up and out of all that and onto another plane altogether, one of ineffable joy and affirmation, a kind of rapture.'[19] John Russell, writing in the *New York Times*, described this finale as being 'as awesome a moment as we shall ever see on a stage'.[20]

To celebrate the end of an incredibly hard year, the success of *Tristan*, and the imminent opening of the retrospective at LACMA, Hockney decided to throw a New Year's Eve party with a Scottish theme. The invitations featured a mock-heraldic crest, and to give the studio a 'Palm Court' atmosphere, he and Ian Falconer painted the floor with a faux oriental rug, and hired a dance band. There were two hundred guests, valet parking, and the event was covered by the local rag, the *Hollywood Reporter*, whose gossip columnist, George Christy, known for his waspish tongue, gave an amusing flavour of the evening. '"I wish I could take him home with me, he's run up all these Scottish kilts that you're seeing tonight on David and himself and all these other attractive men. I wouldn't mind his sewing a fine seam or two for me,"[21] sighed Coral Browne about artist Ian Falconer, the protégé of David Hockney, who co-hosted the party, along with David and "comedic actor" Butch Kirby, with the dress code being "Black Tie, Kilt, or Any Old Drag". Coral Browne, who one guest winked could give "bitch lessons"[22] (of the most amusing kind), and Vincent Price were seated near the dance band that was playing "Putting on the Ritz".'

Christy continued: 'As more guests arrived, David was concerned

Invitation to the Hogmanay party 1987–88

A kilted David
Hockney at the
Hogmanay party

about his two dachshunds, Stanley and Heinz, who appeared bewildered by the crush of people . . . Before midnight, Scottish bagpipers played while Camilla McGrath snapped photos of the kilted crowd. San Francisco author, Armistead Maupin (in a kilt) and his chum, Terry Andersen (also in kilt) were back from a month's holiday on the island of Lesbos ("had to see where the poet Sappho was born") . . . On the stroke of 12 o'clock Gemini Gallery's Sid Felsen and his bride, Joni Wey, held a long kiss . . .' He finished his piece with a description of Vincent Price at the end of the night. 'With the wait for the cars being a while, Vincent scrambled into the bushes for a pee. Very English that.'[23] This did not amuse his wife when she read it. 'I had Coral Browne on the phone the next morning,' Scheips remembers, 'eating my head off and asking me, "Why did you ask that awful George Christy?"'

Unfortunately the evening ended on a sour note, with the theft of one of Hockney's favourite paintings, the *Painted Lady* image of Celia that had graced the cover of French *Vogue*, and which, along with a series of Victorian menu cards given to him by Billy Wilder, had been hanging in a little foyer that led to the living room and the TV room. 'At two or three in the morning,' Scheips recalls, 'after the guests had gone home, Butchie and Ian had invited a bunch of kids to come up to have an after-party as there was still so much booze and food left over. I was exhausted, so I went up to David's room and told him I was leaving and should I keep the security on all night, and he said, "Oh no, love, it'll be fine." The next morning, when I came up, the painting of Celia was gone, and it's never, ever been found. The last thing I heard about it was a theory that one of these boys stole it as a prank and then got very nervous about it and probably destroyed it. It has never surfaced again, and most of those boys are dead from AIDS.'[24]

When *David Hockney: A Retrospective* finally opened in the Robert O. Anderson building of the Los Angeles County Museum of Art on 4 February 1988, it was the climax of two years of planning. Though the curators, Maurice Tuchman and Stephanie Barron, had been working on Hockney to agree to it for several years before that, he had made it clear that he wanted to wait until he was fifty. Together they had secured loans of 250 works, including paintings, drawings, photographs, prints, stage sets and illustrated books, from all over the world, for what Hockney considered 'a journey, not a retrospective or a mid-career survey'. The costs for this, mostly paid for by the sponsorship of AT&T, were enormous, over $1 million, and were largely made up from the charges for insurance, transportation and crating. The latter was an art in itself, with each piece of art loaned to the museum arriving in an individually built, form-fitted box, generally made of wood and lined with paper and foam, and set inside another box – a crate within a crate, each one costing between $700 and $1,000. As for the transportation costs, they not only included trucking and air fares, and customs-clearance fees, but also often the cost of a courier to travel with the art. By the mid-eighties this had become common practice for foreign loans, after one too many incidents of paintings being left on the tarmac in the rain.

By the day of the Hockney opening, Los Angeles was gripped by 'Brit Fever', as it heralded the start of a three-month, and one-time-only, arts festival, UK/LA 88 – A Celebration of British Arts, which included orchestral and rock concerts, art shows, film and theatre, as well as an official visit by the Duke and Duchess of York, on board the royal yacht *Britannia*. The hot ticket, however, was an invitation to LACMA's private-view party, at such a premium that sixty couples signed up to be 'President Circle Patrons' of the museum, at $5,000 a throw, just in order to get one. For this eye-watering amount, they still had to queue to get into the museum, queue to get into the exhibition, and queue to get a piece of the giant chocolate cake decorated in icing sugar with a reproduction of *A Walk Around the Hotel Courtyard, Acatlán*. 'What if they gave a party and everybody came?' asked the correspondent for the *Los Angeles Times*. 'That's what happened Wednesday night at the Los Angeles County Museum of Art when "David Hockney: A Retrospective" opened and 1,500 or 2,100 or 2,800 friends showed up. Friends of the artist, of LACMA, of AT&T, and big names from UK/LA flooded the museum, waves of black-tied partygoers surging between the tables crowding the Times Mirror Central Court. And, amazingly, everybody in this extraordinary, eclectic mix seemed to be having a wonderful time . . . "Are there only 2,500 people? Is that all we invited?" kidded Zack Manna, the corporate advertising manager of AT&T . . . Beside him, Hockney beamed and did a nervous little dance as friends lined up to kiss him hello. Lighting a cigarette, he said with Manna that this party was great – but Manna should have made his and Butch Kirby's New Year's Eve bash.'[25]

However much he might have made light of it, this show was of great importance to Hockney. It was only his second retrospective, and there could be few greater accolades than this one, which, after LA, was due to go to the Met in New York, and then to London's Tate Gallery. Much had happened in the intervening years since the retrospective at the Whitechapel in London in 1970, when his precocious talent had astonished critics and public alike. By now he was a fully-fledged celebrity, admired by those who knew the name of no other artists, courted by the rich and the famous, and by committees who wanted a poster for their society benefit. He had been memorialised in books and on film. He had embraced painting, drawing, photography, print-making, computer graphics and film-making, and his theatre sets were as eagerly awaited and closely scrutinised by opera lovers as the singing.

There was a downside to this, pointed out by William Wilson, the art critic of the *LA Times*, who interviewed him before the opening. 'The British artist,' he noted, 'has changed remarkably little since he materialized in Los Angeles back in the '60s. Same shock of blond hair, same owl-round glasses and ironically self-effacing manner supported by a jaw that somehow recalls a crab claw. At some level you don't want to mess with this exceedingly nice man. "I'm not hearing too well today. My little dog chewed up two of my hearing aids. Here, look at this." He pulls a lump of plastic from his pocket that looks like a small nut-meat or possibly a mouse's brain. "Easy to mistake that for a chicken bone." He's always been remarkably candid, modest and funny. A critic once praised a painting of his in a show of modern portraits in London. The artist squeezed his cheeks together in consternation. "I saw that show. They hung me next to a Matisse. I said, 'Good heavens. I can't hang next to Maa-teese.'"'

Wilson went on to point out that Hockney's 'sheer popularity and prolix production have caused observers to worry that he is somehow a lightweight dandy flitting over the surfaces of one enthusiasm after another, frittering away immense talent that rests lopsided on his head like a tipsy crown of golden laurel. He has seemed like some updated film biography of Franz Liszt surrounded by friends begging him to get down to serious composing while he gads about playing flashy concerts for the adoring masses.'[26] It was a sound point and understandable considering that most people viewed the artist's work only in bits and pieces over time, without considering the journey he might be engaged in, so here was the opportunity for the doubters to be won over, to see that he was more than just a frivolous *flâneur*.

The show, laid out by Hockney himself, encompassed his entire life, beginning with his *Self Portrait* from 1954, in which he is seated on his bed wearing a pair of pinstriped trousers and a black-and-white striped tie, and ending with *Pearblossom Hwy*. There was also a special room that re-created his studio and included his models for *Tristan und Isolde*, together with a generous helping of 'Home Made Prints', framed in a manner that would not have disgraced an El Greco. In between, the viewer was led through a sequence of themed rooms devoted to the nature of representation, with names such as 'Flatness and Depth', 'Breaking the Frame' and 'Elusive Surfaces'. The museum had not stinted on the catalogue, for which they had commissioned new photography, as well as a series of introductory essays by both friends, such as Henry Geldzahler and Ron Kitaj, and critics like Christopher Knight, Gert Schiff and Ren Weschler.

In a way, the exhibition ended *in* the catalogue, the final twenty-three pages of it comprising eleven 'Home Made Prints'. A short handwritten multicoloured note on the last page explained that these were not reproductions in the ordinary sense, but original works, in that this was the only form in which they existed. 'They were proofed first on an office copying machine,' Hockney wrote, 'without which it would not have been possible to construct them. New technologies have started revolutions that need not frighten us. They can be humanized by artists. The office copier has opened up commercial printing as a direct artist's medium.'[27]

Sixteen thousand people passed through the exhibition in its first week, setting it on its way to becoming one of the museum's record-breaking shows, garnering Hockney myriad new fans, and confounding his critics, who universally praised it. 'Trooping the 150 or so Hockneys in LACMA's Anderson Gallery,' wrote William Wilson, 'is enough to make a believer out of the most fanatical hair-shirt art monk. (Everybody else is already convinced.) This is superb stuff.'[28] While John Russell, writing in the *New York Times*, commented, 'Given the scale of the show, every visitor will find things in it that he doesn't like. But it is the work of an artist who digs deep within himself without ever appearing to do so.'[29]

Almost as soon as the retrospective had opened, Charlie Scheips gave in his notice. In the previous few months he had found himself becoming increasingly isolated. He no longer had a role at the studio where Hockney and Falconer were working obsessively on the opera, and he felt like he was treading on toes at the office on Santa Monica Boulevard from where he had been helping organise the retrospective. 'I kind of felt like a man without a country,' he recalls, 'and I looked around me, and I saw these people like Mo and Jimmy and I thought to myself, "I'm thirty years old and I don't want to be fifty and dealing David's cigarettes and drinking his booze and doing all that stuff." I wanted to be a museum director.'[30] Though he had briefly mentioned his concerns to Hockney before Christmas, he had taken them no further until the museum show had opened. 'Then one day we went out to lunch at Muse restaurant on Beverly Boulevard, just the two of us, and David said, "I don't think you're happy, love. What shall we do about it?" And I said, "I don't know but the retrospective's over and the opera's over, and maybe you want to take a rest. So maybe I should leave and do something else."'[31] After further discussions, he left before the show moved to New York and London. That Hockney considered anyone leaving him, for whatever reason, to be some form of betrayal was reflected in the fact that Scheips was not invited to the opening of either of these shows.

England was due to see the retrospective at the Tate in October, though for a while it looked like they would only see a part of it owing to Hockney's continuing support for a cause that he had fought for all his life. It had reached his ears, through his editor and friend Nikos Stangos, that the British government under Margaret Thatcher was planning to bring onto the statute books, as part of the Local Government Act, a clause known as Section 28, banning local councils from 'promoting' homosexuality, and schools from 'promoting the teaching of the acceptability of homosexuality as a pretended family relationship'. That it had widespread support can partly be explained by the general fear that then existed about the spread of AIDS, which, through ignorance, was largely blamed on the homosexual community.

When Hockney heard about this, he 'went mad', he told the *Sunday Times*, and asked for all the details to be sent out to him so he could consider his response. He began by writing a furious letter to the paper, explaining that this was just the kind of thing that had driven him to leave England, and recalling how, when he had asked to see a copy of Cavafy's *Poems* in Bradford Public Library, he was told that it was not considered suitable to be on the open shelves. He had been incensed by whoever it was who had taken the decision to hide the book away. 'I deeply detested the person who had done this,' he fumed, 'because I am an Englishman. As I set off from Bradford, I was determined that myopic nannies would not interfere. I came across them again and again and complained and shouted as much as I could. Nanny England was to me a hideous perversity that was, as I saw it, denying my own heritage . . . To read now about Clause 28 doesn't, I'm sad to say, surprise me. Thatcherism is a fraud because it doesn't go far enough. It is freedom for the businessman but not for the artist. It is crude and philistine . . .'[32]

There was some confusion about what happened next. The *Sunday Times* reported that Stangos told them that Hockney had telephoned him to say he would consider withdrawing all the work he personally owned from the forthcoming Tate show, if it was thought this would strengthen the hand of opposition to the government's proposals. This would have had a devastating effect on the exhibition, since it amounted to a quarter of all the work to be shown. Meanwhile, he had also told a *Guardian* reporter, 'I will never exhibit in England again.'[33] The threat certainly put the wind up the arts establishment. 'I, like a great many other people in Britain,' said the director of the Tate, Nicholas Serota, 'would be dismayed if his show should not come to the Tate.'[34] Though the tabloids tended to support the government, with the *Sun* commenting about Hockney, 'We can get away without his paintings. In fact he can stay away permanently,'[35] The Times, in a leader, observed, 'There is too much truth in what Mr Hockney says, alas, for it to be swept aside with chauvinist contempt . . .'[36] As the furore surrounding the rumours increased, Hockney panicked and made a conflicting statement to the Sunday Telegraph, saying, 'The Sunday Times tried repeatedly to get me to say I would consider cancelling the retrospective. I repeatedly denied it,' and eventually telling the Sunday Times that he could not in effect withdraw from the Tate exhibition because of contractual obligations. The attitude of the gay community to Hockney's statements was well summed up by John Cox, who wrote to him, 'As for Clause 29,* God knows what you actually did or did not say, write or threaten, but it was good that you spoke out.'[37] In the end, Hockney admitted defeat. 'Yes, it will come to the Tate,' he said. 'And I hope it might bring pleasure to somebody. Because I am very English, I now just want a quiet life.'[38]

A quiet life, however, was not to be, for it was rarely without its drama, the latest being the final decline of Mo McDermott. In September, Ann Graves had written to Hockney, 'I'm so sorry to hear Mo is drinking – Thank God we don't really understand those sort of addictions. I know you have gone out of your way to do your utmost in the situation, but you must keep telling yourself it's an illness and any way he behaves is not a personal thing.'[39] Then in January, Hockney had received a postcard from McDermott that suggested he was on the mend. 'Do take care, you are again working overtime and we're all looking forward to the Retrospective in February. I adored Tristan and was so Proud to be an early part of it. I'll call and come and see you soon. I'm well and taking every day as it comes . . . the going away to Guatemala + the South certainly helped. L.A. after 9 years was pretty awful in many ways. Here's to a lovely Happy 1988. Love, Mo.'[40] The trip to South America had been a failed attempt to try to get back together with Lisa, but they had both started drinking again, which infuriated Hockney as he thought about them sitting drinking

* Clause 28 was renamed Clause 29 after small changes to the legislation.

rum-and-Cokes on Copacabana Beach, ignoring the doctor's warnings. It was really the last straw, however much McDermott claimed to be regretful. 'In my Alcoholic-Schitsophrenic [sic] manifestations,' he had written to him, 'I did not seem to appreciate your kindness, help and friendship. I do want you to know now I always did and always will. My deepest Apologies again for all the ways I've hurt you, I didn't really mean to.'[41]

In April, he was back in hospital, this time on a last warning. 'He went to hospital in a really bad state,' Maurice Payne recalls, 'where they told him that if he had one more drink he'd be dead, so what did he do? He came out of hospital and poured himself a drink straight away and that was the end.'[42] 'George came round. Dad, I've got some really bad news,' Ossie Clark noted on 6 May. 'I knew from his faltering voice immediately he said Da'ad. "Mo's dead!" "Ohhh," as though I knew already – he has been so on my mind. So many people loved him. Although it was still a shock, I accepted it – no tears: "Well we must drink to dear Mo," but my voice cracked and I said no more, washed a glass and drank a sip of clear vodka.'[43]

Hockney was deeply saddened by the death of Mo McDermott, who was one of his oldest and most loyal friends. 'Mo always told me,' Paul Hockney says, 'that he was still in love with David even though he'd married Lisa.'[44] For years Hockney had put up with the drinking and drug abuse, the continual payment of fees for clinics and hospitals, admission to which had often ended up with Mo back on the bottle as soon as he was released, and the selling of pictures both given as gifts and stolen. He had done so because he loved him, and they made each other laugh. Even Mo's thieving could be a subject for one of Hockney's jokes. When he had once retrieved half of a torn-up drawing from a waste-paper basket, and had managed to sell it, Hockney referred to it as 'Half a Mo'. But Hockney was also angry, because McDermott's death was, in his eyes, akin to suicide, during a period when so many of his friends were dying of AIDS, all of whom would have given anything to go on living – friends like Nick Wilder, his first dealer in LA, who died one week later on 1 2 May, and Sheridan Dufferin, co-owner of the original Kasmin Gallery, who died on 29

A Visit with Christopher & Don, Santa Monica Canyon, **1984.** Oil on 2 Canvases, 72 × 240″

A Walk Around the Hotel Courtyard, Acatlán, **1985.** Oil on 2 Canvases, 72 × 240″

Cover for French Vogue, December 1985–January 1986

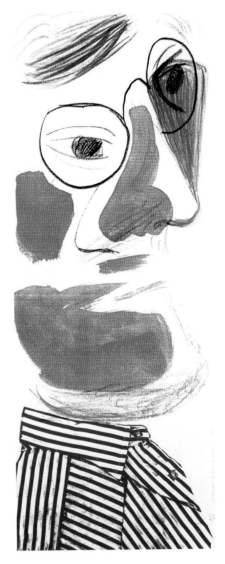

Self-Portrait, July 1986.
Home-Made Print on 2 Sheets of Paper,
edition of 60, 22 × 8 ½″

Pearblossom Hwy., 11–18th April 1986 (Second Version). Photographic Collage, 71½ × 107″

Bradford Bounce, Feb. 1987. Colour Xerox (2 panels), 15 × 22″

1˝ scale model for Tristan und Isolde, Act III, 1987

Pacific Coast Highway and Santa Monica, 1990. Oil on Canvas, 78 × 120˝

Turandot, Lyric Opera of Chicago, 1992. Poster, 72 × 36″

Model for Act I, Scene 2 from Die Frau Ohne Schatten, 1992.

The Eleventh V.N. Painting, 1992. Oil on Canvas, 24 × 36˝

Dog Painting 1, **1994.** Oil on Canvas, 24 × 24″

Self-Portrait, *January 19, 1997.*
Oil on Canvas, 13 ¾ × 10 ¾″

Jonathan Silver, February 27, 1997.
Oil on Canvas, 13 ¾ × 10 ¾″

May. It was scarcely surprising that Ossie Clark noted in his diary on 16 June, after he had just seen Hockney in London, 'DH been and gone and very depressed.'[45]

While in London, John Cox had spoken to Hockney about the possibility of him designing the Richard Strauss opera *Die Frau ohne Schatten* for Covent Garden. He said, 'David, the defiant imagination must take wing, the Phoenix must rise again with an immortal "Frau ohne Schatten".'[46] After the success of *Tristan*, Hockney was keen to further explore his new ideas of staging, and he loved the Strauss opera and knew that it was meant to be grand and exciting theatre, as well as visually challenging. Moreover he had hated almost all the productions of it he had seen. He had, however, decided that he now wished to have two years of uninterrupted painting, so it was agreed with the new head of Covent Garden, Jeremy Isaacs, that it should be the first new production of the 1992/93 season.

Unusually, the first painting he undertook after the retrospective was a commission from the organisers of the International Festival of Photography at Arles. It was in 1888 that Van Gogh had rented a studio in Arles, the Yellow House, and had invited Gauguin to join him there, and had done several paintings of sunflowers to decorate his room in anticipation of his arrival. To celebrate the centenary of this event, various contemporary artists, including Rauschenberg, Lichtenstein and Hockney, had been invited to create a homage to Van Gogh. Hockney chose to do a painting of Van Gogh's chair in reverse perspective. He liked the picture so much that after giving it to the Van Gogh Foundation in Arles, he did another version for himself. He also came across an illustration of the painting that Van Gogh had done of Gauguin's chair and painted his own version of that, again in reverse perspective. These were followed by a whole series of works further exploring the spatial ideas of perspective, which included a number of interiors of Montcalm Avenue, and a huge landscape, *The Road to Malibu*, reminiscent of his earlier painting *Mulholland Drive: The Road to the Studio*.

The inspiration for this last picture was the fact that after the retrospective, he had bought a house overlooking the beach in Malibu, a twenty-one-mile strip of Pacific coastline that lies to the south of the Santa Monica Mountains and is famous for its warm, sandy beaches. It had been Ian Falconer's idea. 'Butchie and I had a friend called James Curley,' he remembers, 'whose father, Walter, had been US Ambassador to Ireland under Nixon, and he had a beach house in Malibu. I was out there one day and James pointed out a house that was for sale. It was a very good 1930s house, solidly built, on a rocky promontory with a deck next to it. It was very pretty. Not Hollywoodish, but just a lovely old-fashioned beach cottage. I called David up and told him about it and he came down the same day and he bought it.'[47]

The cottage had belonged to an elderly lady and her husband who had been among the pioneers who had moved down to the beach in the early 1930s, when the then privately owned land was opened up by the building of the Pacific Coast Highway. They had built the house and raised a family there. She was an amateur painter, and had added a small studio at the back of the house with an electric stairlift for access. Fifty years later, it was the perfect place for an overworked, stressed-out Hockney to escape to with the dachshunds. He fell quite in love with it at the beginning and started to spend most of his time there. What he particularly liked about it was the fact that it had a double-length deck. 'To be able to walk along that wooden deck with the water at your feet,' he told Paul Joyce, 'gives you a feeling of real connection to the sea. Here I'm on the edge of the largest swimming-pool in the world – the Pacific Ocean. Beyond me is nothing but sea . . . Studying the movement of the water sends one into a profound meditative state. When you live this close to the sea, where it literally comes up and splashes the windows, it is not the horizon line which dominates, but the close movement of the water itself. It's like fire and smoke, endlessly changing, endlessly fascinating. I've noticed that the dogs don't look out of the windows in the hills, but here they'll sit and watch the sea with me for hours. I go to sleep and wake up to the sounds of the sea.'[48] The dachshunds also benefited because the stretch of beach in front of the house was one of the few places in LA where dogs could run free and was thus known by the name of 'Doggie Beach'.

Hockney loved the studio there – he thought it was one of the nicest he had ever worked in. It was also one of the smallest, 'not much bigger than my bathroom', Gregory Evans commented, and this limited the size of the canvases he could use there. As luck would have it, he had a large supply of small ones, 16½ inches by 10½ inches in dimension, having bought a hundred of them to use with the Canon copier, and he immediately began to paint on them. He painted the little house itself, its interior, its exteriors, what was behind, which was all the landscape, and he painted what he had never painted before, in spite of having established himself in the previous two decades as the definitive painter of California's light and scene, which was the ocean. 'I didn't paint it,' he said, 'because I hadn't really seen it. Now that I'm here, of course, it's become one of my main preoccupations . . . It's endlessly fascinating watching the water. It gets to be like watching fire: intoxicating, hypnotic.'[49] When Nikos Stangos was visiting to start work on a second volume of memoirs, his lover David Plante remembers Hockney staring out of the window and endlessly repeating, 'We're living on the edge of the Western World, the edge of the Western World.'[50]

As well as painting the waves, he also painted little flower studies as a memorial to all the friends he had recently lost, not vases of flowers, but living plants in pots. Most of all, however, he painted his living friends and family, small portraits done rapidly from life with a strong concentration on the face; portraits of, among others, Peter Goulds, Maurice Payne, John Hockney, Paul Hockney, Bing McGilvray, Karen Kuhlman, Don Cribb, Henry Geldzahler and, of course, his mother. 'I felt I wanted to look at my friends' faces again,' he said, 'and I painted them rather quickly and crudely, but, as the paintings accumulated, they seemed quite interesting. Most of the people I had painted didn't like them – I don't think I'm that much of a flatterer. Nevertheless it was useful for me to look at people again – they were all people I knew. If the best ones are of my mother, it is perhaps because I know her best.'[51]

Just as he had done with the portrait of Henry Geldzahler, he placed the completed paintings on the Canon copier to make a unique reproduction of each of them. 'I . . . became very excited by the result,' he recalled. 'The colours from the Canon machine were intense and very, very close to the originals. But what was it, this copy? A photograph but not a photograph? A copy without a conventional camera . . . However, unlike a colour photograph, where the colours seem to exist below the surface of the print itself, here was colour which sat on top of the paper, giving it an incredible luminosity. What were they then? Not "home made" prints, because there I made the images in stages via the machine. So they are not copies, but originals in an unlimited edition, just made by using a copier. I wasn't sure what to do with them, or where this would lead, but I knew instinctively that it would lead somewhere. So I made a lot of prints and gave them away to my sitters.'[52] Soon the little studio in Malibu was filled with faces. They were company for Hockney, and a permanent reminder that despite the death that was so ever-present, life carried on.

A number of the new paintings were added to the retrospective when it travelled to the Tate Gallery in October, where Hockney hung them himself in a special room at the end. London, much to the dismay of the artist, was rife with Hockneymania: there was the opening at the Tate, followed by a dinner for forty at Lindy Dufferin's, five other exhibitions of prints, graphics and photography at various London galleries, the publication of two new books – one on photography, the other a biography – and an episode of *The South Bank Show*, the television arts programme hosted by Melvyn Bragg, devoted to him. Like some pop star before a global tour, there was also a press conference for three hundred journalists from around the world. 'Numbered tickets were handed out,' reported the *Sunday Times*. 'Security men were on the door. Photographers argued and jostled for front-row seats. At least two lenses ended up broken. "It's more like Madonna at Wembley than a retrospective at the Tate," said one.'[53] His celebrity status meant that there was little peace at home either. 'Even in his London studio,' noted the journalist Geordie Greig, 'suitcase left unpacked, clothes strewn around the pine floor, any relaxation was short-lived. Within ten minutes, the telephone rang four times, the doorbell three times and Hockney found himself conducting conversations with three sets of people. It was only 10.15am on Wednesday. "It's been like this all week and it's getting too hectic," he said, leaving the receiver off the hook.'[54]

Ossie Clark, whom he had failed to ask to the opening, wrote to him, rather than telephoned. 'David, it no longer surprises me that you're never in touch; though sometimes I wonder why. I did think I might receive an invite, this time, to your Reception at the Tate, but not so far which just proves how right my mother's advice was, never expect anything and you'll never be disappointed.'[55] The night before the private view on 24 October, he was 'very thrilled to find a buff envelope delivered by hand, foolscap and folded, addressed to Mr Ossie Clark. I recognised Hockney's style, realised it was an invitation at last. I was so excited I delayed opening it . . .'[56]

Writing about the exhibition in the *Sunday Times*, Marina Vaizey made the point that Hockney's celebrity was in danger of obscuring his achievement since it prevented people from taking him seriously. Seeing this show might make those detractors think again. 'The show displays,' she wrote, 'his wonderful way with line, outstanding draughtsmanship, and above all his absorption with brilliant blues, greens, reds, lately perhaps influenced by his stage designs. But what gives Hockney's art its cutting edge, lifting it above the beguilingly decorative, is his obsession with visual codes and language.' She finished by stating, 'He is certainly one of Britain's greatest artists this century.'[57] Other reviewers were less enthusiastic. While lauding his skill as a draughtsman, Richard Shone in the *Observer* decried his 'gawky poster-colour palette' and his 'bizarre pastiches', writing, 'He is on a tightrope, absurdity and impasse grinning up from one side, comfort in the arms of tradition beckoning from the other.'[58] In the *Guardian*, Tim Hilton commented, 'David Hockney was not a *wunderkind* a quarter of a century ago. Nor is he nowadays Peter Pan. He is the lost boy of contemporary painting . . . There's a lot of the boring old northern art schoolmaster in what he says about representation versus abstraction, the falsity of the avant-garde and so on. At the same time he wants to be always having new ideas – and the results are lamentable.'[59]

Such words might seem harsh, but they need to be seen in the climate of the times. A new wind was blowing through the British art world, and it emanated from London's docklands, where, only a month previously, another wunderkind had taken over the empty Port of London Authority Building in Surrey Docks, a vast disused warehouse, and mounted an exhibition of work by sixteen young and unknown British artists, many of them his contemporaries at Goldsmiths College. Damien Hirst, who was working part-time at the Anthony d'Offay Gallery, had prepared the space for the show himself, along with fellow student Angus Fairhurst, installing lighting and touching up the place, and even painting two of his 'Spot' pictures, *Edge* and *Row*, directly onto the warehouse walls. The show was titled *Freeze*, after the catalogue description of one of the exhibits, Mat Collishaw's macro photograph *Bullet Hole*, a backlit transparency of a gunshot wound to a human head, and featured work by artists who were to be collectively labelled by the press the YBAs, Young British Artists, including Gary Hume, Sarah Lucas, Michael Landy and Angus Fairhurst. A brilliant self-publicist, Hirst persuaded the property development company Olympia & York to sponsor an expensive-looking catalogue, which he distributed around galleries and bookshops, as well as working overtime to persuade notable curators, journalists and collectors to attend, including Richard Shone, Nicholas Serota, Charles Saatchi and Norman Rosenthal. The result was that through what Hirst's tutor at Goldsmiths called 'a combination of youthful bravado, innocence, fortunate timing, good luck, and, of course, good work',[60] the show caught people's imagination.

As for Hockney, he remained unfazed by the critics' opinions. 'It doesn't matter what people think,' he told Geordie Greig. 'I think the world is beautiful. I really do. Colour is a wonderful thing. In the 19th century the Impressionists were painting much prettier pictures and they are now getting the attention they deserve.'[61] He had the confidence to know where he was going, irrespective of whether or not other people understood, an attitude he took from his great hero. 'Picasso said he never made a painting as a work of art. It was all research, a logical sequence and it was about time. I understand that remarkably well . . . Of course it's a struggle. I see it as my own journey discovering things constantly. In life there is only love and fear . . . We are either destructive or creative. And I plan to remain creative.'[62] Indeed, he was about to move his creativity in a completely new direction.

CHAPTER TWELVE

TENNIS

In August 1989, Hockney wrote to Kitaj from his house in Malibu:

> I will finish this letter and hopefully put it in an envelope and post
> it to you. It will be taken by aeroplane from here to London, you
> will receive it in a few days, perhaps a week, that time is <u>now</u>,
> exactly when you are reading this for the first time.
>
> What I would like to suggest with all this nonsense is that you
> go out (into the street) and in the Kings Rd buy a fax machine.
> With this machine you could receive this letter the moment I
> have finished it. You can keep the copy and send me one back at
> any time, you can draw, write, collage, etc and we will both have a
> record, the same one but reversed in positive and negative.
>
> It strikes me as a wonderful knew [sic] way to communicate
> [. . .] Please do it. They cost about £1,000 but are priceless in
> what they can do. I write many letters and never post them. I tend
> to think I've communicated when I've written it down. People
> find ten page letters to themselves amongst the newspapers here.
> With this machine I can deliver them myself.[1]

Hockney had been experimenting with the commercial fax
machine ever since Karen Kuhlman had bought one for the office
sometime in 1988. Though there was nothing new in the technology,
newspapers having used it for years to send photographs down the
wire, as soon as he saw the machine, he realised the possibilities it
held, first and foremost as a means of communication for deaf people.
He bought one for himself and one for his sister, Margaret, who lived
in Bridlington and was also, like him, profoundly deaf. They began
to exchange messages via fax and Hockney started to refer to it as 'a
telephone for the deaf', because you didn't have to speak or hear when

using it. 'Then I realised,' he said, 'you could draw and send drawings. It was also a printing machine, and if you realised how it printed, you could draw accordingly, so that you could always make good pictures. It's an electronic printing, a different kind of printing. The speed with which you could do it was almost spontaneous, like painting. I was very thrilled to be able to do that. Exploring the fax was quite simple. For instance to use the half-tones, I found in the end you didn't put a wash on, you put an opaque grey on, then it would print that as a half-tone with dots, and it would look like a wash. If you put a wash on it you couldn't read it.'[2] By endless experiments and testing different mediums, he soon came up with a way of transmitting a drawing so that it always came out clear at the other end. He discovered that, used right, the printing could actually be quite beautiful.

He began to fax drawings to his friends all over the world, to begin with just single sheets, but progressing, as he became more experienced, to pictures made up of more than one sheet that had to be assembled at the other end. Bing McGilvray, who was then working at Tower Records in Boston, was one of the recipients. 'He would send me these faxes of the Malibu Sea,' he recalls, 'of the coffee table in the den with the roaring ocean in the background, pictures of his dachshunds, and they increasingly got bigger and bigger. When they started there'd be one sheet, then there'd be four that you put together, then eight, and eventually my boss kept saying, "What the hell is all this stuff?" He'd come in on the morning and there'd be twenty-four pieces of paper on the floor.'[3]

'As people became aware of what I was doing,' Hockney told Paul Joyce, 'they would call and ask me to send the latest fax. First I would send a detailed plan of how the pages should be pasted together, followed by the work itself. My phone bills became enormous! Then I realised that people have different kinds of fax machines at the other end – old ones and new ones. The old ones were incredibly slow sometimes. Once I send one to an old machine, they rarely get another!'[4] Since the faxes were sent from Hockney's house in Malibu, which had the Pacific Coast Highway on one side and opened out onto the beach on the other, they often had the ocean as their subject. 'Many of them,' he wrote, 'were

Fax: *Yes. Another Sea Picture*

made up from paintings of the sea, stretched on one machine, reduced in another way, crammed in, pasted up, made into a collage and then into a fax . . . Next to the fax machine I had a new black and white laser copier with which I now began to do all kinds of things, not just reduce: I could use it to bend images, play with variations or put one image inside another. One fax shows how the machine can tilt the image, so I have written on it, "Mind-bending fax coming soon."[5] Since the sea was now playing such an important role in his life, he sent the faxes as if from a large company, which he named 'The Hollywood Sea Picture Supply Company'. Alongside them was a note explaining that if people wanted to keep them, they should make a copy on good-quality paper, as the thermal paper on which the fax was printed would not last.

Gradually the faxes became increasingly complex and much bigger, starting with sixteen-page images and going up to twenty-four. As he began to send out the larger ones, the first image he sent out had to be of the whole picture, reduced from its full size to one page, with a grid drawn on it and accompanied by a note which read, 'The following [however many] pages make up this picture.' Each picture was then sent through numbered according to where it would be placed on the grid, so that whoever received them could put them together. As this became more successful, it gave him a wonderfully subversive idea. He had been asked to show his work at the São Paulo Biennale in Brazil, which was taking place in the autumn of 1989. Founded by Ciccillo Matarazzo, an Italian-Brazilian industrialist, this was, after Venice, the second-oldest art biennial in the world, and he was keen to participate. They wanted to do a painting exhibition, but it was proving very difficult to persuade owners to lend again so soon after the retrospective. So Hockney came up with a novel plan which he suggested to the curator of the proposed show, his old friend Henry Geldzahler, who had been the recipient of many of the new fax paintings.

'I cheekily suggested,' he recalled, 'that since the recent work had all been done on the telephone, why not do a big fax exhibition? Henry had already seen quite a lot of the faxes and I told him I'd now learnt how to make them bigger. So we got a map of the room in São Paulo and made an exact model of it so that we could make some faxes specifically to fit the wall.'[6] The idea he put forward was that the entire exhibition of his work would be sent by fax, and he would not make an appearance at all. This was not quite what the organisers had in mind, and many people dismissed it as a joke, horrified that he was sending faxes to an important biennial, but Hockney persisted that this was the only way they were going to get any works, so in the end they were forced to go along with the proposal. Since no artist had ever done this before, they had to concede that it was an original idea.

It had its problems, though, as was soon discovered by Richard Schmidt. 'We were supposed to transmit them two weeks in advance,' he recalls, 'and they were supposed to install them themselves. However, it soon turned out that the phone lines in Brazil were so bad that the faxes either took ages to come through, or else wouldn't transmit at all. This was something we had never contemplated, so panic set in.'[7] They realised that the only way to do it at such short notice was to transmit them from one room to another in California, and physically carry them down to Brazil. So Schmidt, representing Hockney, was sent down to São Paulo, carrying suitcases full of faxes, to meet up with Henry Geldzahler and put the whole thing together.

The work was to be shown in a room in the Ciccillo Matarazzo

Pavilion, a three-storey building designed by Oscar Niemeyer in the Parque do Ibirapuera in São Paulo, and Hockney had devised four very large pictures, one for each wall. The prints that were stuck onto the grid were made on the best-quality archival paper, so as to last. 'The first thing I remember,' says Schmidt, 'was running round town trying to find plain white glue to paste them all up to the walls. Then I hired a helper or two and we worked for three days to get it all up in time for the opening.'[8] When the show was finally over, the organisers asked Hockney what they should do with the faxes, which had little value. 'I told them,' he said, 'Well, you could send them back by fax.'[9]

What they actually did when the exhibition was dismantled was to cut down the walls with the faxes still glued to them, and put the large panels into storage with the view that if kept carefully they might eventually have some value since they were dated and part of Hockney's *oeuvre*, and would never be sent out again. 'The fax show in Brazil caused quite a stir,' wrote Hockney. 'But many people saw the philosophical side, the interesting side, the use of printing to make original works. I assume that even though people think my work is very popular, it often takes them time to see what I am really doing, to see what it is I am exploring, that it is not just a wild thing, but something that grows out of something else, and will grow into something else again.'[10]

One person who absolutely understood what Hockney was up to was a Yorkshire entrepreneur called Jonathan Silver, with whom he had been friends since the 1960s. Silver was the son of a Bradford textile manufacturer named Sidney Silver, who owned two clothing factories and a number of Wimpy Bars. While a pupil at Bradford Grammar School in 1963, aged thirteen, he had met Hockney after writing to him to ask if he would design a cover for a school magazine project he was working on. Hockney, who had just won the Royal College of Art gold medal, was amused by what he considered a cheeky letter, and replied that he would think about it, and would meet Silver in Bradford when he came home for the Christmas holidays. They met in one of his father's Wimpy Bars, in Broadway, and Hockney was immediately seduced by the charm and enthusiasm of the young boy

twelve years his junior. He agreed
to design the cover, and eventually
sent Silver a painting, which was
a typical sixties psychedelic take
on the Bradford Grammar School
tie.

Over the years, whenever he
was back in Bradford, a friendship
blossomed, which was based on
their mutual appreciation of each
other's enthusiasm for life and
art. Silver had boundless energy,
which could take off in a thousand
directions. After studying art and
textiles at Leeds University, he
started a clothing business called
Jonathan Silver Clothes, which
soon expanded into a chain of
thirteen stores across the country.
He even had his own factory,
called Noble Crest. His love of
art then prevailed, and in
November 1978 he opened a
gallery in Manchester called Art
and Furniture, in which the art,

Jonathan Silver at the 1853 Gallery, standing in front of *Tennis*

primarily works by Hockney, was hung in furnished rooms as it
would be in a private home, except that the furniture was also for
sale. Two years later he gave this up to go into business with another
local entrepreneur, Sir Ernest Hall, buying and developing two great
Yorkshire mills, C. & J. Hirst in Huddersfield, a cloth mill, and Dean
Clough in Halifax, the headquarters of Crossley carpets.

After two years working on Dean Clough, he sold his half and
took his wife, Maggie, and their daughters, Zoe and Davina, on a
round-the-world trip, ending up in La Jolla, a town north of San Diego,
California, where they rented a house. One day, while on a visit to

Hollywood, totally by chance they ran into Hockney. 'We had gone into LA for the day,' Zoe Silver recalls, 'and we were standing on the street in Rodeo Drive, when one of us looked across the road and saw David. He was quite unmistakable. It was 1986 and he looked so different to everyone else who was there, because he was so graphic. So we ran across the road to say hello, and he was fumbling around in his pocket to find a laundry ticket. When he saw us he just said, "Oh, hello. Come to tea," so we went to his house and me and my sister swam in the pool, which was very exciting as we knew all about him and his swimming pools.'[11]

For Silver, visiting Hockney's studio and seeing all the work he was engaged in was fortuitous, because on his return home to Bradford he saw that another important mill was for sale, the Italianate-style Salts Mill, in the model village of Saltaire, which was by then in a sad state of dilapidation. The creation of the great philanthropist and wool merchant Sir Titus Salt, the man who had invented the fashionable cloth alpaca, Salts Mill was, at the time of its completion, the largest industrial building in the world. More importantly, it stood at the centre of a self-sufficient community that had its own shops, hospital, school, library, park and church, along with good houses for the workers, each with its own supply of fresh water, sanitation and gas. In its heyday, the mill was turning out eighteen miles of worsted cloth a day, but by the 1980s it had become, like so many other north-country mills, the victim of the decline in the British manufacturing industry that was a by-product of the Thatcher years. 'Jonathan bought it,' remembers his brother, Robin, 'without at that time really having an idea as to what to do with it, other than that, as it was in Bradford, it should house a David Hockney gallery.'[12]

Silver opened the 1853 Gallery on the ground floor of Salts Mill in 1987. Dedicated to Hockney's work, and with his full approval, the collection comprised pictures owned by Silver himself, which he had bought over the years, work lent by Hockney and by other members of his family, and a number of his works that were bought just to put on show. Enough work was eventually gathered together for Silver to be able to advertise it as being the largest collection of works by David

Hockney in the world. So when Silver, who was a natural showman, was on a trip to LA in 1989 and saw the large faxes that were being sent to Brazil, he immediately wanted one for the gallery. 'He said . . . will you send one to Bradford?' Hockney recalled. 'I said, I'll send one tomorrow if you want. He said, "Oh no, hold it, hold it, wait a minute, let *me* tell you when to send it. I'll fix a time."'[13]

The reason Silver, who Hockney used to say was 'publicity mad', was so keen to control how and when the fax was sent was that he wanted to make an event out of it as a means of garnering as much press as possible for the gallery. 'To Jonathan,' says his brother, 'it was all about the mystery of what it was going to be and of creating a huge event out of the simple process of a fax being received.'[14] So it was that on the evening of 10 November 1989 approximately four hundred people, all invited by fax, and comprising members of Silver's and Hockney's families, their friends, people who had been supportive of the Mill and lots of press, turned up for a proper Yorkshire knees-up with loads of drink, plenty of food and an art happening thrown in. To record it all, Yorkshire Television had provided two film crews, one to record the events in Bradford, the other to capture Hockney sending out the fax from his studio in LA.

'David Hockney's latest work of art,' wrote Martin Wainwright in the *Guardian*, 'arrived in his home city of Bradford last night in a welter of spray-on glue and sheets of fax paper, and to the sound of Wagner's *Ride of the Valkyries*. Sheet by acid-sprayed, conservation-guaranteed sheet, 144 pieces of a huge jigsaw of tubes and angles beeped and fluttered from four laser facsimile machines in Sir Titus Salt's former alpaca mill, while 5,000 miles away at his home in California, Mr Hockney – already master of computer, photocopy and snipped-photograph art – was feeding the composite picture into his own fax.'[15] While the party in Saltaire was getting under way, it was 11 a.m. in Hockney's studio in Montcalm Avenue and total calm prevailed as Hockney, accompanied only by his brother Paul, and his assistants Richard Schmidt and Jimmy Swinea, fed the first sheet into his fax, a simple message that read, 'We are starting now, love David'. As it came out at the other end, Silver, sporting a ponytail and designer

stubble, waved it about triumphantly, shouting, 'This is from David –
DH in the Hills! We've got contact!' and they were off, to loud cheers
and applause from the assembled guests as each sheet was stuck to the
grid.

'Bent over the light-flashing, peeping fax machines,' recorded
Wainwright, '. . . Jonathan Silver checked detailed assembly instructions
previously faxed by the artist . . . While the fax winked and peeped
on its artistic way, following in the steps of the great etchers and
lithographers of the past, tributes to fax from Hockney were passed
around. In a (faxed) letter to his old Bradford Primary, he tells the
pupils: "It seems to me fax will spread everywhere as it is such a useful
instrument and a wonderful way to communicate with each other."
. . . Fax art is not valuable. Each copy is a copy which anyone else can
copy again, says Hockney. "You can frame them, or you can throw them
away."'[16] As the last page came through from the peace and calm of the
studio, in Saltaire they were well behind in completing the picture.
There the party was getting rowdier and rowdier until eventually there
was a massive roar from the crowd as the last piece of the jigsaw was
put in place, and they discovered the name of the 'painting' to be *Tennis*.
Silver had the completed work enclosed in nine Perspex boxes, with an
enormous frame made specially for it.

Laura Hockney was among the revellers. 'I must let you know,'
she wrote, 'what a wonderful evening we had with the fax picture. I
have never enjoyed anything like it! Everything was so well organised . . .
Your ideas & arranging for such a big technical venture was overwhelming. Congratulations for the marvellous brainwork & Jonathan's
co-operation at this end. All his staff had worked very hard all
week. There were reporters & photographers from near & far. It
was all so exciting. I hope I did you justice in answering all their
questions . . . A great aunt of Jonathan's says she feels sure Bradford
will now be so important it will take London's place as capital of
England! I hope you are as pleased at your end as we are here. It
is thrilling.'[17]

So successful was the event that Hockney repeated it in Japan, an
occasion that was shown on Japanese TV. 'The contrast there was quite

amusing,' wrote Hockney. 'Whereas in Bradford the kind of people in   *Fax: Tennis*
the audience were slightly drunk, running around and singing, in Japan
it was a whole little team of young people, probably art students, all
with white gloves, running and putting it up. We then made an even
bigger fax of the sea, the last one, I think, which was made of 288 pages.
That was sent to Japan as well as to Hawaii and to a few other places.
With that, I finished with the faxes.'[18]

During the summer of 1989, a new lover came into Hockney's life.
John Fitzherbert was a handsome, rather roguish young Englishman
in his early twenties whom Hockney had first met in London in
1985 when Fitzherbert was working as a cook for John Dexter. Born
in Littlehampton, Sussex, in 1966, and adopted soon after, he had
spent most of his childhood in South Wales where his adoptive
mother bred horses on a small farm. After her death, when he was
fifteen, he had moved to London to be with his birth mother, a
relationship that never really worked out, and aged nineteen he had
left home to find work in the theatre. He knew by then that he was

gay and felt that the theatrical world was probably the best place to be. While looking for employment, he had met Riggs O'Hara, an actor who lived with John Dexter, and they offered him a job cooking and driving for them. 'John and David were doing a revival of the triple bill in London,' he recalls, 'and I was cooking for John when David came over for lunch. There was quite a bit of flirting went on, and then word got back to me that David had said it was one of the best lunches he'd ever had. Before he left he said, "Why don't you come out to LA for a holiday?"[19]

The following year Fitzherbert and O'Hara, who were then in a relationship, took up the invitation, and on their return to London, Fitzherbert painted the walls of their apartment yellow to remind him of Hollywood and the California sunshine. LA had ruined London for him. He couldn't get the boys, the beach and the sun out of his mind. 'Something in my head just said I had to be in Hollywood,' he remembers, 'so when things began to go pear-shaped with Riggs, I rang up David and asked him if he would like someone to go out and cook for him. I lied to him and told him I had a diploma, and he said, "Come out for a month and see how it goes."'[20]

When Fitzherbert arrived in the Hollywood hills in 1989, Hockney was spending most of his time in Malibu. Richard Schmidt was running the studio at Montcalm Avenue, and Ian Falconer had moved out of the annexe and was living down the hill, leaving Butch Kirby there alone, causing some stress to Hockney, who wanted him out. 'Butchie used to string him along,' says Fitzherbert. 'The trouble was that he was quite a good actor. He could cry on call and then David didn't know what to do. When I was first there I hung out with Butchie quite a lot. He showed me around, and he was telling everyone that I was his driver. I had a crush on him, because he was the typical American blond and was funny and good-looking. He was also very bitchy. One night I made an advance to him and he turned round and said, "I don't sleep with the help!"'[21] When finally all Hockney's patience with Butchie ran out, he employed Bing McGilvray to go into the house and start redecorating the rooms, after a few days of which Butchie got the message and left.

Apart from Fitzherbert, there were no rivals for Hockney's affections at this time other than the two dogs, Stanley and Little Boodgie, who had replaced Rupert after he was run over on the street. These two could do no wrong in their master's eyes and ran free after Hockney, wherever he was, even winding themselves round his legs as he drove. House-training was not an option. 'David was not good at discipline with the dogs, who would piss all over the furniture,' Ian Falconer remembers. 'There was a kind of watermark all along the bottom of the sofa and the chairs where the dogs had pissed, and they would shit everywhere and David's attitude was "Oh, just leave it until it dries up and then you can pick it up". Of course he didn't notice how much it stank!'[22]

Hockney's friend Jonathon Brown recalls how the dogs used to defecate in his shoes, and wrote an amusing account of a post-dinner visit to Dennis Hopper's Frank Gehry-designed house in Venice, where their behaviour was less than perfect. 'Here as we talked and took our Burgundy and glanced at the art, the dogs amused themselves too. For one of them, little Boodgie, I am sure, this meant a fine crap in the middle of the floor . . . I already had an inkling that David's sense of the soul's right to liberty included what elsewhere might be regarded rather as a lack of house-training and I assumed his friends knew what to expect . . . I saw Hopper approach with a look that summoned his *machete*: he marched up to the scene of the grime and came close to remonstration, but with some effort held back ever so slightly. It was a display of the horsemanship of etiquette of a high order . . . David was aware of the turd at any rate, and turned and said, "Oah", which didn't entirely pacify the situation. He added, in helpless retrospective instruction: "Little Boodgie, no; NO!" Gesture as language: David wagged his finger in the exaggerated manner of a silent-film character, more to seem to make an effort than to achieve anything. As Hopper's look of a chain-gang murderer increased in intensity, David added "Oah, it'll be dry in the morning, Luv, and you can just pick it up." It's not that this did the trick, but it left Hopper with only two manly choices – silence or murder. He chose silence, but he looked murder. On the way home, David said to me, "I'm not sure Dennis was too pleased with Little Boodgie. Do you think he was annoyed?"'[23]

Gradually a relationship developed between John Fitzherbert and Hockney, whose worsening hearing exacerbated his feelings of loneliness. 'He paid me a lot of attention and always talked to me as an equal,' Fitzherbert recalls. 'He was fun and had a twinkle in his eye, and he was incredibly interesting and funny.'[24] There were many reasons why this should have been an idyllic time for Hockney. The

Malibu house oozed charm, he loved the sea, the dogs were free to run wild on Doggie Beach, he was painting portraits again, and Fitzherbert had reinvigorated his sex life. The days had a lovely rhythm to them, beginning with watching the sun rise on the wooden deck. In the early part of the morning a sitter would arrive and Hockney would take them up to the studio to begin work. There was a large open fireplace on the deck, and around midday a barbecue lunch would be served, after which the portrait would be completed. In the evening Hockney and Fitzherbert would have drinks on the deck and watch the sun set, and friends often came over for dinner. Jonathon Brown, who visited in the summer of 1989, recalls what a brilliant cook Fitzherbert was. 'We ate fantastically twice a day. I remember that when I came back from my fortnight in Malibu, my girlfriend told me, "You didn't come off the plane, you rolled off it"';[25] and there were some memorable parties. 'We had marvellous parties out there,' says Ian Falconer. 'I remember once we did a party for Billy Connolly and Billy Wilder. David called it "The Billy Party". It was just a dinner party on the deck, lit by lanterns, but it was actually a bit awkward because Billy Connolly and Billy Wilder didn't get along that well, the clashing accents for one thing!'[26]

Over all this potential happiness, however, there still hung the ever-present shadow of AIDS, the death knell of which had sounded for so many of Hockney's friends in New York that visits to the city had become almost too painful for him. The latest was his long-time dealer from the André Emmerich Gallery, Nathan Kolodner, who died in August, and he had also only recently heard that Ian Falconer had been told he was HIV-positive. This cast a pall on the burgeoning relationship with Fitzherbert. 'John got me back into sex again,' he recalls, 'but I told him that this was a bad time of my life. A lot of friends of mine were very ill and I had to keep going to NY to see them and they were not people who he knew so I don't want to burden him with it. I was having a bit of a hard time, and I became very scared myself. I remember once going to New York and visiting three separate hospitals. It was the worst time of my life.'[27] Fitzherbert recollects that 'Every other week there was a funeral, a memorial or a hospital visit. The list of casualties was just phenomenal.'[28]

One way that Hockney had of dealing with the sadness and depression that sometimes overwhelmed him was to take long drives in his red convertible Mercedes up into the Santa Monica Mountains, a range of hills to the west of the Los Angeles Basin that stretch from the Oxnard Plain in south-west Ventura County to the Hollywood Hills. He liked to go in the evening so that he would catch the setting sun, and he would drive to the music of Wagner that blasted out from extra-powerful speakers that he had had installed in order to accommodate his increasing deafness. The more he did this, the more he began to realise that the music perfectly suited the majesty of the mountains. 'I slowly choreographed a drive,' he said, 'that's an hour and a half long, through the Santa Monica Mountains, mostly with the music from *Parsifal*. It matches everything the eye sees and the ear hears.'[29] He called it 'The Wagner Drive', and the more he did it, the more he refined it, till it might have started in Malibu with American music – a march by Sousa and 'America' from *West Side Story* – followed by Strauss's 'Blue Danube Waltz', then, as the car nosed its way up into the mountains, progressing to 'The Entrance of the Gods' from *Das Rheingold* and the prelude to *Parsifal*, and other Wagner favourites. The climax would come just as the car reached Saddle Peak Road and rounded a final bend, where to the music of 'Siegfried's Funeral March', there would be revealed, at the very moment the sun was sinking behind the hills, a 200-mile panorama from Santa Monica Bay across all of Los Angeles, away to the San Bernadino Mountains. For those lucky enough to take the drive, usually a one-on-one experience, it was akin to being immersed in a movie.

'It was a thrill,' John Cox remembers, 'with David at the wheel driving like a Valkyrie. The Wagner drive was seeing the landscape with that music, very much through David's eyes. I was impressed by the sheer care with which it had been crafted. He would do a stretch at a very, very regulated speed, so that when we turned a corner or went round a bend, a new theme would come in which would be absolutely appropriate to the landscape we were looking at. It was awesome really. He was ambitious enough to want to sort of incorporate the entire landscape and the entire score and the act of driving through it into one huge, almost global concept. It was land art in a very big way.'[30]

The drives through the mountains also led to a series of experimental landscapes that echoed his earlier 'journey' paintings such as *Mulholland Drive: The Road to the Studio*, in that he created in them an amalgam of views, a changing perspective that gave the viewer the feeling that they were moving along the road as well. One of the best of these, *Pacific Coast Highway and Santa Monica*, a multiple view of Santa Monica Bay and the mountains, he described as 'in a sense, a great big drive through the mountains'. 'You go up the road, you look out at space, and you see the whole of Santa Monica Bay,' he told a reporter from the *LA Times*. 'The Santa Monica Mountains are absolutely ravishing, and I've noticed that most of the people I took from Los Angeles didn't know them. I was shocked actually. It's so near and beautiful. On a Sunday, when everybody's crowded down on the Pacific Coast Highway, there's nobody up there. If it were Yorkshire on a Sunday, there'd be crowds up there having picnics.'[31]

At the beginning of 1990, Hockney was at the centre of a controversy in Yorkshire. A regular contributor to local civic projects in his home town, he had accepted a commission to design the cover for the 1990 Bradford Telephone Directory, for which he had produced a painting titled *Bradford and District*, depicting, in a simple style, the town hall, the Cow and Calf Rocks on Ilkley Moor, and some terraced houses, factories and mills against a background of rolling Pennine moorland. The subscribers to the local exchange were not, however, impressed, and flooded the Bradford daily newspaper, the *Telegraph & Argus*, with letters describing it as 'childish', 'monstrous' and 'disgraceful'. 'Proud Tyke, Keith Naylor,' wrote the *Daily Mirror* correspondent, 'was so angry he sent his directory back to BT. "It's the sort of thing you expect in a junior school," he said. It was a challenge the *Mirror* couldn't resist. We commissioned Class 7K at Calversyke Middle School to do their versions of 52-year-old Hockney's work.'[32] They then ran the results on a full page against the original with the banner headline 'SPOT

THE HOCKNEY'.[33] This did not prevent there being such a flood of worldwide orders for the directory from places as far afield as Dallas, Seattle, Geneva and Germany that BT decided to print an extra five thousand copies. One London collector even ordered five hundred for himself, prompting Kasmin to remark, 'If people are buying the phone book because they think it will be worth something, I should think they are misguided.'[34] Even Hockney's greatest fan, his mother, had her doubts. 'She had the cover pinned up on her kitchen wall,' remembers Hockney's old friend, the antiquarian book dealer George Lawson, 'and I might have raised my eyebrows slightly, because she said, "Oh well, you can't win them all!"'[35]

If certain Bradfordians were less than impressed by Hockney's latest work, this was not the case in California's Silicon Valley, where many of the world's leading computer companies were based and new technologies were moving ahead at a pace. Knowing of his interest in computers and photography, and keen to involve one of the world's leading artists in their discoveries, Russell Brown, the art director at Adobe, and John and Thomas Knoll, the inventors of Photoshop, invited Hockney to a three-day workshop on computers and printing. He accepted and travelled up there early in 1990 with Richard Schmidt, John Fitzherbert and the two dogs. 'I found out that my Canon printing machine could be plugged up to a computer,' he wrote, 'so that you could draw on the computer and print immediately. This was very interesting to me. And at this conference somebody showed us a still video camera that could also, with another bit of small equipment, print immediately through your laser printer. It took photographs on a disk, not on film, and I thought that might be exciting, so I bought one. It was rather expensive, I thought, £2,000 for what essentially looked rather a simple camera. It turned out that the reason it cost that much was that they only made 400!'[36]

The camera, a Canon RC 470, was at the forefront of new technology. It was not yet a true digital camera, but it recorded analogue images on special two-inch-square video floppy disks, which could then be inserted into a disk drive to be viewed on a computer. Hockney was intrigued by the fact that it was a camera without film.

Now he could print colour images himself, via his computer and laser copier; there was no longer any need for the one-hour Fotomat. He started playing with it immediately, and though the first results were a little fuzzy, he soon got the hang of it as he began to understand how it recorded colour. 'I realised colour was coming out in a different way,' he wrote, 'no film was being used, the camera was seeing and putting digits onto a disc. I then put the disc into a little machine tied to the printer and you could print the photographs practically any size. If you printed four on a page, they were more sharply focused and the colour seemed rather rich and rather unphotographic . . . I was struck by the strong quality of the colour.'[37] To get people's feedback and to show them the different way of doing colour photography that was not really photography at all in the original sense, he took a series of pictures of details around his house and put them into a little book called *40 Snaps of My House, August 1990*, fifty copies of which he sent out to friends.

Once he had mastered the intricacies of the new camera, he used it to take portraits, beginning a project that was to last the better part of a year in which he photographed visitors to the house. Each person was recorded life-size standing in front of the painting *Pacific Coast Highway and Santa Monica*, and when that had to go off to an exhibition, he painted another similar picture to replace it. 'I realised that having a common background,' he said, 'set up a kind of *gestalt* that made a link.'[38] Everybody that came to the studio or the house was inveigled into posing, whoever they were – friends, reporters, plumbers, framers, car cleaners, opera producers, art dealers, etc., etc. 'I shoot full-length portraits,' he explained, 'moving the camera vertically in stages down the bodies of my subjects, usually ending up on my knees, taking about five or six different portions which we'd then paste together. In this way it was possible to make *images* approaching life-size . . . The colour of the laser prints was quite unusual and intense – unlike any other kind of photographic reproduction. By shooting so close to the subject one avoided the grainy effect caused by atmosphere between camera and subject, which is often characteristic of ordinary colour photography.'[39]

Among the subjects photographed for the portrait project was Barbara Isenberg, a reporter for the *LA Times*, who had come to do an interview. 'I joined four other volunteers,' she described in her article, 'in front of the artist's huge, still unfinished painting of the Santa Monica Mountains . . . The artist lines all of us up in front of the canvas. We all stare straight ahead. Hockney picks up his new camera and starts shooting. Since the video camera images will appear on the video monitor in a specific order – which Hockney has learned through experimentation – the artist takes his photographs in that order. He crouches and moves from person to person taking pictures. The first picture is the first person's head. The second picture is the second person's head. Methodically, he moves from one person to the next, shooting everybody's head before he returns to the first person and starts shooting upper torsos. Lower torsos are next. Then legs. And finally feet. That done, Hockney pulls a small floppy disc out of the still video camera, pops it into the still video playback unit and everybody watches a composite photograph take shape on the video monitor. One by one, the photos appear on the screen exactly as shot – heads, torsos, feet. The screen now is filled with our composite image. Looking at it, smiling, Hockney is clearly pleased. He moves a few feet to his color laser copier, where he pushes a button and makes copies of the screen for each of us. He stamps the 8½-by-11-inch print twice, first with a stamp that reads "There is no such thing as an unlimited edition," then with a stamp that reads "hand stamped, David Hockney."'[40]

Another model for the portraits was Bing McGilvray, who had left Hockney's employ back in 1986 as a result of a bad drug problem, and had gone home to Boston to live with his parents. In 1990, Hockney suggested that he should come back to work on two operas he had to design back to back. These were *Die Frau ohne Schatten* and Puccini's *Turandot*. Hockney was already committed to the Strauss, having made a promise to John Cox that he would do it for the 1992/93 season at Covent Garden, but could not resist the challenge of taking on his first Italian opera when San Francisco Opera approached him to do *Turandot*, which was to be a joint production with Chicago, where it would open in January 1992. It was a huge commitment, in which he was assisted once again by Ian Falconer, who designed the costumes, and Richard Schmidt, who set up the model and was in charge of all the technical work with the lights. Knowing what an enormous job he was taking on, he asked McGilvray to join them as an extra pair of hands.

McGilvray's strength was his video expertise, having studied the subject at UCLA. This was needed because Hockney had recently acquired a number of Sony Hi8 Handycams. These were the first portable video cameras made for the commercial market, and with their arrival at his studio there began a new obsession with videoing everything that was going on. 'He was quite amazed by the new camera,' McGilvray remembers. 'The VCR itself had only been about less than ten years, so they had really advanced the technology pretty quickly. The idea was that you could hold it in your hand rather than prop it on your shoulder so you were very mobile with it, and the quality for the time was quite remarkable.'[41] To begin with they were almost entirely used to record the design of *Turandot*.

This time Richard Schmidt constructed a model that was even bigger than the one for *Tristan*, at one and a half inches to the foot, and they had a new system of blinds installed in the Montcalm studio so that they could work on the lighting during the day. The miniaturised lighting system was now so accurate that Hockney could study precisely the effects wrought on the painted drops by the superimposition of shafts of light through coloured filters. 'We set up three cameras so we were making a record of what we were doing from three different angles,' says McGilvray. 'David would design the set and put in all the little characters, work out how to move them, play the music, and then when he thought he had the scene ready, we would shoot the entire scene with all the lighting changes, so we'd have it on tape, synchronised. Then I would go and edit it together. These were long days, because when Richard went home at five o'clock, there was still hours of watching the videos back. But it was very exciting, and by the end of it, we had the entire opera on video before we even stepped into the theatre to rehearse it. It was quite incredible.'[42]

It was draining for Hockney, who drove himself on in spite of signs that he was not in the best of health. As much as a year earlier, David Plante, on a visit to Malibu with Nikos Stangos to record material for a new book, had noticed that he was not on his usual form. 'David was in a terrible state,' he recalls. 'He would go away for the whole day and then come back in the evening looking exhausted and saying, "Oh, I'm sorry, love, but I've got to go to bed now." And he would go upstairs. Sometimes days went by and nothing was done . . .'[43] Like others before him, McGilvray noticed that once Hockney started work on a major project, there was no stopping him, and his hours were random. 'He just created his own schedule which was pretty frantic. Then there would be days when he would say he couldn't get out of bed, so no one worked that day. He works himself into a frazzle and then collapses.'[44]

There was also something else that was causing him much stress and reminding him of a time of great unhappiness. It had been brought to his attention that a number of drawings by him were being offered for sale at Sotheby's by Mo McDermott's ex-wife, Lisa Lombardi. Since it was soon discovered that they were not registered as having left the studio, as all works going out for sale would have been, it was clear that Mo must have taken them without permission. 'I wouldn't have minded,' he later told John Cornwell, 'but I'd already given him about $8,000, a gift to help him out . . . As it turned out they weren't even my drawings, they were Richard's. I was just incredibly angry.'[45]

Things came to a head in November. 'We were sitting about one evening at Montcalm watching videos,' McGilvray recalls, 'and David suddenly said he wasn't feeling well and was going to go and lie down. He couldn't make it up the stairs to his bedroom. We tried to get him to stand up, at which point we realised this was very serious. Then we got him into the car and John drove him to hospital where he was diagnosed with having suffered a heart attack.'[46] Hockney was hospitalised for a week in Cedars-Sinai Medical Center on Beverly Boulevard, where he underwent an angioplasty. Karen Kuhlman remembers that seeing him in hospital was very frightening. Apart from a warning to slow down, the one good thing that came out of his illness was a reconciliation with Gregory Evans.

CHAPTER THIRTEEN

VERY NEW PAINTINGS

Gregory was one of the first people Hockney called from his hospital bed. He had seen him only intermittently over the previous five years, and they had been almost completely estranged for the past year. 'We really didn't speak at all,' Evans recalls. 'I didn't see him at any time and in fact I almost forgot him.'[1] Though much of Evans's life during this time had been spent going to AA meetings and trying to keep sober, he had also dipped his toes in the world of commerce, having opened a store on North Robertson Boulevard specialising in fabrics and antique teapots. 'I'd always wanted a shop, and I was fascinated with teapots and stuff like ceramics from the twenties and thirties,' he says. 'It seemed to be something that was in front of me and that I could do and wanted to do, and could maybe make a living from, so I put it together. I found a premises on Robertson, just below Melrose, with a charming little storefront. It sold teapots and cups and saucers, and textiles.'[2]

The shop, called simply Gregory Evans, thrived for a while, selling mostly to people in the arts and entertainment businesses, and Evans travelled all over Europe, buying tea paraphernalia and choosing fabric from Celia Birtwell. Being a one-man business, however, which initially had been fun, began to seem like a chore after a couple of years, and he started to undertake interior-decorating jobs for friends, including buying furniture for Hockney's Malibu home, before eventually closing the shop completely. Seeing Hockney in the hospital wiped away any feelings of antagonism between them, and Evans was brought back into the fold by first agreeing to help with the new book of memoirs to be edited by Nikos Stangos. It was tentatively titled *That's the Way I See It*, though Evans, in usual waspish form, liked to refer to it as 'The New Testament'.

When he left hospital at the end of the month, Hockney made

a few concessions to his health, installing a treadmill in the studio, taking himself off each day for long walks, and eating healthier food. Otherwise things were soon back to normal, and he was once again buried in work, the two operas taking precedence. He had said yes to *Turandot* because, as well as being his first Italian opera, it was set in mythical China and had elements of fantasy to it. He relished the challenge of making it visually extravagant, while getting away from the kitsch, in the form of overdone chinoiserie and too many dragons, that so often accompanied this opera. He took his inspiration from the Chinese red that he had seen everywhere on his travels through the country back in 1981. 'And I wanted to avoid the C19th Chinese look,' he said, 'and concentrate instead on the harshness of China – harsh edges, strong diagonals. We started with red walls and then dressed the chorus in black, to stand out against them. The costumes were boldly abstract, rather than elaborate.'[3]

After the problems with Jonathan Miller on *Tristan*, the subject of who was going to direct the *Turandot* was a sensitive one. The first choice was the distinguished Iranian opera director Lotfi Mansouri, who also ran San Francisco Opera, but after a few initial meetings, he pulled out, having seen that Hockney had such strong ideas about the piece that he had, to all intents and purposes, really taken over directorial control. When Ardis Krainik, the effervescent and dynamic director of the Lyric Opera of Chicago, saw what was happening, she decided to give Hockney his reins and appointed one of her directors, Bill Farlow, to work with him on the staging. It turned out to be a smart move.

The designs were completed by the end of March and were sent off to San Francisco, where the sets and costumes were to be made in the company workshops. After making intermittent visits there to check on their progress, Hockney needed to go to Chicago to work on the lighting. He decided to make a vacation of it and drive there from LA, a distance of two thousand miles through some of the most spectacular parts of the American West – states like Nevada, Utah and Colorado, as well as the Corn Belt states of Nebraska, Iowa and Illinois. Early in July, Hockney, Fitzherbert, Schmidt and McGilvray, accompanied by the two dogs, Stanley and Little Boodgie, and equipped with assorted video cameras, set off for Chicago. They took two vehicles: his own Lexus and a hired RV in which they could, to quote Hockney, 'sleep, cook, shit and shower'.[4] Unfortunately, as it turned out, they rented it not because of its reliable make, but because it was the craziest-looking one they could find. Sensing that the journey might not be without incident, Ian Falconer chose to meet them in Chicago.

'David had got it into his head,' McGilvray remembers, 'that we were going to film our trip, which was going to be some kind of Magical Mystery Tour, and we did shoot hours and hours of video. Nobody knew exactly which way we were going. We'd take it in turns to drive and in the morning David would decide he wanted to look at this canyon or that town. It was all just day by day.'[5] The outward journey, which took a week, went fairly smoothly, though they soon gave up the idea of sleeping in the RV as it was too small. 'John cooked, we never ate in restaurants,' Hockney recalled, 'we did stay in motels sometimes . . . We had to find Holiday Inns because they allow dogs. The cheaper the motel, usually, the more likely they'd be to have signs saying "No Pets." From Denver to Chicago it is not as interesting. You drive on a great plain through Nebraska and Iowa and into Illinois, 600 miles of rather flat wheatland, a bit monotonous. Nevertheless we had a lot of fun driving there.'[6]

On their arrival in Chicago, straight off the dusty path, they stayed at the luxurious Mayfair Regent Hotel, overlooking Lake Michigan, where Sir Georg Solti had lived during the time that he was running the Chicago Symphony Orchestra. 'We stayed at the grandest hotel,' said Hockney, 'because they would take dogs. We were probably the only people who ever arrived in an R.V. at the front door of that hotel . . . They have special rooms for guests with dogs, where it doesn't matter if they pee on the floor.'[7] Every day for a week they went to the opera house and worked with the lighting director Duane Schuler. As he sensed the lighting and the music synchronising perfectly, Hockney became increasingly excited. 'We had worked out a glorious ending,' he wrote, 'as though you were in a heart. In fact, we thought everything would work very well, however it was directed. It fit the music and was visually exciting with the music.'[8]

After a week of intense work, and two weeks in each other's company, it is perhaps not surprising that the journey back to LA did not run quite so smoothly. Hockney was a little tense and wanted things done his way, while Fitzherbert and McGilvray were like naughty schoolboys, getting stoned and egging each other on, and not obeying the maestro's orders. 'It was kind of a mad trip,' McGilvray recalls. 'There were no cellphones in those days so we weren't really communicating with each other and often one person didn't know where the other person was going. So there was a lot of "Look, he's pulling over"; "No, he's not pulling over"; "We've missed that light and now they've gone off and we don't know where they are." One time John and I were in the Lexus and we took off in completely the wrong direction to where we were supposed to be going. David had to call Karen Kuhlman from a payphone somewhere to call the Lexus, which had a carphone, to tell us to turn around right away. He was absolutely furious when we got back.'[9] The dogs also caused tension because they were very frisky, and everyone had to be constantly careful not to let them jump out of the car and run into the traffic as soon as the door was opened, and that led to a lot of shouting.

The final straw came, however, when the RV broke down on a sunny afternoon in August, somewhere in Colorado, just past the Continental Divide. 'It was absolutely beautiful,' wrote Hockney, 'you couldn't have broken down in a more spectacular place. We were videoing our journey . . . When the R.V. broke down, and we started rowing, I told Bing to keep the cameras going. Richard, who was the most mechanical of the four of us, had to try and get under the R.V. to see what had happened.'[10] When Schmidt was unable to fix whatever was wrong, they decided to leave the RV where it was and drive the Lexus into the nearest town, which was sixty miles away, and have the RV towed in the next morning. So far as Hockney was concerned, the $300 it was going to cost to get the tow was worth paying, as they would be able to film it. 'I realised that's the artist in me: use it, don't see it as a disaster, just put it on a video; we'll laugh at it then, this marvellous picture of a tow-truck and this big clumsy thing being drawn up the Rocky mountains.'[11]

Schmidt, however, who was more than a little exasperated about the whole situation, got up early in the morning and left with the tow truck to collect the RV without telling Hockney, so the event was never filmed. When he returned, Hockney was beside himself with anger. 'David just went off on one of his rants,' Fitzherbert remembers. 'He had a very bad temper and used to love screaming and shouting, and we'd all end up shivering and shaking. He loved that rage. It was almost like it was some kind of medicine for him. In the end the three of us ended up staying in a motel and he stayed in the RV because no one wanted to be with him.'[12]

The next day Schmidt decided he'd had enough, and was going to drive the repaired RV back to LA on the Interstate. This was not quite what Hockney had in mind, as it had been his intention to take the back roads, passing through Monument Valley and up to the Grand Canyon. He told the fuming Schmidt to take the Lexus, and that he would drive the RV on the route he wanted. 'I want to see Monument Valley, we want to see the Grand Canyon,' he told him in no uncertain terms, 'we're going to risk it – if we break down, we'll manage.'[13] At this point Schmidt caved in. 'Just as I was ready to drive off in a fury,' he recalls, 'we all had one big group hug and kissed and made up. It was just like family arguing over nothing.'[14]

Once again the convoy set off, along the back roads, through deep gorges, stopping by a lake for lunch and a swim, and arriving at Monument Valley, immortalised by John Ford in so many of his Westerns, just as it was getting dark. The two motels there, the View and Goulding's Lodge, were full, so they all ended up having to sleep in the RV. Hockney was keen to watch the dawn rise over the valley, but by now he was feeling a little contrite and did not dare wake up the others in case they got annoyed with him all over again. He crept out on his own, only to be surprised by McGilvray, who had also woken up early. 'I asked him where he was going,' he remembers, 'and he replied, "Oh, love, I'm just off to see the sun rise." So I asked if I could go with him. Off we went and I think that was the most amazing day I ever had with him. There was just him and me, and we drove out to Monument Valley and saw the most spectacular event I'd ever seen; and he just knew it was going to be like that.'[15]

Hockney described it as being the kind of dawn that David Lean would have waited six months to film, and they captured quite a bit of it on video. 'As the dawn broke on the eastern sky, on the western sky you saw a great storm, heavy grey clouds moving towards us . . . We then drove about as the sun rose and as it rose it first hit the tops of what are the great monuments. It looked like gold, while behind us the storm was coming forward with lightning flashing. And then, as the sun was coming up, appeared a perfect rainbow, with lightning flashing in the middle. What with that, and the sun hitting the tops of the monuments, it was like Moses coming to speak.'[16]

As soon as he got back to the studio, Hockney started painting intensively. Richard Schmidt had taken a well-deserved holiday, so he was alone. His mind was whirling with inspiration, from the crashing waves of the ocean, from the perspective tricks of the *Turandot* designs, from the plants and flowers, the caves and cliffs, the rocks and steep inclines of Monument Valley, and the shadows cast by the intense Californian sunlight – all these were incorporated into a series of experimental landscapes. Though these paintings were primarily abstract, they contained references to things that were instantly recognisable. 'When [Richard] came back after two or three weeks, he looked at the paintings, looked at the space in them, and saw what the trip had done. In *Iowa Again, 1991*, the wood surface at the bottom side on the left might suggest the table in the R.V. and there are references to windows, corn growing, fields. Richard realised that the space in these pictures had been greatly affected by the trip.'[17]

Hockney's obsession with video cameras was continuous all through this period. When he went to Paris in November 1991, to oversee the staging of the *Parade* triple bill at the Théâtre de Châtelet, he equipped each member of 'the Circus' with one. Jonathon Brown, fresh off the train from the Gare du Nord, remembers arriving at the stage door and 'Almost immediately I found myself among perhaps nine or even more of us who were to be equipped with Hi8 video cameras, also more or less the latest thing . . . This was the phase of ceaseless camcording and the team of us was stationed about the various corners of the auditorium to make a record of the rehearsals from every angle and to verify the sight lines even from . . . the Gods, the topmost of the cheap seats.'[18] Strict instructions were issued that the cameras had to remain on a fixed lens, a lesson taken from Hockney's favourite film director, Jacques Tati, who liked to let the viewer do the zooming in. As well as filming in the theatre, they also took footage of an exhibition of Daumier's *Idylles Parlementaires*, dachshunds with a street musician, and at the Café Voltaire, where he just left the camera running on the table to record anything that happened.

The trip to Paris cheered Hockney up no end. 'These were the happiest of days,' Brown recalled. 'In the café, David would tell his jokes – how Toulouse-Lautrec was so superstitious, he would never walk under a black cat – and on stage he would pick up props and mime a music-hall routine. In the queue for the great Géricault exhibition at the Grand Palais . . . he would make a loud cough behind the person in front and then make as if to flick debris from their shoulder. Schoolboy stuff: we never stopped laughing really. He has an ability to get away with corn, it's a key to his humour, and when he says, standing at the Eiffel Tower, "Ah, yes, the Arc de Triomphe, won'erful . . .", you let him get away with it.'[19] They ate out for every meal, lunching at the Café Zimmer, across from the theatre, and dining most nights at his favourite haunt, La Cafetière, where, while doing a drawing of the owner, Jean Romestant, he suddenly opined, 'I shouldn't really draw after all the wine.'[20]

Hockney's happiness in Paris was brought to an abrupt end by the news of another death from AIDS, that of one of his closest friends, Tony Richardson, who died on 14 November, and in whose Paris apartment on the Cour de Rohan he had spent so many happy days back in the early seventies. Though he would never get used to it, by now Hockney had a way of dealing with the loss of so many friends. 'You think about them every day and then you stop it,' he told Jeremy Isaacs on the BBC programme *Face to Face*, 'because there's too many actually, and it would rather drive you mad if you think about it. Slowly you begin to realise that it's become part of your life. It's something you never, ever expected. I've got a lot of friends who are in the same predicament and they always say they have to block it out of their minds at times, otherwise it's difficult to live.'[21]

He was able to bury himself in opera, now beginning work on *Die Frau ohne Schatten*. Regarded by many as Strauss's greatest opera, it is a complex story set in a Far Eastern island kingdom, involving two sets of characters: the Emperor and his spirit Empress, who is searching for a shadow, and a poor dyer and his wife, who is bribed to give up her shadow to the Empress in return for great riches. When John Cox was made Director of Productions at the Royal Opera House in 1988 and decided to put on this opera, he only had one person in mind to design it. 'I liked the idea,' he recalls, 'that the leading man in *Die Frau* was like a Hockney character, in that his profession was colour. He was a dyer and his life was dominated by the production of colour for consumption by other people, and I thought, "That's just like David Hockney." The choice had a kind of inevitability about it.'[22]

As he gradually became more involved in the design, Hockney began to incorporate ideas taken from the abstract paintings he had been working on, which were hanging all around the studio. 'The first thing I made for *Die Frau*,' he wrote, 'was an abstract representation of a river, like a snake. I put little dots on it which were actually derived from the textures that were appearing in these paintings. *Turandot* is mostly architectural interiors; even the garden, which is nearest to nature, is a Chinese garden, stylised, formal, not raw nature. In *Die Frau*, on the other hand, we are dealing with nature in the wild – landscapes, forests etc, – and I knew these paintings were going to influence its design.'[23] One of his most striking ideas, that the dyer's house should have colours running down the walls, inspired by the Souk of the Dyers he had seen in Fez, was translated into a collage, *Running Construction*, in which he tested how gravity would make the colours run.

It was a frantic schedule and while Richard Schmidt once again acted as technical assistant, Hockney also recruited Gregory Evans to help in the creative process of designing the set. 'It was a lot of work,' Cox remembers, 'as *Die Frau* is in every way one of the most complex operas in the repertoire. It is scenically very complex and makes extraordinary demands.'[24] In the middle of the process, they all had to up sticks and decamp to Chicago for rehearsals for the opening of *Turandot*.

The team arrived in Chicago on a bitterly cold Boxing Day, checking in at the Mayfair Regent, along with Stanley and Boodgie, whose refusal to pee outside because of the cold eventually led to Hockney being charged for the recarpeting of the entire suite. That was to be the least of their troubles. When Hockney arrived at the theatre with video cameras to film the rehearsals, the unions, fearing exploitation, banned them. 'The unions objected to the fact that we were filming the production,' Bing McGilvray recalls, 'because they thought we were going in some way to use whatever we shot to make money, and that caused a bit of friction. David was saying, "Well, I've been doing this brand-new production using these tools, and now all of a sudden you're telling me I can't use them." He explained to them that they were just tools and he wasn't going to use them for anything except for himself, to see if he had missed anything in rehearsal. In the end there was a compromise of some sort reached, but they wouldn't let us use the cameras as much as we would have liked to, and he was not very happy about that.'[25]

As rehearsals progressed, it became clear to everyone working in the theatre that Hockney was very much in control and was as good as directing the show himself. '"It just looks so good," he half demands and half asserts,' wrote Geordie Greig, sent over from London to cover the rehearsals for the *Sunday Times*. 'He leaves his makeshift desk in the middle of the stalls – where he likes to sit chewing liquorice and taking notes – and dashes down the opera-house aisle, his turquoise shirt-tail flapping loose. The rainbow-like figure moves agilely round his abstract Chinese roofs before shouting to a startled singer playing the Emperor, "I want you to move three feet forward and to have your chair eighteen inches lower." This is a precision artist's opera. After months shaving millimetres off his model theatres, Hockney knows exactly what he wants.'[26]

There were, however, dark mutterings that this time he had gone too far in his unrestrained use of colour, with the stage being enveloped alternately in luminous blue and incandescent red light, which illuminated mysterious vistas, steps and tunnels, with vanishing points that seemed to defy reality. 'I knew I wanted a lot of colour,' he said. 'It is something I have never been afraid of. Like Cézanne, I believe the purer the colour the purer the form.'[27] There were hints in the press that Hockney's China was going to be nothing less than garish. 'What no one but he knew,' wrote Jonathon Brown, who was helping with the videos, 'was that once the lighting was pulled back and the different subtleties of gel had been fixed, the red hue would achieve a spread of tonal range we associate with lacquer; and that only in the final scene, with a chorus of at least 100 singing of the triumph of love, would we be swum into an intricate filigree of several drops, all in a blood-pumped chasm of orgasmic vermilion. It prompted David Graves to whisper in my ear at the final rehearsal, "Really, I don't know how David of all people can do it – pure fanny!"'[28]

Opening on 11 January 1992, this production, once again, had little to do with opera and everything to do with Hockney, and the music critic of the *Chicago Tribune*'s statement that it was a show 'from which you emerge literally humming the scenery'[29] said it all. It was a view largely echoed by the other critics, such as the *Observer*'s Andrew Porter, who wrote that 'Chicago's Turandot was musically and dramatically null, but visually – in David Hockney's glowing sets – an unforgettable vision of Puccini's opera'.[30] At the final curtain, 'Turandot melted in Calaf's embrace within what looked like the giant auricle and ventricle of a glowing red heart. The audience went wild.'[31] Charged with enthusiasm, Hockney rushed back to LA to finish work on *Die Frau*, and to use all the ideas, fermenting within him, that he had gained from working on these two operas to begin painting again. As soon as the designs were completed and shipped over to London in April, Richard Schmidt was instructed to take down the model and pack it up and everyone was sent away. 'I wanted to be absolutely alone,' Hockney recalled. 'In the theatre you are always working with people . . . So the moment the designs had gone off to London, I retreated to Malibu and started painting in my small studio down there in early May. I didn't want anybody around.'[32]

The series of paintings on which Hockney now began to work were unlike anything else he had ever done, and were quite likely to shock his followers. They were works that attempted to combine representation

and abstraction, and they came directly out of the operas, in particular
his observations about the lighting of the stage and how it was possible
to manipulate a surface with projected light to cause a certain kind
of abstraction to occur. The paintings were like journeys that led the
viewer into a fantastical landscape filled with disappearing roads,
swirling and interconnecting spheres, monumental megaliths, caves,
tunnels and cones. One might be forgiven for believing that they were
painted while the artist was on an acid trip, though he told the journalist
John Cornwell, 'I get these strange ideas in the morning before I'm
fully awake. Just when I'm between sleeping and waking. I suppose it's
because the mind is free then.'[33] The first pictures in the series were
given titles, as usual, but he soon realised that he was engaged in a
different way of seeing and thinking about painting, and so he coined
the term 'Very New Paintings' for them, from then on giving them only
numbers to identify them.

'Someone said that *The V.N. Paintings* are abstract narratives,' he
told Paul Joyce. 'Certainly a great deal of thought and feeling have gone
into them. For example, here at the beach I am between two great
forces of nature, the mountains and the sea. The mountains were made
by a great force of nature . . . while below the other thrust continues,
the endless movement of the sea. These forces are present, I believe, in
the paintings. They are also quite sexual . . . These things were on my
mind when I was painting them. Perhaps these paintings seem a jumble
to the viewer at first. They take time to unfold. They're a bit mind-
boggling, but they are meant to be. The viewer can roam freely within
them, finding his or her own space. That's why there are no figures in
them. You construct your own space mentally.'[34]

Hockney constantly experimented with different finishes, mixing
up the media himself and using systems of glazes, sometimes working
wet on wet, at other times waiting for a colour to dry tacky and then
putting other colours on top, or scraping through to get effects. As he
progressed, the paintings became more and more complex, and he was
sometimes working on two or three at the same time while he waited
for a particular colour to dry. 'By the time I had done about eight,' he
recalled, 'I was beginning to enjoy the little studio where I painted very

much. I did these paintings for myself and as I put them up they seemed to grow from one to another. Gregory came down at that time and he thought there were sexual allusions in them. He said I love this room, sitting in it, and I said, Well, I do too.'[35]

Three *V.N. Paintings*, numbers 12, 13 and 14, were done in Bridlington, where Hockney travelled in June to see his mother. In the previous two years Laura Hockney's health had deteriorated considerably. In December 1990, she had celebrated her ninetieth birthday, and though her sight, hearing and mental facilities remained excellent, her arthritis had got much worse and she had started to have falls. When Margaret Hockney moved to Bridlington with her partner, Ken Wathey, both of them retired from the nursing profession, it was decided that it would be best for Laura to leave Bradford and come to live with them, and in December 1991 they bought a former hotel on Kingston Road, overlooking Bridlington South Bay. It had a ground-floor flat into which Laura moved in January 1992, happily enough in spite of the wrench of leaving Bradford.

'Every day I think of you,' she wrote to Hockney in February, '& thank you with all my heart for your love & kindness to me. You have helped me so much over the years. Growing old is not easy & the creaky joints can't be oiled . . . It was so hard to leave Hutton Terrace – my kind neighbours & familiar rooms – every corner of them I knew. We old folk are a liability to our younger folk who naturally want to live their own lives. I know I am not "with it" and not able to keep up with this wonderful age we live in. You should just see me as I write this. On table to my left – a masterpiece of telephones with 3 "one number push buttons" – a "life line". Margaret, with her quick & clever brain went & bought an extra phone with 20 more (1 number press buttons) & she has fixed them all up for me & I wear another press button round my neck. David it is so marvellous! I only need a secretary . . .'[36]

As his mother began a new life in Kingston Road, an old and valued relationship came to an end in London. The economic recession under which Britain had been struggling since the late eighties had claimed many victims, and the art world was as hard hit as everyone else, with a number of major London galleries closing their doors. These included Wolfgang Fischer, opposite Christie's in King Street, and now Kasmin's in Cork Street, which he had run for ten years with an American partner. After many years of success fuelled by the economic boom in the early eighties, the business then just stopped. 'You've got to be very convinced of what you're doing in the face of no possibility of making money, only of losing,' Kasmin commented. 'This is a long recession to sit out . . .' He was also disillusioned, however, by the greed and business that took over in the early days of Thatcher's Britain. 'All those people in the Eighties buying things to leave in warehouses. The auctioneers and some collectors and dealers got a great adrenalin rush from all this, but I never really did. I began to feel less and less part of it because the money thing just wasn't my game . . . I could never get into it. I always liked dealing with people who used it. You know, that old-fashioned thing: people putting art on the walls and looking at it.'[37] When asked how he felt about his dealer closing down after so many years, Hockney was philosophical. 'I'm not a person of nostalgia. I just live for now.'[38]

He dropped by the gallery on the day of the private view of its closing exhibition, a mixed show that included his etching of a fish and chip shop that he had done while at Bradford School of Art. 'I thought in a rather kinky show,' explained Kasmin, 'why not have a kinky Hockney?'[39] He had come to say that he was too tired to attend the opening. 'He looks like David Hockney,' noted the journalist Simon Garfield, who was in the gallery at the time: 'green shirt, red tie, beige suit, two-tone suede and leather beige shoes, light blue raincoat, lime green umbrella, tortoise-shell glasses, and a hearing-aid which is half bright blue and half bright red . . . He is over from Los Angeles for three weeks to visit his mother and receive an honorary doctorate from the Royal College of Art.' Hockney did not spare Garfield his wit. 'Being a doctor is not that much use really. You still can't write prescriptions for your own drugs. Someone asked me how it felt. I said: "Take two aspirins and call me in the morning."'[40]

Garfield also recorded a typical example of Hockney banter:

HOCKNEY: I'll be coming back here to start the opera around 20
   October. *Die Frau ohne Schatten* will hit the fans at Covent
   Garden on 16 November. Hit the fans. Get it? The Schatten will
   hit the fans.
KASMIN: Oh, the Schatten.
HOCKNEY: That was a joke. I won't explain any more. Kas has no
   ear for music whatsoever.
KASMIN: Thank God David doesn't write music.
HOCKNEY: Well, my friend Henry thought that *The Magic Flute*
   was my best score ever.[41]

Hockney returned to Malibu after that, only stopping work on
the *V.N. Paintings* when he had to travel back to London for *Die Frau
ohne Schatten*. Covent Garden was then going through a very difficult
period and as rehearsal time was shorter than usual, he rented Placido
Domingo's flat, which was very close to the opera house. '*Die Frau ohne
Schatten*,' he recalled, 'was the least time I was ever given to stage an
opera and even by the dress rehearsal not everything was lit right . . .
Therefore on each of the subsequent five nights, adjustments were
made. The last performance was without doubt the best, the only one
when all the cues were correct with the music.'[42] John Cox remembers
them having to sacrifice a major rehearsal onstage, because the management under Jeremy Isaacs decided to put in an extra performance of
their current hit show, *Porgy and Bess*. They also overlapped technically
with the ballet. 'It got technically very hairy indeed,' he recalls, 'so
when we came to the first night, it wasn't frankly ready. The bad things
were mostly to do with flying cues, so they didn't come in at the right
time, or they got caught on bits of scenery that were nothing to do with
our show, but which happened to be hanging in the grid.'[43]
   'Hockney's opera sets upstage the work of career set designers'
ran the byline for Tom Sutcliffe's review in the *Guardian*. 'But they also
upstage the music.'[44] As it turned out, career set designers had nothing
to worry about as this was to be the last opera Hockney designed.
Though the main reason for this was that his ever-increasing deafness
meant he simply couldn't properly hear the music any more, a small

part of it was his frustration with the whole process of opera, where the result of weeks and weeks of work was only seen for what amounted to a few hours, and where the attitude of the management towards artists could be condescending. 'When we did *Die Frau* at Covent Garden,' he told a reporter from the *Guardian*, 'I must have spent seven months preparing it, and we gave them a three-and-a-half-hour videotape of a model we had done with all the lighting changes and all the music cues. I sent it to them saying "This is what it should be like," but then they didn't give us time to light it, they took time away. In the end I just felt, "Oh, I can't be bothered to do this anymore."'[45] After the last performance, he returned to California and the solitary pursuit of painting, telling Geordie Greig, who came out to interview him for the *Sunday Times*, 'I have simply retreated to do something on my own. After two very big pieces of theatre, working with other people and compromising decisions, I want to work on my own, so I now just sit by the sea and do my own thing. I sit in silence and do my pictures.'[46]

When the *V.N. Paintings* were shown at New York's André Emmerich Gallery in late January 1993, the critics were bemused, and at the press show Greig witnessed an attempt by Henry Geldzahler to persuade Hockney to explain them. 'David once said to me,' he enthused, 'the architecture of Los Angeles is the only architecture in the world which makes you smile. It is the same with these pictures, which have an architectural feel. To me they feel very inhabited. Think of ballet and architecture.' But Hockney was having none of it. 'They lapse into silence and awkward smiles,' wrote Greig. 'The journalists peer quizzically at the new works, which are as bright as Matisses and elusively unnarrative . . . And this most loquacious of artists . . . is reticent about this new work. "The paintings are about movement, but that is about all I can say. I sit by the sea, which is in a state of constant motion, and just let my thoughts run. I did that in Malibu and at Bridlington in Yorkshire . . . I think they speak for themselves. If not, it doesn't matter. They speak to me," he says in good humour, with a smile and a shrug.'[47] The climax of the *V.N. Paintings* came in a show at the LA Louver Gallery that opened in April 1995, when Hockney exhibited a number of panoramic variants of this group, including the vast *Snail's Space*, which at seven feet by twenty-two feet came close to matching Picasso's *Guernica* in size.

These paintings did not, however, stand alone in this show, which had the somewhat cumbersome title of *Some very large new paintings with twenty-five dogs upstairs and some drawings of friends*. Hockney had indeed been busy after the first series of *V.N. Paintings*, returning to a more traditional mode of work, in part a reaction against his recent,

Jonathan Silver, Dec 30th, 1993

almost continuous involvement with images produced by cameras, photocopiers, fax machines, computers and laser printers. This began with a series of crayon drawings of his friends and family, large-scale portraits of them at half-length, mostly seated and holding the artist and the viewer with a fixed stare. They were powerful images in which he scrutinised his sitters with an intensity that reached deeper into their souls than anything he had done previously. 'These drawings were made,' he explained, 'at the same time as I was painting invented spaces in strong colour with gouache. As the spaces got deeper, so I realised was the psychological exploration in the drawings.'[48]

One of the friends he drew was Jonathan Silver, who described the experience thus: 'Being drawn by David is intense, exhausting and very rewarding. He does not let you sit necessarily in a comfy position, asking you to position your eyes at an angle, or to turn your head to the side. To watch David drawing is equally exhausting – he seems to be in his own world of examination transcendentally in a passage of his own time and space – gazing at you with a penetration right into the centre of your soul. His face twists and turns, his eyes dart about and screw up, his whole body is acutely heightened in a dynamo of intense scrutiny. His lips move up and down like the sea, and often his tongue is out!! Emerging from one of these sessions, usually about two hours, you feel as if there has been a union between artist and model – that union being transferred by crayon onto paper. The bigger the effort made in the union between the two of us, the stronger the picture. At the end I feel exhausted, simultaneously liberated . . .'[49]

The drawings were also an attempt to reach out to the living at a time when the litany of death never stopped, the latest casualty being his oldest and dearest friend, Henry Geldzahler, who was dying of pancreatic cancer. 'I hope . . . you are getting through all the sadness of Henry's mortal illness,' Ann Graves wrote to him. 'I know it is a hard thing to bear, all we have been through the last few years as relatively young people losing those close to us. I know it is particularly tough for you as your relationship with Henry is very special.'[50] Before Geldzahler died in August 1994, Hockney visited him at home on Long Island where, after months of chemotherapy, he had finally decided that even though it might lengthen his life, it would not improve the quality, and had withdrawn from treatment to let nature take its course. 'Henry handled dying very well,' Arthur Lambert remembers. 'He was very well cared for, was on a cocktail of painkillers, which he loved, and had his friends around him, so under the circumstances his death was as good as it could have been.'[51] Hockney's subsequent series of poignant drawings of Geldzahler on his deathbed would have delighted his old friend whose greatest joy had always been to be the artist's model. 'He asked me to draw him when he was dying,' Hockney recalled. 'I went to visit him a lot and I wouldn't have drawn him, because I would have felt it was a bit of an intrusion. He asked me to read to him. Then he did say, "Draw me," and he wasn't looking terrific, but I drew him.'[52]

Geldzahler's death hit Hockney hard. He had expected to watch him grow into a crotchety old man. It was followed within a month by that of Kitaj's wife, Sandra Fisher, who died of a sudden stroke. He retreated back to Malibu and his dachshunds, which he proceeded to paint in every imaginable position. They were small oil sketches, out of necessity painted very quickly. 'In order to draw them,' he wrote, 'I

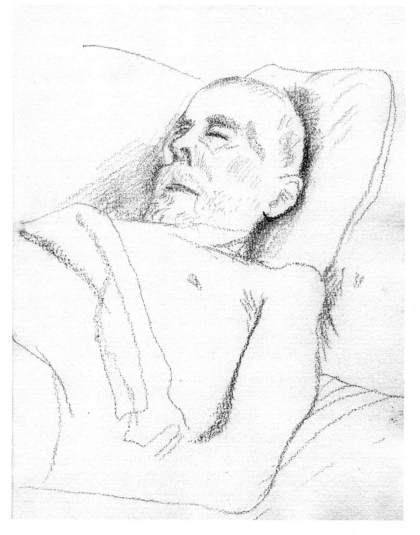

had to leave large sheets of paper all over the house and studio to catch them sitting or sleeping without disturbance. For the same reason I kept canvases and a fresh palette ready for times when I thought I could work. Everything was made from observation, so speed of execution was important. They don't stay long in one position and one knock on the door is enough to make them leap up.'[53] These expertly realised and sharply observed sketches depicted the two dogs in the kinds of poses that are so well known to dog lovers – curled upon cushions, drinking water from a bowl, lying on their backs, sitting on laps, propped up in armchairs – and did so with great charm and no sentimentality.

When he had done one he particularly liked, he would send it out to his friends by fax. 'We love to get the faxes,' replied Ann Graves after receiving one, ' – even on a fax we can see what's going on with the boys. They are really lovely, not just paintings of dogs but of individuals – Stanley and Boogie by someone who knows and understands them. The one of them together gives such a sense of dogginess you can almost inhale the warmth. The faxes of the big paintings however are pretty impossible to read. A bit like being taken out for a meal and then being told you may only look through the window . . .'[54] People clamoured to buy the dachshund paintings when they were put on show the following year, upstairs at the LA Louver, but they were not for sale. 'I wanted desperately to paint something loving,' he said. 'In the last six months of last year, I lost four friends . . . I felt such a loss of love I wanted to deal with it in some way. I realised I was painting my best friends. They sleep with me; I'm always with them here. They don't go anywhere without me and only occasionally do I leave them. They're like little people to me. The subject wasn't dogs but my love of the little creatures.'[55]

Whether it was as a result of the deaths of so many of his friends, or stirrings of homesickness, there were signs at this time that Hockney was becoming disillusioned with California. After years of rejoicing in its lifestyle, he had begun to despair of new draconian forces showing themselves right across America. 'A crude peasant mentality now governs everything,' he complained to Geordie Greig in the *Sunday Times*. 'They want to stop people enjoying themselves and to pit their own narrow-minded views on to other people's lives.'[56] Where he had once complained of the punitive licensing laws in England that discriminated against the working class, his new gripe was against similar laws in the US that banned smoking in many American cities, including LA. 'My joke has always been,' he said, 'that I'm shocked the city council has not stopped the flight to Paris, a very dangerous city for Angelinos, as secondhand smoke comes out of the restaurants and cafés and might just drift into the path of a passing Angelino. On D Day, Eisenhower smoked 80 cigarettes. Do you think he did not need them?

Nobody will mention this today, but that's because weak people who have never faced life and death struggles seem to have taken over and haven't this imagination to put themselves in somebody else's shoes.'[57]

Though Hockney's disillusionment with America may not have amounted to more than the odd gripe against LA, in his home town of Bradford hordes of disaffected teenagers, predominantly of Asian origin and fed up with being constantly picked on by the police, had gone on the rampage over two nights in the suburb of Manningham, leaving a trail of burned-out cars and shattered windows that amounted to a million pounds' worth of damage. Jonathan Silver immediately contacted Hockney for his help with a 'Healing Festival' to be held in the summer of 1995. His contribution was to send fifty of the dog paintings and drawings for an exhibition in the 1853 Gallery, where dog-leash 'barriers' roped them off from the public. 'A lot of art critics,' Silver commented, 'go for sheep in formaldehyde, dismembered bodies and other grim, grey subjects. This is cheerful, pleasant and colourful – just what Bradford needs.'[58] Hockney opened the exhibition, pointing out the emotion that was at the heart of the new works. 'The dogs think nothing of them, really,' he said. 'They'd just as soon pee on them. They don't care about art since, I might point out, they're simply on to higher things – the source of art, which is love.'[59] Ironically, Jonathan Silver's 'Healing Festival' was taking place just as he had been diagnosed with pancreatic cancer, news of which would have a profound effect on Hockney and would eventually bring him back to England.

CHAPTER FOURTEEN

GARROWBY HILL

At the beginning of 1996, Hockney's old friend Peter Adam visited him in California and found him in a melancholy mood, 'sitting opposite me, reciting the long list of the departed, people he had known, shared a bed with or a drink. The emotion is still visible on his pale face as he lists the tragedies which had reached almost everybody he knew: "Nick died six years ago, Jean Léger, Nathan Kolodner, who looked after me at Emmerich, Joe McDonald, Jacques, Mark and John." So many people, the most shining, the most brilliant, the most hopeful – friends aged thirty, thirty-five or forty years old. The American hero of so many of his paintings, the sexy image of life and physical pleasure, the icon of healthy living, the American Dream, was no more.'[1] For all of these friends, beginning with Joe McDonald, it had been his habit to paint them a vase of flowers and give it as a get-well card. Jonathan Silver was no exception. As soon as he heard of the diagnosis of cancer, Hockney flew to Yorkshire to be with him, and painted *Sunflowers for Jonathan*, inscribed, 'Get well soon, love David H', which was delivered to his bedside after his operation.

Flowers were very much on Hockney's mind, as he had recently attended the exhibition *Claude Monet, 1840–1926* at the Art Institute of Chicago. It had greatly inspired him. 'I came out of that exhibition,' he wrote, 'and it made me look everywhere intensely. That little shadow on Michigan Avenue, the light hitting the leaf. I thought: "My God, now I've seen that. He's made me see it."' . . . I came out absolutely thrilled.'[2] He began to look at the world anew, almost as if through Monet's eyes. Early one morning, soon after returning from London, he was in the sitting room at Montcalm Avenue enjoying a cup of tea and reading the *New York Times* when he underwent a defining experience. 'I noticed it was beginning to get light outside,' he recalled; 'I switched off the lights inside and just sat . . . with my cup of tea watching the dawn come up . . . Every minute, the light changed: dark blue, then a lighter blue, then a whole range of greens, then the redness before the sun. A whole palette of colours. A living Monet! It remains here in my head, that image, I'll never forget it.'[3]

Hot on the heels of the huge Monet exhibition came another show from which he drew inspiration: *Vermeer, Royal Cabinet of Paintings, Mauritshuis*, in The Hague. Here he was astonished by the condition of the paintings and the vibrancy of the colours, as well as by the supreme craftsmanship of the artist. He devoured what it could teach him. 'He put the paint on so carefully,' he noted, 'in transparent layers so you get those vibrant blues . . . I've learned a lot about transparent glazes in oil painting over the years; I've made it my business to. Seeing how Vermeer handled the paint, and beyond that how he controlled the light on to his subjects, sent me back into the studio with tremendous energy.'[4] Hockney was quick to choose exactly the right place in his studio to paint the series of flower studies, picking a spot at the far end of the room, at the top of the stairs just outside the bathroom. He saw that this was where the northern light came down in just the right way. It was the beginning of an intense period of painting. 'When I start painting,' he told Paul Joyce, 'I get into a good routine. I'm disciplined enough to concentrate for hours. I love it! It's terrific when I really get painting: squeezing the paint out and using it so it doesn't even have time to get a skin on it; working in the evenings where I'll set something up; and then continuing on it first thing in the morning. And as soon as I get going, I develop. I'm never short of what to do. Just give me enough time, and I'll work it out.'[5]

It was a good time to be back at the easel, as there were few distractions. His relationship with John Fitzherbert had temporarily foundered, partly owing to a row over drawings Fitzherbert had sold, and partly as a result of the usual dissatisfaction caused by their age difference. Also, Hockney's deafness, which was so bad now that he couldn't hear the sound of his paintbrush on the canvas, was making him increasingly isolated. The days when he used to love going out to parties and openings, and just to chat to anybody around, were over.

He couldn't cope with large gatherings any more, and even visits to restaurants or small dinner parties were difficult. 'You lose interest in going into a room with 30 people talking,' he said. '. . . you've no idea how deeply embarrassing it is when people think you're being rude and you just haven't heard them. You give up because of that. And you have to realise that people aren't sympathetic to you . . . In hotels they say "Smoking or non-smoking?", but they don't say "Do you want a volume control for the telephone?", which I need or I can't use it.'[6]

Though he tried hard to hide the hurt of losing Fitzherbert, for the first time in his life Hockney began to admit that loneliness was his 'greatest suffering'.[7] It was the inevitable consequence of both being in love with much younger men, and being an artist, a profession in which he freely admitted 'you never put your relationship first; work comes first'. When Peter Adam asked him if he had ever contemplated suicide, he replied, 'We all have sometimes, but it lasts a short time. When you go to the Grand Canyon, you can drive to the edge and just go on driving, but I know the minute I would go over the edge, I would regret it . . . We have a deep desire to survive, because we like the experience of loving.'[8] Hockney's work, his love of life and his mother's adage, deeply embedded in him, that there was always somebody worse off elsewhere, sustained him through tragedy that never seemed to go away, the latest being the shocking and violent death of one of his oldest friends. On 6 August 1996, Ossie Clark was murdered in his flat, stabbed thirty-seven times by a 28-year-old Italian drifter, Diego Cogolato, whom he had picked up in Holland Park a year previously. Hearing the news had deeply saddened Hockney, but brought back happy memories of the far-off days when he and Ossie had been inseparable.

When he was done with the flowers, Hockney started on a series of portraits, head shots of his friends and family painted in vivid colours using bold brushstrokes, all posed against an emerald-green background. They were merciless in the way they depicted sadness and frailty, such as in the studies of his mother and in one brutally honest self-portrait. 'Those portraits were painful to me,' he recalled, 'including [of] myself. When I looked at myself, I just saw pain in my face. Some people said, "It didn't even look like you." And I thought

"Oh, you've no idea what I look like when I'm on my own looking in a mirror. You've no idea what I see." I must admit thinking it was one of the worst times of my life.'[9] Altogether he painted twenty-seven of these portraits, designed to be sold as a single work, and to be first shown by his new dealer, Annely Juda, an 82-year-old German Jew who was the doyenne of British art dealers. A small woman with a steely, no-nonsense character, her reputation as the most discerning of dealers went before her and Hockney, after the closing of the Kasmin Gallery, had been only too happy to align himself with her and her son David.

At a time when the art world in London was the domain of young British artists like Damien Hirst, Rachel Whiteread, Tracey Emin and Gary Hume, it was a brave move to put on a high-profile show, *Flowers, Faces and Spaces*, that consisted primarily of paintings of vases of flowers, the staple theme of greetings cards and office calendars, especially since it was his first large-scale exhibition in a commercial London gallery for over a decade. The fuss was expected, with over a thousand people a day pouring into the gallery after it opened in May 1997. What came as a surprise was the virulence with which most of the critics attacked it. '. . . our most famous painter just doesn't seem to be able to paint anymore,' wrote Tom Lubbock in the *Independent*. 'The truth is without the [Hockney] name there wouldn't be such cause to write these pictures up. They aren't very good and they aren't very good in perfectly normal ways.'[10] In the *Evening Standard*, Brian Sewell cited the flower paintings as 'evidence of steep decline', adding, 'That Hockney should now claim that the vulgar, cheap-jack daubs that he offers as his work have even the most tenuous connection with Vermeer is laughable';[11] while Martin Gayford, in the *Telegraph*, wrote, 'As a series, the flower paintings teeter on the edge of banality, and quite a few don't just teeter.'[12] Hockney put on a brave face, telling the *LA Times*, 'It's what I think that counts . . . I know what I'm doing.'[13]

Hockney returned to LA with an idea in his mind that his next painting should be a great Western landscape, a painting on a vast scale that would be made up of an amalgamation of many views drawn from memory. 'I would take the drive to Santa Fé and back,' he recalled, 'Twelve hours from here, and I did that twice in three weeks as well. People in Santa Fé thought I was crazy. I said the drive was the marvellous bit of it. Twelve hours of intense visual pleasure . . . Now I was planning to do a Western landscape on a big scale, by using memory, meaning not one view, but many views as I drove. Now, what is this collective space, that I got from twelve hours continuous travelling, in my head? I wanted to make something of that.'[14] Instead, however, he found himself travelling across the Yorkshire Wolds.

Ever since Henry Geldzahler had died, Hockney's Bradford friend Jonathan Silver had taken his place as a telephone companion. Jonathan was, he said, 'the first thing in Bradford, outside my family, that was exciting and interesting . . . We met because he was keen on pictures . . . He had a very sophisticated eye, and he could talk about pictures in an interesting way, he really *looked* at them . . . He was an amazing person – dynamic, intelligent. You did grow to love him, he was very special.'[15] So it had come as a shock to Hockney when, while staying with his mother for Christmas in Bridlington, it was revealed that Silver was suffering from the same virulent form of pancreatic cancer that had killed Geldzahler. Though the early prognosis had been promising, the cancer had steadily worsened, until by the early summer of 1997, it was diagnosed as terminal. As soon as Hockney heard this, he flew to Yorkshire. 'When I saw him,' he recalled, 'I could see he was deteriorating, he was very ill. I mean, you saw it in the face. After all, I'd seen this before. I realised, I can't just fly back to LA. What would I do there? So, I decided I'll stay here.'[16]

By the summer of 1997, the loft of his mother's house in Bridlington had been converted at Hockney's expense into a large studio, which was primarily used by Ken Wathey, a keen amateur painter, and by Hockney, whenever he was over. He moved into the house and every couple of days, or sometimes even daily, he would drive to visit Silver who was by then living at home in Wetherby, the other side of York, a journey of sixty miles that took him right across the Wolds. It was August, and the weather was steadily improving after two months of almost continuous rain that had given the landscape an unusual lushness. The sun shone and the corn was turning gold, and as he drove, Hockney began to recall the beauty of this remote area, with its rolling chalk hills and little valleys, its red-brick farmhouses dotted about on the horizon, its clumps of woodland and, above all, its big, big skies, which appealed to his growing love of open spaces. 'I realised,' he said, 'I had fallen in love with the landscape . . . driving rather slowly because there's no one else on the roads, and going to see my ailing friend made me see the living aspect of the landscape. I must admit it was a glorious summer, it was incredibly fine. I was there just as they were beginning to cut the corn so you'd get these golden fields and then these great big machines, like insects laying eggs, leaving these big bales. Some days were just glorious, the colour was *fantastic*. I can see colour. Other people don't see it like me obviously.'[17]

On arrival at Silver's house, he would feel helpless in the face of his friend's deterioration, and when he asked him if there was anything he could do for him, he always got the same answer: 'Why don't you paint East Yorkshire?' Before the building of the Humber Bridge in the 1970s, the East Riding was a relatively remote place, cut off for centuries by the river. It was a place that was on a road to nowhere, and had thus been largely neglected by artists, who had tended to concentrate on the more romantic areas of West Yorkshire, topographical studies of which had been painted over the years by, among others, Turner, Alexander Cozens and Thomas Girtin. Hockney's first three paintings took him back to his love of journey pictures. Every time he visited Jonathan, he was driving a round trip of 120 miles, and in *North Yorkshire*, the first that he completed, the swooping lines invited the viewer to take a ride around a picture in which the road the eye was led down formed an outline that more or less approximated the shape of Yorkshire on a map. Two more works in a similar vein, *The Road Across the Wolds* and *The Road to York Through Sledmere*, followed, both of which captured the feeling of what it was like to drive through a place, rather than being frozen in one position, and which concentrated on the land rather than the sky. 'When you're driving,' said Hockney, 'you don't really look at the sky . . . You keep your eye on the road. And in fact with some of these — *The Road Across the Wolds*, for instance, — I was consciously piling horizons one atop the next, such that when you were at one place in the painting, that's the horizon you'd see, whereas a bit further along, you'd see this other horizon line. They're fairly complicated paintings actually.'[18] Silver's wife, Maggie, remembered well the day Hockney brought this painting to show him. 'David and a friend brought the beautiful picture to our house in the back of a hired van with the paint still wet and David bearing the paint splashes on his jumper. It was displayed against the fireplace for Jonathan to see from his couch and it was a very special moment we all shared.'[19]

While the paintings gave Silver's spirits a much-needed boost, they were the cause of some tension between Hockney and his mother, who was used to enjoying his undivided attention while he was in Yorkshire. Having been under the impression that her favourite, unmarried son had come to Bridlington solely to see her, she did not take kindly to the fact that, for the first time in his life, he was not putting her first. Though she was fond of Silver, she slightly disapproved of the amount of time Hockney was spending with him, however ill he might have been. 'She's a very very strong-willed woman,' he told the journalist Lynn Barber. 'Tough as old boots, frankly. I remember when Diana died, saying to my mother, "That's very sad isn't it?" and she said, "Oh yes, very sad. Is there any more tea in that pot?" And I assume if you're 97, you take a very different view of death.'[20] Nevertheless, he was quite hurt by her apparent lack of emotion, expressing his feelings in a drawing that showed his mother seated, staring straight ahead, apparently ignoring her son's distress, Jonathan Silver in profile next to her, and himself curled into a foetal ball to the side.

The final painting that Hockney did for Silver was of Saltaire, the place in which he had invested so much of his love and energy. It was an obvious choice too, because it was a place Hockney had been visiting since he was a child when on bank holidays the whole family used to take the tramway up to the top of Shipley Glen, walking past the then busy mill, over the Leeds–Liverpool canal and the River Aire. 'I wanted him to see it as I see it now,' Hockney recalled, 'and also for him to know how I remembered it as well . . . By that I mean, for instance, the rows of houses to the right of the mill never came down the hill like that. You would actually have to be *inside* the mill looking out to achieve that perspective effect. But I grew up in Bradford in small terraces jammed together just like that, and I remember Saltaire as a busy working mill – literally the hub of the whole community. The workers' houses crowded down towards the mill. It was the focus of their whole working lives.'[21] When he told Silver of his intentions, all he said was, 'Show how big the mill is.'[22]

Silver's health was by now in steep decline. 'He was fading away,' Hockney told Ren Weschler, '. . . You know, the face begins to cave in . . . And I was in a turmoil, really.'[23] Working against the clock, Hockney walked the streets around the mill, taking photographs from every angle and doing sketches, before starting work on the painting back in Bridlington. It was such a large picture, ten feet by four feet, that it had to be painted on two canvases, since the studio was not big enough to take a single canvas of that size. It also had the practical element that he could fit both canvases in his car and drive over to Wetherby to show to Silver when it was finished. In the meantime, he kept him up to date with how it was progressing by showing him daily drawings and photographs. 'I'd been showing him snapshots as the painting developed,' he told Weschler, 'and actually he was quite talkative. But it was during that time that he told me not to worry so much about him, to get back to work . . . "You just paint those pictures, David. Don't do anything else . . . You paint those pictures. Celebrate life."'[24]

The painting was completed about ten days before Silver died, on 24 September 1997, and Hockney later said that when he looked at the picture, he saw not the death of his close friend, but his life. Silver's doctors told Hockney that his visits and the excitement they generated in Silver almost certainly prolonged his survival by a few months. Hockney was devastated by the loss, but after the funeral he dealt with it by returning to California to continue with his Yorkshire paintings, pictures that were intended to be a celebration of life, and joy in the beauty of the world, beginning with a large double canvas, *Double East Yorkshire*, which depicted the autumn, a time when the harvest is in and new life is ploughed into the ground. Painting this landscape lifted his spirits, something that Silver's wife noticed when Hockney returned to

Bradford for the memorial service, which took place in a room in the Salts Mill hung with his pictures. 'When you and the crew are around,' she wrote, 'it is as though everyone at Salts Mill has been injected with a life-enhancing elixir which makes people smile a lot and like each other better. You bring excitement and thrill, we all love seeing you and being with you and you make us all want to get up in the morning . . . Johnny loved and believed in you. David, you didn't let him down right to the end.'[25]

In November, Laura had finally moved into a nursing home, her frailty and constant falling having become too much of a responsibility for Margaret and Ken. Her mind, however, remained as sharp as ever. As usual, Hockney spent Christmas with his mother in Bridlington. 'I'm 60 years old,' he told Lynn Barber, 'and I've spent 58 Christmases with my mother. And she's 97 so I can't stop now, can I?'[26]

Hockney returned to California at the beginning of 1998, and began work on the last of this series of East Yorkshire views, a picture that he had always had in mind. It was of the extraordinary view from the top of Garrowby Hill, the highest point on the Wolds, which he used to walk his bicycle up when as a teenager he was a farmhand at Foxcovert Farm, Huggate. From the summit there is a 160-degree view across the Vale of York, all the way to the Pennines, a distance of fifty miles, and on the horizon you can see factory chimneys and cooling towers to the south, and the great cathedral tower of York Minster to the north. 'It also imparts,' said Hockney, 'this marvellous feeling, how you're about to take off and fly. A momentary sense of soaring.'[27] It was this feeling that made him see a connection with the American West.

Though he had a few photographs of the plain of York, the painting was done largely from memory. 'You can't photograph the landscape from any position to accord with the painting,' he recalled. 'I painted it . . . then I said "The next painting has to be of the Western landscape, and we'll start with the Grand Canyon."'[28] Hockney settled on the Grand Canyon as a subject for a painting after exhibiting a huge, forty-foot-wide version of his 1982 photo-collage of it at the Museum Ludwig in Cologne in December 1997, as part of a photographic retrospective of his work mounted there by its director, Reinhold Misselbeck. On seeing it in position, however, in the vast central room, he was disappointed by the impact it made: 'what I noticed was how the image did not read from a great distance. It seemed to lose its presence, its impact, as you stepped back.'[29] He realised that the reason for this was that photographic printing inks simply did not have the luminosity of paint. They seemed powdery compared to the vibrancy of the colours he had seen at the Vermeer show in The Hague, where he had spent hours studying how Vermeer had made his images glow by building up thin layers of colour one atop the next. 'I joked,' he said, 'that Vermeer's colours will last a lot longer than MGM's, but it's true . . . the photocollage mural in Cologne, as impressive as it was, couldn't hold a candle to that kind of presence. I turned to Richard [Schmidt] and said "I should *paint* the Grand Canyon."'[30]

When Hockney told Peter Goulds what he had in mind, Goulds encouraged him to make a trip to Washington where the National Gallery was holding a major show of the work of the nineteenth-century landscape painter Thomas Moran, an American artist who had originally hailed from the north of England, having been born in Bolton, Lancashire, no more than forty miles from Hockney's own home town of Bradford. The son of a hand-loom weaver who had emigrated to Philadelphia in search of work in the textile industry, he had attended art school before finding work as an apprentice in a Philadelphia firm of wood engravers called Scattergood and Telfer, from where he had gone on to study under the maritime painter James Hamilton, known as 'the American Turner'. Moran soon became known for his grandiose paintings of the American West, in particular the Yellowstone region, his work providing a major contribution to the creation of the Yellowstone National Park. Latterly he also painted a number of views of the Grand Canyon, which was often referred to as 'the despair of the painter' for the problems it presented to artists. When Hockney saw these in Washington, they inspired him to tackle the subject and try a new approach, in which he would attempt to convey not information about the topography and geology of the canyon, but the experience of space.

There was an additional impetus for Hockney to embark on this ambitious project, which was an offer of a retrospective exhibition tracing his ideas about space and landscape at the Pompidou Centre in Paris, to open in January 1999. After measuring the end walls of what was to be the final room of the show, he decided to produce one painting for each of these to the maximum size they could accommodate, which was close to twenty-five feet in width. The first of these, *A Bigger Grand Canyon*, followed the layout of his 1982 photo-collage, and was painted on sixty small canvases, the same number as there were individual snaps in the collage. It was done entirely from memory. 'I deliberately decided not to go again before I did it,' he said. 'It was January, not the best time to see the Grand Canyon . . . There might be a lot of mist and I'd see nothing. I might as well be looking at Bridlington. So I decided not to go. I didn't want to be influenced by atmospherics. I wanted to paint it how I remembered it, with real colour and pigments, strong pure colour put on right . . . it had to be carefully planned . . . working long days, every day. Terrific. Once I'm started, I'm gone!'[31]

When Lynn Barber visited him early in 1998, she saw a sketch of the painting up on the wall, though then comprising only sixteen canvases. She had not interviewed him since he was in his twenties and was amused to find how, at the age of sixty, he had reverted to 'pure Yorkshireman – the jutting jaw, the pursed mouth, the Alan Bennett haircut',[32] but she also noticed how his increasing deafness was turning him into something of a monologist, with a habit of throwing in fillers such as 'frankly', 'I must say' and 'I would point out' to cover pauses. 'It gives him a slightly hectoring, soapbox tone,' she wrote. 'But – more – you get the sense he has talked too much to himself. It seems absurd to call him a recluse when he is surrounded by more gofers than most film stars, but there is a touch of the Ancient Mariner about him. His theories, ideas, opinions come tumbling out as if he has been hoarding them through months of solitude.' His humour, however, remained as strong as ever, and she laughed at the good jokes displayed in his studio. '. . . a headline from the *New York Times* saying "Science confronts the unknowable – less is known than people think" and a sign saying "Thank you for Pot Smoking".'[33]

A Bigger Grand Canyon was the largest painting Hockney had ever done, four feet longer than *Mulholland Drive: The Road to the Studio*. He liked to recount how one night, leaving a dinner early, he ran into Ed Ruscha. 'I said "Well, I'm going home now. I go to bed early. I get up very early. I'm doing this large painting of the Grand Canyon." And he said "Well, in miniature of course." Which I thought was very witty. For, of course, whatever size we do it, it will be a miniature.'[34] The painting was done entirely in the studio, between January and March 1998, and the sixty different canvases gave it the equivalent number of vanishing points, creating for the viewer a tremendous feeling of space. It featured virtually no sky, painted as it was from the perspective of someone looking down into the canyon, which covers an area of nearly 5,000 square miles, and in places is over a mile deep. In September he started work on a second, even larger version, this time done from life, and painted from a specific spot, Powell Point, named after the explorer, Major John Wesley Powell, who in 1869 became the first man to successfully explore the Colorado River through the Grand Canyon. Hockney chose this vantage point because 'I found a quiet spot for me to sit'.[35] The new picture comprised sixty canvases, on which he painted a skyscape. 'The second,' he recalled, ' – which I called *A Closer Grand Canyon* because you feel closer to it – was done from drawings after sitting there for a week. I took the chair right to the edge to make sure I could sit comfortably for quite a while. I'd be out very early when the sun had just risen. I'd just sit there.' He did this for seven days, from dawn till sunset.

'I'd just think about the space,' he said. 'I'm not afraid of the canyon. The first people who went there thought it was something to fear, but I don't see it that way. It is about the only place on earth that really makes you look in every direction. You feel small. And the longer you look the more thrilling that becomes.'[36] In this painting the vastness of the sky stretching into infinity creates a powerful sense of the hugeness of the landscape, while the viewer is so convincingly placed at the very edge of the south rim as to induce a sense of vertigo. Hockney was delighted with the completed work, joking with Marco Livingstone that he felt he had 'out-Turnered Turner'.[37]

Hockney had not been idle in the period between the production of
the two Grand Canyon paintings. As had so often been the case after
the death of someone close to him, he had been drawing his friends, in
this case going back to one of his first-learned skills, that of etching,
and working again with his most long-standing and skilled collaborator
in the field, Maurice Payne. At Hockney's suggestion, early in 1998
Payne had moved into Montcalm Avenue, where he had created and
equipped a fully functioning etching studio and adjoining workspace,
the first set up in the garage, the second in part of the living room.
Having done this, and being used to the way the artist worked, he had
then developed a strategy of leaving prepared etching plates all around
the house, in the hope that something would catch Hockney's eye and
he would then pick them up and draw on them as spontaneously as
he might in a sketchbook. It turned out to be a strategy that repaid in
spades, resulting in around fifty etchings made during the year that
Payne spent in LA.

Visiting Montcalm Avenue in June 1998, Paul Joyce, who was
working on a book of interviews with Hockney, gave a vivid description
of the scene he found there. 'On the last evening of my visit,' he wrote, 'I
arrived at David's house in the Hollywood Hills for dinner, as arranged,
to find no visible evidence of dinner but much of etching procedures.
David and Maurice Payne, his master printer of thirty years and more,
were locked in silent communication, unshaven, grimed and ink-
stained . . . Together they had produced twenty stunning and completely
different images which . . . would be major works when editioned.
Maurice clearly felt this and was trying to get the series completed,
but David still pressed on, experimenting with and extending the
possibilities of the medium . . . The image David had been working
on was a near-life-size head of Maurice, in half-profile. David was still
unhappy about the amount of hard line detail, particularly around
the mouth and eyes. This meant that he had to physically attack the
plate with a burnishing tool, flattening lines by carefully gouging out
surrounding layers of copper. This took a great deal of strength in hand
and forearm and, although David is not over muscular, he is wiry and
extremely strong. He worked hard on the plate for about ten minutes

and, apparently satisfied, he told me that this was the third "state" or working of the plate, and it would probably go to six or seven before they were finished.'[38]

Watching Payne making the final preparations to the plate, first drawing the ink across it, then working it into every line, before wiping it away and finally using a fine dusting of French chalk to eradicate any last traces, Joyce understood how the production of a fine etching was a true partnership between artist and printer. 'When at last the plate was prepared to the satisfaction of

Paul Joyce. London.
2nd June 1999

both, Maurice selected a sheet of heavyweight paper, full of water and resting between sheets of blotting paper, wiping off the excess moisture and placing it beneath a cloth facing the plate on the printing press. Then he turned the heavy press slowly but incredibly smoothly, like an old-fangled clothes mangle until plate and paper had travelled right through the drum mechanism . . . As David said, watching Maurice, "No machine could ever be programmed to do this, ever."'[39]

The resulting etchings, both colour and black and white, and mostly done to a large scale, were self-confident demonstrations of technical brilliance, and a reminder to people of where Hockney's origins lay. They comprised still lifes, studies of Stanley and Boodgie, and striking portraits of Celia Birtwell, Maurice Payne and his girlfriend Brenda Zlamany, all of which were notable for being drawn not with a single-point pen, but with special brushes that Hockney designed himself using different thicknesses of wire which produced a network of spidery lines. Watching him at work, Payne was struck by how perceptive he was. 'He is very insightful,' he says. 'Sometimes it's as if he sees things that are there, but aren't actually there. For example when he did a portrait of Brenda, my girlfriend, he didn't realise that she had been trying to get pregnant for some time and at that moment actually was not pregnant. Well, he was doing that portrait of Brenda and when you look at it, you wonder whether he knew something that I didn't know. In the portrait she is sitting there with all her curly hair and her hand is resting over her stomach. This big old hand is not exactly like a hand is, but it tells you everything. When I was printing those etchings I thought to myself that it must have been very close to the time that she actually did get pregnant. The trouble with David is he can read your mind. It's not worth lying to him or pulling the wool over his eyes. I've tried that and he sees through it straight away. I've learned now with him that there's no point in making a story up about anything. You might just as well be direct with him.'[40]

The work on this series of etchings happened to coincide with an invitation from Gérard Régnier, the director of the Musée Picasso in Paris, to mount an exhibition of Hockney's work to tie in with the Pompidou show. 'It's frightening at times thinking what to do in the Picasso Museum,' Hockney wrote to Régnier, 'to look at all interesting compared to what is there, but my suggestion now is to make a show of the etchings I have been obsessively doing recently. Since you were here I have been doing portraits – very strong and dense, already there are about 45 etchings . . . I'm realy [sic] drawing on copper with wire brushes (Picasso would have loved the medium) . . . The work is I think more than just some etchings. I think it would work very well, in fact I've confidence enough that the range of subject and the range of graphic exploration would make it very strong.'[41] Dialogue avec Picasso was to be the first exhibition by a living artist at the Musée Picasso, and one of the highlights of Hockney's career.

CHAPTER FIFTEEN

SECRET KNOWLEDGE

In January 1999, while Paris was in the throes of Hockney-worship, with
shows simultaneously running at the Pompidou, the Musée Picasso and
the Maison Européenne de la Photographie, two French artists were
enthralling the gallery-visiting public in London. As the Royal Academy
was pulling in the crowds with *Monet in the 20th Century*, the National
Gallery had an equally important show of the work of the neoclassical
painter Jean-Auguste-Dominique Ingres, a deeply unfashionable artist
in comparison to Monet. Ingres, who was born in Montauban in 1780,
was the son of a minor sculptor, stonemason and painter of miniatures,
Jean-Marie-Joseph Ingres, who from an early age gave him encouragement and instruction in drawing and music. Though the French
Revolution disrupted his education, the young Ingres eventually made
it to Paris where he worked in the studio of Jacques-Louis David,
before being accepted into the École des Beaux Arts. While studying
there he was awarded the Prix de Rome, a scholarship given by the
French government allowing students to study at the Académie de
France in Rome, to where he moved in 1806, enjoying a period of
relative prosperity over the next few years as a portraitist of Napoleonic
officials and dignitaries.

In 1815, with the fall of the Napoleonic Empire and the subsequent
French evacuation of Rome, Ingres, who had opted to remain in Italy,
found himself stranded there without patronage. 'The fall of the Murat
family in Naples,' he wrote to a friend, 'has ruined me with paintings
that were lost or sold without payment.'[1] Things became so desperate
that to stave off starvation – there was no more bread in his house and
the baker had cut off his credit – he was reduced to selling himself as a
portrait artist to the numerous Grand Tourists passing through Rome in
the aftermath of the Napoleonic Wars. Many of these were English, who

for twenty years had been denied the sun of Italy, and, lured by street urchins who were paid a commission to recruit them, they flocked in droves to his house at 34 Via Gregoriana, just down the street from the Villa Medici. Though some were members of the aristocracy, such as Lord and Lady Glenbervie, Sir John Hay and his sister Mary, and Lady William Henry Cavendish Bentinck, the majority, Mrs Charles Badham and Mr and Mrs Joseph Woodhead for instance, were part of an entirely new phenomenon, the middle-class traveller. Ingres, who had higher aspirations than being a jobbing portraitist, thought the work beneath him and it was said that to the visitors who knocked on his door to ask, 'Is this where the man who draws the little portraits lives?', he would answer sarcastically, 'No, the man who lives here is a painter.'[2]

Whatever Ingres may have thought about them, this series of perfectly executed drawings, each of them not much bigger than eight by twelve inches, are today regarded as among his finest work. Hockney had first come across them while an art student in Bradford, at a time when they were held up as an ideal in drawing: sensitive, full of character and uncannily accurate about physiognomy. He visited both the Monet and the Ingres shows. 'I spent hours at each,' he recalled, 'and each seemed to leave me more exhilarated . . . Especially the Ingres, which I went back to three times – . . . in particular the drawings. Now, for someone like me, trained in the conventional Caracci tradition – you know, plumb line, the extended thumb, gauging relative proportions, and so forth – those pencil portraits of Ingres's were mind-boggling. For one thing their size – how small they turn out to be when you see them in person. The images are . . . incredibly detailed and incredibly assured. If you draw at all, you know that's very rare and not at all easy.'[3]

Hockney became increasingly fascinated by the immense, time-consuming care of Ingres's technique. He bought the catalogue and took it back to LA where he further studied it, reading it over and over till he knew almost every word. He scrutinised the drawings, intrigued by how uncannily true to life they were, particularly in the relationship of the eyes to the nose and mouth, always ending up asking himself the same question: how was it done? He could not understand how Ingres achieved such accuracy on such a small scale, so took some of the drawings and enlarged them on his Xerox machine so that he could examine the line more closely. While studying the blow-ups one morning, he was struck by how much they reminded him of some of the Warhol drawings that he had seen in New York at a show called *Studio Still-Lifes*. They had the same clean, fast and completely assured line. He knew, however, that Warhol's were traced using a slide projector, and immediately wondered whether it was possible that Ingres had done his the same way, through using some other optical device.

He then recalled that while he was studying at art school he had once been shown a camera lucida, an optical device invented in 1807 by William Wollaston, an English doctor/chemist who was captivated by optics, the purpose of which was to aid artists in the accurate rendering of perspective. The camera lucida was basically a prism balanced at the end of a stick that allowed the superimposition of a subject onto the surface of a piece of paper, so that both could be seen simultaneously. With mounting excitement, Hockney instructed Richard Schmidt to scour the local art shops to see if he could find one. As the device is nowadays something of a rarity, it was not an easy task, but Schmidt eventually tracked one down for the sum of over two thousand dollars. It was immediately set up on a flat drawing table in a corner of the studio, within a small alcove that was cordoned off with screens and curtains, and the first subject was Schmidt himself. What Hockney found was that the device enabled him to accurately place the eyes, nose and mouth, before then drawing from direct observation, or 'eyeballing' as he called it.

One of his next subjects, Paul Joyce, compared the experience of being drawn in this way to what it must have been like having a portrait photograph taken in the nineteenth century, when the slowness of the film emulsion necessitated a long exposure. Another sitter, Ren Weschler, recounted it thus: "'Sit there,' Hockney commanded, and then spent a few moments adjusting my pose. "Perfect," he said. "Stay like that." He fetched a sheet of Arches paper and a canister of sharpened pencils, laid the page beneath the prism, and set to work. The first part of the session lasted about an hour, but Hockney used the camera lucida itself for only two or three minutes – quickly and, yes, with startling assuredness, sketching out the tangle of my hands, legs and sleeves, and then, turning to my face, laying in the general shape of my head. Muttering, "this is the crucial part," he posited, with the faintest of pencil stabs, the coordinates of my pupils, the corners of my eyes, my nostrils, the lay of my glasses over my ears, the edges of my mouth. After that, he reverted to a more standard posture, gazing past the hovering prism, as if it weren't even there, and probing my face and then the page, back and forth. His own face was becoming increasingly scrunched up with concentration, so much so that at one point his earpiece began to screech (he plucked it out and set it aside); his tongue, animate, prehensile, lolled and darted from one side of his open mouth to the other in evident syncopation with his drawing hand (it was as if he were thinking with his tongue). Only once or twice thereafter did he bother to look through the prism, for minor adjustments.'[4]

Over the next year, the camera lucida was to become the dominant tool in Hockney's work, though sadly he was never to have the opportunity of using it for a portrait of his mother. Though her mental faculties had remained good, Laura's physical condition had deteriorated since moving into the nursing home. Her will to survive, however, was undiminished, and, aged ninety-eight, was driven by a determination that she would beat Barbara Cartland to reach her hundredth birthday, and at least equal the age of her other rival, the Queen Mother. By early May, however, it was clear that her days were numbered, so the family gathered round her in Bridlington, with the exception of John, who was on his way from Australia. 'We kept telling her where he would be at a particular time,' Margaret Hockney remembers, 'and I'm pretty sure she hung on for his coming. He eventually arrived and he had about three hours with her.'[5]

Laura's death was the end of an era, and in her passing Hockney lost not only a beloved mother who had been the still heart of his career, but a subject to whom he had returned time and time again. Even during these last few days, he continued to make drawings of her. 'She had four children around her,' he recalled, 'and she was 98 and she only spent her last three days in bed. So she was blessed really. I'm sad, of course.

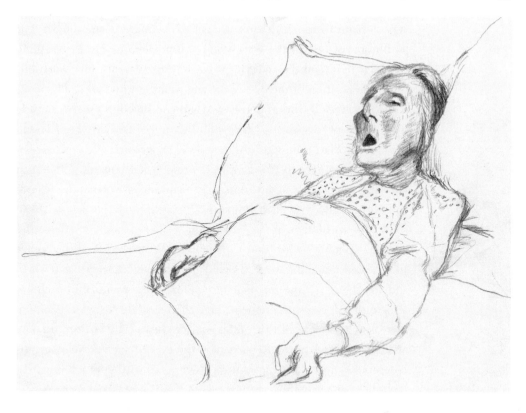

After all, she was the person I've known all my life.'[6] She died on 11   *Mum, 1999*
May, only seven months short of her ninety-ninth birthday, and on the
following day he told Marco Livingstone, 'Up until yesterday, I always
knew exactly where my mother was. If I wanted to have a chat with her
I could phone her and she would drop whatever she was doing to talk
to me.'[7] To another friend he wrote, '[Death] has a strange effect, even
when you expect it. My mother was . . . a keen Bible reader, waiting
"to be called", and, I admit, she seemed to know. But to live into the
nineties must be just enough. My mother would say to me it's no fun
being old. She had such bad arthritic hands she couldn't switch off a
light . . .'[8]

   In the weeks and months following his mother's death, Hockney
dealt with his grief in the way that he had on so many previous occasions,
by obsessively drawing his friends, and in so doing mastering the art of
using the camera lucida. 'At first,' he wrote, 'I found the camera lucida

very difficult to use. It doesn't project a real image of the subject, but an illusion of one in the eye. When you move your head everything moves with it, and the artist must learn to make very quick notations to fix the position of the eyes, nose and mouth to capture "a likeness". It is concentrated work. I persevered and continued to use the method for the rest of the year – learning all the time.'[9] He stayed in London throughout May, June and July, completely engrossed in the process of making the camera lucida drawings, working flat out, his enthusiasm knowing no bounds as he captured the likenesses of family, friends and acquaintances of all ages, and producing enough finished works to show fifty-six of them at the Annely Juda Gallery in a show called *Space and Line* opening on 30 June 1999. On his return to LA at the end of July, he continued the work, drawing portraits of his American friends, and for the first time introducing colour in the form of gouache as an additional pictorial element; and all the while he was becoming increasingly convinced that optical devices had probably been used by artists as far back as the Renaissance. The earliest such device that was commonly known was the camera obscura, consisting of a box with a pinhole in one side through which light from an external scene passed to strike a surface inside, upon which the scene was reproduced upside down. Canaletto was known to have used one in his scenes of Venice, and it is thought that Vermeer may also have used one to facilitate the painting of his interiors. 'Once I started seeing it in Ingres,' he told Ren Weschler, 'I began to notice lens- or mirror-based imagery, in all sorts of other places, including before Ingres, and in fact . . . hundreds of years before.'[10] Hockney's belief was strengthened by the fact that strong lighting was required to use the camera lucida successfully, and strong lighting created deep shadows, a combination he began to see over and over again in the works of the great masters such as Caravaggio and Velázquez.

Like a dog with a bone, Hockney was determined to be proved right in his theories. Needing a good researcher to dig out evidence, he pulled in his old collaborator, David Graves, and together they began a detailed study of the work of the old masters going all the way back to the sixteenth century, as well as searching through hundreds of books and texts. His starting point was a woodcut by Dürer, *Artist Drawing a Lute*, dated 1525, which demonstrated a very cumbersome method of drawing a lute in perspective, involving two men and a mass of complicated measuring equipment. This he compared with a painting by Caravaggio from 1595, *Young Boy Singing and Playing the Lute*, in which the artist had rendered a lute in complex perspective, seemingly effortlessly, as well as including a violin in the picture. Was this really achieved, he wondered, using Dürer's incredibly complicated drawing machine? 'The flow of my thought,' he wrote, 'is that somewhere between 1525 (Durer's engraving) and 1595 (Caravaggio's boy with a lute) a lens was developed that, combined with the natural phenomenon of a camera (hole and dark room) became a tool for artists. This, it seems to me, would explain the new found naturalism of these painters, and the thrill people had when looking at them.'[11]

Caravaggio was known for working in the dark, posing his models in cellars, but he left no notes or preparatory sketches behind to show just how he did it. 'I believe,' speculated Hockney, 'he would pose his models at one end of the cellar and then put his lens, which he would carry around with him in a bag, in the middle of the room on a stand and drape a curtain wall around it. The tableau is projected through the lens to where he stands with his brush and canvas, when he quickly sketches guidelines which he can then fill in while the models take a break.'[12] He thought that many other painters would have used a similar technique, which in his mind explained the great leap forward in painting during the sixteenth century, when faces and bodies became more expressive. Artists were secretive about their methods, he suggested, because projecting images through lenses or onto mirrors was still a bit close to magic and risked accusations of heresy. So painters and their sitters kept quiet about how the trick was done.

If Hockney had a notion, as he began to expound his theories, that they would be received within the art world as the revelations of a genius, he was to be gravely mistaken, as was foreseen by John Walsh, the director of the Getty Museum and a long-time admirer of his. 'David will often take a sound general observation,' he said, '. . . and then push and push it, way, way out to the very limit and beyond.

Which is fine: it's what makes him an artist, that divine confidence of his. But in this latest discourse, marvelously suggestive as several of his suggestions are, I fear David may well find himself sailing against the wind. For before the seventeenth century, where's the evidence? Where's the testimony of sitters or other contemporaries, or the treatises of the artists themselves? We have vast inventories, often compiled for inheritance purposes at the time of the artists' deaths, every single brush accounted for – and where are all the lenses and other devices you'd expect to find listed, if David were right? It's pretty dicey.'[13]

Walsh's prediction was indeed prescient, for Hockney soon found that the weight of opinion within the art-historical world was against him, while within the artistic world he was regarded as a traitor to the cause for having dared to suggest that great artists might ever have required any mechanical assistance in the production of their works. 'Hockney's claim,' wrote a *Sunday Times* journalist, 'that the Old Masters were exam cheats who employed mysterious optical devices to trace the visible world onto their canvases has been greeted with the reaction it deserved: belly laughs and scorn.'[14] Hockney got a T-shirt printed with the words 'I KNOW I'M RIGHT', and ploughed on with his researches, as well as continuing to master the camera lucida, participating in a millennium show at the National Gallery in London in June 2000 called *Encounters: New Art from Old*. Each contributing artist was invited to take inspiration from a work in the collection and, as a tribute to Ingres, whose pencil drawings had been shown there a year earlier, Hockney chose to portray a cross section of the gallery's wardens as *12 Portraits after Ingres in a Uniform Style*, all drawn using the camera lucida.

The strain, however, was getting to him, caused by a combination of grief, loneliness and overwork. 'Towards the end of 1999,' Gregory Evans recalls, 'David went through a period of intense depression. He was taking a lot of drugs. I was living in the house next door and he used to call me up sounding terrible and ask me to come over. Sometimes I would find him unconscious on the floor, having passed out. I was seriously worried that he might take his own life.'[15] When he came over to London in November, David Graves noticed how run-down he was. 'He had some really bad days,' he remembers, 'when he was feeling cold and he would lie by the fire in his dressing gown.'[16] At the beginning of December he had a complete collapse and went off to Baden-Baden in Germany for a few days, to take the waters and recover. In true form, Hockney took it lightly, writing to a friend, 'Gregory said I'd possibly over-faxed myself.'[17]

Reinvigorated by his trip to the spa, he returned to England to spend his first Christmas without his mother, and to complete the series of the National Gallery wardens, a project that was to prove particularly popular with the paying public, who enjoyed the fact that they might come face to face with the subjects portrayed in the drawings. He then returned to LA, accompanied by David and Ann Graves, to further pursue his theories of how the old masters worked, which was now to be the subject of a book. In mid-February, writing to Martin Kemp, Emeritus Professor of History of Art at Oxford, who had been following Hockney's researches with interest and an open mind since they had been introduced the previous autumn, he informed him, 'We've started work on the book. We're making a wall of 500 years of painting that will be 70 feet long. David Graves and I are piecing it all together . . . we have a rich visual story going on here and we are adding more to it all the time. I think it will excite you.'[18]

What Hockney and Graves had actually done was to clear the long far wall of his Montcalm Avenue studio, which ran the length of the tennis court over which it had been built and stood two storeys high, install a colour photocopier in the middle of the space and, drawing on his comprehensive collection of art-history books, proceed to cover the wall with photocopied images of European paintings, overlapping them in chronological order, from 1350 to 1900, with northern Europe above and southern Europe below. The resulting 'Great Wall', as his assistants quickly named it, allowed Hockney at a glance to survey the history of Western art and to work out when optics might first have been used. His immediate deduction was that it was at the time of Van Eyck and his followers, a conclusion which initially seemed impossible as there was no evidence from that date that lenses had yet been invented.

Detail from
The Great Wall

The game-changing moment came when he met Charles Falco, an experimental physicist and motorbike enthusiast, then chair of the condensed matter/solid state physics programme at the University of Arizona in Tucson. Falco's work had made him an authority in both quantum and standard optics, and having read about Hockney's researches, he approached him, offering him his expertise, and was immediately invited up to the studio. After studying the 'Great Wall' and hearing Hockney's doubts, he explained to him that though lenses may not have existed in 1430, convex mirrors, which appear in many Flemish paintings of that date, certainly did, and their concave flip sides were capable of projecting images of outside reality onto a darkened flat surface, which could then be traced in the same way as with a focusing lens. Trying out this theory using his shaving mirror, placing it in a darkened room and finding it projected an image – the folds on Richard Schmidt's shirt, through a peephole onto a wall – was what Hockney referred to as a 'eureka eureka moment'. It proved to him that artists could indeed have used such techniques before the invention of lenses in the 1600s. All this was further grist to his mill, and having a scientist as eminent as Falco on his side gave greater weight to his theories, and to the considerable amount of evidence he and Graves managed to amass, which was published in 2001 in his book *Secret Knowledge: Rediscovering the Lost Techniques of the Old Masters*.

The book received massive attention, and it was accompanied by an *Omnibus* film made for the BBC. When all was said and done, however, and in spite of a number of artists and distinguished art-world figures publicly stating that they believed he was on to something, the overwhelming consensus, in the absence of the smoking gun of a written description in diaries or letters of a great artist actually using a device, was that his theory was entirely speculation. There was furious debate, culminating in a two-day conference in December 2001 arranged by the New York Institute for the Humanities called 'Art and Optics: Toward an Evaluation of David Hockney's New Theories regarding Opticality in Western Painting of the Past 600 Years'. Two dozen artists, museum curators and scientists were invited to the Greenwich Village campus of New York University to discuss his hypothesis, and the event was chaired by Ren Weschler, who, having recently pulled a leg muscle, was able to use his crutch as a gavel to call the often rumbustious audience to order. The event attracted hundreds of New Yorkers, who, as well as listening to the debates, were able to see and try out the same sort of lenses and the cameras obscura and lucida that Hockney contended were used centuries ago by Van Eyck, Velázquez and others.

Among the first to speak was Susan Sontag, who took Hockney to task over his assertion that optical devices were mere tools to help artists and in no way diminished their reputations. 'If David Hockney's thesis is correct,' she said, 'it would be a bit like finding that all the great lovers of history have been using Viagra . . . What David Hockney does is start from the position of a practicing artist. "I couldn't draw like that." Therefore the presumption is they couldn't do it.'[19] Chuck Close, who painted from photographs of faces, followed on, stating that it was obvious that any artist would use every tool possible to make the job easier. At the end of two days of always lively and occasionally fractious argument between sceptics and supporters, which Close suggested should have been titled 'Look Back in Ingres', Hockney got to speak, by which time he seemed to have had enough.

'When it was Hockney's turn to sum up,' reported the *LA Times* correspondent, 'he did not claim any conclusive outcome. "The paintings I agree are absolutely magical," he said. "We will never actually know how they were done." He seemed ready to let others figure that out. All the research had cost him not only money, but month after month away from his painting. "I now want to allocate my time back in the studio," he said.'[20] He told Weschler, 'I've been getting bored with the whole controversy . . . I had other things I needed to be doing. Like Painting! I needed to be getting back to painting. For a short time, but only a very short time, I wondered if there were some way I could adapt optics to my new purposes. But I quickly realised that no, the trouble with optics is the trouble with photography: it's not *real* enough, it's not true enough to *lived* experience. The Chinese say that painting draws on three things: the eye, the heart, and the hand. And I longed to return to the hand.'[21]

Hockney spent the better part of two years working on *Secret Knowledge*, and that period was not uneventful in other spheres, the most important of these being his getting back together with John Fitzherbert. In the years since they had split up, Fitzherbert had been living down the hill on Willoughby Avenue with his brother, Robbie, in a house paid for by Hockney, who always liked to keep his old friends within spitting distance. They had hooked up again when both were in London, and the relationship had rekindled in a fresh and exciting way. After three years of being on his own, this made Hockney extremely happy, and he and Fitzherbert returned together to LA, where they settled into a domestic routine of work, delicious meals and seeing friends. But Hockney's exhaustion, from overworking on the *Secret Knowledge* book, was soon noticed by Fitzherbert. 'We'd go to dinner at people's houses,' he recalls, 'and all of a sudden David would fall asleep. He'd have had a few drinks, and after a while people began to think it was a bit rude. He'd have these bouts of just getting really tired. Then his doctor, Dr Wilbur, had the idea it might be pancreatitis, which is partly triggered by alcohol, and by caffeine in all the tea that David used to drink.'[22]

Pancreatitis is a painful illness and saps the energy of the sufferer, and in spite of having Fitzherbert to look after him, as well as his faithful housekeeper, Elsa, Hockney felt very low. It was a situation that was not improved when in May 2001 his beloved dog Stanley passed away, leaving only Boodgie to follow him around. Then in November, at the very moment that there were numerous calls on his time connected to the publication of *Secret Knowledge*, he lost yet another close friend to AIDS. Jeff Burkhart was a raconteur with whom he would speak most days on the telephone. A Hollywood writer, Burkhart was also the author of a successful book called *Hollywood's First Choices*, about the great casting decisions made in the movies 'He had an amazing Jewish wit,' Fitzherbert remembers, 'and David adored him. We all did, except for Henry Geldzahler, who didn't get on with him because their personalities clashed. They were too similar. We had loads of fun with Jeff, who would come to lunch most days at Montcalm. He was one of those people who always sang for his lunch. He was so entertaining.'[23] Unfortunately he also had a serious cocaine habit and died from the complications of both AIDS and drug abuse, leaving another big hole in Hockney's life. Brought down by this, and exhausted by the whole *Secret Knowledge* project, Hockney decided to spend some time back in England.

CHAPTER SIXTEEN

GEORGE
AND MARY CHRISTIE

Early in March 2002, Lucian Freud told Hockney that he might be prepared to sit for him for a portrait, on the condition that he returned the favour. Hockney knew well who would be getting the better deal if he were to agree to this, as it was common knowledge that the average time required of a sitter by Freud was a hundred hours, while half a day would suit Hockney nicely. It was not the first time that Freud had put the proposal, and on previous occasions Hockney had politely refused using the truthful excuse that he would not be in England long enough for the portrait to be completed. On this occasion, however, he was intending to stay longer, so his response was that he was prepared to 'make a start'.

So one morning in late March, Hockney found himself walking through Holland Park to Freud's studio, noticing as he went that there were buds on the trees heralding spring, and thinking how exciting the English seasons were compared to those in California. Freud worked in the morning and in the evening, leaving the afternoon free, and Hockney had chosen the morning slot, that being his best time of day. He arrived at eight thirty at the studio, one of two used by the artist, this one being on the top floor of a large house in Holland Park. There was no lift, and Hockney noticed how nimble and fit Freud was as he almost ran up the six flights of stairs.

Every artist's studio is unique, and Freud's cannot have presented a more stark contrast to Hockney's large airy space with its neat and tidy workspaces, brushes and paints perfectly arranged, canvases stacked in special shelving, and the floor meticulously clean. Here the walls were covered in paint, owing to Freud's habit of not putting the tops back on the tubes after he had squeezed out the colour. This caused the oil paint to cake up on them, which he would then flick off onto the wall with a swipe. 'He has been doing this on the studio wall for the past forty years,' Hockney recalls, 'so it is thick with many years' layers. Like a wall in the life rooms at the art schools of the fifties that I knew, but this was all done by the same hand – a rare and beautiful thing in itself.'[1] The walls were also used as a message pad. The floor too was covered in paint, and in the corner of the room were bundles of rags, torn from old linen sheets that Freud's assistant, David Dawson, would pick up in Brick Lane, and which were used as both paint rags and aprons. There was little in the room other than a bed, a couple of chairs, an easel and a paint cart, and the light came from a glass roof directly above that gave very good lighting on the face, its amount being controlled through louvres.

Knowing that it was not unusual for Freud to abandon a painting if he was not happy with it, Hockney came prepared to cooperate fully with his demands, deciding to always wear, for example, a particular jacket and a blue shirt. His only stipulation was that he should be allowed to smoke. 'He agreed,' Hockney remembers, 'but told me not to mention it to Kate Moss who was his other subject at the time.'[2] He was then given a low chair to sit in with a reachable ashtray on the floor beside it. When it had been put in place, David Dawson made paint marks round the legs so it could be put back in precisely the same position with reference to the overhead light and the easel each time he returned for a sitting. Freud then went through his preliminary ritual, as described by the art critic Martin Gayford, who sat for Freud the following year. 'First, he rummages around and finds a palette, thickly encrusted with worms and gouts of dried pigment. Then he spends a considerable amount of time carefully cleaning a zone at the bottom left near the thumbhole. There follows more casting around for suitable brushes and tubes of paint that lie around in mounds on a portable trolley and on top of a cupboard near the wall. From the pile of old ragged sheets in the corner of the studio he selects a clean section, tears off a square and tucks it into his waistband, like a very informal butcher or baker . . . The rag-apron is used for wiping brushes and occasionally the palette knife . . .'[3]

It wasn't vanity that persuaded Hockney to agree to the sitting, but a natural curiosity from a fellow portrait painter to see his technique, and during the three months he spent sitting for Freud, little escaped his notice. 'His method of painting is very good,' he recalled, 'because being slow it means you can talk. If you're going to draw someone in one hour, you can't really chat to them because you haven't got that long, and you want to watch the face. But if you do have longer and you talk, you get to know and watch the face do a lot of things, and obviously that's part of his method. Sometimes he'd come very close to look . . . looking and peering and peering, and coming closer, closer. He has this energy which comes across to you as well. I thought I daren't fall asleep . . .'[4] They talked a lot, mostly gossip about mutual friends and other artists, and while Hockney was amused by Freud's pithy putdowns, Freud enjoyed Hockney's smoking jokes. He admired Hockney and liked to refer to him as 'the Yorkshire Master'.[5]

The one thing that struck Hockney as unusual was the fact that whenever the telephone, which was in another room, rang, Freud would go and answer it, though it gave Hockney an opportunity he did not miss. 'If we took a break and he was on the phone,' he said, 'I would do drawings of things in the studio: the ashtray and worn footboards with a big hole – perhaps where the rat came through I thought. I liked the old fashioned Bohemia of it all – the plates with old beans on them from last night, or even last week. It was like student days, very appealing after very clean New York lofts.'[6] These drawings were done in a series of landscape-shaped sketchbooks, of a particular size he had found which would fit into his pockets. He used new pens he had discovered with brown inks that dried quickly and didn't fade. 'I was constantly drawing,' he said, 'which in turn makes you look harder, look more, *see* more, remember more . . . And I realised, this is fun!'[7] When he showed some of his sketches to his friend George Lawson, he commented, 'How did you manage all these, David, when he was painting you?', to which Hockney replied, 'Well, he spent all his time on the fucking telephone!'[8]

When Freud eventually came to sit for Hockney in August 2002, for a pen-and-ink drawing, it was a very different story. He was a difficult

Lucian Freud

25 August 02
LM.

subject, losing attention, twisting about and eventually falling asleep, though he was to return for a second, more successful, sitting, on that occasion with his assistant, David Dawson. 'I got one or two things out of it,' wrote Hockney, 'but I thought *his* portrait very good indeed. All the hours I sat were layered into it; he had always added, rarely taken anything away. It really shows.'[9] It was, he thought, a remarkable work by a great artist. When Hockney showed a photograph of it to one of his sitters, he first said that he thought the painting made him look older. 'And yet when he sat here for me,' he recalled, 'and he looked at my face for seven hours, he told me, "I begin to see now what Lucian Freud was seeing."'[10] Hockney himself thought it was a good likeness. 'I just assumed it, actually,' he said, 'because of his method of scrutiny. It's a scrutiny that's hard work. Not many people could look at a face for 120 hours, and constantly be doing something with it – not overlaying things, but constantly finding something that gives it a shimmer of life.'[11] His approval must have pleased Freud, who once told the art historian John Richardson, 'Unrealistic as it sounds, I want each picture that I'm working on to be the only picture that I'm working on – to go a bit further the only picture that I've ever worked on, and, to go even a bit further, the only picture that anyone has ever done.'[12]

In the time that Hockney was not sitting for Freud, he was hard at work on his own portraits, revisiting a medium which he hadn't touched for years, and which has so often been derided as being the refuge of the 'Sunday painter', and that was watercolour. His interest was sparked off by seeing some of the pictures he had done on his two trips to Egypt, in 1963 and 1978, which were included in the catalogue for an exhibition of his work that was being mounted in Cairo. Among them, he was particularly struck by two watercolours from 1963, which inspired him to have another go at the medium. What interested him was the way watercolour was more immediate and direct. '. . . it's more lively,' he said. 'The thing is it does take a while to master the techniques – having to work, say, from light to dark, because unlike with oils, you won't be able subsequently to daub a light colour over a dark one. Everything has to be thought out in advance – and I realised it would take time to master all this. I had to ask myself, was I going to be willing to take six months to learn all this? Well I was, and I did, and it took even longer, mastering the medium, innovating new techniques, but by the end I'd broken into this looser, more immediate way of being present to my material.'[13]

He began in New York at the start of 2003, where he was stopping over en route to London, with a number of still lifes, and some views of Central Park from his hotel-room window. Then, when he arrived at Pembroke Studios, he worked on studies of the bonsai trees he kept there, as well as sketching the gardens around the studio and the trees that were coming into blossom. He used the best sable brushes, since they retain moisture better and produce richer layers of colour than standard horsehair brushes, and as he honed his technique, he also began to experiment with his friends visiting the studio, beginning in the early days with single images painted on first one and then two large sheets of watercolour paper. He had a new confidence in his understanding of the topography of the human face, which came from having worked with the camera lucida and having made 280 drawings of individual sitters, and the challenge of capturing a likeness no longer held any fears for him. He now abandoned optical devices and photography, stating boldly, 'I'm quite convinced painting can't disappear because there's nothing to replace it. The photograph isn't good enough. It's not real enough.'[14] When he wasn't practising with watercolour, he was making large pen-and-ink portraits that incorporated far more detail of the subjects than he would previously have chosen to include, and which concentrated on the nuances of character, the faint smile, the half-closed eyes, the twitching lip or the nervously entwined fingers.

As he started to master the medium of watercolour, it occurred to Hockney that he had found the solution to a problem that up till now he had been unable to solve. Three years previously he had accepted a commission from Sandy Nairne, the director of the National Portrait Gallery, to paint his old friends Sir George and Lady Christie, who together had run Glyndebourne Opera for forty years. Normally this was not something he would ever have done, having vowed, after painting Sir David Webster for the Royal Opera House, never to accept commissions again. However, because the Christies were old friends and he deeply admired them, he agreed to it. 'But I did keep telling them,' he recalled, 'I wasn't ready yet. I had to find a way to make portraits in the twenty-first century that were interesting, and I didn't know how to do it.'[15] Watercolour suddenly seemed the obvious answer.

The painting of the Christies was to be one of over thirty four-panel double portraits, all made on the same scale and with the subjects identically posed in each one, sitting on two office swivel chairs, placed on bare floorboards against a pale green back wall. Hockney painted from a standing position looking down on them. In working rapidly with two people together just feet away, he had set himself a challenge: to reinvigorate the portrait. 'Watercolour makes you work fast,' he says. 'It makes you therefore think fast about painting. You seem to do it more intuitively. You get a liveliness in speed, probably sacrificing at times accuracy of some things. Every mark put down counts. You can't remove them. You have to work from light to dark. But it is painting and drawing all in one. I just do them with a brush. To catch lively expressions is not easy. The tiniest little marks, especially around the mouths and eyes, and an amazing difference happens with them. It has to be direct somehow through my heart, my eye and my hand.'[16] Certainly the picture of the Christies, dressed as if for Glyndebourne – him in black tie, her in a white silk dress and jewellery – was unlike anything else then hanging in the National Portrait Gallery. It was painted on four large sheets of paper, measuring four feet by three feet in total, and was a considerable technical achievement. Portraits had never been done on such a large scale in watercolour. Thus the full-length double portrait is seldom attempted and one painted entirely from life in a day was unheard of. Hockney liked to joke, 'What was the phrase you used to say about people who weren't very good-looking? You'd say, "Well, they're no oil painting." I could use that here: None of my sitters were oil paintings, so I used watercolor.'[17]

After his own sitting with his partner Stephen Stuart-Smith, Marco Livingstone wrote of the complex strategy involved in painting a watercolour on this scale, 'that involves knowing from the beginning what the next five moves will be. The degree of fast-thinking demanded is not unlike that required of a world-class chess player. And not just any world-class chess player, but one who can keep all this in his head while continuing to draw and paint with a relaxed hand. In spite of the many hours of intense work that went into the making of this portrait, there is no sign anywhere of it being laboured . . . I remember my astonishment at seeing Stephen's left shoe suddenly take on a more convincing weight when Hockney quickly painted in the outline of the sole in a continuous line, gracefully twisting his wrist in a single action.

It seemed so simple and it took no more than a few seconds. But the confidence to find such an elegantly straightforward solution and to perform the task, without hesitation, only comes from a combination of innate ability and an experience to match.'[18]

Just as he had been with the double portraits all those years before, Hockney was interested in the story within the relationships. It was the curiosity of a man who was happy to admit that he had never been very successful in his own. 'Two people have something,' he reflects, 'and there is a story. It's bound to happen. Each couple have some relationship, man and wife, brother and sister, gay lovers, two brothers. I mean any couple is interesting.' As he got going he was soon painting up to four couples a week, and his need for more and more subjects necessitated a return to his old London life and friends, some of whom he hadn't seen for nearly thirty years. 'He was trying to grasp onto people he knew,' recalled the theatre director Anthony Page, 'friends from the past that would give him something personal to paint about.'[19] As he observed them and put their personal relationships under intense scrutiny, they in turn observed him, noticing, for example, how when he stared at them he would screw up his eyes, which Norman Rosenthal's wife, Manuela Mena Marqués, described as being 'like swords'.

One of his sitters, Lindy Dufferin, pointed out that 'It's quite a daring thing to do, because really he's penetrating into the private feelings of his sitters and he's trying to say what their relationships are. It's almost like spying on somebody.'[20] Her comment was borne out by Manuela, who admitted that, after looking at the portrait of herself and her husband, in which she reaches out to touch him, yet he doesn't appear to respond, 'I really meditated about myself and our relationship.'[21] And just as these double portraits sought to catch the emotions between two people, they equally revealed Hockney's own relationship to his sitters. John Fitzherbert, for example, said that he probably got more from the picture than he ever did from his lover. 'When he paints me,' he reflected, 'sometimes it tells me more about his relationship with me and how he sees me. I get quite a lot of that from the pictures, and since we've been in England, they've all been rather touching.'[22]

Hockney himself was not interested in what the subjects thought about the results. 'I'm doing them for myself,' he said, 'not for the sitters, and frankly what they think of them I never ask. I'm unconcerned, anyway. After all, I'm not giving my pictures to the sitters.'[23] In the film *David Hockney: Double Portrait*, made by Bruno Wollheim, there is an interesting exchange between Anthony Page and his partner, Ken Palmer, that captures their views on how they think Hockney has seen them, and is indicative of the kinds of conversations that must have gone on between all the sitters.

'Poor Ken looks like a caged animal,' comments Page.

'I don't,' replies Palmer. 'That's very insulting.'

'You do,' says Page. 'You look like something looking through a cage.'

'I think it's got intensity about it,' replies Palmer.

'It does have intensity, but it has a certain amount of angst,' says Page.

'Look at you, you look disapproving,' says Palmer.

'I was watching your nicotine, Ken, I'm sorry,' says Page. 'I was feeling like Mayor Bloomberg . . . Ken is looking more pent up and I'm looking reflective.'

'I don't think I was pent up,' says Palmer. 'I was just trying to be comfortable. I just wanted to sit as comfortably as possible and I didn't want to have a smile on my face. I think we just sat there and he painted what he saw.'[24]

When the new double portraits were finally revealed to the public at the beginning of 2003, in two exhibitions, at the National Portrait Gallery and at Annely Juda, the critical reception was either lukewarm or downright hostile, calling them uneven, clumsy, unflattering and caricatured, with Brian Sewell adding, 'The portraits are little short of frightful.' Though Hockney's reaction was 'It's what I think that counts, always', Lindy Dufferin jumped to his defence, suggesting that the critics had the wrong approach. 'David's a kind of naive philosopher about life and I think these watercolours excite him because he's exploring a philosophical angle about the transiency of life. He looks for the second in time, and catches an aspect of this person when they are caught off balance. And that's what I think is important in these portraits. They almost come out sometimes very awkward, so when you're looking at them with a critical eye, you say, "oh that hand or that foot, the head is too big", or something, but you're missing the point. What he's saying is, that is what it was like for me at that moment, and you either accept it or you don't. And I think it's very exciting to see something of the moment, however dotty it is.'[25]

On 1 February 2003, Hockney flew back to LA for what proved to be the last prolonged amount of time he was to spend in California. John Fitzherbert accompanied him, but their renewed life at Montcalm Avenue was short-lived. In the months that had passed since 11 September 2001, when three hijacked planes piloted by terrorists had hit the Twin Towers and the Pentagon, the US Immigration Service had brought in a string of laws to tighten the visa process and other restrictions on immigrants. This was because it had been established that some of the hijackers had entered the country legally through the visa process, while others had overstayed their visas and were in the country illegally. Many innocent people subsequently fell foul of these new laws, passed in a climate of fear in which the concept of immigration was suddenly viewed through the lens of 'homeland security'.

John Fitzherbert was one of them. On 2 May 2003 he flew to London for a week, returning to LA on 13 May, where he was detained by customs at the airport after they found out that on a previous occasion he had outstayed his visa by one day. No amount of arguing, or explaining who he was, could soften the hearts of the customs officers, and he was held overnight. The unenviable task of telling Hockney fell to Karen Kuhlman. 'I had the sad job of having to relay the news to David,' she recalls, 'as I had sent my assistant to fetch John from LAX, and received the distraught call from the airport that he wouldn't be coming home.'[26] The next morning Fitzherbert was deported back to the UK. In the following weeks Hockney used his celebrity to pull every string he could think of to get Fitzherbert's visa renewed, while his friend Rita Pynoos, who had friends in the Clinton administration, did her best to help too, but all to no avail. Hockney was beside himself. 'One day I received a call from David,' Fitzherbert remembers, 'in which he said he didn't like being in LA any more without me, and so he was going to return to London.'[27] Thus, as Ren Weschler put it, 'in yet another triumph for Homeland Security, one of the most identifiable and beloved chroniclers of the life and light of California no longer felt at home in his adopted home state'.[28]

Back in London in early June, Hockney continued his love affair with watercolour, but now concentrated more on nature, experimenting with views of Holland Park, and the trees and gardens around the studio. When the declining health of his sister Margaret's partner, Ken Wathey, took him up to Bridlington, he stayed on after Wathey's death in July, both as a comfort to Margaret 'and as an excuse to enlarge the subject matter of his landscapes. 'A couple of days after Ken died,' says Margaret, 'David and I went on a picnic to Millington. He really loves that area. He'd known it since he used to work on the farms up there.'[29]

There is some very beautiful and remote countryside close to Bridlington, and he and Margaret took to going for drives to look at places he remembered from his childhood. The more he saw of the Wolds, the more he felt drawn to it, partly from a sense of nostalgia, but also by a growing belief that he had finally found his next great subject.

CHAPTER SEVENTEEN

THE ARRIVAL OF SPRING IN WOLDGATE

Hockney spent Easter of 2004 staying in Italy with his old friend Drue Heinz, widow of the heir to the Heinz foods empire, and a renowned philanthropist and supporter of the arts. Her house, Casa Ecco, at Cadenabbia, on the west shore of Lake Como, was a charming pink *castello* with crenellations and Gothic doors and windows, and was surrounded by a mixture of formal and English-style gardens. Tall mountains loomed up in the background. Here Mrs Heinz would generously entertain groups of writers and artists who would gather together to discuss their work in a series of what she liked to call *conversazioni*. Hockney liked to go there simply to paint.

It was a cold, wet April, and snow was still to be seen on the Alps at the far end of the lake, but as a fellow guest, the biographer Jeremy Lewis, noted, the bad weather in no way impeded Hockney. 'Despite the rain,' he wrote, 'David Hockney painted every day on the terrace, perched under an umbrella, the occasional raindrop adding verisimilitude to his watercolours. He smoked incessantly, was deaf as a post, talked wonderfully well about every subject known to man and wore flamboyant check suits with huge pockets in the lining from which he withdrew brushes, paints, a sketchbook and a collapsible canvas bucket . . . One afternoon he said he would like to paint me in ink and watercolours, so I hurried off to my room to wash my hair . . . We had two long sessions in his cottage down by the gates: he sat very close leaning forward on a stool staring intently and breathing heavily, his pens in his mouth when not in use, a cigarette in his free hand; I wasn't sure what I was supposed to do, apart from sitting still, so I stared back with equal intensity. Every now and then he would lean back and light a fresh cigarette, and we would talk about this and that till it was time to resume. I was immensely chuffed at his wanting to paint me . . .'[1]

As soon as he arrived back in England, Hockney headed off to Bridlington. Over the previous two years, alongside the portraits, he had been experimenting with painting landscapes in watercolour, first in Norway and Iceland, and then in Spain, all countries where he knew he would find perfect light, and now he had returned from making Alpine views in northern Italy. All the time, however, he was conscious of the fact that he was just sightseeing and painting views. East Yorkshire, on the other hand, held emotional ties for him. His ancestors had worked the land there, as he himself had done as a teenager on Foxcovert Farm. He began to really explore the area, driving off the beaten track up every little road he could find. 'I began to notice it was very beautiful,' he recalls, 'a cultivated landscape, unlike West Yorks, and very unspoiled. It's still the same, amazingly the same, as it was fifty years ago. And the great thing is it's not crowded.'[2]

A new assistant, to whom he had been introduced by David and Ann Graves, accompanied Hockney on these journeys. Jean-Pierre Gonçalves de Lima, or J-P as he came to be known, was a young Parisian, who was a brilliant musician and accordion player. He and Hockney had hit it off straight away, and he had begun helping out part-time in the London studio. Soon he had become an indispensable right hand to Hockney, driving him around so that he could study the scenery. The more he observed, looking long and hard, the more he saw and understood, stopping from time to time to make drawings in a Japanese sketchbook that opened out like a concertina. 'I set out one day,' he remembered, 'with . . . Jean-Pierre driving, I was sitting in the passenger seat, and every few yards I'd have him pull over and stop so that I could sketch a particular stalk of grass or weed in the low roadside hedge . . . Each one quite distinct, quite different. The point being the more you draw, the more you see, and then you start seeing everywhere, order emerging out of chaos, an order you can draw on the next time you take on the subject of an entire foreground hedge.'[3]

In attempting to master watercolour as a medium for painting landscape, Hockney was boldly placing his toe in waters that had produced some of the greatest of English art, notably the eighteenth- and nineteenth-century landscapes of artists such as Turner, John Sell Cotman, David Cox and John Varley. In setting himself up in competition with these much-celebrated painters, he had at least one advantage. They had concentrated their work on the magnificent and dramatic scenery of West Yorkshire, a countryside of deep gorges and crags, rushing rivers and waterfalls, with romantic names like Gordale Scar, Brimham Rocks and Malham Tarn, never venturing into the more gentle agricultural landscape of the east. That until now had been the province of the local amateur, a situation that was about to change quite dramatically.

In 'Little Gidding', the last poem of his *Four Quartets*, T. S. Eliot wrote:

> We shall not cease from exploration
> And the end of all our exploring
> Will be to arrive where we started
> And know the place for the first time.

Nearing seventy, Hockney felt he was ready for this moment. He remembered the old Chinese adage that painting is an old man's art, and was conscious that he was by no means the first artist to return in his later years to landscape painting. During the last years of his life, for example, Van Gogh had drawn and painted a series of intense pastoral views at Arles and Saint-Rémy in the south of France. Hockney had also read somewhere a statement made by some young artist in the news that 'The artist doesn't paint now, just as we don't go to work on a horse'. 'I was amused by that,' Hockney says, 'and I cut it out and blew it up and stuck it on my studio wall in London because I realised that what he meant was that something has taken over from painting, and that is photography. And I thought that's wrong. So I thought to myself, Well, if you think that's wrong then you've got to do something about it, and that's one reason I decided to come and paint last summer.'[4]

After filling several books with preparatory sketches, he was ready to take out his pad and start painting from nature, working out of his car, which J-P would park at the side of the road. Since using watercolour requires speed, he used pre-mixed colours, kept in childproof pill bottles that he could slip into his pockets. There was no pencil underdrawing. He painted directly onto the paper, leaving no room for error, and he worked in all weathers, one painting, *Valley, Millington*, even bearing the marks of raindrops that had fallen on the paper. The results of those first few months, which taught him so much about painting freely again with the hand, were shown as a single work, *Midsummer: East Yorkshire, 2004*, consisting of thirty-six paintings ranged six by six on a wall, first at the 1853 Gallery, Salts Mill, and then, the following year, in London at the Gilbert Collection in Somerset House.

By the time this new work was showing in London, Hockney had abandoned watercolour and was painting in oils again. He had started in Los Angeles, on a return trip there in March 2005, when he had undertaken a series of portraits of his closest American friends. Working on these had reminded him of the advantages of oil paint. 'I went back to oil painting,' he says, 'and when you've been doing watercolours, oil paint is like a luxury medium. You can do what you want with it. I mean with watercolour, you have to work from light to dark. With oil paint you can do whatever you want, so going back to it was rather thrilling. I'd been doing portraits in LA first, and then I thought, Well, I'll go back to Brid and do East Yorks again in oils.'[5] It was to be the beginning of one of the most fertile periods of his life as an artist.

From the beginning of July he painted every day from dawn to dusk, revisiting the sites of many of his watercolours, as well as exploring new territories, leading to the discovery of places to which he would return time and time again, and to which he liked to attach nicknames such as 'The Dump' and 'The Tunnel'. He soon became a familiar figure, standing at his easel in the fields, his little white van used for transporting materials parked to one side, and the faithful J-P always close by, recording each creation on a digital camera. He worked on two-by-three-foot canvases, of which he had ordered scores, because he thought anything bigger would be a bit difficult, and he worked fast, taking on average two hours to complete a picture. Nothing was planned. 'It just happened,' he recalled. 'That's partly the excitement. You don't know what it will really look like, you don't know where it will lead. That's the excitement for me, especially at my age.'6 The subjects were various – lush meadows, rolling landscapes, the harvest, roads and tracks receding into the distance, single trees, groups of trees, roadside verges, valleys and endless big skies – and his output was prodigious, often painting two or three pictures a day, and completing thirty-two in that first month. Sometimes at the end of the day, he would take a painting back home with him and put it up in his bedroom, where brushes, paper and paint were always at hand. 'I go to sleep looking at my paintings,' he said, 'and when I wake up – wow! – I have a completely different response to them. I always have paper by the bed, because your mind is freer then, and it's in a special state.'7

Weather held no fear for him, and the paintings are full of mist and rain and snow. 'To do landscapes,' he said, 'you've got to know the place rather well. You've got to love it actually. You've got to know where the sun will be. In the summer I should be out at 6 in the morning, because if it's sunny the light from 6 till 9 is magic. Of course to paint in the winter, you've got to prepare yourself. You need thick clothing and things. I mean we often looked like Michelin men. The first winter I spent here I began to see how beautiful the winters were. There was far more colour than I expected. Occasionally a farmer would come and talk to me. They didn't think I'd exaggerated colour. They thought my paintings were very accurate, and talking to them I noticed that they knew just how beautiful it is here.'8

It was an exciting time for Hockney, and the more he painted it, the more he fell in love with East Yorkshire. London was temporarily abandoned, with David Graves left to look after the studio. John Fitzherbert also moved up to Bridlington, where he ran the house and did the cooking, while J-P, now employed on a full-time basis, and referred to by Hockney as 'the only Parisian in Bridlington', looked

after the attic studio, made sure there was a constant supply of paints
and paper, and acted as artist's photographer. Margaret Hockney, too,
had a role to play, one that turned out to be much more important than
she could have imagined. A keen amateur artist, she had, since the death
of Ken Wathey, been exploring computer art, and had become quite an
expert at it, specialising in making scanned images of flowers, plants and
vegetables. 'David came over in 2004,' she recalls, 'and painted some
landscapes in watercolour, and at that time I had started doing scanning
on the computer. I got involved in scanning the watercolours for him,
and showing him how to send them to LA by email. All of a sudden he
had the eureka moment and realised how handy the computer could be
for him. He had used computers in the past of course, but this was the
first time he realised that there were a lot of things up here that I was
doing that he hadn't been aware of. He had done computing with an
art program years before, but he discovered now that it had all become
much speedier, and he saw a new potential.'[9]

The potential Hockney saw was how the computer could be used
to make his pictures bigger – and not just the watercolours. Though he
had started with canvases that measured two feet by three feet, after
the first month he had moved on to a slightly larger size of three feet
by four feet. His next move was to scale upwards further by placing
two canvases side by side on an easel, giving him an area of six feet by
eight feet on which to paint. 'I thought they were quite big then,' he
says, 'but slowly I began to see, when I'd done quite a few and I'd put
them up in the studio, and I saw eight on a wall together, I thought, My
God, if that could be one landscape, it would be very powerful, and
there must be a way to do that.'[10] As Hockney became more ambitious,
J-P came up with various methods of coping with the problems that
are encountered by anyone painting en plein air, the main one being the
wind, from simply leaning the easels against the high sides of the van
to using guy ropes and sandbags to stabilise them, until eventually it
became possible to paint on all six canvases at once. Now he could paint
the big dynamic landscapes he had been envisaging.

To cope with the larger number of canvases required, Hockney
invested in a Toyota pickup truck, of the type used by the Taliban in

Afghanistan, and equipped it with a series of large shelves in the back on which canvases could be transported without touching one another. Its powerful engine and four-wheel drive also meant that he could now explore even the most rutted farm track without difficulty. The first six-canvas paintings were of Woldgate Woods, an area of trees situated on Woldgate, a Roman road running from Bessingby Hill on the outskirts of Bridlington to the village of Kilham, seven miles to the west. It was a favourite spot of Hockney's, offering woodland views as well as panoramic vistas, south across the Holderness Plain to the North Sea, and north over the rolling fields of the Wolds towards Scarborough. The subject was the arrival of spring, and was a single view painted from within the canopy of trees at a point where three paths met. While the first of these paintings took three weeks to complete, from 30 March to 21 April 2006, his confidence grew to such an extent that the next one, *Woldgate Woods II*, was done in two days, on 16 and 17 May, without any sacrificing of quality, as was *Woldgate Woods III*, on 20 and 21 May. Curiously, their size, six feet by twelve feet, induced feelings not of monumentality, but of intimacy, drawing the viewer right into the action. 'Once I moved to the bigger scale,' he recalls, 'I realised that this was better. The watercolours were painted essentially with the wrist. The small oil paintings are painted with your elbow, and when you get to the bigger ones you're painting with your shoulder, and when you get to put a few together you're painting with your whole body, and that got more and more exciting. You get bolder. But as I then got more confident I was drawing with bigger brushes, so you're responding directly to the space you're in and that's what gives the pictures that feeling that people think they're in the landscape. They're closer to it.'[11]

Hockney was on a roll and increasingly exhilarated by working on a larger scale. While in LA during the summer, for the opening of a retrospective of his portraits at the Los Angeles County Museum of Art, he was looking at reproductions of some of the six-canvas Yorkshire landscapes when he was suddenly struck by one of his flashes of inspiration. 'There were nine of them,' he remembered, 'in three rows of three. I hung them by my bed . . . and I saw that there were images of fifty-four canvases up there. Then it came to me that it was possible to make a picture that size . . . using digital photography to see what you're doing. Then I thought, "My God! It would be an enormous painting."'[12] He worked out that the way to do it would be by first making a drawing of the subject, then dividing it up into identical rectangular pieces, scanning it and using this to create the equivalent of a jigsaw on the computer, each piece of the jigsaw representing an individual canvas. As each canvas was completed it would be photographed and slotted into its position on the computer screen, thereby enabling the artist to see the progress of the entire composition while still painting from life. 'I used the aspects of the computer,' he said, 'that permit almost instant reproduction . . . That enables you to build up the rectangles and see them together, so I can see immediately what's happening in the picture. Technology is allowing us to do all kinds of things today . . . It wouldn't have been possible to paint this picture without it. All you could do would be to blow up a drawing.'[13]

He was convinced it could be done and early in 2007, Edith Devaney, a senior curator of contemporary art at the Royal Academy, received a telephone call. 'David called me at the beginning of the year,' she recalls, 'and said, "Edith, can you do something for me? Can you procure me the end wall of Gallery III for the Summer Exhibition, for a painting I'm going to do?" Since we have a hundred or so Academicians all wanting the best space for their work, that was quite an ask.'[14] Hockney told her that he was planning to create the largest picture ever painted *en plein air* for the Summer Exhibition, made up of fifty canvases measuring forty feet by fifteen feet. This being the draw, and seeing it as an opportunity not to be missed, Devaney managed to fight her way through all the politics and persuade the exhibition committee and the Royal Academy Council to agree to his request. 'When I told him,' she remembers, 'he laughed and said he had wanted to make sure it went from corner to corner since, knowing how the Summer Exhibition worked, he knew that if there was any room on either side, they would hang little pictures round it.'[15]

The subject he had chosen, found after hours of driving round little side roads, was a stand of trees on the outskirts of the village of Warter.

Garrowby Hill, 1998. Oil on Canvas, 60 × 76″

A Closer Grand Canyon, 1998. Oil on 60 Canvases (16 × 24″ each), 81 ½ × 293″

George and Mary Christie, 2002.
Watercolour on Paper (4 sheets), 48 × 36″

Trees & Puddles. East Yorkshire, 30 III 04. Watercolour on Paper, 29 ½ × 41 ½″

Road and Cornfields. East Yorkshire from Midsummer: East Yorkshire, **2004.** Watercolour on Paper, 15 × 22 ½″

Late Spring Tunnel, May, **2006,** Oil on 2 Canvases (48 × 36″ each), 48 × 72″

The Big Hawthorn, 2008.
Oil on 9 Canvases (36 × 48″ each), 108 × 144″

Bigger Trees Near Warter or/ou Peinture sur le Motif pour le Nouvel Age Post-Photographique, **2007.** Oil on 50 Canvases (36 × 48″ each), 180 × 480″

661, 2009.
iPhone Drawing

March 31st 2011,
The Atelier, 4pm.
Still from 18-Screen
Video

Sept 04 2011,
The Atelier, 11:30am,
'A Bigger Space for
Dancing'. Still from
18-Screen Video

The Arrival of Spring in Woldgate, East Yorkshire in 2011 (twenty eleven). iPad Drawings

He loved trees, especially in winter. 'You notice that the trees aren't skeletons in the winter,' he says. 'They're absolutely alive but they're looking for the light, reaching for not much light, and all the branches seem to go up. And you notice when gravity pulls them down again, then the life force pushes them back up. In a sense the tree in winter is like the life force made visible to us. It's the biggest plant there is and when you think about them they look like veins, they look like our brains.'[16] Having committed to the project, Hockney now knew that it was touch and go as to whether or not he would actually be able to do the picture in time. He wanted to paint the winter trees and he had worked out that he had only about two weeks before spring arrived and the leaves began to appear; two weeks in which to cover six hundred square feet of canvas. It was a huge technical challenge, and he was working so close to the subject that he couldn't see the painting as a whole until it was finished and hung. The image was in his head. 'In your head you can go anywhere,' he said. 'You can even go to the very edge of the universe. You'll never get there on the bus or spaceship or whatever they think of.'[17] It was also in drawings, which he kept refining, and which he propped up on an easel at the end of his bed. 'At night I lie in bed looking at them. It's 24-hours-a-day painting.'[18] He slept little, and even stopped shaving during the weeks he was working on this picture.

The scale of a project such as this required more help than could be given by J-P, whose main task now was the photographing of the individual canvases and knitting them into the computer grid, so Hockney called in reinforcements in the form of Richard Schmidt, who flew over from LA, John Fitzherbert, seconded from cooking duties, and a new young assistant, a seventeen-year-old Bridlington boy called Dominic Elliott, the son of a local GP. He also rented a warehouse on an industrial estate on the outskirts of Bridlington and employed carpenters to build a wall in it so that he could see the finished picture hung up in its entirety, before it went down to London. When he saw it for the first time, he considered it finished, and partly as a joke, partly as a declaration, he designed a flyer to announce it – in the style of one that might have been used in the nineteenth century – which was a dig at the infamous *Sensation* exhibition that had caused such a stir at the Royal Academy in 1997.

COMING UP AT THE ROYAL ACADEMY
A BIGGER SENSATION
A HANDMADE OIL PAINTING
Recently done en plein air by D. Hockney. R.A.

BIGGER TREES NEAR WARTER

OR/OU

'PEINTURE SUR LE MOTIF POUR LE NOUVEL AGE POST-PHOTOGRAPHIQUE.'

'The painting,' he stated, 'is a real Royal Academy picture. The Big One. When you go into a room to see it, you might say, "Wow!" But the other word would be "How?"' As to the question 'Why?', his answer was, 'Because you can. That's why dogs lick their balls. Because they can!'[19]

Hockney's excitement with the new work was boundless, and he couldn't wait to see it hanging in Burlington House. 'As the sprawling summer showing opened to the press yesterday,' noted the *Guardian*, 'it emerged that he came in to supervise personally the 50 canvases which make up his gigantic and gigantically named Bigger Trees Near Warter or/ou Peinture en Plein Air pour L'Age Post-Photographique. Getting the biggest painting ever shown in the 239 years of the exhibition onto the wall took most of two days – directed, magisterially, by the great man from the comfort of a borrowed wheelchair.'[20] When the Exhibitions Secretary, Norman Rosenthal, saw it up, he said, 'It's fucking good. Great proportions,'[21] while Martin Gayford, writing in the *Telegraph*, declared, 'The effect is completely extraordinary. It's like standing in front of a real tree.'[22] Meanwhile, Hockney, his confidence bubbling over, couldn't wait to spread the word. 'David told me he'd done the biggest painting in the world,' said Damien Hirst. 'It was going to go in the record books for the biggest outdoor painting. I love it that he's excited about that. You kind of think that when you get older you wouldn't have any interest in breaking records, but it's great that David now is exactly the same as he's always been.'[23]

At some point after the Summer Exhibition had opened, Hockney asked Edith Devaney if he could try an experiment. He told her that he had made two facsimiles of the painting, which, after the rest of the exhibition had been taken down, he wanted to hang on the walls either side of the original. 'Very few of us saw that,' Devaney recalls, 'but for twenty-four hours we had the gallery full of the three identical paintings. It was like being in a wood, and that immersive experience was very, very exciting. David and I talked a lot about this and very quickly it occurred to me that there was something very interesting to come and to tap into. I knew he had this great body of work from Yorkshire behind him, but I also knew there was more to come. It was to do with the immersion and the scale and all of those things.'[24] Devaney was convinced that they should invite Hockney to exhibit at the Royal Academy, in spite of the fact that Norman Rosenthal was certain that he would never agree to do it. When Hockney was told, however, that there would be scope in the show for lots of new work, he was immediately interested, and eventually said yes to a show in 2012. Although Rosenthal's feelings were tinged with sadness, as he was leaving the Royal Academy after eleven years and thus would not be involved with the planning of the exhibition, both he and Devaney were jubilant.

Now nearing his seventieth birthday, Hockney, who had always liked to refer to himself as an 'English Los Angelino', was well settled back into English life. Having bought a nearby bungalow for Margaret, he had now taken over the charming, slightly eccentric house in Bridlington. It was painted inside in bright primary colours, with vases of tulips usually dotted about, giving any visitor the impression that they were inside a David Hockney painting, while on the top floor the windows of the studio looked out across *les toits de Brid* to a view of the North Sea beyond. From early in the morning his days were spent painting, and the little leisure time he had, he would pass reading – history, biography and science being his favourite subjects. The isolation suited him. 'The advantage here is that you're just too far from London for people to come for a day,' he says. 'So you're outside of that orbit of London and that's an enormous advantage. When people do come and stay, at least we know when they're coming. Every morning I wake up here, I think, All the day is mine.'[25]

The happy side of Hockney revelled in the idiosyncrasies of life in the country, which were the subject of much laughter. 'You can make a joke about anything,' he told Bruno Wollheim. 'Everything is funny. Practically everything, anyway.'[26] It had amused him immensely, for example, when the police had flagged him down on a road where few cars ever travelled. 'We were driving up Woldgate,' he recalled, 'a tiny little road on which you'd be lucky to see three cars in an hour, when four police, three men and a woman, jumped out, and gave us each a ticket for not wearing seat belts. One of them was lecturing us along the lines of "Death is lurking everywhere", and I was looking at the signs of spring behind him, and thinking, "Well, life is lurking every-where too." I said to J-P, "It was worth a £60 fine just for the story."'[27]

He found humour in the names of some of the local villages, saying he thought Burton Fleming sounded like the name of a movie star, while Wold Newton could be a Las Vegas crooner. The local news-papers were another source of amusement, with their lurid headlines such as – STEAM ROLLER HORROR ON HIGH STREET, SEVERED EAR FOUND IN YORKS CAR and SEX TRADE MOVES TO LEAFY SUBURBS. He once found himself in a remote village, where not only were there no cars passing through, but there were no cars parked anywhere, let alone any other sign of life, only to see a poster outside the post office proclaiming MAYHEM ON THE STREETS FEARED. 'We call the *Driffield Times*,' he says, 'the News of the Wolds.'[28]

There was also an angry side to him that showed itself in frequent rants against the things he disliked about life in twenty-first-century England, a country he increasingly perceived as being run by prigs and bossyboots. In 2002, he had joined the Countryside March in London, more as a protest against bossiness rather than for any strong feelings about fox-hunting, and had had hundreds of badges printed proclaiming

'END BOSSINESS SOONER'. Later he was upset by the cultural vandalism that he felt would be generated by proposed legislation to imprison anyone found possessing images of child abuse, laws that could so easily lead to innocent people being convicted, such as the photographer Nan Goldin, whose pictures of young children were intended purely as art. 'I am out of step with the mean spirit of our age,' he wrote to the *Guardian*. 'I told a friend I had been to a house in Lincolnshire where in three rooms there must have been pictures of a few hundred naked children and a lot of naked adults as well. He looked shocked until I told him they were painted by Antonio Verrio between 1688 and 1698, at Burghley House in Stamford. I detest the cultural vandalism that contaminates New Labour. I hope they go – and soon.'[29]

Most of all he loathed 'the fucking Blairs'[30] and had a particular contempt for Gordon Brown, who he considered 'a prig, P.R.I.G, a dreary aesthetic Calvinistic prig, who I'm sure will never be elected in England'.[31] He used to say, 'If that fucking Gordon Brown came to my house, I'd kick him in the fucking balls,' toning it down if anyone expressed their horror at these sentiments to 'Well, I wouldn't be very polite to him'.[32] It was its attitude towards smokers that was the main reason for his intense dislike of the government. 'I have utter contempt for it,' he wrote. 'I feel I am entitled to my opinion. I don't mind prigs but when they want to take my little corner as well, I have a right to argue against their dreary view of life contaminating mine . . . In the Labour Party – let's get a lot more human in our observations – the 80-year-old Mr Benn is a happy pipe smoker; Mr Robin Cook took up "healthy" fell walking, it killed him; same with Mr Smith; Tony Banks another non-smoking vegetarian health fiend falls over with a stroke at the age of 61 . . .'[33]

In the autumn of 2005 he even attended the Labour Party Conference to protest against their plans to ban smoking in public places, appearing on Radio 4's *Today* programme to indulge in a vociferous argument with an anti-smoking MP called Julie Morgan, whom he considered nannyish. 'Death awaits you whether you smoke or not,' he told her. 'Pubs are not health clubs. People go to drown their sorrows.'

When she said it was important to protect non-smokers, he replied, 'Why must every place be suitable for you? What about me? Can't there be some place suitable for me? You destroy bohemia.' Becoming increasingly irate when she protested that it was important to protect children from the dangers of smoke, he said, 'I think you are too bossy, chum. You are dreary, absolutely dreary. Some people want to live and they don't want to live like you do . . . You get rid of smoking and they are all on anti-depressant pills. You think that's better. I don't.'[34] Interviewed afterwards by Jasper Gerard for the *Sunday Times,* he told him, 'They say smoking is bad for you, but they used to say the same about wanking. Even if it was, you can always wear glasses.'[35]

The ban on smoking in public places became law on 1 July 2007, a week before Hockney's seventieth birthday. It did little for his peace of mind. 'On July 1 2007,' he wrote in the *Guardian,* 'the most grotesque piece of social engineering will begin in England . . . imposed easily by a political and media elite. They think it will lead to healthier people and a cleaner atmosphere. They believe they can change people easily . . . I don't think they can. People will stay at home and do drugs instead – legal and illegal . . . I smoke for my mental health. I think it's good for it, and I certainly prefer its calming effects to the pharmaceutical ones (side effects unknown) . . . Two months ago I started the largest painting I've ever done: 15ft x 40ft. The moment I began I found myself running up the stairs (with a fag) and realised some people are more in tune with a life force than others. I can't be the only voice like this. In England people should speak up more, defend themselves, but it's hard against all the forces at work. Two million anti-smoking signs are going up on July 1, including inside Westminster Abbey. The uglification of England is under way by people with no vision. I detest it.'[36]

When Tate Britain gave a party for Hockney's seventieth birthday, Nicholas Serota, the director, announced after dinner that they were going to make an exception and turn off the smoke alarms for ten minutes so that he could enjoy a cigarette. It was an honour that would have been granted to no one else. Likewise, guests who gathered for another birthday celebration at Sledmere House, the East Yorkshire home of Sir Tatton Sykes, a friend of Hockney's and the owner of

the mansion that featured so prominently in the painting *The Road to York Through Sledmere*, were actively encouraged to smoke – glasses filled with multicoloured Sobranie cocktail cigarettes, and large boxes of cigars were placed on each table. The party took place on 22 July 'in celebration of 70 years and 13 days', and was for his family and friends only. It consisted of a dinner cooked by Ossie Clark and Celia Birtwell's son Albert and was followed by dancing to a live band and the letting off of a ton and a half of fireworks. There was even a cake incorporating a reproduction in icing of *The Road to York Through Sledmere*. It was a glittering occasion, attended by all the Hockney siblings, each one

Invitation to David Hockney's 70th birthday dinner

of whom gave a little speech about their memories of growing up with their artist brother.

John, the youngest brother, spoke first, sharing memories that extended from childhood mischief to being taken on the 'Wagner Drive' and ending with the words, 'Though I am acutely aware that David's seventy years of living have not always been happy, as life isn't, tonight surely is at least the greatest gift we all give – the love of all who are here, and some in spirit! Thank you, David, for your gift to us and to the world.'[37] Speaking last, Paul brought the house down with a story about Henry Geldzahler. In the summer of 1970 Geldzahler had been visiting David in London, when he ran short of money. Having no bank account in England, he asked to borrow £250. David duly made out a cheque to him for that amount, but when he took it to a bank,

they wouldn't cash it as they
didn't know Geldzahler and he
had no ID. To solve this problem,
David wrote a letter to the bank,
enclosing a drawing he had done
of Geldzahler. 'Dear Sir,' he
wrote, 'this is Henry Geldzahler.
He looks like this.' Geldzahler
couldn't bring himself to get
the cheque cashed, and had it
framed along with the drawing.
He knew a good investment when
he saw it.

At the end of dinner Hockney
was dragged up to join his brothers
and sister in a performance of
'Wild Woodbines', a music-hall
song that his father used to sing
every Christmas. It was a warning
against the perils of smoking,
and told the story of Little Billy
Williams who found a penny
in the garden and spent it on a
packet of five cigarettes, which he proceeded to smoke, ending with
the lines:

David Hockney and
his birthday cake,
in the entrance hall
of Sledmere House

> Five little whiffs and in five little jiffs
> He was lying in the tramway lines,
> His face greener than the label
> Of Little Billy's Wild Woodbines.

Standing behind the others, Hockney looked as if he wished the floor
would open up and swallow him!

*

David Hockney and his siblings performing 'Wild Woodbines'

The prospect of such a major show at the Royal Academy in 2012 focused Hockney's mind, and he set to work painting every day from dawn till dusk, untroubled by the weather as usual, aware only that by the end of 2011 he had to have painted enough pictures to fill most of the space in the ten galleries that make up the ground floor of the Royal Academy. He had set himself a colossal task into which he threw himself like a man possessed. 'I am so excited by all this,' he told Ren Weschler. 'Really, it's completely rejuvenated me. I was seventy in July, but I feel thirty, frankly – or, alright, maybe forty. In any case, I know this is hardly the end of things . . . things are barely just beginning.'[38]

Though he was very careful in the planning of his work schedule, there were times when no amount of planning could prepare him for the reality. One of these was the flowering of the hawthorn blossom, which is a sight to be seen on the Yorkshire Wolds where many of the hedgerows are planted with this dense, spiky shrub, the *Crataegus monogyna*. In late spring it bursts into flower with an eruption of creamy white petals that assail the nostrils with their heady, honeyish scent.

When they arrive depends on the weather, and they are at their best for a week, two at the most. Hockney fell totally under their spell in, as he referred to it, 'Action Week'. He became stoned by the beauty of the hawthorn, and produced quite magical, almost surreal paintings that looked as if they had been painted on acid. 'When the hawthorn blossom was at its height in late May and early June,' he recalled, 'we had two weeks of unbelievable madness. The blossom was fabulous. In Japan there would be ten thousand cars driving around the lanes looking at it. Here, we were the only ones . . . We were doing eighteen-hour days and I wouldn't sleep much in case I missed the sunrise. Afterwards I collapsed and was in bed for a week . . . But I wouldn't have dared collapse if the blossom had still been out. I'd have found the energy.'[39]

With more and more paintings being completed, and a growing desire to make them bigger and bigger, early in 2008, inspired by the experience of renting the large space to hang *Bigger Trees Near Warter*, Hockney took a lease on a vast warehouse on the same industrial estate, with thousands of square feet of floor space, and a fleet of wheelchairs for him and his assistants to move about in it at speed. It was as big as a film studio and was flooded with even daylight that came from the ceiling above. 'When I signed the lease for five years,' he said, 'I felt twenty years younger. I stopped feeling frail and started feeling energetic.'[40] It was an energy that resulted in the period between 2007 and 2009 being the most productive of his entire career, and the studio soon filled up with an extraordinary variety of landscape paintings that reflected his love of nature, and in particular trees, which were represented in all their variety, from summer woodlands to dead stumps rising out of the ground like Indian totem poles.

Devaney had always wanted the 2012 show to demonstrate the way Hockney had mastered photography as well as painting, which is why she was fighting hard to persuade the Getty Museum in Malibu to lend her *Pearblossom Hwy.* What at that stage she was not prepared for was the fact that another new technology was about to come along to distract him. Hockney had done paintings using a computer twenty years previously when he played with the Quantel Paintbox, but had

The warehouse
studio in
Bridlington

abandoned it because he had found it too slow. He made a mark on the screen and it was seconds before it appeared. Encouraged by Margaret, however, to learn how to use Adobe Photoshop, he found it was now possible to draw very freely and fast with colour on the computer. This led to a number of experiments making inkjet computer drawings on paper, which were a mixture of drawing and collage, and which included landscapes, as well as a series of studio portraits. 'Photoshop is a terrific medium,' he said. 'What you are really doing is drawing in a printing machine. You don't look at your hand, you look at the screen. Then I print it out, see what it's looking like, see what colours you get. So you actually use the colours that the printing machine makes . . . Then I discovered how good it would be for portraits because of the freedom you have to alter things. You can do that amazingly. In a watercolour portrait, once you put things down that's it.'[41]

Margaret Hockney was something of an early enthusiast of the Apple iPhone, buying one soon after it had been released in June 2007. Her brother Philip had brought one over from Australia. 'We were having dinner at Sewerby Grange,' she recalls, 'and Philip came out with this iPhone. I could hardly get my hands on it because they were all looking at it. The result was we all had one within the next month and absolutely took to it.'[42] Hockney used his mostly for text messaging, rather than phoning, and he was also amused by the various software applications, known as apps, that were beginning to appear, such as one which turned the iPhone into a virtual electric razor, another into a harmonica, and one which made it look as though the screen were a goldfish bowl with goldfish swimming round and round it. He got great pleasure demonstrating these to friends. Then Margaret told him about a new drawing app called Brushes. 'When I saw the Brushes app,' she remembers, 'I told David that it looked good. He wasn't too keen to begin with, but it didn't take him long to realise what he could do with it and he was soon sending us the results of what he was doing. That's how it all started.' [43]

Hockney was entranced by the Brushes app and had soon mastered the technique of using it. 'With the IPhone I often drew with my thumb,' he wrote. 'I could hold it in my right hand and my thumb could reach every corner of the screen as it was small and the fulcrum of the thumb is within the thumb . . . I could then have a cigarette in my left hand to help me concentrate.'[44] He was soon producing beautiful drawings of such subjects as a vase of sunflowers, a glass on a tray, slippers by the bed, a bowl of fruit, the rooftops outside his bedroom window, and his dressing gown hanging on the bathroom door, with breathtaking accuracy. 'Who would have thought,' he commented, 'that the telephone would bring back drawing?'[45] He kept the iPhone by his bed, so that when he woke up early on a summer's morning he could draw the dawn from his bedroom window. 'It's at its most beautiful,' he said, 'between 5.15 when the sun has been up a little bit and you get its shadows, until about 8.30. Most people sleep through it. I wake when it starts getting light, and I do little drawings of the dawn, while I'm still in bed. Would Turner have slept through such terrific drama?

Absolutely not! Anyone in my business who slept through that would be a fool. I don't keep office hours.'[46] Soon all Hockney's iPhone-owning friends were receiving daily doses of his art, little miniature Hockneys on a miniature electronic canvas. His favourite subjects were sunrises and flowers. 'I draw flowers every day,' he said, 'and send them to friends, so they get fresh flowers every morning. And my flowers last.'[47]

For the better part of a year, Hockney hardly ever had the iPhone out of his hand. To people who would tease him by saying, 'We hear you've started drawing on your telephone,' he would reply, 'Well, no actually, it's just that occasionally I speak on my sketchpad.'[48] Then on 27 January 2010, at a press conference at the Yerba Buena Center for the Arts in San Francisco, Steve Jobs, the CEO of Apple, announced the arrival of the iPad, a tablet computer that went on sale in April 2010. Hockney ordered several right away, and it immediately replaced the iPhone as his drawing tool of choice. He had no problem carrying it around as all his jackets were already made with a poacher's pocket to carry his sketchbooks. 'I got one of the first iPads,' he recalled. 'It took me some months to learn the techniques, but by then I knew how to get anything I wanted, almost. It's a superb medium for some things. Turner would have loved it. You can be very, very subtle with transparent layers. The light changes quickly here so you have to choose how you want to depict it. I realised how fast I can capture it with the iPad, a lot faster than watercolours for example . . . You can choose a new colour or a new brush more rapidly. You don't have to wait for anything to dry.'[49]

The iPad also had one feature that was completely new. 'You could play the drawing back with the press of a button,' he wrote. 'I had never seen myself draw before, this also seemed fascinating to everybody I showed them to. The only thing like this before was Picasso drawing on glass for a film.'[50] Just as he had done with the iPhone drawings, likewise Hockney sent his iPad images out to friends on a daily basis, which begged the question, were they reproductions? 'Well no,' he thought, 'they are exactly the same as I had on my phone: it was just a digital file that I had sent them; so in theory they were identical, at least to the naked eye. They would differ slightly . . . only because each

David Hockney
working on the
iPad

surface of an iPhone is a physical thing and therefore each one would
have tiny differences on its physical surface. So how would one see
them collectively? You could download them onto the computer but
then they are a different size.'[51] This prompted him to find a way of
mounting an exhibition of the work, a challenge that was eventually
taken up by the Fondation Pierre Bergé–Yves Saint Laurent in Paris,
who, in October 2010, put on a show of the digital drawings, which were

emailed to their headquarters on the Avenue Marceau and exhibited on a series of iPhones and iPads. Nothing was for sale. 'As of yet,' Hockney wrote, 'I simply give away the drawings by sending them via email. Like many people I haven't figured out a way to be paid for them. But as they give a lot of my friends pleasure, what does it matter?'[52] For Hockney, who was the first major artist to have an exhibition of work produced entirely on the iPhone and iPad, it brought back memories of his 1989 show in Brazil that was entirely delivered by fax. 'The Fondation need not email them back to me,'[53] he commented.

The astonishing amount of work that Hockney was producing throughout this period speaks volumes about his tenacity and energy, which often left his much younger assistants unable to keep up with him. All the more so because at the same time that all this was going on he had also become involved with an extremely complex form of film-making. In September 2009, Edith Devaney and Marco Livingstone, who was to be co-curator of the Royal Academy show, took a trip up to the new Bridlington studio, now jokingly referred to as 'the Atelier', after the French word for an artist's workshop where a principal master, assistants, students and apprentices all work together. There they had seen many new paintings, this time done from memory rather than en plein air, such as tightly painted scenes of felled timber rendered in strong, bright colours, as well as an enormous panoramic inkjet print of trees along Bessingby Road. Impressive though this was, there was more to come. 'David said, "I've got something interesting to show you,"' Devaney recalls, 'and he brought us to the studio in the house and showed us this film work. It was very wobbly on a single camera and you could see the tax disc on the front of the jeep. Marco said, "What do you think of this? Could this really go in the show?" And I said, "We have to grit our teeth and be brave, Marco." After all, we may have been taking a risk, but the person taking the biggest risk was David.'[54] The film, which had been shot hand-held by Hockney himself at hedge height, was of a progression along a hedgerow billowing with hawthorn blossom, and it was quite clearly the beginning of something bigger.

By January 2010, Hockney was seriously experimenting with film, using the best Hasselblad digital cameras, and had hired a new technical assistant, Jonathan Wilkinson, to help him. Martin Gayford saw one of their first attempts, a drive through Woldgate in the snow, and thought it 'remarkable. It was projected at a slower speed than real time, creating a slow progression through the frozen landscape that had a strangely powerful emotional effect . . . At this solemn pace, the experience reminded me of *L'Année Dernière à Marienbad*.'[55] The film was shot with one camera, though after he had shown it he then projected another experimental film, with the screen this time split into four, each separate part showing different images of a journey down the road. This was an attempt to make a new kind of 'joiner' and was inspired by his having revisited the experimental film he had made for *The South Bank Show* in 1983. Watching it had convinced him he was on to something that could be incorporated into the Royal Academy show, and would attract a whole new audience. 'I think you are going to get a lot of young people in because of the videos and bigger ways of filming,' he emailed Devaney. 'I think they will interest a lot of people, in fact anybody at all who is interested in picture making. We are just joining two nine-camera pictures together, so it's as though eighteen cameras were used, a bigger picture is made this way. Right on, I say, and up yours Harriet Harman!'[56]

By June he was flying. 'You will see when you come here,' he wrote, 'how much we have developed our films, moving into new territory. We haven't as yet really seen what we've made, as we can only see them with all their rich colour and full high definition glory on nine separate screens, otherwise it's just a reproduction. That only dawned on me lately, and is very interesting in itself, as you can't just put it on the internet as it has only one screen. The relationship with the paintings and drawings is obvious, indeed I am saying all the things I am showing have their basis in drawing including the video work . . . We are using the video camera like a brush, we are very excited. I have stopped thinking of these as films, indeed nine screens makes them objects like paintings, more new territory. We are on a very creative roll, sometimes I don't sleep much pondering the many levels to all this, and they seem to me very big indeed.'[57]

The making of these films was a highly complex and sophisticated operation using the very latest high-definition digital technology. It was technology that did not exist as a kit, but had to be pieced together by Hockney and Wilkinson bit by bit as they went along. By using numerous lenses knitted together, they hoped in effect to make a single fluid lens that was much more akin to the human eye. 'We began with cameras just a bit bigger than a mobile phone,' Hockney emailed Gregory Evans, 'but the difficulty was in composing the picture, I realised we needed a nine screen monitor in the back of the jeep so I could "draw" the composition. Sometimes this "drawing" took an hour or so, and was more difficult in the summer, trying to see so much detail to match up on very small screens. I then decided if we were really to go into this we should use the best small cameras we could find and high definition as well. We built a frame to hold them on the front of a jeep, and all the wire from them fed into the monitors I was looking at. We drove as slow as possible, JP got very good at it, almost keeping a steady five miles an hour for an hour or so. We knew the optimum lighting conditions for every nearby road and any direction. In May, June and July this meant very early in the morning if we were travelling west. Early evening if we were travelling east. Jonathan and Dominic walked at the side occasionally altering the exposure of individual cameras at my suggestion as I was the only one seeing the whole picture. Skill is practice, and we got better at it, and eventually moved the cameras onto a new frame made for the side of the jeep, and very low down almost on the road so we could get all the wonderful variety of grasses and wild flowers that grow in such abundance by the roadside . . .'[58]

When Devaney saw the new films, like everyone else who had seen them she was captivated by the fact that everything, from the very tops of the trees to the tiniest blade of grass, was in such clear and sharp focus, leaving no detail obscured. She also saw how right she had been to fight for the inclusion in the exhibition of *A Closer Grand Canyon* and *Pearblossom Hwy.*, both of which were so obviously connected to the films. Hockney was thrilled by them and couldn't wait to get to LA and show them to all his friends in the film business. After arranging and attending a special viewing in the studio on Santa Monica Boulevard, he emailed Devaney: 'We finally got the eighteen screens up, and quite spectacular they are. I now realise they will need a room of their own with seats, as what we have found is that people want to watch them for quite a while. Mesmerising is what they said, and of course I watched them watching . . .'[59] As the lights went up he proudly told them, 'From now on we shall be calling Bridlington, Bridlywood!'[60]

The show was scheduled to open in mid-January 2012, and at the beginning of 2011 Hockney still had one room to fill in the Royal Academy, Room III, the largest of the galleries and said to be the most difficult to hang. It had been a cold and snowy December and early January, and he had been recording the winter scene in Woldgate on his iPad. He was able to do this sitting in his car, it being far too cold for him to paint outside. Jonathan Wilkinson had recently taken possession of some new software which allowed iPad drawings to be printed on a much larger scale, and when Hockney saw his winter paintings blown up to five feet high, the possibility occurred to him that he might use the iPad to record all the seasonal changes in Woldgate over the next few months and show them as a single work in Gallery III. 'It then seemed obvious,' he wrote. 'I calculated that I could show it in this room with about 70 pictures, two rows of 35. I began to build it.'[61]

From 1 January till 8 June, Hockney was to be found in Woldgate, recording the changing days, starting when the ground was hard with ice and snow, through days of rain and mist, the appearance of snowdrops, followed by daffodils, the first buds on the trees, the bursting of the buds into leaves, the flowering of wild garlic in the woods, the explosion of the hawthorn blossom, on and on until every inch of hedgerow, verge and woodland was a dense mass of greenery. 'The iPad is becoming a fantastic tool for me,' he emailed Marco Livingstone on 30 April. 'I have done about 65 already. What is really good about it is its speed. No other medium using colour is as fast. You can get things down very fast, meaning you can capture quick lighting effects like nothing else. The spring is just spectacular this year and I am getting it down. The winter ones now look very wintry. I am very confident it will be one of my major works.'[62]

He named the completed work *The Arrival of Spring in Woldgate, East Yorkshire in 2011 (twenty-eleven)* and it consisted of fifty-one iPad paintings depicting different aspects of spring, hung in two rows, one above the other, and one huge, 32-canvas oil of the woods that covered the far wall of Gallery III. 'I thought it was kind of cathedral-like in the end,' Edith Devaney recalls. 'The way we hung it, the pictures were almost like stained-glass windows with the great altarpiece at the end.'[63]

Though *The Arrival of Spring in Woldgate* brought the painting for the exhibition to a conclusion, it was by no means the end of the work. The filming carried right on into September when it moved from *en plein air* into the Atelier where they used eighteen cameras to film *A Bigger Space for Dancing*, a ballet choreographed by Wayne Sleep. It was a nail-biting time for Devaney and Livingstone as they waited to find out if everything would be ready for the New Year opening. Hockney had pushed it to the limit.

When Lucian Freud died on 20 July 2011, the British press were all too keen to pass the mantle of 'Britain's Greatest Living Painter' on to Hockney, a label he had little time for. In the New Year's Honours List of 2012, however, he did, as Freud had also done, accept the award of Order of Merit, the most prestigious honour for achievement in the arts and held by only twenty-four living recipients. In fact, awards such as this meant little to him. 'I don't care about the greatest living painter thing,' he said, 'nor do I think life's about prizes. I'm just busy working.'[64] He had turned down the offer of a knighthood in 1990, and had been angry in 1997 when he had been appointed a Companion of Honour without his knowledge. Someone else had apparently opened the envelope and had accepted on his behalf, giving him no chance to reject it. 'I was a bit annoyed about that,' he said. 'It's OK for some people, but it's not for me. I never claimed to be a respectable person. I smoke dope.'[65] He had decided to accept the Order of Merit because it was the personal gift of the Queen and he felt it would have been ungracious to turn it down.

However much Hockney may have dismissed the label of greatest living painter, he was quite aware of how much was hanging on the upcoming show, particularly since this was the year the Olympics came to London and *David Hockney: A Bigger Picture* was the first event in the Cultural Olympiad. A row had already broken out in the press because a reporter who had interviewed him in Bridlington had seen a jokey notice attached to one of the exhibition posters that read 'All the paintings and drawings in this show were personally hand done by the artist himself', and in an interview with the *Radio Times*, Hockney had admitted that when he wrote this he had in mind Damien Hirst, who was known to employ students to help him paint certain series of pictures. 'It's a little insulting to craftsmen,' he said. 'I used to point out, at art school you can teach the craft; it's the poetry you can't teach. But now they try to teach the poetry and not the craft.'[66] This had resulted in numerous headlines of the 'Hockney attacks Hirst' variety. Whether he liked it or not, he knew his reputation was very much at stake.

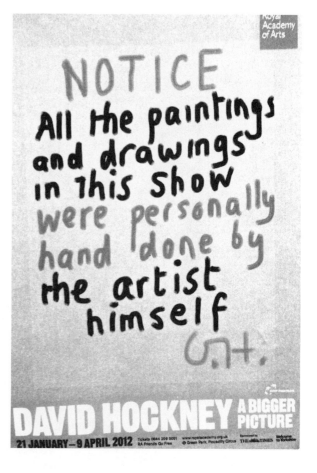

A notice in the Bridlington studio

He need not have worried. Norman Rosenthal, emerging from a preview, simply said, 'This is by far the best thing that David has ever done,'[67] and by and large both the critics and the public were inclined to agree, the latter attending in record numbers, with, perhaps unsurprisingly, over 50 per cent travelling down from Yorkshire.

1134, an iPad
drawing of spoof
reviews

'If you define a great art work,' wrote Rachel Campbell-Johnston
in *The Times*, 'as one which can lead you to a new way of looking,
which can deepen your perceptions and intensify your feelings, then
Hockney with this show surely proves his greatness.'[68] Martin Kettle,
writing in the *Guardian*, called it 'a bold assertion about the place of
skill, craftsmanship and beauty in the making of art',[69] while Andrew
Graham-Dixon, in the *Telegraph*, loved the 'joyous palette of zinging

yellow, sappy green, fluorescent purple, screaming pink and candied orange'.[70] There were some detractors, however, and they made their disdain quite clear. Andrew Lambirth in the *Spectator* found many of the paintings 'crudely brushed, crudely coloured and crudely composed', while he felt the iPad drawings resembled 'nothing so much as a sample room of schmaltzy greetings cards'.[71] As for the *Evening Standard*'s Brian Sewell, he found the accumulation of work 'the visual equivalent of being tied hand and foot and dumped under the loudspeakers of the Glastonbury Festival', and considered 'half the pictures are fit only for the railings of Green Park'.[72] After the latter review was published, Hockney sent round an iPad drawing to selected friends on which he had scrawled graffiti over a painting of some woods in Yosemite National Park, which read: '"WORSE THAN SUMMER SHOW" – R. SEWELL, Evening Standard; "SHOULD PAY MORE ATTENTION" – A. KUNT, Head Prefect, Daily Telegraph; and "PIGMY ARTIST" – A. Sure, Guardian.'

On the morning after the private view, Hockney emailed Edith Devaney: 'What a night! It was very hard work for me, but people did seem to look at the work and enjoy it, as I'm sure now many more people will in the next three months. One should laugh at the grunge critics, who are much too keen to tell you about themselves and how they are much better than anybody in the crowd. Amusing really. My fellow artists told me how impressed they were, and I could tell it was genuine. Nevertheless I'm glad it's over, the social bit anyway. I like people in all their variety, but for now just in small numbers. Enjoy your triumph, Edith, it was a marvellous five years. Thank you.'[73]

Aged seventy, in 2007 Hockney had embarked on the most intense five years of his life, producing work for the Royal Academy show. At a time when the attention of the British art scene was largely focused on the young, the cynical, the conceptual and the inaccessible, he had thrown them a challenge and tackled a subject that was unashamedly romantic and unfashionable, and was largely seen as the territory of the amateur hobbyist. It was a brave move, but he was able to pull it off because he had already been at the cutting edge of art, he had mastered the camera, he had adopted the new technologies long before anyone else, he had been and still was an anarchist, just like his father before him, railing against the curtailment of personal freedoms. Just because he was seventy-five by the time of the show, it did not mean he had any intention of stopping. 'I'm still too excited about what I will do tomorrow,' he said. 'You don't retire doing this. You just do it till you fall over. It's an interesting life. My mind is occupied. That's what you want at my age, but I always wanted it. In fact I'm greedy for it.'[74] For most people the end of five years of hard, hard graft might have seemed like an anticlimax. Not for David Hockney. 'It's not an end,' he said, 'it's another beginning. I'm only just finishing my middle period.'[75]

NOTES

PROLOGUE

(Appearing on page 8)

1   *That's the Way I See It*, David Hockney, Thames & Hudson, 1993, p. 29

CHAPTER ONE
MY PARENTS AND MYSELF

(Appearing between pages 9 and 35)

1   Interview with DH, February 2011

2   Interview with Arthur Lambert, February 2011

3   DH to JC, June 1975

4   *That's the Way I See It*, David Hockney, Thames & Hudson, 1993, p. 31

5   'A Visit with David and Stanley', Lawrence Weschler, in *David Hockney: A Retrospective*, LACMA/Thames & Hudson, 1988, p. 84

6   *David Hockney*, Marco Livingstone, Thames & Hudson, 1996, p. 183

7   Diary of Laura Hockney

8   Ibid.

9   Ibid.

10   Ibid.

11   Ibid.

12   Interview with Don Cribb, October 2012

13   Ibid.

14   Interview with DH, May 2011

15   *City Boy*, © Edmund White, Bloomsbury, 2009, p. 57

16   Interview with Don Cribb, October 2011

17   Diary of Laura Hockney

18   Ibid.

19   Ibid.

20   *Yorkshire Post*, 26 September 1977

21   *Portrait of David Hockney*, Peter Webb, Chatto & Windus, 1988, p. 153

22   *Words in Pictures*, Charles Ingham, University of Essex, 1986, p. A88

23   'Special Effects', Anthony Bailey, *New Yorker*, 30 July 1979, p. 65

24   'Hockney's Vision of Style', Nikos Stangos, *Art & Design*, No. 1/2, 1988, p. 39

25   Ibid.

26   *Portrait of David Hockney*, op. cit., p. 158

27   *That's the Way I See It*, op. cit., p. 31

28   Interview with DH, May 2011

29   *The Ossie Clark Diaries*, ed. Henrietta Rous, Bloomsbury, 1998, p. 72

30   Interview with Marinka Ellidge (née Watts), February 2012

31   *That's the Way I See It*, op. cit., p. 32

32   'Little Billy Williams' was a music-hall song that Kenneth used to sing every Christmas

33   Diary of Laura Hockney

34   Ibid.

35   Ibid.

36   Ibid.

37   DH to HG, 2 January 1977

38   Interview with Gregory Evans, May 2012

39 'Hockney Abroad: A Slide Show', *Art in America*, February 1981, p. 136

40 DH to KH and LH, 29 January 1976

41 Ibid.

42 Ibid., 6 February 1976

43 Interview with Gregory Evans, May 2012

44 DH to KH and LH, 29 January 1976

45 Sid Felsen to Paul Cornwall-Jones, 5 April 1976, Kasmin Letters and Papers, Getty Center, Los Angeles, CA

46 *David Hockney*, op. cit., p. 184

47 *Hockney at Work*, dir. Peter Adam, BBC Films, 1981

48 *Portrait of David Hockney*, op. cit., p. 162

49 *Liberation: Diaries, Volume 3, 1970–1983*, Christopher Isherwood, ed. Katherine Bucknell, Chatto & Windus, 2012, p. 502

50 DH to KH and LH, 3 April 1976

51 DH to RBK, 8 April 1976

52 DH to KH and LH, 3 April 1976

53 Diary of Laura Hockney

54 DH to RBK, 8 April 1976

55 Ibid.

56 Ibid., 11 April 1976

57 Ibid., 8 April 1976

58 Diary of Laura Hockney

59 Ibid.

60 Ibid.

61 Ibid.

62 *Liberation: Diaries, Volume 3*, op. cit., p. 511

63 Ibid., p. 512

64 Ibid.

65 Ibid., p. 513

66 Diary of Laura Hockney

67 *Words in Pictures*, op, cit., p. A71

68 *Guardian*, 21 August 1975

69 *Gay News*, No. 100, August 1976

70 Diary of Laura Hockney

71 *Gay News*, No. 100, August 1976

72 Diary of Laura Hockney

73 *Gay News*, No. 100, August 1976

74 Interview with Peter Schlesinger, February 2011

75 *Gay News*, No. 100, August 1976

76 Ibid.

77 Interview with Gregory Evans, September 2010

78 *Gay News*, No. 100, August 1976

79 Diary of Laura Hockney

80 Ibid.

81 Ibid.

82 Ibid.

CHAPTER TWO
THE BLUE GUITAR
(*Appearing between pages 36 and 61*)

1 *That's the Way I See It*, David Hockney, Thames & Hudson, 1993, p. 31

2 *Times Literary Supplement*, 21 January 1977

3 *Words in Pictures*, Charles Ingham, University of Essex, 1986, p. A89

4 *Times Literary Supplement*, 21 January 1977

5 Interview with Maurice Payne, February 2012

6 *That's the Way I See It*, op. cit., p. 32

7 DH to HG, 2 January 1977

8 *David Hockney: My Early Years*, David Hockney, Thames & Hudson, 1976, p. 9

9 *Hockney: The Biography*, Christopher Simon Sykes, Century, 2011, p. 73

10 Diary of Laura Hockney

11 Interview with Paul Hockney, October 2012

12 *Yorkshire Post*, 22 October 1976

13 Diary of Laura Hockney

14 *David Hockney: My Early Years*, op. cit., p. 295

15 *The Times*, 26 November 1976

16 *Listener*, 4 November 1976

17 *Spectator*, 6 November 1976

18 *Times Literary Supplement*, 3 December 1976

19 DH to HG, 9 December 1976

20 *Opening Accounts and Closing Memories: Thirty Years with Thames & Hudson*, Trevor Craker, Thames & Hudson, 1986, p. 166

21 DH to HG, 2 January 1977

22 Ibid.

23 Ibid.

24 Ibid.

25 DH to HG, 5 February 1977

26 *Hockney Paints the Stage*, Martin Friedman, Thames & Hudson, 1983, p. 35

27 Interview with Gregory Evans, September 2010

28 *Portrait of David Hockney*, Peter Webb, Chatto & Windus, 1988, p. 164

29 Interview with Gregory Evans, May 2012

30 *A Chequered Past: My Visual Diary of the 60s and 70s*, Peter Schlesinger and Manolo Blahnik, Thames & Hudson, 2004, p. 110

31 DH to HG, 17 February 1977

32 Interview with DH, July 2012

33 Ibid.

34 Ibid.

35 DH to HG, 5 February 1977

36 Diary of John Kasmin, Kasmin Papers, Getty Center, Los Angeles, CA

37 Ibid.

38 Ibid.

39 Ibid.

40 Ibid.

41 Ibid.

42 Ibid.

43 Interview with John Kasmin, April 2012

44 Diary of John Kasmin, op. cit.

45 Ibid.

46 Ibid.

47 DH to KH and LH, 1 April 1977

48 Diary of John Kasmin, op. cit.

49 Ibid.

50 Ibid.

51 Ibid.

52 Ibid.

53 Ibid.

54 Ibid.

55 *That's the Way I See It*, op. cit., p. 36

56 'Special Effects', Anthony Bailey, *New Yorker*, 30 July 1979, p. 60

57 Diary of Laura Hockney

58 Ibid.

59 *I Don't Know Much About Art, But I Know David Hockney*, Jonathon Brown, MER Publishing, 2007, p. 40

60 Ibid., p. 41

61 Interview with Jonathon Brown, June 2013

62 Interview with Marinka Ellidge (née Watts), February 2012

63 Ibid.

64 *New Review*, January/February 1977

65 Ibid.

66 'Special Effects', op. cit., p. 63

67 *Words in Pictures*, op. cit., p. A71

68 DH to HG, 17 February 1977

69 *Portrait of David Hockney*, op. cit., p. 167

70 *Art Monthly*, December 1977/January 1978, p. 8

71 Interview with Maurice Payne, March 2012

72 Diary of Laura Hockney

73 Ibid.

74 Ibid.

75 Ibid.

76 Ibid.

77 Ibid.

78 Ibid.

79 Ibid.

80 Ibid.

81 Interview with George Lawson, September 2012

82 Diary of Laura Hockney

83 *Art Monthly*, December 1977/January 1978, p. 8

84 *Observer*, 24 July 1977

85 *Guardian*, 20 July 1977

86 *The Times*, 2 August 1977

87 *Observer*, 29 May 1977

88 *Guardian*, 1 June 1977

89 Quoted in 'Robbie', a BBC *Tonight* special, 13 August 1977

90 Ibid.

91 Ibid.

92 *Guardian*, 6 September 1977

93 Ibid.

94 *Art Monthly*, November 1977, p. 6

CHAPTER THREE
PAPER POOLS
(*Appearing between pages 62 and 81*)

1　Interview with John Cox, March 2011
2　Interview with Aaron Kasmin, May 2012
3　Ibid.
4　Diary of Laura Hockney
5　*Observer*, 28 May 1978
6　Diary of Laura Hockney
7　'The Fun of David Hockney', Hilton Kramer, *New York Times*, 4 November 1977
8　'Special Effects', Anthony Bailey, *New Yorker*, 30 July 1979, p. 35
9　Glyndebourne programme notes by DH.
10　Interview with David Graves, January 2013
11　'Hockney Magic', *Sunday Times*, 28 May 1978
12　*David Hockney*, Marco Livingstone, Thames & Hudson, 1996, p. 193
13　Interview with John Cox, March 2011
14　'Portrait of the Artist as a Naughty Boy', John Mortimer, *Sunday Times*, 6 July 1980
15　'Special Effects', op. cit., p. 48
16　Interview with George Lawson, September 2012
17　'Special Effects', op. cit., p. 54
18　Interview with DH, March 2011
19　Diary of Laura Hockney
20　Ibid.
21　DH to RBK, 25 April 1978
22　*That's the Way I See It*, David Hockney, Thames & Hudson, 1993, p. 36
23　Ibid., p. 37
24　Ibid., p. 38
25　Interview with John Cox, March 2011
26　Diary of Laura Hockney
27　*Hockney Paints the Stage*, Martin Friedman, Thames & Hudson, 1983, p. 64
28　*Sunday Times*, 1 June 1978
29　*Guardian*, 29 May 1978
30　*The Times*, 29 May 1978
31　*New Statesman*, 16 June 1978
32　'Hockney at Home', William Green, *Vogue*, September 1978
33　'Mr Hockney's Guitar Music', *Observer*, 22 January 1978
34　'Special Effects', op. cit., p. 67
35　DH to HG, 31 July 1978
36　'Special Effects', op. cit., p. 49
37　Ibid.
38　DH to HG, 31 July 1978
39　DH to RBK, 11 June 1978
40　*That's the Way I See It*, op. cit., p. 33
41　*The Art of Collaboration*, Jane Kinsman, The National Gallery of Australia, April 2003
42　*Paper Pools*, David Hockney, ed. Nikos Stangos, Thames & Hudson, 1980, p. 9
43　Interview with Ken Tyler, November 2012
44　*Paper Pools*, op. cit., p. 10
45　Interview with Ken Tyler, November 2012
46　Ibid.
47　*That's the Way I See It*, op. cit., p. 47
48　Interview with Ken Tyler, November 2012
49　DH to LH, 19 September 1978
50　Interview with Ken Tyler, November 2012
51　*Paper Pools*, op cit., p. 21
52　'Hockney Abroad: A Slide Show', *Art in America*, February 1981, p. 141
53　Ibid., p. 39
54　Ibid., p. 48
55　Interview with Ken Tyler, November 2012
56　DH to Jonathan [surname unknown], July 1978
57　*Words in Pictures*, Charles Ingham, University of Essex, 1986, p. A49
58　Ibid.
59　Ibid.
60　DH to RBK, 5 November 1978
61　Ibid.
62　Ibid.

CHAPTER FOUR
SANTA MONICA BLVD.
(Appearing between pages 82 and 106)

1   *Art Newspaper*, No. 228, October 2011, p. 82
2   Interview with Peter Goulds, October 2011
3   Ibid.
4   Ibid.
5   'An Interview with David Hockney', Peter Fuller, *Art Monthly*, Part 1, November 1977
6   Interview with DH, September 2011
7   *That's the Way I See It*, David Hockney, Thames & Hudson, 1993, p. 50
8   *David Hockney and His Friends*, Peter Adam, Absolute Press, 1997, p. 114
9   Diary of Laura Hockney
10   Ibid.
11   Ibid.
12   Ibid.
13   Ibid.
14   Ibid.
15   Interview with George Lawson, September 2012
16   *Words in Pictures,* Charles Ingham, University of Essex, 1986, p. A36
17   Diary of Laura Hockney
18   Ibid.
19   Ibid.
20   Ibid.
21   Ibid.
22   Ibid.
23   *That's the Way I See It*, op. cit., p. 134
24   Interview with Gregory Evans, June 2012
25   *That's the Way I See It*, op. cit., p. 134
26   *Face to Face*, BBC TV, 10 November 1993
27   Diary of Laura Hockney
28   Vincent van Gogh to Theo van Gogh, 5 June 1888, The Letters of Vincent van Gogh, Van Gogh Museum, Amsterdam, www.vangoghletters.org
29   'CALENDAR', *Los Angeles Times*, 11 February 1996
30   *David Hockney*, Marco Livingstone, Thames & Hudson, 1996, p. 193
31   Diary of Laura Hockney
32   Ibid.
33   *That's the Way I See It*, op. cit., p. 134
34   *Telegraph & Argus*, 17 February 1979
35   Ibid., 23 February 1979
36   Interview with Paul Hockney, October 2012
37   Diary of Laura Hockney
38   DH to LH, 24 February 1979
39   LH to DH, 8 March 1979
40   VR to DH, 25 February 1979
41   *Guardian*, 16 February 1979
42   *Observer*, 11 February 1979
43   *Words in Pictures*, op. cit., p. A38
44   'No Joy at the Tate', *Observer*, 4 March 1979
45   Ibid.
46   *The Times*, 18 February 1976
47   'No Joy at the Tate', *Observer*, 4 March 1979
48   'Buying the Best', *Observer*, 11 March 1979
49   Ibid.
50   Ibid.
51   DH to RBK, 8 August 1979
52   *Words in Pictures*, op. cit., p. A89
53   *True to Life: Twenty-five Years of Conversations with David Hockney*, Lawrence Weschler, University of California Press, 2008, p. 64
54   *That's the Way I See It*, op. cit., p. 52
55   *True to Life*, op. cit., p. 66
56   *That's the Way I See It*, op. cit., p. 48
57   DH to RBK, 8 August 1979
58   *Words in Pictures*, op. cit., p. A91
59   Interview with Maurice Payne, February 2012
60   *Portrait of David Hockney*, Peter Webb, Chatto & Windus, 1988, p. 178
61   Diary of Laura Hockney
62   Ibid.
63   Interview with George Lawson, September 2012
64   Diary of Laura Hockney

65 *One Hundred Great Paintings*, dir. Peter Adam, BBC Films, 1980

66 Ibid.

67 *Words in Pictures*, op. cit., p. A89

68 Interview with Don Bachardy, September 2010

CHAPTER FIVE
MULHOLLAND DRIVE
(Appearing between pages 107 and 134)

1 DH to RBK, 8 August 1979

2 *As Much as I Dare*, Arnold Wesker, Century, 1994, p. 505

3 *Hockney Paints the Stage*, Martin Friedman, Thames & Hudson, 1983, p. 127.

4 James Levine – Principal Conductor and Music Director of the Met; Anthony Bliss – Executive Director of the Met, referred to by Dexter as 'Miss Blisskins'

5 *The Honourable Beast: A Posthumous Autobiography*, John Dexter, Nick Hern, 1993, p. 145

6 *That's the Way I See It*, David Hockney, Thames & Hudson, 1993, p. 53

7 *The Honourable Beast*, op. cit., p. 154

8 Ibid., p. 145

9 *That's the Way I See It*, op. cit., p. 56

10 *Hockney Paints the Stage*, op. cit., p. 157

11 Interview with Gregory Evans, July 2012

12 DH to RBK, 8 August 1979

13 *That's the Way I See It*, op. cit., p. 53

14 *David Hockney and His Friends*, Peter Adam, Absolute Press, 1997

15 *That's the Way I See It*, op. cit., p. 57

16 *The Honourable Beast*, op. cit., p. 152

17 Interview with DH, November 2012

18 *I Don't Know Much About Art, But I Know David Hockney*, Jonathon Brown, MER Publishing, 2007, p. 58

19 *The Honourable Beast*, op. cit., p. 152

20 Diary of Laura Hockney

21 *Ambit*, No. 83, London, 1980, pp. 3–7

22 Ibid.

23 Interview with Celia Birtwell, September 2012

24 *Ambit*, No. 83, op. cit., pp. 3–7

25 Ibid.

26 Ibid.

27 Ibid.

28 DH to RBK, 26 January 1980

29 LH to DH, 7 January 1980

30 *That's the Way I See It*, op. cit., p. 62.

31 Ibid., p. 161

32 JD to DH, 29 November 1978

33 *New York Times*, 15 February 1981

34 *The Honourable Beast*, op. cit., p. 160

35 Ibid.

36 Interview with David Graves, January 2013

37 *The Honourable Beast*, op. cit., p. 161

38 Ibid.

39 Ibid.

40 *New York Times*, 23 May 1980

41 DH to RBK, begun 20 May, sent 19 August 1980

42 *That's the Way I See It*, op. cit., p. 62

43 *David Hockney*, Marco Livingstone, Thames & Hudson, 1996, p. 221

44 Diary of George Lawson, June 1980

45 *David Hockney and His Friends*, op. cit., p. 111

46 *Portrait of David Hockney*, Peter Webb, Chatto & Windus, p. 189

47 Interview with David Graves, January 2013

48 *Hockney at Work*, dir. Peter Adam, BBC Films, 1981

49 *Hockney Paints the Stage*, op. cit., p. 173

50 Interview with DH, November 2012

51 LH to DH, 14 August 1980

52 *The Times*, 15 July 1980

53 *Guardian*, 11 July 1980

54 *The Times*, 15 July 1980

55 *David Hockney and His Friends*, op. cit., p. 108

56 *Not Drowning but Waving*, Peter Adam, André Deutsch, 1995, p. 426

57 DH to RBK, 19 August 1980

58 DH to RBK, 12 September 1980

59 *New York Times*, 12 October 1980

60 Ibid.

61 *That's the Way I See It*, op. cit., p. 68

62 Ibid.

63 *Not Drowning but Waving*, op. cit., p. 426

64 Ibid., p. 427

65 Ibid., p. 428

66 Ibid.

67 *Hockney at Work*, op. cit.

68 *Portrait of David Hockney*, op. cit., p. 190

69 *That's the Way I See It*, op. cit., p. 67

70 *Hockney at Work*, op. cit.

71 *After Dark*, February 1981, p. 49

72 Interview with Bing McGilvray, February 2013

73 *After Dark*, op. cit., p. 49

74 *David Hockney*, op. cit., p. 226

75 *True to Life: Twenty-five Years of Conversations with David Hockney*, Lawrence Weschler, University of California Press, 2008, p. 65

76 *That's the Way I See It*, op. cit., p. 68

77 *Hockney at Work*, op. cit.

78 *Sunday Times*, 18 January 1981

79 *Listener*, 22 January 1981

80 *The Times*, 20 January 1981

81 *Hockney at Work*, op. cit.

82 *After Dark*, op. cit., p. 49

CHAPTER SIX

PARADE

(Appearing between pages 135 and 156)

1 *New York Times*, 20 February 1981

2 'A Risky Venture at the Met', John Rockwell, *New York Times*, 15 February 1981

3 *That's the Way I See It*, David Hockney, Thames & Hudson, 1993, p. 69

4 *The Honourable Beast: A Posthumous Autobiography*, John Dexter, Nick Hern, 1993, p. 161

5 *Hockney Paints the Stage*, Martin Friedman, Thames & Hudson, 1983, p. 173

6 *David Hockney: A Retrospective*, LACMA/Thames & Hudson, 1988, p. 20

7 Interview with Gregory Evans, March 2013

8 MM to DH, 29 January 1981

9 *Gay and Steamy: The Career of the Club Baths*, Erik Mitchell, Yahoo Voices, yahoo.com/gay-steamy

10 Interview with DH, September 2011

11 Interview with Ian Falconer, November 2012

12 Ibid.

13 *New York Times*, 15 February 1981

14 *That's the Way I See It*, op. cit., p. 69

15 *Guardian*, 6 April 1981

16 *New York Times*, 22 February 1981

17 *Guardian*, 6 April, 1981

18 *That's the Way I See It*, op. cit., p. 69

19 LH to DH, 18 March 1981

20 *That's the Way I See It*, op. cit., p. 71

21 *Hockney Paints the Stage*, op. cit., p. 200

22 Ibid., p. 138

23 *China Diary*, Stephen Spender and David Hockney, Thames & Hudson, 1982, p. 7

24 *That's the Way I See It*, op. cit., p. 78

25 *China Diary*, op. cit., p. 9

26 Ibid., p. 10

27 Ibid., p. 13

28 Ibid., p. 15

29 Ibid., p. 16

30 Ibid., p. 191

31 Ibid., p. 190

32 Ibid., p. 20

33 Ibid., p. 190

34 Ibid., p. 81

35 Ibid., p. 87

36 Ibid., p. 102

37 Ibid., p. 109

38 Ibid., p. 116

39 *That's the Way I See It*, op. cit., p. 78

40 Ibid., p. 82

41 Ibid.

42 Ibid., p. 83

43 *Hockney Paints the Stage*, op. cit., p. 194

44 Ibid., p. 203

45 Ibid., p. 204

46 Ibid., p. 197

47 Ibid., p. 199

48 DH to RBK, 5 September 1981

49 DH to HG, 2 September 1981

50 Ibid.

51 DH to RBK, 5 September 1981

52 Ibid.

53 JC to DH, 20 November 1981

54 Ibid.

55 *New York Magazine*, 21 December 1981

56 *New York Times*, 5 December 1981

57 *Hockney's Homes*, Henry Geldzahler, unpublished manuscript in Beinecke Library, Yale University, New Haven, CT

CHAPTER SEVEN

DRAWING WITH A CAMERA

(Appearing between pages 157 and 183)

1 Interview with Ian Falconer, November 2012

2 *David Hockney and His Friends,* Peter Adam, Absolute Press, 1997, p. 118

3 Ibid.

4 Interview with Ian Falconer, November 2012

5 Ibid.

6 Ibid.

7 *Portrait of David Hockney*, Peter Webb, Chatto & Windus, 1988, p. 232

8 Interview with Gregory Evans, March 2013

9 Ibid.

10 Interview with Ian Falconer, November 2012

11 *Cameraworks*, David Hockney, Thames & Hudson, 1984, p. 8

12 *The South Bank Show*, LWT, 13 November 1983

13 'Looking at Pictures', David Hockney, Introduction to *The Artist's Eye*, National Gallery, 1981

14 *Hockney on Photography*, Paul Joyce, Jonathan Cape, 1988, p. 15

15 *That's the Way I See It*, op. cit., p. 89

16 *Cameraworks*, op. cit., p. 11

17 Interview with Ian Falconer, November 2012

18 *Photographs*, exhibition catalogue, International Exhibitions Foundation, 1986, p. 32

19 *Cameraworks*, op. cit., p. 11

20 Ibid.

21 Ibid., p. 13

22 Interview with George Lawson, October 2012

23 DH to SS, 17 May 1982, Stephen Spender Archive, Bodleian Library, Oxford

24 Ibid.

25 Ibid.

26 *Photographs*, op. cit., p. 26

27 *Cameraworks*, op. cit., p. 17

28 *New York Times*, 13 June 1982

29 *The Times*, 6 July 1982

30 DH to IF, 14 June 1982

31 Ibid.

32 *That's the Way I See It,* David Hockney, Thames & Hudson, 1993, p. 136

33 Interview with Ian Falconer, November 2012

34 *Photographs*, David Hockney, Petersburg Press, 1982, p. 7

35 *Portrait of David Hockney*, op. cit., p. 207

36 DH to RBK, 14 August 1982

37 *Cameraworks*, op. cit., p. 20

38 DH to RBK, 8 September 1982

39 'Rare Cancer Seen in 41 Homosexuals',

Lawrence K. Altman, *New York Times*, 3 July 1981

40 *New Selected Journals 1939–1995*, Stephen Spender, Faber & Faber, 2012, p. 613

41 *City Boy*, © Edmund White, Bloomsbury, 2009, p. 284

42 Ibid., p. 287

43 LH to DH, 27 July 1982

44 Interview with Bing McGilvray, February 2013

45 DH to RBK, 8 September 1982

46 *Cameraworks*, op. cit., p. 22

47 Ibid., p. 21

48 Ibid., p. 22

49 *New York Times*, 27 October 1982

50 HG to DH, 11 October 1982

51 DH to HG, 2 November 1982

52 Ibid.

53 *Cameraworks*, op. cit., p. 21

54 Ibid., p. 23

55 'David Hockney's Photo Graphics', *Vanity Fair*, May 1983

56 *Hockney Paints the Stage*, Martin Friedman, Thames & Hudson, 1983, p. 38

57 Interview with Ian Falconer, November 2012

58 DH to HG, 2 November 1982

59 *The Ossie Clark Diaries*, ed. Henrietta Rous, Bloomsbury, 1998, p. 120

60 *Listener*, 11 November 1982

61 *Portrait of David Hockney*, op. cit., p. 209

62 *The Ossie Clark Diaries*, op. cit., p. 133

63 Ibid., p. 122

64 Diary of Laura Hockney

65 Ibid.

66 Ibid.

67 Ibid.

68 DH to HG, 2 November 1982

69 *That's the Way I See It*, op. cit., p. 98

70 *Cameraworks*, op. cit., p. 33

71 Diary of Laura Hockney

72 Interview with David Graves, January 2013

73 Diary of Laura Hockney

74 Ibid.

75 Interview with Ian Falconer, November 2012

CHAPTER EIGHT
HOCKNEY PAINTS THE STAGE
(Appearing between pages 184 and 204)

1   *The Yard Man: Meet Madison Square Park's Secret Weapon*, Sarah Douglas, Galleristny.com

2   *That's the Way I See It*, David Hockney, Thames & Hudson, 1993, p. 138

3   Ibid.

4   Interview with Richard Schmidt, March 2013

5   *Cameraworks*, David Hockney, Thames & Hudson, 1984, p. 37

6   Interview with David Graves, February 2013

7   DH to RBK, 17 February 1983

8   *The South Bank Show*, LWT, 13 November 1983

9   *Japanese Gardens*, Günter Nitschke, Taschen, 2003, p. 92

10 *Hockney on Photography*, Paul Joyce, Jonathan Cape, 1988, p. 56

11 *That's the Way I See It*, op. cit., p. 100

12 DH to RBK, March 1983

13 'AIDS Anxiety', Michael Daly, *New Yorker*, 20 June 1983

14 *The Ossie Clark Diaries*, ed. Henrietta Rous, Bloomsbury, 1998, p. 133

15 *New Selected Journals 1939–1995*, Stephen Spender, Faber & Faber, 2012, p. 613

16 LH to DH, 7 April 1983

17 AU to DH, September 1987

18 *The Ossie Clark Diaries*, op. cit., p. 134

19 *New York Times*, 20 April 1983

20 Interview with David Graves, January 2013

21 *The Ossie Clark Diaries*, op. cit., 28 April 1983

22 Interview with David Graves, January 2013

23 Interview with Ian Falconer, November 2012
24 LH to DH, 7 April 1983
25 *Cameraworks*, op. cit., p. 38
26 Ibid.
27 *New York Times*, 20 May 1983
28 *L.A. Herald Examiner*, 3 July 1983
29 *Guardian*, 20 July 1983
30 *The Times*, 4 November 1983
31 *The Face*, September 1983
32 *Cameraworks*, op. cit., p. 39
33 Interview with Ian Falconer, November 2012
34 *Hockney Paints the Stage*, Martin Friedman, Thames & Hudson, 1983, p. 140
35 *Sunday Times*, 21 February 1988
36 Ibid.
37 Ibid.
38 Ibid.
39 Interview with David Graves, January 2013
40 DH to RBK, 17 February 1983

41 *New Selected Journals 1939–1995*, op. cit., p. 613
42 *That's the Way I See It*, op. cit., p. 155
43 DH to RBK, 17 February 1983
44 Interview with Ian Falconer, November 2012
45 *New Selected Journals 1939–1995*, op. cit., p. 653
46 Ibid.
47 Interview with David Graves, January 2013
48 *Los Angeles Times*, 18 January 1987
49 Ibid.
50 *Portrait of David Hockney*, Peter Webb, Chatto & Windus, 1988, p. 217
51 Interview with Peter Goulds, March 2013
52 *That's the Way I See It*, op. cit., p. 140
53 'A New Stage', Paul Froiland, *Horizon*, November/December 1983, p. 45
54 *The Times*, 6 August 1985
55 Interview with David Graves, January 2013

CHAPTER NINE

A WALK ROUND THE HOTEL COURTYARD, ACATLAN

(*Appearing between pages 205 and 225*)

1 'A New Stage', *Horizon*, November/December 1983, p. 45
2 'David Hockney's Journey to a New Cubism', Douglas C. McGill, *New York Times*, 7 October 1984
3 *True to Life: Twenty-five Years of Conversations with David Hockney*, Lawrence Weschler, University of California Press, 2008, p. 71
4 Ibid., p. 72
5 DH lecture on *A Day on the Grand Canal*, Sci-Arc Media Archive
6 DH to SS, undated letter
7 *True to Life*, op. cit., p. 74
8 'David Hockney's Journey to a New Cubism', op. cit.
9 Interview with Gregory Evans, March 2013
10 *That's the Way I See It*, David Hockney, Thames & Hudson, 1993, p. 141
11 Interview with Gregory Evans, March 2013

12 Ibid.
13 DH to RBK, 21 May 1985
14 Interview with Ken Tyler, November 2012
15 Ibid.
16 Interview with Paul Hockney, February 2013
17 Interview with Peter Goulds, March 2013
18 Nathan Kolodner to Gregory Evans, 1 November 1984
19 *Portrait of David Hockney*, Peter Webb, Chatto & Windus, 1988, p. 216
20 Interview with Ian Falconer, November 2012
21 Interview with Ken Tyler, November 2012
22 *Hockney on Art: Conversations with Paul Joyce*, David Hockney & Paul Joyce, Little, Brown, 1999, p. 111
23 Interview with Ken Tyler, November 2012
24 Ibid.
25 *That's the Way I See It*, op. cit., p. 154
26 DH to RBK, 31 May 1985

27 *That's the Way I See It*, op. cit., p. 154

28 DG to DH, undated letter, 1985

29 Interview with David Graves, January 2013

30 AG to DH, undated letter

31 *The Times*, 31 July 1985

32 *The Ossie Clark Diaries*, ed. Henrietta Rous, Bloomsbury, 1998, p. 177

33 Ibid.

34 *Sunday Times*, 4 August 1985

35 *The Ossie Clark Diaries*, op. cit., p. 178

36 *Sunday Times*, 4 August 1985

37 *Listener*, 22 August 1985

38 *Guardian*, 1 August 1985

39 *Observer*, 4 August 1985

40 LH to DH, 1 August 1985

41 *That's the Way I See It*, op. cit., p. 106

42 Ibid., p. 107

43 Ibid., p. 106

44 Ibid.

45 Interview with David Graves, February 2013

46 *Portrait of David Hockney*, op. cit., p. 230

47 Interview with DH, February 2013

48 *Portrait of David Hockney*, op cit., p. 230

49 Interview with Gregory Evans, March 2013

50 PH to GE, 31 January 1986

CHAPTER TEN
PEARBLOSSOM HWY.
(Appearing between pages 226 and 254)

1 *Celia Birtwell*, Celia Birtwell, Quadrille, 2011, p. 157

2 LH to DH, 8 January 1986

3 DH to SS, undated letter.

4 www.thebambamblog.com

5 *Painting with Light,* dir. David Goldsmith, York Films, 1987

6 Ibid.

7 Ibid.

8 Interview with Jerry Sohn, March 2013

9 'David Hockney', Robert Becker, *Interview*, December 1986, p. 160

10 From the introduction, 'A Life in Portraits', Marco Livingstone, *Faces*, Laband Art Gallery/Thames & Hudson, 1987

11 'David Hockney', *Interview*, op. cit., p. 160

12 *Home Made Prints*, David Hockney, Knoedler Gallery, 1986

13 *True to Life: Twenty-five Years of Conversations with David Hockney*, Lawrence Weschler, University of California Press, 2008, p. 53

14 *Hockney on Art: Conversations with Paul Joyce,* David Hockney & Paul Joyce, Little, Brown, 1999, p. 133

15 *That's the Way I See It,* David Hockney, Thames & Hudson, 1993, p. 121

16 'David Hockney', *Interview*, op. cit.

17 Interview with Charlie Scheips, November 2012. The art dealer Richard Gray later took the Grants and Hockney for lunch at the Tremont Hotel. A woman spotted Grant getting into the limousine and begged through the window for an autograph. Hockney quoted Grant as replying, 'My mother told me never to sign anything.'

18 Ibid.

19 From *Pearblossom Highway,* an unpublished MS by Charlie Scheips

20 Ibid.

21 *Guardian*, 4 July 1987

22 Interview with Charlie Scheips, November 2012

23 Ibid.

24 DH to SS, April 1986

25 Interview with Charlie Scheips, November 2012

26 *That's the Way I See It*, op. cit., p. 112

27 Interview with Charlie Scheips, November 2012

28 *Hockney on Art*, op. cit., p. 133

29 DH to SS, April 1986

30 Interview with Charlie Scheips, November 2012

31 Ibid.

32 *Guardian*, 21 October 1986

33 *That's the Way I See It*, op. cit., p. 171

34 Interview with Ian Falconer, November 2012

35 *True to Life*, op. cit., p. 93

36 *That's the Way I See It*, op. cit., p. 172

37 DH to John Cox, 3 March 1989

38 *Vincent Van Gogh: Verzamelde Brieven*, vol. 3, ed. V. W. Van Gogh and Johanna Van Gogh-Bonger, Wereldbibliotheek, 1973, p. 95

39 Vincent van Gogh to Theo van Gogh, 18 September 1888, The Letters of Vincent van Gogh, Van Gogh Museum, Amsterdam, www.vangoghletters.org

40 *That's the Way I See It*, op. cit., p. 173

41 Ibid., p. 172

42 Ibid., p. 178

43 *The Ossie Clark Diaries*, ed. Henrietta Rous, Bloomsbury, 1998, p. 187

44 Interview with Celia Birtwell, September 2012

45 Interview with DH, July 2012

46 Interview with Celia Birtwell, September 2012

47 *The Ossie Clark Diaries*, op. cit., p. 195

48 Ibid., p. 206

49 Ibid., p. 208

50 MM to DH, 25 February 1987

51 MM to DH, 12 March 1987

52 AG to DH, 29 March 1987

53 DG to DH, 9 April 1987

54 Interview with Charlie Scheips, June 2013

55 MM to DH, undated letter

56 CB to DH, 22 March 1987

57 *The Ossie Clark Diaries*, op. cit., p. 188

58 *Hockney on Art*, op cit., p. 155

59 *That's the Way I See It*, op. cit., p. 178

60 'David Hockney', *Interview*, op. cit., pp. 160–61

61 *Telegraph & Argus*, 3 March 1987

62 *Observer*, 1 June 1986

63 *Observer*, 31 May 1987

64 *Guardian*, 6 June 1987

65 *That's the Way I See It*, op. cit., p. 187

66 Ibid., p. 190

67 'Hockney on the Beach', Lawrence Weschler, *Interview*, August 1989

68 *Sunday Times*, 21 February 1988

CHAPTER ELEVEN
THE ROAD TO MALIBU
(*Appearing between pages 255 and 277*)

1 Interview with Charlie Scheips, May 2013

2 Ibid.

3 Interview with Ian Falconer, November 2012

4 *True to Life: Twenty-five Years of Conversations with David Hockney*, Lawrence Weschler, University of California Press, 2008, p. 85

5 'The Middle Age of Mr Hockney', Gordon Burn, *Sunday Times*, 21 February 1988

6 *Guardian*, 21 May 1987

7 Interview with Charlie Scheips, May 2013

8 LH to DH, 27 August 1987

9 *Sunday Times*, 21 February 1988

10 Ibid.

11 *A Day on the Grand Canal with the Emperor of China*, dir. Philip Haas, 1987

12 *Los Angeles Times*, 13 January 2008

13 DH to JC, 3 March 1989

14 *In Two Minds: A Biography of Jonathan Miller*, Kate Bassett, Oberon Books, 2012, p. 255

15 *New York Times*, 14 March 1991

16 *Los Angeles Times*, 6 March 1988

17 *Guardian*, 18 December 1987

18 JW to DH, 9 December 1987

19 *True to Life*, op. cit., p. 95

20 *New York Times*, 8 December 1987

21 *Hollywood Reporter*, 7 January 1988

22 Ibid.

23 Ibid.

24 Interview with Charlie Scheips, May 2013

25 Marylouise Oates, 'LACMA fills house for

Hockney party', © *Los Angeles Times*,
5 February 1988. Reprinted with permission

26 William Wilson, 'Hockney's cheeky look at
today's history', © *Los Angeles Times*,
7 February 1988. Reprinted with permission

27 *David Hockney: A Retrospective*, Thames &
Hudson, 1988, p. 312

28 *Los Angeles Times*, 7 February 1988

29 *New York Times*, 17 June 1988

30 Interview with Charlie Scheips, June 2013

31 Ibid.

32 *Sunday Times*, 6 March 1988

33 *Guardian*, 8 March 1988

34 *Sunday Times*, 6 March 1988

35 *Sun*, 7 March 1988

36 *The Times*, 3 March 1988

37 JC to DH, 1 April 1988

38 *Sunday Times*, 13 March 1988

39 AG to DH, 24 September 1987

40 MM to DH, 5 January 1988

41 MM to DH, 15 January 1988

42 Interview with Maurice Payne, February 2012

43 *The Ossie Clark Diaries*, ed. Henrietta Rous,
Bloomsbury, 1998, p. 242

44 Interview with Paul Hockney, February 2013

45 *The Ossie Clark Diaries*, op. cit., p. 244

46 JC to DH, 1 April 1988

47 Interview with Ian Falconer, November 2012

48 *Hockney on Art: Conversations with Paul Joyce*,
David Hockney & Paul Joyce, Little, Brown,
1999, p. 178

49 'Hockney on the Beach', Lawrence
Weschler, *Interview*, August 1989

50 Interview with David Plante, September 2012

51 *Hockney on Art*, op. cit., p. 187

52 Ibid., p. 182

53 *Sunday Times*, 30 October 1988

54 Ibid.

55 *The Ossie Clark Diaries*, op. cit., p. 273

56 Ibid., p. 274

57 *Sunday Times*, 30 October 1988

58 *Observer*, 30 October 1988

59 *Guardian*, 29 October 1988

60 Michael Craig-Martin, Myartspace>blog,
August 2007

61 *Sunday Times*, 30 October 1988

62 Ibid.

CHAPTER TWELVE
TENNIS
(Appearing between pages 278 and 299)

1 DH to RBK, 28 August 1989

2 *Hockney's Fax*, Yorkshire TV Great North
Show, 1990

3 Interview with Bing McGilvray, June 2013

4 *Hockney on Art: Conversations with Paul Joyce*,
David Hockney & Paul Joyce, Little, Brown,
1999, p. 183

5 *That's the Way I See It*, David Hockney,
Thames & Hudson, 1993, p. 190

6 Ibid., p. 198

7 Interview with Richard Schmidt, March 2013

8 Ibid.

9 *That's the Way I See It*, op. cit., p. 199

10 Ibid., p. 204

11 Interview with Zoe Silver, June 2013

12 Interview with Robin Silver, June 2013

13 *That's the Way I See It*, op. cit., p. 204

14 Interview with Robin Silver, June 2013

15 *Guardian*, 11 November 1989

16 Ibid.

17 LH to DH, 11 November 1989

18 *That's the Way I See It*, op. cit., p. 205

19 Interview with John Fitzherbert, June 2013

20 Ibid.

21 Ibid.

22 Interview with Ian Falconer, November 2012

23 *I Don't Know Much About Art, But I Know David
Hockney*, Jonathon Brown, MER Publishing,
2007, p. 52

24 Interview with John Fitzherbert, June 2013

25 Interview with Jonathon Brown, June 2013

26 Interview with Ian Falconer, November 2012

27 Interview with DH, August 2012

28 Interview with John Fitzherbert, June 2013

29 *Los Angeles Times*, 16 September 1990

30 Interview with John Cox, July 2013

31 *Los Angeles Times*, 16 September 1990

32 *Daily Mirror*, 29 January 1990

33 Ibid.

34 Associated Press, 30 January 1990

35 Interview with George Lawson, September 2012

36 *That's the Way I See It*, op. cit., p. 206

37 Ibid.

38 Ibid., p. 207

39 *Hockney on Art*, op. cit., p. 188

40 'The Art on the Cover', Barbara Isenberg, *Los Angeles Times*, 16 September 1990

41 Interview with Bing McGilvray, June 2013

42 Ibid.

43 Interview with David Plante, September 2012

44 Interview with Bing McGilvray, June 2013

45 *Sunday Times*, 10 October 1993

46 Interview with Bing McGilvray, June 2013

CHAPTER THIRTEEN
VERY NEW PAINTINGS
(*Appearing between pages 300 and 319*)

1 Interview with Gregory Evans, March 2013

2 Ibid.

3 *That's the Way I See It*, David Hockney, Thames & Hudson, 1993, p. 218

4 Ibid.

5 Interview with Bing McGilvray, June 2013

6 *That's the Way I See It*, op. cit., p. 219

7 Ibid.

8 Ibid.

9 Interview with Bing McGilvray, June 2013

10 *That's the Way I See It*, op. cit., p. 220

11 Ibid.

12 Interview with John Fitzherbert, June 2013

13 *That's the Way I See It*, op. cit., p. 220

14 Interview with Richard Schmidt, March 2013

15 Interview with Bing McGilvray, June 2013

16 *That's the Way I See It*, p. 221

17 Ibid.

18 *I Don't Know Much About Art, But I Know David Hockney*, Jonathon Brown, MER Publishing, 2007, p. 58

19 Ibid., p. 64

20 Ibid., p. 66

21 *Face to Face*, BBC TV, 10 November 1993

22 Interview with John Cox, July 2013

23 *That's the Way I See It*, op. cit., p. 224

24 Interview with John Cox, July 2013

25 Interview with Bing McGilvray, July 2013

26 *Sunday Times*, 12 January 1992

27 Ibid.

28 *I Don't Know Much About Art*, op. cit., p. 60

29 *Chicago Tribune*, 13 January 1992

30 *Observer*, 27 December 1992

31 *Chicago Tribune*, 13 January 1992

32 *That's the Way I See It*, op. cit., p. 229

33 *Sunday Times*, 10 October 1993

34 *Hockney on Art: Conversations with Paul Joyce*, David Hockney & Paul Joyce, Little, Brown, 1999, p. 189

35 *That's the Way I See It*, op. cit., p. 233

36 LH to DH, 17 February 1992

37 *Independent*, 26 July 1992

38 Ibid.

39 Ibid.

40 Ibid.

41 Ibid.

42 *That's the Way I See It*, op. cit., p. 240

43 Interview with John Cox, July 2013

44 *Guardian*, 16 November 1992

45 *Guardian*, 26 April 1997

46 *Sunday Times*, 24 January 1993

47 Ibid.

48 *Hockney's Portraits and People*, Marco Livingstone & Kay Heymer, Thames & Hudson, 2003, p. 189

49 'What it's like to be drawn by David Hockney', Jonathan Silver, exhibition notes, 1853 Gallery, Salts Mill, 1994

50 AG to DH, 29 July 1994

51 Interview with Arthur Lambert, February 2011

52 *Los Angeles Times*, 11 February 1996

53 *Dog Days*, David Hockney, Thames & Hudson, 1998, p. 5

54 AG to DH, March 1995

55 Q&A with David Hockney, Barbara Isenberg, *Los Angeles Times*, 5 April 1995

56 *Sunday Times*, 4 April 1995

57 Ibid.

58 *Guardian*, 27 June 1995

59 Sotheby's Catalogue of Sale of the Collection of Mark Birley, 31 March 2013, p. 133

CHAPTER FOURTEEN
GARROWBY HILL
(Appearing between pages 320 and 334)

1 *David Hockney and His Friends*, Peter Adam, Absolute Press, 1997, p. 132

2 *Hockney on Art: Conversations with Paul Joyce*, David Hockney & Paul Joyce, Little, Brown, 1999, p. 203

3 Ibid., p. 205

4 Ibid., p. 206

5 Ibid.

6 *Sunday Times*, 27 April 1997

7 Ibid.

8 *David Hockney and His Friends*, op. cit., p. 134

9 DH interview with Lawrence Weschler, 7 March 1998

10 *Independent*, 6 May 1997

11 *Evening Standard*, 8 May 1997

12 *Telegraph*, 10 May 1997

13 *Los Angeles Times*, 26 May 1997

14 *Hockney on Art*, op. cit., p. 231

15 'Home Boy', Lynn Barber, *Observer*, 15 March 1998

16 *True to Life: Twenty-five Years of Conversations with David Hockney*, Lawrence Weschler, University of California Press, 2008, p. 100

17 'Home Boy', *Observer*, op. cit.

18 *True to Life*, op. cit., p. 104

19 *Mail Online*, 14 January 2012

20 'Home Boy', *Observer*, op. cit.

21 *Hockney on Art*, op. cit., p. 232

22 *True to Life*, op. cit., p. 106

23 Ibid., p. 107

24 Ibid., p. 106

25 MS to DH, November 1997

26 'Home Boy', *Observer*, op. cit.

27 *True to Life*, op. cit., p. 109

28 *Hockney on Art*, op. cit., p. 232

29 *True to Life*, op. cit., p. 111

30 Ibid.

31 *Hockney on Art*, op. cit., p. 227

32 'Home Boy', *Observer*, op. cit.

33 Ibid.

34 *True to Life*, op. cit., p. 114

35 *David Hockney: Space and Line*, Annely Juda Fine Art, 1999, p. 19

36 'Hockney's Final Frontier', Tim Adams, *Observer*, 30 May 1999

37 *David Hockney: Space and Line*, op. cit., p. 15

38 *Hockney on Art*, op. cit., p. 239

39 Ibid., p. 240

40 Interview with Maurice Payne, February 2012

41 DH to GR, 12 June 1998

CHAPTER FIFTEEN
SECRET KNOWLEDGE
(Appearing between pages 335 and 347)

1 'A Look Back at Ingres', Gary Tinterow, *Travel + Leisure,* September 1999

2 *Portraits by Ingres: Image of an Epoch,* Gary Tinterow, Philip Conisbee and Hans Naef, Harry N. Abrams, Inc., 1999, p. 111

3 *True to Life: Twenty-five Years of Conversations with David Hockney,* Lawrence Weschler, University of California Press, 2008, p. 117

4 Ibid., p. 121

5 Interview with Margaret Hockney, July 2013

6 'Hockney's Final Frontier', Tim Adams, *Observer,* 30 May 1999

7 *Independent,* 17 May 1999

8 DH to Martin Kemp, 19 October 2000, quoted in *Secret Knowledge: Rediscovering the Lost Techniques of the Old Masters,* David Hockney, Thames & Hudson, 2006, p. 310

9 Ibid., p. 12

10 *True to life,* op. cit., p. 123

11 *Secret Knowledge,* op. cit., p. 262

12 *Sunday Times,* 30 January 2000

13 *True to Life,* op. cit., p. 13

14 *Sunday Times,* 6 February 2000

15 Interview with Gregory Evans, March 2013

16 Interview with David Graves, September 2013

17 DH to Martin Kemp, 6 December 1999, quoted in *Secret Knowledge,* op. cit., p. 282

18 Ibid., 18 February 2000

19 *Los Angeles Times,* 3 December 2001

20 Ibid.

21 *True to Life,* op. cit., p. 190

22 Interview with John Fitzherbert, July 2013

23 Ibid.

CHAPTER SIXTEEN
GEORGE AND MARY CHRISTIE
(Appearing between pages 348 and 358)

1 *Evening Standard,* 22 July 2011

2 Ibid.

3 *Man with a Blue Scarf: On Sitting for a Portrait by Lucian Freud,* Martin Gayford, Thames & Hudson, 2010, p. 31

4 *David Hockney discusses Lucian Freud,* DH interview, www.youtube.com/watch?v=_4OGC9pj86g

5 He referred to DH in these terms during a conversation with the author

6 *Evening Standard,* 22 July 2011

7 *True to Life: Twenty-five Years of Conversations with David Hockney,* Lawrence Weschler, University of California Press, 2008, p. 190

8 Interview with George Lawson, September 2012

9 *Evening Standard,* 22 July 2011

10 *Los Angeles Times,* 12 January 2003

11 Ibid.

12 Interview with John Richardson from a film by David Dawson, 2011

13 *True to Life,* op. cit., p. 197

14 *Hockney's Portraits and People,* Marco Livingstone & Kay Heymer, Thames & Hudson, 2003, p. 214

15 *David Hockney: Double Portrait,* dir. Bruno Wollheim, Coluga Pictures, 2003

16 Ibid.

17 *Los Angeles Times,* 12 January 2003

18 *Sitting for Hockney,* Marco Livingstone, Annely Juda Gallery, 2003

19 Ibid.

20 Ibid.

21 Ibid.

22 Ibid.

23 Ibid.

24 *David Hockney: Double Portrait*, op. cit.

25 *Sitting for Hockney*, op. cit.

26 Interview with Karen Kuhlman, March 2013

27 Interview with John Fitzherbert, July 2013

28 *True to Life*, op. cit., p. 198

29 Interview with Margaret Hockney, June 2013

CHAPTER SEVENTEEN
THE ARRIVAL OF SPRING IN WOLDGATE
(Appearing between pages 359 and 390)

1 *Grub Street Irregular*, Jeremy Lewis, Harper Press, 2008, p. 207

2 Interview with DH, June 2006

3 *True to Life: Twenty-five Years of Conversations with David Hockney*, Lawrence Weschler, University of California Press, 2008, p. 201

4 Interview with DH, June 2006

5 Ibid.

6 *David Hockney: Nur Natur, Just Nature*, Kunstalle Würth, Swiridoff Verlag, 2009, p. 193

7 *The Times*, 2 September 2006

8 Ibid.

9 Interview with Margaret Hockney, July 2013

10 Interview with DH, June 2006

11 Ibid.

12 *A Bigger Message: Conversations with David Hockney*, Martin Gayford, Thames & Hudson, 2011, p. 70

13 Ibid., p. 73

14 Interview with Edith Devaney, September 2013

15 Ibid.

16 Interview with DH, June 2006

17 *David Hockney: A Bigger Picture*, dir. Bruno Wollheim, Coluga Pictures, 2009

18 Ibid.

19 Ibid.

20 *Guardian*, 7 June 2007

21 *David Hockney: A Bigger Picture*, op. cit.

22 *Telegraph*, 26 May 2007

23 *Guardian*, 7 June 2007

24 Interview with Edith Devaney, September 2013

25 Interview with DH, June 2006

26 *David Hockney: A Bigger Picture*, op. cit.

27 Ibid.

28 Interview with DH, June 2006

29 *Guardian*, 4 June 2008

30 *The Times*, 2 September 2006

31 *Guardian*, 25 February 2006

32 Interview with DH, April 2010

33 *Guardian*, 25 February 2006

34 BBC Home Page, 28 September 2005

35 *Sunday Times*, 2 October 2005

36 *Guardian*, 15 May 2007

37 Seventieth birthday message to DH, from John Hockney

38 *True to Life*, op. cit., p. 222

39 *A Bigger Message*, op. cit., p. 229

40 Ibid., p. 76

41 Ibid., p. 97

42 Interview with Margaret Hockney, July 2013

43 Ibid.

44 *Fleurs Fraîches: Dessins sur iPhone et iPad*, Fondation Pierre Bergé–Yves Saint Laurent, 2009, p. 9

45 Ibid., p. 8

46 *Guardian*, 24 June 2009

47 *A Bigger Message*, op. cit., p. 88

48 *New York Review of Books*, 22 October 2009

49 *David Hockney: A Bigger Picture*, Royal Academy Catalogue, 2012, p. 67

50 *Fleurs Fraîches*, op. cit., p. 9

51 Ibid., p. 8

52 Ibid., p. 9

53 Ibid.

54 Interview with Edith Devaney, July 2013

55 *A Bigger Message*, op. cit., p. 156

56 DH to ED, 12 May 2010

57 DH to ED, 30 June 2010

58 DH to Gregory Evans, 12 July 2011

59 DH to ED, 4 October 2010

60 Ibid.

61 *David Hockney: A Bigger Picture*, op. cit., p. 226

62 DH to ML, 30 April 2011, quoted in *David Hockney: A Bigger Picture*, op. cit., p. 37

63 Interview with Edith Devaney, July 2013

64 *The Times*, 2 January 2012

65 Ibid., 23 May 2012

66 *Mail Online*, 3 January 2012

67 Conversation with the author, January 2012

68 *The Times*, 16 January 2012

69 *Guardian*, 19 January 2012

70 *Sunday Telegraph*, 22 January 2012

71 *Spectator*, 28 January 2012

72 *Evening Standard*, 19 January 2012

73 DH to ED, 18 January 2012

74 *David Hockney: A Bigger Picture*, op. cit.

75 Interview with DH, January 2012

BIBLIOGRAPHY

BOOKS

Adam, Peter, *Not Drowning But Waving*, André Deutsch, 1995

Adam, Peter, *David Hockney and His Friends*, Absolute Press, 1997

Bassett, Kate, *In Two Minds: A Biography of Jonathan Miller*, Oberon Books, 2012

Birtwell, Celia, *Celia Birtwell*, Quadrille, 2011

Brown, Jonathon, *I Don't Know Much About Art, But I Know David Hockney: Thirty Years of Friendship in Seven Chapters*, MER Publishing, 2007

Clark, Ossie, *The Ossie Clark Diaries*, ed. Henrietta Rous, Bloomsbury, 1998

——, *Cameraworks*, Thames & Hudson, 1984

——, *Photographs*, Petersburg Press, 1982

Craker, Trevor, *Opening Accounts and Closing Memories: Thirty Years with Thames and Hudson*, Thames & Hudson, 1986

Dexter, John, *The Honourable Beast: A Posthumous Autobiography*, Nick Hern, 1993

Eliot, T. S., *Selected Poems of T. S. Eliot*, Faber & Faber, 2009

Friedman, Martin, *Hockney Paints the Stage*, Thames & Hudson, 1983

Gayford, Martin, *A Bigger Message: Conversations with David Hockney*, Thames & Hudson, 2011

——, *Man with a Blue Scarf: On Sitting for a Portrait by Lucian Freud*, Thames & Hudson, 2010

Hockney, David, *David Hockney: My Early Years*, Thames & Hudson, 1976

——, *Dog Days*, Thames & Hudson, 1998

——, *Paper Pools*, ed. Nikos Stangos, Thames & Hudson, 1980

——, *Secret Knowledge: Rediscovering the Lost Techniques of the Old Masters*, Thames & Hudson, 2006

——, *That's the Way I See It*, Thames & Hudson, 1993

—— & Paul Joyce, *Hockney on Art: Conversations with Paul Joyce*, Little, Brown, 1999

Ingham, Charles, *Words in Pictures*, University of Essex, 1986

Isherwood, Christopher, *Liberation: Diaries, Volume 3, 1970–1983*, ed. Katherine Bucknell, Chatto & Windus, 2012

Joyce, Paul, *Hockney on Photography*, Jonathan Cape, 1988

Lewis, Jeremy, *Grub Street Irregular*, Harper Press, 2008

Livingstone, Marco, *Faces*, Laband Art Gallery/ Thames & Hudson, 1987

——, *David Hockney*, Thames & Hudson, 1996

—— and Kay Heymer, *Hockney's Portraits and People*, Thames and Hudson, 2003

Nitschke, Gunter, *Japanese Gardens*, Taschen, 2003

Schlesinger, Peter and Manolo Blahnik, *A Chequered Past: My Visual Diary of the 60s and 70s*, Thames & Hudson, 2004

Spender, Stephen, *New Selected Journals 1939–1995*, Faber & Faber, 2012

——, and David Hockney, *China Diary*, Thames & Hudson, 1982

Stevens, Wallace, *Collected Poems*, Faber & Faber, 2006

Tinterow, Gary, Philip Conisbee and Hans Naef, *Portraits by Ingres: Image of an Epoch*, Harry N. Abrams, Inc., 1999

Van Gogh, Vincent, *Vincent Van Gogh: Verzamelde Brieven*, vol. 3, ed. V .W. Van Gogh and Johanna van Gogh-Bonger, Wereldbibliotheek, 1973

Webb, Peter, *Portrait of David Hockney*, Chatto & Windus, 1988

Weschler, Lawrence, *True to Life: Twenty-five Years of Conversations with David Hockney*, University of California Press, 2008

Wesker, Arnold, *As Much as I Dare*, Century, 1994

White, Edmund, *City Boy*, Bloomsbury, 2009

NEWSPAPERS AND MAGAZINES

Adams, Tim, 'Hockney's Final Frontier', *Observer*, 30 May 1999

Altman, Lawrence K., 'Rare Cancer Seen in 41 Homosexuals', *New York Times*, 3 July 1981

Amory, Mark, 'Hockney Magic', *Sunday Times*, 28 May 1978

Bailey, Anthony, 'Special Effects', *New Yorker*, 30 July 1979

Barber, Lynn, 'Home Boy', *Observer*, 15 March 1998

Becker, Robert, 'David Hockney', *Interview*, December 1986

Bragg, Melvyn, 'Mr Hockney's Guitar Music', *Observer*, 22 January 1978

Burn, Gordon, 'The Middle Age of Mr Hockney', *The Times*, 21 February 1988

Burns, Charlotte, 'The Man Who Moved to LA and Stopped Making Films', *Art Newspaper*, No. 228, October 2011

'CALENDAR', *Los Angeles Times*, 11 February 1996

Checkland, Sarah Jane, 'A New Perspective to Hockney', *The Times*, 31 July 1985

Christy, Desmond, 'Luna Mission', *Guardian*, 4 July 1987

Christy, George, column in *Hollywood Reporter*, 7 January 1988

Daly, Michael, 'AIDS Anxiety', *New Yorker*, 20 June 1983

'David Hockney's Photo Graphics', *Vanity Fair*, May 1983

Davie, Michael, 'Painting by Large Numbers', *Observer*, 31 May 1987

Feaver, William, 'Full House: ART', *Observer*, 24 July 1977

Froiland, Paul, 'A New Stage', *Horizon*, November/December 1983

Fuller, Peter, 'An Interview with David Hockney', *Art Monthly*, Part 1 November 1977, Part 2 December 1977/January 1978

Garfield, Simon, 'Time, Gentlemen', *Independent*, 26 July 1992

——, 'Birthday of an Old Master', *Guardian*, 26 April 1997

Gayford, Martin, 'A Yorkshire genius in love with his iPhone', *Spectator*, 24 June 2009

Geldzahler, Henry, 'Hockney Abroad: A Slide Show', *Art in America*, February 1981

Green, William, 'Hockney at Home', *Vogue*, September 1978

Greig, Geordie, 'Portrait of the Artist and His Californian Dog', *Sunday Times*, 30 October 1988

——, 'The Bright Stuff', *Sunday Times*, 12 January 1992

——, 'Mind Expanding', *Sunday Times*, 24 January 1993

——, 'LA Goes Barking Mad', *Sunday Times*, 4 April 1995

Gross, Miriam, 'No Joy at the Tate', *Observer*, 4 March 1979

Harlow, John, 'Hockney Finds Trade Secrets of the Old Masters', *Sunday Times*, 30 January 2000

Harris, Dale, 'The Met Falls under the Hockney Spell', *Guardian*, 6 April 1981

Higgins, Charlotte 'R.A. Summer Exhibition', *Guardian*, 7 June 2007

Hilton, Tim, 'The Draughtsman's Cop-out', *Guardian*, 29 October 1988

Hockney, David, 'David Hockney's Faces',
    Los Angeles Times, 18 January 1987
——, 'David Hockney Pays Tribute to Painter
    Lucian Freud', *Evening Standard*, 22 July 2011
—— and R. B. Kitaj, 'R.B. Kitaj and David
    Hockney in Conversation', *New Review*,
    January/February 1977
Hodgkin, Howard, diary quoted in *Ambit*, No. 83,
    1980
Isenberg, Barbara, 'The Art on the Cover',
    Los Angeles Times, 16 September 1990
——, 'A Painter Gets Back to the Business of
    Painting', *Los Angeles Times*, 5 April 1995
——, 'Drawing on the Inside', *Los Angeles Times*,
    11 February 1996
Januszczak, Waldemar, 'Summer of the
    Umpteenth Doll', 6 June 1987
Kramer, Hilton, 'The Fun of David Hockney',
    New York Times, 4 November 1977
Larner, Gerald, 'Salome Stars in Hollywood
    Opera', *Guardian*, 21 October 1986
——, 'Shipping the Light Fanstastic', *Guardian*,
    18 December 1987
McGill, Douglas C., 'David Hockney's Journey
    to a New Cubism', *New York Times*, 7 October
    1984
Mortimer, John, 'Portrait of the Artist as a
    Naughty Boy', *Sunday Times*, 6 July 1980

Oates, Marylouise, 'LACMA fills house for
    Hockney party', *Los Angeles Times*, 5 February
    1988
Reid, Norman, 'Buying the Best', *Observer*,
    11 March 1979
Rockwell, John, 'A Risky Venture at the Met',
    New York Times, 15 February 1981
Sarler, Carol, 'The Flowerpot Man', *Sunday Times*,
    27 April 1997
Shawe-Taylor, Desmond, 'A Sense of Magic in
    Glyndebourne', *Sunday Times*, 4 June 1978
Stangos, Nikos, 'Hockney's Vision of Style', *Art &
    Design*, No. 1/2, 1988
Taylor, John Russell, 'With the Benefits of
    Hindsight', *The Times*, 15 July 1980
——, 'Galleries', *The Times*, 6 July 1982
——, 'Inspired Pairing of
    Brilliant Invention and Pop', *The Times*, 6
    August 1985
Tinterow, Gary, 'A Look Back at Ingres', *Travel +
    Leisure*, September 1999
Wainwright, Martin, 'True Fax Revealed About
    Hockney Art', *Guardian*, 11 November 1989
Weschler, Lawrence, 'Hockney on the Beach',
    Interview, August 1989
Wilson, William, 'Hockney's cheeky look at
    today's history', *Los Angeles Times*, 7 February
    1988

FILMS AND TELEVISION

'Robbie', a BBC *Tonight* special, 13 August 1977
One Hundred Great Paintings, dir. Peter Adam, BBC
    Films, 1980
Hockney at Work, dir. Peter Adam, BBC Films,
    1981
The South Bank Show, LWT, 13 November 1983
Painting with Light, dir. David Goldsmith, York
    Films, 1987
'Hockney's Fax', *The Great North Show*, Yorkshire
    Television, 1990

Face to Face, BBC TV, 10 November 1993
David Hockney: Double Portrait, dir. Bruno
    Wollheim, Coluga Pictures, 2003
David Hockney: A Bigger Picture, dir: Bruno
    Wolheim, Coluga Pictures, 2009
'David Hockney discusses Lucian Freud',
    DH interview, www.youtube.com/
    watch?v=_4OGC9pj86g

CATALOGUES AND EXHIBITION NOTES

David Hockney: A Bigger Picture, Royal Academy, 2012

David Hockney: A Retrospective, LACMA / Thames & Hudson, 1988

David Hockney: Space and Line, Annely Juda Fine Art, 1999

Fleurs Fraîches: Dessins sur iPhone et iPad, Fondation Pierre Bergé–Yves Saint Laurent, 2009

Hockney, David, *Home Made Prints*, Knoedler Gallery, 1986

Kinsman, Jane, 'The Art of Collaboration', National Gallery of Australia, April 2003

Livingstone, Marco, *Sitting for Hockney*, Annely Juda Gallery, London, 2003

Photographs, exhibition cataloue, International Exhibitions Foundation, 1986

Silver, Jonathan, 'What it's like to be drawn by David Hockney', exhibition notes, 1853 Gallery, Salts Mill, 1994

Sotheby's Catalogue of Sale of the Collection of Mark Birley, 31 March 2013

Würth, Kunstalle, *David Hockney: Nur Natur (Just Nature)*, Swiridoff Verlag, 2009

ARCHIVES

Diaries of Laura Hockney, Hockney Archive, Bridlington, Yorkshire

Diary of John Kasmin, Kasmin Papers, Getty Center, Los Angeles, CA

The Letters of Vincent van Gogh, Van Gogh Museum, Amsterdam, www.vangoghletters.org

Stephen Spender Archive, Bodleian Library, Oxford

INDEX

Figures in italics indicate illustrations. 'DH' indicates David Hockney.